A Cultural History of Dress and Fashion
General Editor: Susan Vincent

Volume 1
A Cultural History of Dress and Fashion in Antiquity
Edited by Mary Harlow

Volume 2
A Cultural History of Dress and Fashion in the Medieval Age
Edited by Sarah-Grace Heller

Volume 3
A Cultural History of Dress and Fashion in the Renaissance
Edited by Elizabeth Currie

Volume 4
A Cultural History of Dress and Fashion in the Age of Enlightenment
Edited by Peter McNeil

Volume 5
A Cultural History of Dress and Fashion in the Age of Empire
Edited by Denise Amy Baxter

Volume 6
A Cultural History of Dress and Fashion in the Modern Age
Edited by Alexandra Palmer

A CULTURAL HISTORY OF DRESS AND FASHION

VOLUME 3

A CULTURAL HISTORY OF DRESS AND FASHION

IN THE RENAISSANCE

Edited by Elizabeth Currie

BLOOMSBURY ACADEMIC
LONDON • NEW YORK • OXFORD • NEW DELHI • SYDNEY

BLOOMSBURY ACADEMIC
Bloomsbury Publishing Plc
50 Bedford Square, London, WC1B 3DP, UK
1385 Broadway, New York, NY 10018, USA
29 Earlsfort Terrace, Dublin 2, Ireland

BLOOMSBURY, BLOOMSBURY ACADEMIC and the Diana logo are trademarks
of Bloomsbury Publishing Plc

First published in Great Britain 2017
Paperback edition published 2021
Reprinted 2023

Selection, editorial matter, introductions © Elizabeth Currie, 2021

Elizabeth Currie has asserted her right under the Copyright, Designs and Patents Act, 1988,
to be identified as Editor of this work.

Cover design: Sharon Mah
Cover Image © DEA/Getty Images

All rights reserved. No part of this publication may be reproduced or transmitted in any form or by any
means, electronic or mechanical, including photocopying, recording, or any information storage or
retrieval system, without prior permission in writing from the publishers.

Bloomsbury Publishing Plc does not have any control over, or responsibility for, any third-party
websites referred to or in this book. All internet addresses given in this book were correct at the
time of going to press. The author and publisher regret any inconvenience caused if addresses have
changed or sites have ceased to exist, but can accept no responsibility for any such changes.

A catalogue record for this book is available from the British Library.

A catalogue record for this book is available from the Library of Congress.

ISBN: HB: 978-0-8578-5751-4
HB set: 978-1-4725-5749-0
PB: 978-1-3502-0470-6
PB set: 978-1-3502-0489-8
ePDF: 978-1-3501-1414-2
eBook: 978-1-3501-1413-5

Series: The Cultural Histories Series

Typeset by RefineCatch Limited, Bungay, Suffolk
Printed and bound in Great Britain

To find out more about our authors and books visit www.bloomsbury.com
and sign up for our newsletters.

CONTENTS

LIST OF ILLUSTRATIONS		ix
Introduction *Elizabeth Currie*		1
1	Textiles *Maria Hayward*	19
2	Production and Distribution *Susan Vincent*	37
3	The Body *Isabelle Paresys*	57
4	Belief *Cordelia Warr*	75
5	Gender and Sexuality *Ann Rosalind Jones*	95
6	Status *Catherine Richardson*	117
7	Ethnicity *Eminegül Karababa*	135
8	Visual Representations *Anna Reynolds*	153
9	Literary Representations *Gerry Milligan*	175
NOTES		193
BIBLIOGRAPHY		223
NOTES ON CONTRIBUTORS		245
INDEX		247

LIST OF ILLUSTRATIONS

INTRODUCTION

0.1   *Usher to the Grand Selim with Parrots*, Jacopo Ligozzi, brush and gouache on vellum, c. 1580–5.   2

0.2   John Bulwer, *Anthropometamorphosis: Man Transformed* (London: William Hunt, 1653), title page.   3

0.3   Detail from the *Portinari Altarpiece*, Hugo van der Goes, 1480–3, oil on canvas.   4

0.4   *To Each His Own Pastime*, "Elck Sijn Tijt-Verdrijff," Adriaen van de Venne, seventeenth century, drawing in red chalk and wash.   6

0.5   Jean Bourdichon, illumination showing the poet Jean Marot handing over his work *Le Voyage de Gênes* to Anne of Brittany, Tours, c. 1508.   8

0.6   Giacomo Franco, *Habiti d'huomeni et donne Venetiane* (Venice, 1609).   10

0.7   Wenceslaus Hollar, *Ornatus muliebris Anglicanus, or, The Severall Habits of English Women* (London, 1640).   12

0.8   *William Drury of Hawstead, Suffolk*, unknown artist, 1587, oil on canvas.   14

0.9   Signboard of the Venetian Silk Guild, sixteenth century, oil on canvas.   16

0.10   Cesare Vecellio, *Ornamento nobile, per ogni gentil matrona* (Venice, 1620).   17

0.11   Needlework long cushion, *The Judgement of Solomon*, c. 1575–1600, linen canvas worked with wool and silk in tent stitch.   18

CHAPTER 1

1.1   A woman's linen jacket embroidered with silk and metal thread and spangles, c. 1600–25.   20

1.2   A piece of velvet cloth of gold with loops of silver-gilt thread, Italy, c. 1475.   21

1.3   A hand-knitted woman's jacket made from silk and metal thread (silver), Italian, c. 1600–20.   23

1.4   A woman's linen smock embroidered with silk, 1575–85.   25

1.5   A man's doublet made from watered wool, silk taffeta, linen, and whalebone, sewn with silk and linen threads, decorated with a silver-gilt and a silver-gilt and silk braid, 1615–20.   27

1.6 A man's collar made from linen and edged with bobbin lace, with
tassels of knotted linen thread, probably English, c. 1630–40.   28

1.7 Chinese silk made into a coverlet, sixteenth to eighteenth century.   30

1.8 A linen and cotton towel, dyed with either indigo or woad, Italian,
1400–1500.   32

1.9 A piece of silk damask, Italian, second half of the fifteenth century.   34

CHAPTER 2

2.1 *Two sewing women*, by Geertruydt Roghman and Claes Jansz Visscher,
Amsterdam, 1648–50.   38

2.2 Miniature from *Splendor Solis*, by Salomon Trismosin, fol. 32v,
Germany, 1582.   39

2.3 Woodcut from Spanish tailoring book *Geometria y traca* by
Diego de Freyle, Seville, 1588.   40

2.4 *The Shoemaker*, woodcut by Jost Amman illustrating Hartmann
Schopper's *Panoplia omnium illiberalium mechanicarum* (Book of Trades),
Frankfurt, 1568.   41

2.5 *Der Tuchhändler* (*The Draper*), miniature from Schachzabelbuch des
Konrad von Ammenhausen, by Hans Schilling, 1467.   42

2.6 *The Tailor*, woodcut by Jost Amman illustrating Hartmann Schopper's
Panoplia omnium illiberalium mechanicarum (Book of Trades), Frankfurt,
1568.   43

2.7 Fashion doll, "Pandora," 1590s.   44

2.8 *The Hatmaker*, woodcut by Jost Amman illustrating Hartmann Schopper's
Panoplia omnium illiberalium mechanicarum (Book of Trades), Frankfurt,
1568.   46

2.9 Early seventeenth-century doublet.   49

2.10 Suit made from quilted ivory satin from another source, with applied
silk braid, England, 1635–40.   50

2.11 An elaborately slashed, sixteenth-century leather doublet, British.   51

CHAPTER 3

3.1 *Emperor Charles V and dog*, Jacob Seisenegger, 1532.   59

3.2 French lady wearing a Renaissance farthingale with hoops, in the front
of a map of Bourges. Georg Braun and Frans Hogenberg, *Civitates
orbis terrarum, Coloniae Agrippinae*, typis T. Graminaei, 1572.   60

3.3 *The French Queen Anne of Austria with the Dauphin (future King
Louis XIV)*, French school, before 1643.   60

LIST OF ILLUSTRATIONS xi

3.4 *Portrait of a Lady*, Rogier Van der Weyden, c.1460. 62

3.5 Cortigiana Veneta, in Pietro Bertelli, *Diversarum nationum habitus*, Patavii, apud Alciatum Alcia et Petrum Bertellium, 1594–96. 62

3.6 *A Ball at the Valois Court* (detail), French school, c. 1580. 63

3.7 *Richard Sackville, 3rd Earl of Dorset*, Isaac Oliver, 1616, portrait miniature. 64

3.8 *Painter's Family*, Jacob Jordaens, c. 1621–2. 65

3.9 Woman's smock, probably made in England from Dutch linen and Flemish lace, 1620–40. 68

3.10 A six section silver pomander engraved with flowers, made in Western Europe, 1600–50. 72

CHAPTER 4

4.1 Fifteenth-century dalmatic, silk with metal embroidery, Italian. 76

4.2 Bishop's gloves, first quarter of the seventeenth century, Spanish. 77

4.3 *The Circumcision of John the Baptist*, designed by Antonio del Pollaiuolo, probably from the Baptistery cope, 1460s. 78

4.4 *The Baptism of Saint Augustine*, Benozzo Gozzoli, 1464–5, fresco from the choir chapel, Sant'Agostino, San Gimignano. 81

4.5 *Saint Francis in Meditation*, Francisco de Zurbarán, 1635–9. 82

4.6 *Mary Queen of Scots in white mourning*, after François Clouet, nineteenth century after an image of 1561. 84

4.7 *De gli habit antichi e moderni di diverse parti del mondo*, Cesare Vecellio, Damiano Zenaro, Venice (1590). 84

4.8 *Philip II of Spain holding a rosary*, Alonso Sanchez Coello, 1573. 85

4.9 *Portrait of Baldassare Castiglione*, Raphael, 1514–15. 86

4.10 Engraving from Jost Amman, *Gynaeceum, siue, Theatrum mulierum*, S. Feyrabend, Frankfurt (1586). 87

4.11 John Bulwer, *Anthropometamorphosis: man transformed: or, the artificial changeling*, William Hunt: London (1653, 2nd edition). 89

4.12 Chasuble of Robert Thornton, early sixteenth century with later alterations. 92

CHAPTER 5

5.1 *Self-Portrait*, Albrecht Dürer, 1498, oil on panel. 96

5.2 *Flora*, Rembrandt van Rijn, probably early 1650s, oil on canvas. 97

5.3 *Portrait of a Lady in a Black Dress with Pearls*, English School, c. 1590. 97

5.4 *Portrait of Sir Walter Raleigh*, unknown English artist, oil on panel, 1588. 98

5.5	Title page engraving, Artus Thomas, *Les Hermaphrodites* (Paris, 1605).	100
5.6	Cesare Vecellio, Nobile Francese, *Degli Habiti antichi e moderni di diverse parti del mondo* (Venice, 1590), 275.	102
5.7	Cesare Vecellio, Meretrici publiche, *Degli Habiti antichi e moderni di diverse parti del mondo* (Venice, 1590), 145 verso.	103
5.8	*Portrait of Guidobaldo II della Rovere, Duke of Urbino*, Bronzino (1531–2).	104
5.9	*Venetian Courtesan, Le vere imagini et descritioni delle piv nobilli citta del mondo*, Donato Bertelli (Venice, 1578), plate 28.	107
5.10	*Frances Howard, Countess of Somerset*, Simon van de Passe, engraving (Hollstein, vol XVI, no. 115), state I and state II.	108
5.11	Title page, "Hic Mulier: or, The man-woman," (London, 1620).	110
5.12	Title page, "Haec Vir: or, the Womanish-Man," (London, 1620).	111

CHAPTER 6

6.1	*Robert Dudley, Earl of Leicester*, Anglo-Netherlandish School, c. 1564, oil on panel, Waddesdon.	120
6.2	Lead alloy livery badge, chained bear and ragged staff of Earls of Warwick.	121
6.3	Scarlet doublet belonging to Gustav Adolphus of Sweden, Livrustkammaren, Stockholm, 1620s.	124
6.4	Christopher Wise (c.1566–1628), Mayor of Totnes (1605 and 1621), Nicholas Hilliard, oil on canvas.	130
6.5	Pair of leather gloves, British, 1600–25.	133
6.6	Sir Henry Unton by unknown artist, oil on panel, c. 1596.	134

CHAPTER 7

7.1	Bulgarian village women, Codex Vindobonensis 8626.	137
7.2	Jost Amman, a picture of a wealthy Turkish woman appearing in public with her children, German woodcut, 1577.	139
7.3	*A Greek Girl Living in Pera, Constantinople.*	141
7.4	Greek women, Codex Vindobonensis 8626.	142
7.5	Two Jewish physicians from the album of Lambert de Vos (1574).	144
7.6	Jewish woman from Adrianople (current day Edirne).	146
7.7	*Portrait of an Armenian Woman*, 1618.	147

CHAPTER 8

8.1	*Elisabeth or Cornelia Vekemans*, Cornelis de Vos, c. 1625.	154

LIST OF ILLUSTRATIONS xiii

8.2 *Catherine Carey, Countess of Nottingham*, Robert Peake, c. 1597. 156

8.3 *Man in Pink (Gian Gerolamo Grumelli)*, Giovanni Battista Moroni, c. 1560. 159

8.4 *Moreel Triptych*, Hans Memling, 1484. 160

8.5 *The Peasant Wedding*, Pieter Bruegel the Elder, 1567. 161

8.6 *The Birth of the Virgin Mary*, Domenico Ghirlandaio, 1486–90. 163

8.7 *Portrait of the St. Adrian Civic Guard*, Hendrick Gerritsz Pot, c. 1630. 165

8.8 *Philosophy Presenting the Seven Liberal Arts to Boethius*, Coëtivy Master (Henri de Vulcop?), c. 1460–70. 166

8.9 *A Woman of Nuremberg Dressed for the Home*, Albrecht Dürer, c. 1500. 168

8.10 *The Gallery of the Palace of Justice (La Galerie du Palais)*, Abraham Bosse, c. 1638. 169

8.11 *The Unicorn is Found (from The Unicorn Tapestries)*, 1495–1505. 171

8.12 *Piero de Medici*, Mino da Fiesole, 1452–3, marble. 172

CHAPTER 9

9.1 *Portrait of Laura Battiferri*, Agnolo Bronzino, c. 1555, oil on canvas. 177

9.2 *Diana and Actaeon*, Titian, 1556–9, oil on canvas. 178

9.3 *Aminta*, 1573, Satyr trying to rape Silvia, act III, engraving, Torquato Tasso, Aldine edition, 1583. 180

9.4 *Habiti antichi: overo raccolta di figure delineate dal gran Titiano, e da Cesare Vecellio suo fratello, diligentemente intagliate, conforme alle nationi del mondo.* Cesare Vecellio (Venice, Combi and la Noù, appresso capo Francesco Bodio, 1664). 182

9.5 *Théâtre de tous les peuples et nations de la terre avec leurs habits et ornemens divers, tant anciens que modernes, diligemment depeints au naturel par Luc Dheere peintre et sculpteur Gantois* (manuscript), Lucas d'Heere (1534–84). 183

9.6 *Esther before King Ahasuerus*, Caspar van den Hoecke, seventeenth century, oil on canvas. 184

9.7 *Judith with the Head of Holofernes*, Lucas Cranach, c. 1530, oil on wood. 185

9.8 *Portrait of a Woman, possibly Ginevra d'Antonio Lupari Gozzadini*, attributed to the Maestro delle Storie del Pane, c. 1485–90. 186

9.9 Finely dressed young men in a detail from *Miracles of St Bernardino*, 1473, by Pietro Vannucci, known as il Perugino (c. 1450–1523), tempera on panel. 189

Introduction

ELIZABETH CURRIE

An Italian traveler to London at the end of the fifteenth century reported that the English dressed in a clumsy imitation of French fashions. It was a dual criticism, implying that the English not only chose to copy the clothing of another country but also that the end result was decidedly inferior.[1] A couple of decades later, in one of his *Colloquies*, Desiderius Erasmus poked fun at a man returning from abroad, whose dress showed that he had "changed from a Dutchman to a Frenchman."[2] The contamination of clothing and people by foreign influences developed into a leitmotif in the Renaissance, inspiring William Harrison's famous comparison between a "dog in a doublet" and a fashionable Englishman. In Harrison's *Description of England* (1587), the appearance of Englishmen is rendered unnatural, even dehumanized, by a patchwork assemblage of "High Almain," Turkish, "Morisco," French, Spanish, and "Barbarian"-style dress.[3] Despite exhibiting a keen understanding of different nations' fashions and living in a world increasingly connected by goods, Harrison considered it treacherous of his fellow countrymen to adopt such clothing. It denoted instability and subjugation, as well as constituting a betrayal of local products.

The print revolution of the fifteenth century played a vital role in propagating such strident views on the cultural and political significance of clothing. It ensured the increasing circulation of fashion through word and image, with many different texts dealing with clothing, from prescriptive writings, manuals on etiquette and domestic management, to travel accounts and festival books. The politics of display, morality, gender, status, and authority were reflected in and through clothing, prompting a growing awareness of the implications of sartorial nuances. The issues that feature repeatedly in these very disparate sources shed light on some of the different kinds of identities, including sexual, geographical, and political ones, all bound up in dress. Discussions surrounding fashion became more sophisticated and insistent, just as the garments themselves became more complicated, structured, tailored, layered, laced, hooked, and pinned into place. By the sixteenth century, fashionable outfits required careful deciphering to understand their many parts, a view shared by contemporary commentators who dissected their individual components one by one, speaking about the clothed body using the same language found in scientific and medical treatises, in which the body itself was often seen as "pieced together."[4]

Many cultural forms in the Renaissance examined new ways of thinking about the world, and what it meant to be human, through clothing. Some were influenced by the voyages of discovery pioneered largely by Portuguese and Spanish explorers from the latter part of fifteenth century onwards, to the West Coast of Africa, the Indies, and subsequently America. In the printed costume books that became popular during the second half of the sixteenth century, dress was a mechanism for organizing the entire world, for categorizing and sometimes subordinating other cultures. Kristen Ina Grimes has analyzed the use of dress to map the globe, pointing out the similarities between costume books and cartography, both relying on the "interplay of the strange and the

FIGURE 0.1: *Usher to the Grand Selim with Parrots*, Jacopo Ligozzi, brush and gouache on vellum, c. 1580–5. Photo by DeAgostini/Getty Images.

familiar."[5] Costume and gesture were thought to be crucial in "knowledge construction" about different ethnic groups, reflected in a late-sixteenth-century album of drawings of Turkish people and animals by Jacopo Ligozzi (Figure 0.1).[6] Although the partially naked bodies of the indigenous inhabitants of the Americas conflicted with European ideals of piety and modesty, some writers interpreted these customs as a mark of innocence, far more natural than their own luxurious, embellished, shape-changing fashions.[7] These ideas were elaborated in John Bulwer's *Anthropometamorphosis* (1650), a work described by Stephen Greenblatt as "one of the first to give an anthropological account of dress as well as of the body."[8] Bulwer, an English physician, saw his volume as a "vindication to the regular beauty and honesty of nature," targeting what he considered to be "primitive" practices of shaping the body. By the same token he also condemned the way English fashions repudiated the body's natural state, selecting aspects of dress that exaggerated or deformed the body, such as sugarloaf hats.[9] On the book's title page, a group of culprits approach the throne of nature, including an Englishwoman whose deformity is a pronounced cleavage on her back, created by her low-necked, tight bodice (Figure 0.2).

FIGURE 0.2: John Bulwer, *Anthropometamorphosis: Man Transformed* (London: William Hunt, 1653), title page. Folger Shakespeare Library, Washington DC.

Clothing is relevant to all the major historical debates of the period and this is reflected in the interdisciplinary nature of the scholarship. Of vital importance are the researchers and practitioners, including theatrical and historical dress costumers, conservators, and curators, who foreground object-based research, viewing clothing and textiles as "historic documents."[10] Scholars from the fields of archaeology and anthropology, economics, gender and literary studies, histories of art and philosophy, have increasingly engaged with early modern dress, resulting in very diverse and potentially complementary approaches. We are lucky to have a growing range of sources for the study of fashion from this period. Archival documents are more detailed and some accessories and garments survive, although still very limited in their range and number. This has facilitated various innovative, multi-disciplinary studies and research questions that have moved beyond traditional concerns of conspicuous consumption and normative behaviors to investigate ideas about agency and varied social behaviors and experiences. These are discussed in this volume, which reveals dress's potential to absorb, reflect, and shape a changing spectrum of cultural practices in the early modern period across different themes. This introduction outlines some of the defining features of the contemporary clothing system, such as how, where, and why fashion thrived, and how dress and appearances intersected with cultural constructions of gender and selfhood. In so doing, it highlights concerns that currently shape the study of early modern clothing, while providing a framework for the subjects elaborated in the subsequent chapters.

PERCEIVING THE WORLD THROUGH DRESS

The certainty that dress could act as a mechanism of control, because of its ability to relay fundamental information about the wearer, such as social status, gender, or political beliefs, was deeply embedded throughout this period. As a consequence, clothing had the potential to keep people in their place. It could bind individuals into a carefully structured hierarchy, defining the way they interacted with those around them. As most early modern societies placed great emphasis on rank and genealogical pedigree, dress was a vital touchstone. Peter Stallybrass and Ann Rosalind Jones have described Renaissance garments as acting "as the bearer of names," and we can see high-status individuals literally marking themselves with clothing, as illustrated by Maria Portinari's pointed *hennin* embroidered with her and her husband's initials in pearls (Figure 0.3).[11] Clothing could incorporate

FIGURE 0.3: Detail from the *Portinari Altarpiece*, Hugo van der Goes, 1480–3, oil on canvas. Photo by DeAgostini/Getty Images.

heraldic colors or decorations with family devices and emblems. The wealthiest, who could afford to commission hugely expensive bespoke textiles, often used this for overtly political purposes. Ludovico il Moro, from the Milanese Sforza family, was portrayed in a cloak with a series of devices reflecting his attributes as ruler, while his wife Beatrice d'Este owned a dress embroidered with the harbor lighthouse of Genoa, recently returned to Milanese control.[12] In 1599, the wedding dress of Margaret of Austria was embroidered with monograms and the coats of arms of Castile-León and the House of Habsburg to mark her dynastic union with Philip III of Spain.[13]

The two centuries covered by this book coincide with the "great age of sumptuary legislation," when legal regulations designed to reinforce order, dictating who wore what and when, were at their most prolific in countries such as England, France, Spain, and Italy.[14] The inefficacy of this kind of legislation has been much commented on, but even though their strictures did not always filter through into actual clothing practices, they provide important indicators of changing priorities across time and place.[15] An overview of Italian laws has argued that there was no clear correlation between the type of government and the thrust of law making. Republics were no more democratic in their aims than courts, suggesting that legislation was less political than moral or mercantilist in intent. Laws focused primarily on protecting and regulating economies, social structure, and gender roles.[16] Charles V's law of 1534 was characteristic in emphasizing longstanding worries about wastefulness and seeking to ban clothing and accessories made of the most expensive fabrics, such as brocaded silks, or ones woven with gold and silver threads.[17] In 1580, one of Elizabeth I's laws condemned "the great excess of apparel . . . in the inferior sort."[18] As Ann Rosalind Jones discusses in Chapter 5, Gender and Sexuality, women were not targeted in Henry VIII's sumptuary legislation because it was felt that their appearances were already sufficiently controlled by male relatives, yet in most other countries there was considerable attention to female dress. Jones describes how legislation was just one way of attempting to reinforce permeable gender boundaries and of policing sexuality. Laws often tried to differentiate between the appearances of "good" and "bad" women, using devices such as yellow veils to publicly mark out prostitutes or tightly regulating female dress in the years immediately before and after marriage, when young women had either no husband or children to discourage advances from the opposite sex.[19]

Sumptuary regulations reflected a system of clothing still deeply rooted in notions of decorum and individuals were expected to dress according to their station and to conform to requirements of etiquette and measure. Not surprisingly, specific cultural contexts influenced these ordering principles, as the contributions to this volume demonstrate. In Chapter 7, Ethnicity, Eminegül Karababa analyzes the ways that travelers to the Ottoman Empire, such as the German Hans Dernschwam and Stephan Gerlach, used knowledge systems from their native countries to categorize the new kinds of clothing they saw. Whenever items of dress were completely unfamiliar, they struggled to understand the social groups they encountered. Cordelia Warr explores the relationship between dress, piety, authority, and moral decorum in Chapter 4, Belief. She illustrates how many of the disputes that characterized the religious reformations were reflected in appearances, from ecclesiastical vestments and the habits of religious orders, to the propriety of clothing worn by the laity. Visual hierarchies of dress were used to bolster the notion of monarchy in England, where sumptuary legislation was employed to represent the sovereign as the epitome of magnificence, unparalleled even by the wealthiest and most powerful of his or her subjects.[20] In the seventeenth-century Dutch Republic, it is possible to relate the codified nature of clothing to new cultures of domesticity. Emilie Gordenker has shown that stages of undress adopted in the home followed the layout of domestic architecture, as important guests with more privileged access would be received by their host in more informal attire.[21]

It has been suggested that such forms of protocol were an obstacle to fashion and that the shifting balance between these two driving forces signaled the change from pre-modernity to modernity in dress.[22] Certainly, many Renaissance commentators believed that more traditional forms of dress, with a clear set of rules, were guided by reason, as opposed to new fashions that were governed by desires. One of the frequent moral criticisms of fashion was that it was the enemy of order and good judgment and consequently fueled the disintegration of the natural balance of things. In the Netherlands, Reformed minister Willem Teellinck (1579–1629) cautioned against novel styles of dress because, "when a fashion is merely novel and unusual it is unchristian . . . the new fashions run among people like a pest, and infect many." [23] The dire consequences of fashion and *vanitas* in general constitute the theme of an engraving by Adriaen van de Venne (Figure 0.4). The scene of a fashionably-dressed couple playing battledore is punctuated by a skeleton, emerging from the curtain in the background, his skull turned rather jauntily sideways, as if to follow the shuttlecock arching through the air. The family's latest fashions are lovingly detailed and their frivolity is highlighted by the

FIGURE 0.4: *To Each His Own Pastime*, "*Elck Sijn Tijt-Verdrijff,*" Adriaen van de Venne, seventeenth century, drawing in red chalk and wash. The Metropolitan Museum of Art, New York. www.metmuseum.org

merry-making objects strewn on the floor, including a pipe, playing cards, and wine glasses.

It could be said that this period was unique in maintaining a strong faith in the legibility of clothing and its power to identify, countered by an equally strong fear of this system breaking down.[24] Given clothing's role in providing the foundations for effective social communication, new ways of dressing that subverted this essential rule were sharply criticized. It was an issue that was featured in many sixteenth-century writings, including Stefano Guazzo's *La Civil Conversazione* (1574):

> ... you can see that peasants presume to compete with artisans in the way they dress, and artisans with merchants, and merchants with noblemen, so that once a grocer starts wearing the clothes and carrying the sword of a nobleman, you won't know who he is until you see him in his shop selling his wares.[25]

In 1596, *Wits Miserie*, a moralizing pamphlet by the English poet and dramatist, Thomas Lodge, elaborated on similar themes: "the plowman, that in time past was contented in russet, must now a daies have his doublet of the fashion, with wide cuts, his garters of fine silk Granada, to meet his Sis on Sunday. The farmer, that was contented in times past with his russet frock and mockado sleeves, now sells a cow against Easter, to buy him silken geere for his credit."[26] Like many such reproofs, although its intention was to paint a picture of the wider dissemination of fashion, it simultaneously revealed that there were still clear expectations of what the lower sorts should be wearing, both in terms of colors and fabrics.

FASHION AND MOBILITY

The origins of fashion, as a form of clothing that changes over time and fulfils more than the basic requirements for warmth or modesty, can be traced back centuries before the Renaissance. What became particularly marked over the course of the sixteenth century, however, was a sense of fashion's accelerating pace of change, coupled with an excitement or thirst for the new. In 1590, Cesare Vecellio drew parallels with the waxing and waning of the moon in an account of his struggles to keep abreast with new forms of female dress, highlighting what was considered to be the underlying instability of female nature. Vecellio lamented that "because female clothes are so quick to change, and are more variable than the forms of the moon, it is not possible to include everything there is to say about them in one account. Rather, I am concerned that while I am in the midst of describing one garment, it will be transformed into another, so that it will be impossible to do justice to all."[27] By the early seventeenth century, observers increasingly noted these changes within a specific time frame, relaying a sense of what might be called fashion's "turnover." An Antwerp merchant living in London wrote that: "The English dress in elegant, light, and costly garments, but they are very inconstant and desirous of novelties, changing their fashions every year, both men and women."[28]

The growth in power and influence of the European courts contributed to fashion's growing momentum. In Chapter 3, The Body, Isabelle Paresys draws a link between fashions that modified and exaggerated the human form, including peascod belly doublets, cartwheel ruffs, and farthingales, and the cultures of distinction and bodily control increasingly promoted at court. Such styles molded the body to enforce the sort of posture and deportment that came to be prized as manifestations of civility. Courtiers also accelerated the forms of mobility that fashion thrived upon, through the circulation of people, ideas, and goods. Women such as Eleonora di Toledo and Anne of Austria, whose marriages often required them to move countries taking their entourages with them as well as their native customs, have often been pinpointed as leading fashionable change.[29] Vecellio alludes to this phenomenon in a description accompanying an engraving of "Women's Clothing worn in Florence and Lombardy," explaining that this kind of dress was not originally Florentine, rather it was introduced by the Grand Duchess's ladies-in-waiting or the wives of the courtiers of the Grand Dukes.[30]

The evolution of the headdress known as the French hood illustrates how female alliances and networks were key in popularizing specific styles. It was depicted on the heads of female rulers, such as Margaret of Austria in the early 1490s, or Anne of Brittany in this miniature from c. 1508 (Figure 0.5), through to Mary I and Catherine de' Medici in the 1550s. Women could also ensure that fashions fell from favor: when Anne Bassett returned from France to be a lady-in-waiting to Jane Seymour, the queen ordered her to remove all her French apparel.[31] Court correspondence shows us how easily fashion could

FIGURE 0.5: Jean Bourdichon, illumination showing the poet Jean Marot handing over his work *Le Voyage de Gênes* to Anne of Brittany, Tours, c. 1508. Bibliothèque nationale de France, Paris. MS Fr. 5091. Photo: SuperStock/Getty Images.

cross geographical boundaries. In 1515, Federico Gonzaga wrote to his mother, Isabella d'Este, passing on a request from François I of France for a fashion doll dressed in Isabella's favorite garments, in order to copy them for the ladies of his court.[32] Letters between Anne Bassett's mother, Lady Honor Lisle, and her servant John Husee, detail textiles and clothing sent to her in Calais from English noblewomen of her acquaintance, to equip her for a fashionable laying-in period.[33] The desire to keep abreast of the latest fashions receives a satirical treatment in the shape of Lady Cressingham in Thomas Middleton's play *Anything for a Quiet Life* (1621), who disdainfully tells mercer Walter Camlet:

> The rich stuff which my husband bought of you, the works [designs] of them are too common. I have got a Dutch painter to draw patterns which I'll have sent to your factors, as in Italy, at Florence and Ragusa where these stuffs are woven, to have pieces made for mine own wearing of a new invention . . . If I live another year I'll have my agents shall lie for me at Paris and at Venice and at Valladolid in Spain for intelligence of all new fashions.[34]

Although we are encouraged to laugh at Lady Cressingham's affectations, it is a compelling account of the appetite for innovation in the early seventeenth century. It also conveys a sense of a shrinking globe in terms of fashion, where an English aristocrat could aspire to command a network of buyers and makers stretching across France, Spain, Holland, Italy, and Sicily.

Beyond the courts, urban growth added further potency to the cultural implications of dress. In her study of early modern London and Paris, Karen Newman characterizes fashion as a "signifier of difference itself," linking its rise in late-sixteenth-century English society to "demographic shifts, wider access to education, a developing state bureaucracy, and the accumulation of capital through expanding foreign and domestic trade."[35] By 1500, 109 cities across Germany, France, Italy, England, Spain, and the Netherlands had at least 10,000 inhabitants.[36] One of the largest of these was London, whose population grew between 1550 and 1650 from more than 80,000 to around 400,000 or more.[37] Numerous factors, such as trade networks, location, and proximity to production centers, contributed to the prominence of cities such as Florence, Lyon, Madrid, Bruges, and London. To some extent rivals for an increasingly international market, their success was far from assured. The predominant taste for French styles in the early seventeenth century, for example, had a negative impact on local production in Amsterdam.[38] These centers are early examples of the phenomenon of the fashion capital, regarded as pivotal in histories of fashion from the late seventeenth century onwards. Distinguished by their manufacturing strengths and ability to shape taste, they wield such influence that it has become customary to situate fashion "at the intersection of key cultural and economic processes that shaped the urban order."[39]

In his colloquy on inns, Erasmus claims that town dwellers were more worldly wise because of their exposure to fashion, distinguishing between cities such as Paris, Rome, and Venice "where nothing causes surprises" and the German inns where, "if they set eyes on a foreigner, whose dress gives him an air of distinction, they all stare intently at him, gazing as if at some new species of animal imported from Africa."[40] Cities brought together the main protagonists—consumers, merchants and artisans—to make new types of dress more readily available. They magnified differences but also made them easier to replicate, fostering a spirit of competition. The "melting pot" of city life is illustrated in an engraving by Giacomo Franco from the costume book *Habiti D'Huomeni et Donne*

FIGURE 0.6: Giacomo Franco, *Habiti d'huomeni et donne Venetiane* (Venice, 1609). Folger Shakespeare Library, Washington DC.

Venetiane (1609) (Figure 0.6) showing charlatans performing in St. Mark's Square in Venice. In the foreground are depicted men from Greece, France, Spain, Turkey, and England. The ribald, carnival atmosphere is highlighted by the central female performer, closely scrutinized by an elderly masked man, and the snake held aloft next to her. The whole scene's undercurrent of desire and transgression is compounded by the crowd of foreigners in their contrasting clothing.

With the development of urban centers came a rise in shops, gradually supplanting fairs and markets as the preferred venue to purchase certain categories of goods, including clothing and haberdashery. Scholarly interest in consumption in recent decades has built up a picture of increasingly developed shopping cultures, usually encompassing far more than simple financial transactions. Buying clothing was not always a pleasurable activity, as Martha C. Howell points out: "with abundance and variety came choice, and with choice came anxieties about the quality of one's choice."[41] However, city streets adorned with textiles drew admiration from visitors such as John Evelyn in Venice in 1645:

> Hence I pass'd thro' the Merceria, which is one of the most delicious streetes in the world for the sweetnesse of it, and is all the way on both sides tapistred as it were, with cloth of gold, rich damasks and other silks . . . and with that variety that for neere half the year spent chiefly in this Citty, I hardly remember to have seene the same piece twice exposed.[42]

Already in the fifteenth century, clothing and textiles sellers were clustered together in various different Italian cities, assuring increased visibility as well as facilitating collaboration across workshops. Fabrizio Nevola has shown that Sienese shops offering luxury goods, such as silk, wool, and fur, were located in the most prestigious and well-frequented areas such as the Campo and Strada Romana because "it is known that the guilds and trades are what make the city rich, populated and beautiful."[43] England differed markedly from Italy in that, although shops were established in small towns in most areas of the country by the late sixteenth century, London remained the destination for fashionable consumers, assisted by the completion of the Royal Exchange in 1568. Members of the English upper gentry, including the Le Stranges who traveled from Hunstanton on the Norfolk coast to purchase the latest London wares in the early seventeenth century, demonstrated preferences that were considered to be harmful to rural economies.[44] In 1616, when James I spoke out against this habit in a speech in Parliament, he nevertheless acknowledged the prevailing view that "new fashion is to bee had nowhere but in London."[45]

The focus on the experiences of town and city dwellers has also enabled a greater understanding of the spread of fashion to less affluent social groups.[46] Dress became a commonplace metaphor for social and cultural changes, often conjuring up their associated fears, and was therefore familiar to people from many different walks of life. However, the wider population's practical and physical engagement with fashionable dress is harder to ascertain. In his analysis of *The Economy of Renaissance Florence* (2009), Richard Goldthwaite proposes that Florentine textile "production for the internal market rose to the point of generating some new consumption, without setting off an upward spiral leading to anything like the 'consumer revolution' of the eighteenth century."[47] Similarly, Paolo Malanima has calculated that even in the early seventeenth century only 5–10 percent of Florentines were affected by variations in dress, a percentage that shrank even further for those living in other, more rural, areas of the Tuscan Grand duchy.[48] The fact that modern words for fashion such as "la mode," or "alla moda" did not come into general use until the early seventeenth century is another reminder that fashion was a restricted pleasure.[49]

It is hard to find qualitative evidence, particularly for the fifteenth century, to understand more fully the experiences of ordinary people, although archival records such as testamentary bequests offer some valuable insights.[50] Some of the most rewarding work to take us beyond histories of elite fashion has focused on particular categories of goods, such as ready-made wares, including Joan Thirsk's influential study on the English stocking industry.[51] With an increasing variety in haberdashery and accessories in the sixteenth century, it became possible to add fashionable touches to an outfit without incurring too many burdensome expenses.[52] Work on Italian inventories belonging to the middling or lower sorts has revealed numerous examples of decorative detachable items, such as sleeves, bodices, or partlets.[53] In fifteenth-century Padua, the dowry of Caterina dall'Arzere, the daughter of a mercer, listed woolen dresses with damask and velvet sleeves, while doctors, lawyers, and artisans, including dyers and a kiln worker, owned items woven with silk or metal threads.[54] A Wenceslaus Hollar engraving presents a

FIGURE 0.7: Wenceslaus Hollar, *Ornatus muliebris Anglicanus, or, The Severall Habits of English Women* (London, 1640). Folger Shakespeare Library, Washington DC.

typical view of how fashion might be manifested in a servant's attire (Figure 0.7). While the figure is not shown in the wide lace collar, figured silks, or fur muff used to denote the latest fashions elsewhere in Hollar's *The Severall Habits of English Women* (1640), her dress and cap are nevertheless trimmed with a lace border, as is her shawl, and her shoes are smart enough to be protected by a pair of pattens. These issues are examined in greater depth in Chapter 6, Status. Catherine Richardson analyzes the consumption patterns of different segments of the population to show how social structure was marked out in sartorial terms, through a range of domestic, civic, and royal clothing. Richardson highlights not simply the stark contrasts between these groups, but also interactions and shared practices, particularly among the middling sorts.

IDENTITY FORMATION AND DRESS

Writing on twentieth-century dress, Fred Davis has referred to its role in "ambivalence management," the way it is used to navigate social relations, coupled with other means of self-expression, such as bodily posture or facial expressions.[55] It is a concept that seems highly pertinent to this period also, particularly when travel or city life could lead to more fluid social networks and a higher probability of encountering strangers. The scenarios in which dress led to mistaken identities, both on the stage and in real life, were plentiful. Diane Owen Hughes relates the experience of a Franciscan friar who traveled almost 200 miles from Florence to Recanati in 1437, where he mistook two Christians in the piazza for Jews. It was argued that such an error would not have occurred in a town like Ancona, where Jews were forced to wear a yellow badge, and the episode was used to support the imposition of this kind of branding in Recanati.[56] This is one example of the confusions that could arise when sartorial signifiers were missing or unintelligible. However, there was also a growing appreciation of how these signifiers could be knowingly manipulated. *The Book of the Courtier* gives a further insight into the still problematic scenario of seeing, and being seen by unfamiliar individuals, with Federico Fregoso recommending the courtier "should decide within himself how he wishes to appear and how he would like to be considered, through his clothing, and make sure that his clothing helps him to be seen as such particularly by those who do not hear him speak or see him act."[57]

Similar manipulations and transformations form the subject of Gerry Milligan's Chapter 9, Literary Representations, which explores the notion of text itself as a cloth to be fashioned and refashioned by author and readers alike. Drawing on a variety of genres of Italian writings that discuss dress, particularly as a means of crafting identity, Milligan shows that this kind of self-awareness is not just a characteristic of the *Courtier*'s sophisticated and urbane subject matter, but symptomatic of a much broader phenomenon. The process advocated by Castiglione is a prime example of what Stephen Greenblatt famously described as "self-fashioning."[58] Although noting the challenges of talking about the experiences of selves and consciousness at this time, Peter Burke also proposes that "people were becoming more aware of the difference between an inner and an outer self."[59] As historians of dress have shown in recent decades, clothing provides clear evidence of changing perceptions of selfhood, including more complex interpretations of the notion that the clothed exterior was a simple, straightforward projection of the interior. Nevertheless, such shifts did not supersede a belief in the constitutive power of dress and its ability to manifest moral qualities or attributes. As Martha C. Howell characterizes it: "the period between 1300 and 1600 might be better depicted as a furious contest over the power of material objects rather than an epoch when the material was pacifically abandoned as a manifestation of the real."[60] So Vecellio, for example, still considered dress to be an indicator of character at the end of the sixteenth century.[61] In *The Worthies of England* (1622), Thomas Fuller provides an arresting description of Sir Robert Shirley, the English ambassador, in which he conflates man, country, and clothing: "as if his clothes were his limbs, [Shirley] accounted himself never ready till he had something of the Persian habit about him."[62] In 1638, the English scholar and author Lucy Hutchinson perceived a symbiosis between her future husband's character and his clothing, saying that "he wore good and rich clothes . . . he equally becoming them and they him, which he wore with such unaffectedness and such neatnesse as doe not often meet in one."[63]

For men who sought advancement within the increasingly powerful and rigidly-structured courts of the Renaissance, clothing was a necessary tool to perfect the arts of performance and dissimulation. Harry Berger argues that there was an "increasing emphasis on the need to *perform* status, the need to develop strategies of self-representation and class self-definition."[64] Scholars have frequently drawn attention to the inherent theatricality of court dress and, conversely, it has been suggested that appetites for fashion were encouraged by the concurrent flourishing of the theater.[65] Many portraits from the period can be read as a kind of static performance, complete with curtains and props that

FIGURE 0.8: *William Drury of Hawstead, Suffolk*, unknown artist, 1587, oil on canvas. Yale Center for British Art, Paul Mellon Collection.

combine to construct an image of the individual as he or she "wishes to be esteemed." A portrait of William Drury of Hawstead (Figure 0.8) is a striking example of this, using material attributes to create different layers of meaning.[66] Drury apparently had a particular interest in fashion. He and his wife presented the queen with various remarkable textiles and garments as New Year gifts, including in 1578, "a fore parte of ashe collored satten, embrawdred with clowdes and wormes of golde and silver, lined with yelowe sarceonet."[67] Elizabeth I stayed at Hawstead Hall in 1578 and soon afterwards Drury was knighted, an honor commemorated by his black garter in the portrait. Subsequently, however, he fell from favor. Ellen Chirelstein argues that the word *sconsolato* and the clouded sun refer to his conflicted relationship with Elizabeth. The unusual combination of both field armor and a tilt lance underline his military capabilities as well as his participation in the Accession Day Tilts. Other features, such as the gold, green, and black of the Drury coat-of-arms and the yellow silk hose encasing elongated legs present him as the contemporary ideal of male nobility. As in the portrait of *Catherine Carey, Countess of Nottingham*, discussed by Anna Reynolds in Chapter 8 on Dress and Visual Representations, clothing and accessories can hint at underlying tensions between the advancement of individual status and reverence towards the monarch. Reynolds discusses the impact of the proliferation of art forms and techniques in this period upon depictions of dress, showing how their careful interpretation can fill the gaps when other forms of evidence are lacking.

A text intended for a female readership, Alessandro Piccolomini's *La Raffaella* (1539) is an equally blatant manifesto for the manipulation of appearances as the *Courtier*. Daniela Costa shows how Piccolomini outlines the art "of offering oneself up to the gaze of other people, creating a delicate balance between concealment and display."[68] Written as a dialogue, the much older advisor Raffaella frequently tells young Margarita to manage the way she is perceived by others, such as demonstrating that she is "naturally beautiful, without any artifice. This can be achieved by sometimes pretending in the morning, to whoever comes into the house, that you have only just got out of bed and have hardly had time to get dressed."[69] Work on the appearances of a variety of social groups, including courtesans and young men, suggests that individuals whose status was not defined in more concrete ways had even further impetus to use fashion to forge their identities.[70] The Spanish fashion for farthingales and the Venetian taste for low-cut gowns have both been interpreted as conscious strategies used by women to gain greater visibility.[71] In Italy, women spoke out against sumptuary legislation because dress was fundamental to their sense of worth and social standing. In the late sixteenth century, for example, women in Cesena protested about clothing regulations because they had so few opportunities to take part in civic life.[72]

This growing awareness of the ways dress could mask identities heightened fears about its corrupting influence, often played out in the context of gender roles. Clothing could create unwanted hybrids, as Philip Stubbes warned in his *Anatomie of Abuses* when he asserted that garments "are set downe for signes distinctive between sexe and sexe."[73] Historians have drawn attention to the many forms of the "adulterations" that concerned Stubbes, from cross-dressing practices, the Spanish women known as *tapade* who disguised themselves with veils, or effeminate fashionable youths, to transgressive types of clothing acted out in controlled scenarios, such as at the theater or during carnival.[74] Beyond the realm of gender construction, commentators also criticized the blurring of boundaries between different socio-economic groups. In Italy, Pietro Aretino lamented that, "It is the disgrace of our age that it tolerates the painted portraits even of tailors and butchers," just as Vicente *Carducho in his Diálogos de la pintura* (1633) complained about "ordinary people" having themselves painted in the clothing of their superiors.[75] Representations of artisans tend to show them at work in their best clothes. This functioned partly as a badge of honor, reflecting the significance of "symbolic capital" in shaping identity for artisan groups in Europe, as opportunities to advance status were usually very limited.[76] A sign for the Venetian guild of silk weavers provides an example of this practice, as the weavers wear several-layered outfits dyed with crimson and with fashionable embellishments, a reminder of how central dress was to identity formation at all social levels (Figure 0.9).

MATERIALS AND MAKERS

Over the last few decades, scholars have tackled the longstanding divide between histories of consumption and production, to consider the material qualities of textiles and dress, its design, composition, and construction, within broader cultural and economic contexts. At the same time, the material turn in early modern studies has introduced new ways of thinking about objects and their central role in defining many forms of social interaction. The recent drive to catalog, take patterns from, and reconstruct early modern garments

FIGURE 0.9: Signboard of the Venetian Silk Guild, sixteenth century, oil on canvas. Photo: DeAgostini/Getty Images.

will doubtless have an impact on studies of physical experience and modifications of the body in this period. Investigating making and matter provides an important reminder of the more visceral aspects of clothing in the Renaissance, such as the talismanic properties associated with jewelry, or the practice of deliberately concealing garments to protect buildings.[77] Recent research into preventative medicine in Italy has traced the belief that clothing and perfumed accessories could form a "protective barrier," by purifying the surrounding air as well as by retaining warmth.[78] In a similar vein, Karen Raber has shown that knowledge about the genesis of pearls, as beautiful secretions, linked them to both purity and corruption in contemporary perception.[79]

In Chapter 1 on Textiles, Maria Hayward discusses the many new types of fabrics developed at this time, spurred on by an increasingly international, competitive market. She outlines innovations in fiber combinations, weaving, and printing, as well as improvements in dyeing techniques, sometimes making use of highly prized, imported ingredients, such as logwood or cochineal, from the New World. As Hayward points out, fashionable names were formulated for new hues, indicating their value to the world of trade and commerce. These terms were presumably invented to stimulate demand, or as William Harrison put it, to please "fantastical heads," supplying his own examples of "gooseturd green, pease-porridge tawny, popinjay blue, lusty gallant, the devil-in-the-hedge."[80] The central role of textiles and clothing within the economies of many countries turned them into vehicles of national pride and as such they were ideal diplomatic gifts, as illustrated by the four Florentine straw hats sent from Eleonora da Toledo to Henry VIII.[81] Equally, foreign fabrics could pose a threat, as was the case with Italian and Spanish silks in sixteenth-century England, when the population was encouraged to wear locally-woven broadcloths.[82] Reconstructing geographies of goods and artisans can provide us with another perspective on the notion of mapping the world through text and fashion. Again, the complexities of textile trade and production take us far beyond European shores. To illustrate this, Marta Ajmar and Luca Molà conjure up a fabric woven with silk threads spun in Persia or Syria, dyed with cochineal from Mexico brought back by Spanish traders, and a Turkish alum mordant, the design itself influenced by Oriental or Middle-Eastern motifs, picked out with threads wrapped with metal shipped from sub-Saharan African mines.[83]

As Susan Vincent's study of production and distribution in Chapter 2 reminds us, textiles and clothing provided employment for a significant proportion of the working population in early modern Europe. It can be difficult to unearth information about individual experiences: all too often groups of workers only rise to prominence when caught up in larger historical developments, their freedoms curtailed by protectionist economic measures or religious persecution, as in the case of Huguenot weavers fleeing the St. Bartholomew's Day massacre. However, the objects they created can reveal their skill and inventiveness. Surviving garments whose functional aspects were creatively transformed into the fashionable suggest growing scope for entrepreneurship among artisans. Ulinka Rublack has identified shoemakers in sixteenth-century Augsburg and Antwerp who owed their success to inventive products.[84] The medium of print provided new opportunities for self-promotion, from the Spanish and Italian tailors' books of the second half of the sixteenth century, to Cesare Vecellio's lace patterns described as a "beautiful sight for every princess." (Figure 0.10). In her contribution to this volume,

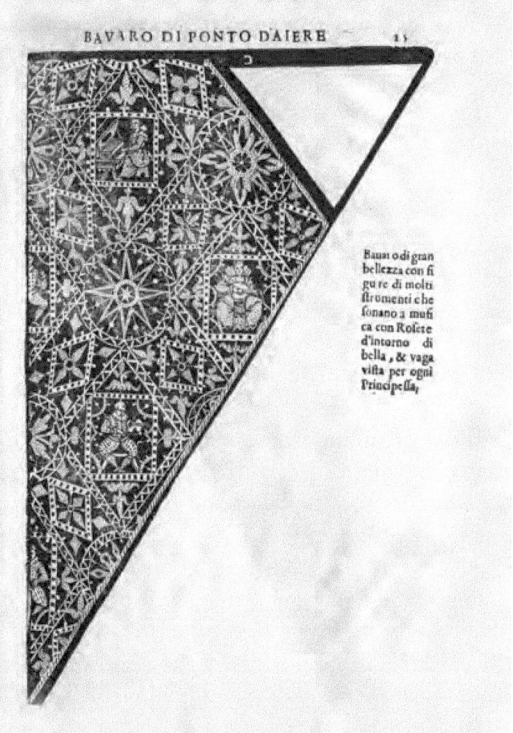

FIGURE 0.10: Cesare Vecellio, *Ornamento nobile, per ogni gentil matrona* (Venice, 1620). Folger Shakespeare Library, Washington DC.

FIGURE 0.11: Needlework long cushion, *The Judgment of Solomon*, c. 1575–1600, linen canvas worked with wool and silk in tent stitch. Hardwick Hall, Derbyshire. © National Trust Images/Brenda Norrish.

Vincent shows that the customer also took an active part in the production of bespoke clothing, bringing expertise and judgment to a process that could often involve a surprising number of individuals including, for example, relatives and domestic servants as well as retailers and artisans.

Juxtaposing production and consumption can help to re-embed clothing within its cultural context. A needlework cushion from Hardwick Hall, Derbyshire, of the Judgment of Solomon depicts men in highly fashionable, silk knitted stockings, similar to those worn by William Drury (Figure 0.11). The knitting sector in this period is one that is often singled out for its innovative nature, aided by the development of the stocking frame. The composition of the embroidered scene is designed to display the stockings of the man on the left to their best effect, rather incongruously so given the threat of violence at its heart. The struggling baby unsettles this depiction of courtly ease and fashionable taste. In similar pieces of needlework, it has been argued that the scenes contain a political message.[85] Here, the association of ostentatiously fashionable men with two peacocks on the right seems intended, a nod to the belief that fashion sat uneasily with Christian virtues. The French preacher Michel Menot, for example, argued that wealth spent on clothing would have been better directed towards the poor: "the very cloaks you wear were bought with the blood of the poorest people."[86] He did not seek to highlight the plight of artisans, but to the modern eye there is a stark distinction between these seemingly effortless appearances and the labor and hardships required to produce them. We know from a recent study of Italian knitting manufacture that thousands of children aged between seven and fourteen years old were involved, typically in the production of less expensive, woolen items, and the pressing need to protect them from violence is cited as one of the driving factors in the rise in knitting mistresses.[87] Evidence of elite courtly life, this embroidery nevertheless reminds us that clothing linked very different social spheres. It epitomizes the spirit of this volume as a whole, as its individual contributors explore many such contrasting and complementary narratives to show us the cultural force of dress and fashion in the Renaissance.

CHAPTER ONE

Textiles

MARIA HAYWARD

INTRODUCTION

In 1606 Thomas Dekker wrote *The Seven Deadly Sinnes of London*. He described clothes-conscious young English men dressing in fabrics and fashions drawn from far and wide:

> His codpiece ... in Denmarke, the collor of his Dublet and the belly in France; the wing and narrow sleeve in Italy; the short waste hangs over a Dutch Botchers stall in Utrecht; his huge slopes speakes Spanish; Polonia gives him the Bootes ... [1]

While he primarily linked different styles of dress to different geographical locations, Dekker could have made his point equally well had he listed where their various materials, trimmings, and accessories had come from. Like many other countries, England was tightly bound into the international textile trade which combined tradition and innovation. This chapter is divided into five sections—fibers, textile production, other materials used to make and decorate clothing, economy and trade, and dyes—to demonstrate why textiles were so important in early modern society.

FIBERS

Textiles woven from natural fibers were the most important of the materials used to make clothes of the sort described by Dekker. The types of textiles an individual selected for themselves and others would reflect their social status and disposable income. Their choices would also depend on the garment they were ordering, whether it needed an outer fabric, interlining, lining, and padding, and on the drape and handle of the textile. One example will serve to illustrate this point. On October 14, 1510, Henry VIII gave John Williams, one of his footmen, a set of clothes as a wedding gift. The clothes needed to reflect the status of both Williams and the king, while also being appropriate to the specific occasion where they would be first worn. Williams was given the following: a gown made from five yards of tawny cloth at 5s per yard, and furred with 139 black lambskins at 3d each, six yards of black damask for a jacket at 7s a yard, three yards of black velvet for a doublet at 11s a yard, three ells of linen for a shirt at 14d the ell, a pair of scarlet hose costing 8s and a bonnet priced at 3s 4d.[2]

The first thing the list highlights is that two main types of fiber were used to make fabric in the early modern period: these were either proteinaceous or cellulosic. Protein fibers included wool, silk, mohair, alpaca, angora, and cashmere, the most common being wool and silk, while linen and cotton were the most popular cellulosic fibers (Figure 1.1).

FIGURE 1.1: A woman's linen jacket embroidered with silk and metal thread and spangles, c. 1600–25. © Victoria and Albert Museum, London.

These could be woven into fabrics with the same fiber being used for the warp (the vertical threads) and the weft (the horizontal threads) or into union or mixed cloths where one fiber was used for the warp and another for the weft.

Williams was given a gown, a mark of male status, which was made from wool cloth. This is not surprising because wool was arguably the most important fiber in the early modern period, both in terms of the quantity produced and its value to the economy. This is linked to two factors. First, the wool fiber is warm, soft, crimped, grows in clusters, does not wet easily and covers the body of sheep (*Ovis aries*). Second, sheep were reared in huge numbers in Europe at this time. It also was suited to Williams's social status as a man from the lower middling sort. The quality of the wool varied greatly depending upon the variety of sheep it came from, while the value was influenced by market trends. The Townsends, a landowning family in Norfolk, owned between 8,000 and 9,000 sheep in the 1480s.[3] The main challenge to English wool came from the very soft, fine wool of the Spanish merino sheep which were raised on the Medina del Campo in Castile. It was exported via Seville and Burgos to Bilbao and then sent to Flanders.[4] Sheep farming and wool production were very important in Spain with 2,000,000 to 3,000,000 sheep migrating each year as part of the pattern of transhumance. However, the *Mesta*, the sheep owners, supplied loans to the crown resulting in a serious imbalance of trade in Spain with emphasis placed on wool rather than cloth. This hindered the development of weaving in Barcelona and Valencia.[5]

Other animal fibers were popular, the most important of these were mohair, the silky hair of the Angora goat (*Ankara keçisi*), cashmere from goats in Kashmir and Nepal, and the hair of the Bactrian camel (*Camelus bactrianus*). The guard hair and the undercoat were used or were mixed with wool. These camels were native to central Asia, ranging from Turkey, to Siberia, Mongolia, and China but there was increasing demand in Europe for these fibers. In 1637, the mayor of Canterbury objected to the number of Walloon weavers working in the city and the "late abundant ymportacion of mohaire or turkey yarne" and the "greate importacions of late yeares from Turkie of yarnes made of camells haire."[6]

Black silk damask and silk velvet were selected for Williams's jacket and doublet, and the desirability of silk over wool is reflected in the price per yard with the cloth costing 5s while the damask cost 7s and the velvet 11s. The high cost of silk was linked to several factors including that the silk worms (*Bombyx mori*) fed only on white mulberry leaves which were native to China. Silk worms produce two silk filaments coated with sericin; once the sericin is removed the silk fibers are fine, soft, long, translucent, and lustrous, qualities that are transferred to the textiles woven from them. Sericulture was widespread in the early modern world with silk worms being raised in China, Japan, and Korea, as well as in India, although the silk from Bengal was quite poor quality.[7] Silk was raised in Andalusia and Sicily from the eleventh century and by the 1500s sericulture had spread to Italy and more specifically to Lombardy, Lower Piedmont, Tuscany, and the Veneto (Figure 1.2).[8] By the seventeenth century, raw silk was being produced in France and James I wanted to establish silk production in England and in Jamestown, Virginia, by encouraging the planting of mulberry trees.

Moving to the cellulosic fibers, Williams was given a linen shirt. Linen was made from the flax plant (*Linum usitatissimum*) which produces a thick, strong, hygroscopic, bast

FIGURE 1.2: A piece of velvet cloth of gold with loops of silver-gilt thread, Italy, c. 1475.
© Victoria and Albert Museum, London.

fiber, which has little elasticity. Between 1450 and 1650, flax was predominantly produced in Western Europe, with the area of production moving towards Poland and Russia over time.[9] When Fynes Morrison (1566–1630), a traveler and writer, stopped in Haarlem in the northern Netherlands in 1593 he observed that "the Citie makes great store of linnen clothes, and hath five hundred spinsters in it."[10] In contrast, production in England and Ireland was relatively small scale. In part this was because flax is very demanding on the soil, so it was planted in rotation with other crops to help keep the soil fertile. It was also labor intensive to produce because the plants needed regular care and weed-free conditions.[11] However, the English government used legislation to promote flax cultivation reflecting the value it attached to linen. An act passed in 1531 required that one rood (a quarter of an acre) of every sixty workable acres was to be used to produce flax and hemp.[12]

The one fiber which did not appear on Williams's clothing warrant was cotton, and this is typical of other warrants issued by Henry VIII to his household and of his own clothing orders. However, this does not mean that cotton was unknown in early modern Europe. Raw cotton (*Gossypium*), sometimes called cotton wool, is a seed fiber which is very fine. It has a short staple or standard length, it is very absorbent, and it can be used as padding as well as being spun into yarn. In the 1500s, India, Persia, Syria, and Egypt were producing raw cotton which was exported by the Portuguese and the Italians, their key market was southern Germany, to supply the weaving industries in Swabia.[13] Spanish settlers also found cotton being grown in Peru and Mexico in the sixteenth century, while John Chardin, a French jeweler and traveler, found cotton growing in Safavid, Persia in the following century. More significantly from a European perspective, cotton was also grown in Calabria and Sicily, as well as in Spain in the area around Cordova and Seville. By the late 1600s, cotton was poised to replace wool as the most widely worn fiber in Europe.[14]

TEXTILE PRODUCTION

The account book of the royal household noted that all the materials used to make the clothes given to Williams were specially bought, indicating that there was a vibrant market for textiles in London. The selection of material and making it up into garments was the culmination of a lengthy and often complex process, the first stage of which was making yarn for weaving, or for sewing or embroidery. Yarn was spun using either a drop or hand spindle or the spinning wheel (the smaller flax wheel and the wool wheel). Spinning gave the thread twist, either to the left or right (known as s or z spun); when two or more threads of similar weight were twisted or plied together they would become stronger. Fancy threads included gimped thread which consisted of a core thread with another wrapped around it, often a fine metal strip (Figure 1.3).[15]

These threads were then woven into textiles on several types of loom, including the treadle loom where the shafts were lowered and raised using foot pedals.[16] Draw looms, a more complex version of the treadle loom, were used to produce patterned fabrics from the sixth and seventh centuries until the start of the nineteen century when they were replaced by the Jacquard loom. The draw loom required a weaver and a drawboy who raised the heddles in the combination required by the design.

Various methods were used to finish fabric and these processes enhanced its visual appearance and its value. Dyeing will be discussed later, but other finishing techniques included raising and shearing the nap and scarlets were so-called from *eskalata* meaning

FIGURE 1.3: A hand-knitted woman's jacket made from silk and metal thread (silver), Italian, c. 1600–20. © Victoria and Albert Museum, London.

"well sheared," as opposed to describing the color.[17] The term "cottoned" was applied to wool fabrics from the fifteenth century which had the nap raised. Woolens and worsteds (made from a smooth yarn of combed long staple wool) were finish by felting. Calendaring resulted in the woolen fabric being put through two rollers either making the surface smooth and shiny or embossing it with a pattern. Cottons and linens would be bleached to make both fibers and fabrics white, either by bleaching in the sun or by a chemical bleaching process.

John Williams's gown was made from tawny cloth which was probably broadcloth, one of the traditional woolen fabrics or "old draperies." The most important of these were broadcloth (wider than 27 inches), worsted (woven from yarn made from combed, long staple, wool), kerseys (woven from carded yarn in a twill weave), and straights (a twilled cloth with a fulled surface and half the width of broadcloth). Woolen textiles were often produced in a variety of plain weaves, usually with a single warp and weft, including tabbies. Tabbies could be warp or weft faced, along with hopsack or basket tabbies. Twills, such as herringbone and diamond twill, were also popular. While produced throughout Europe, Italy was one of the main centers of production of these traditional wool textiles. However, during the course of the sixteenth century the traditional woolens described above faced competition from the "new draperies." Their novelty lay in three main areas—their being were woven from long staple, highly twisted wool including the *ostaden* and *rassen* (the equivalent of English worsted), by the wool being mixed with other fibers such as camel or goat hair (for example grosgrain), or they were designed to look like silk fabrics (such as the mockadoes and corduroy).

Raw silk was imported from Calabria, Granada, and Asia via Genoa and Venice to supply the key weaving centers of Bologna, Florence, Genoa, and Venice from the 1450s.[18] There were also a number of smaller centers including Milan and Siena.[19] During the sixteenth century, silk weaving developed in France at Avignon, Lyons, and Tours and in Germany at Augsburg, Cologne, and Nuremberg reflecting the desirability of silk and its economic value.[20] Bursa was a key silk-producing town when it was part of the Byzantine empire and by the mid-fifteenth century the town was the second most important market for raw silk coming from Persia and Turkey. In 1502, Bursa had over 1,000 looms producing ninety-one types of fabric.[21] By the late sixteenth century, satins (*Atlas*) and cloth of gold or silver (*Serāser*), polychrome silk with metal thread (*Kemhā*), polychrome silk (*Serenk*), velvet (*Kadife*), pile on pile velvet (*Kadife-i dū hāvī*), and with metal thread (*Çātma*) produced in Bursa were traded with Russia for furs.[22] Silk weaving also developed in Constantinople in the 1500s.[23]

Silk weaving in India was focused around Ahmedabad, Cambay, Patan, and Surat.[24] Raw silk as well as silk yarn were imported from China and used to produce *patola*, while silk production was established at Bengal and it gradually replaced Chinese silk.[25] Significant levels of silk weaving also took place in China but the isolationist policies of the Ming dynasty meant that most were for domestic consumption and that the Chinese had little interest in importing Italian silks. Even so, there is evidence to suggest that some Chinese silks did reach Europe via Spain and that these fabrics were probably produced specifically for export. For example, a fragment of slate-blue broderie velvet with the design of flowers and leaves in large stylized vases worked in uncut pile and the ground in cut pile.[26]

Silk textiles were produced in a wider variety of weaves than woolens. These could include satin and damask, which combined a warp- or weft-faced twill with a satin. Complex weaves included velvet (a warp pile fabric) produced with cut loops, uncut loops, a combination of the two and with various heights of pile, and lampas (with two warps and one weft). Examples of these textiles could be found worldwide, including the *riccio sopra riccio* (cloth of gold with uncut and cut pile) woven to shape in Florence to make a set of copes commissioned by the first Tudor monarch, Henry VII.[27]

Light to medium plain weave linens were used for shirts, smocks (Figure 1.4), partlets, and coifs throughout the early modern period, while heavier weight linens or canvas, as they were known, were used as interlinings; complex weaves, such as diaper and damask, were more usually reserved for napery.

Linen weaving took place throughout Europe. For example, during the fifteenth century, Hull was a center for linen weaving while also importing linens from Germany, Ireland, the Low Countries, Prussia, and Scotland.[28] Much of the French linen weaving industry that was focused round Reims was disrupted by the religious wars but production of heavier weight fabrics such as canvas continued to flourish around the Bay of Bourgneuf, Morlaix, Rennes, and Vitré in Brittany.[29]

Lombardy developed cotton weaving in the thirteenth century using locally-produced cotton and cotton imported from Asia via Genoa and Venice.[30] India was the key producer of cotton goods in the sixteenth century, with the main areas of production in the Deccan. Most of this cloth was consumed in the Asian sub-continent but by the late sixteenth century raw cotton was imported into Europe from Asia and the Americas. Raw cotton was imported into England at the end of the sixteenth century and duty was charged at a rate of £3 6s 8d for a hundredweight of raw cotton and £5 for the same quantity of spun cotton.[31] Cotton weaving was established at Manchester but production was small scale.[32] Asian cottons were not common in Europe until the late seventeenth century, when large

FIGURE 1.4: A woman's linen smock embroidered with silk, 1575–85. © Victoria and Albert Museum, London.

quantities of calicos, cottons, and muslins began to be imported and they had a very significant impact on women's fashions.[33]

In addition to fabrics woven from single fibers, this period saw the growing importance of mixed or union cloths some of which would be termed the "new draperies." These included silk and wool camlets and *bourettes*, and silk and linen *oeillets*.[34] In France these sixteenth-century textiles were divided into the "light draperies" (*draperies légères*) and "new light draperies" (*nouvelles draperies légères*). Traditionally, combining fibers was viewed as problematic because this could be a way to defraud the buyer, but it also had many virtues. In particular, the different fiber combinations could meet the demand for novelty, while their being cheaper would facilitate the wish for fashionable change by making them more affordable. In addition, some of the lighter fabrics draped better than some stiffer traditional cloths and many were better suited to being printed. Popular union cloths included linen and wool mixes (for example, linsey woolsey), linen and cotton combinations (for example, fustian), along with cotton with silk, wool, and hemp (for example, bombazine). The popularity and value of these cloths was demonstrated by a request put forward by Pasqualin d'Alessandro and the Venetian silk weavers in 1580:

> We too should be able to make the below-mentioned fabrics that are made all over the world, which are silk *ferandine* with a wool weft, *dobloni* with a wool weft, *buratti* with a wool weft, tabbies with a flax and waste-silk weft, *canevazze* with a waste-silk

and flax weft, twilled *rasetti* with a flax and cotton weft ... are continually imported in very great quantities to the detriment of us poor weavers.[35]

OTHER MATERIALS USED TO MAKE AND DECORATE CLOTHING

While most clothing and accessories were made from textiles, three other materials should to be mentioned briefly. Two of them were skin-based products, namely leather and fur, and both feature in the clothing issued to Henry VIII and his henchmen in November 1510.[36] They received fox fur and black lamb skins to line their gowns, double soled leather shoes, and leather points. Leather was made from the corium, the thickest layer of the skin, from a range of animals, birds, fish, and reptiles, and was preserved by a variety of tanning methods.[37] Leather was used more for men's clothing than for women's, particularly jerkins,[38] doublets, hose, and buff coats, as well as gloves, shoes, boots, purses, and pouches used by men and women.[39] Well-prepared leather brought the tailor a variety of desirable characteristics because it could be very fine, soft, and have high levels of elasticity. In addition, it could be easily dyed, slashed, pinked, stamped, and sewn. While most countries in Europe produced leather, Spanish leather from Cordova was highly prized and often copied with varying degrees of success.

Equally prized by wealthy men and women were the furs of the sable, leopard, or lynx, while home-produced furs such as rabbit, cat, and fox were more widely available. In comparison to the Middle Ages, there was a reduction in the use of fur in the early modern period. Taking squirrel fur as an example, the decline in its popularity in the fifteenth century has been linked partially to changes in taste but also to excessive hunting which reduced the availability of suitable furs.[40] Even so, fur was still a high-status item that was often used to make linings, trimmings for gowns, sleeves, and hoods, as well as fur accessories such as the *zibellino* (a fur tippet worn by women in the late fifteenth and sixteenth centuries).[41] They were often given by men to their wives, such as the sumptuous sable Henry VIII gave to Catherine Howard.[42] While a *zibellino* might be worn at any time, fur use was often seasonal so fur linings were put in for warmth in the winter and taken out in the summer.

The third material, felt, was made from wool and other animal fibers but it did not have a woven structure, which sets it apart slightly from other textiles. It was also possible to felt some animal skins, including beaver and rabbit pelts, using mercuric nitrate. They were made into hats from the mid-seventeenth century (a process called carroting).[43] Wool and fur felts had a variety of properties, providing warmth, insulation, and padding, as well as being waterproof, stretchable, and moldable. Felt was ideally suited to making hats. Felt making was a significant industry with 3,000 felt makers working in sixteenth-century London. In 1576, they established their own guild when they separated from the Haberdashers' Guild.[44] Felt was also an important industry in the south of France, especially in Cévennes and Languedoc, but also in Chartres, Marseilles, Paris, Rouen, and Sedan. The felting guild was the third most important in early sixteenth-century Paris.[45]

While textiles were the primary components of garments, once tailoring became a significant part of how a garment was constructed, a range of additional items was required to complete a piece of clothing. At its most basic, thread was required to sew the seams as well as to baste pieces of fabric together, and to pad stitch. The thread was spun quite tightly to give it the strength required and depending on the complexity of the garment, a variety of threads of different weights, fibers, and colors were required. In addition, wool, silk, or metal wrapped threads might be required for embroidery. Wax, often in the form of candles, was used for searing sewing yarn making it easier to thread the needle and to stop it knotting.

Late sixteenth- and early seventeenth-century Western clothing incorporated padding and stiffenings to create the distinctive fashionable shapes. This was alluded to in a seventeenth-century ruling passed by the Common Council of London seeking to control the clothing of female servants stating that they were not permitted "Any fardingale at all . . . nor any body or sleeves of wire, whalebone or other stiffening saving canvas or buckram only."[46] Whalebone, or to give it its proper name, baleen, was derived from filter-feeding whales. It had the advantage of being strong, light-weight, flexible and it could be cut into narrow strips. A cheaper alternative was bents, the dried stems of grasses. Bents grouped in bundles of twenty were used to stiffen the front of a linen pair of bodies, now in the Rocamora Collection, Barcelona, dating from the early seventeenth century.[47] Cotton wadding or bombast (*bambagio*) was used as the padding layer in quilted doublets as well as nightgowns. Other padding materials included sawdust, bran, and horse hair.[48]

Men's doublets, in particular, made increasing use of a range of fastenings including buttons, many of which were made from a variety of metals ranging from gold and silver to latten and tin (Fig. 1.5).[49]

FIGURE 1.5: A man's doublet made from watered wool, silk taffeta, linen, and whalebone, sewn with silk and linen threads, decorated with a silver-gilt and a silver-gilt and silk braid, 1615–20. © Victoria and Albert Museum, London.

FIGURE 1.6: A man's collar made from linen and edged with bobbin lace, with tassels of knotted linen thread, probably English, c. 1630–40. © Victoria and Albert Museum, London.

Thread and fabric buttons were also readily available. Other fastenings included hooks and eyes, lacing, points, and pins.[50] Fine cords and braids were often used to make points, which secured a man's hose to the lacing band of his doublet, or keep his codpiece in place. Silk and wool trimmings were also used to decorate new clothes and refurbish old garments. The terms "passamenterie," "small wares," and "haberdashery" encapsulated the various, often expensive, items produced by silk women and silk men.[51]

A key development in Europe was the rise of lace made using two different techniques. The first involved the use of threads, bobbins, and a hard pillow to make a plaited and twisted structure from silk, linen and metal thread (Fig. 1.6).

Bone or bobbin lace in late sixteenth- and early seventeenth-century England took its name for the bone bobbin used in its making, while it was known as *dentelle* in France, *merletto* in Italy, and *puntas* in Spain. The second technique, known as needle-lace, developed from embroidery in the early sixteenth century.[52] Lace was made in Flanders, France, Germany, Spain, and Italy, and these countries supplied an increasingly international trade by the late sixteenth century.[53]

ECONOMY AND TRADE

Cloth production was very important to the early modern economy because of the scale of the trade, its financial value, the tax it generated, and because it was a leading form of manufacturing. As a result, the textile trade attracted two main groups of men with entrepreneurial aims. The first formed business groupings that traded in a variety of goods such as textiles, including the Hanseatic League, the Levant Company, the Muscovy Company, and the various East India Companies. The second sought to make the production of cloth more commercial or to develop new areas of production, such as the attempt to introduce silk weaving into England under James I.[54] According to Nicholas Geffe (fl.1586–93), England needed its own silk industry because:

> the making of silk in England ... cannot give better occasion ... weaving satins, velvets, taffeta, and divers sorts of other silken stuffs, by which disposing them the industrious will be ready and willing to work, or being idle, loiterers may be compelled.[55]

There was also investment in technological developments, which helped make the transition from hand to mechanized production. For example, guilds of hand knitters were well established in Paris (1366), Barcelona (1496), Tournai (1429), and Coventry (1496).[56] However, in 1589 William Lee developed the knitting frame and silk knitting frame in 1599. The technology soon spread, partly because Lee did not get the support he had hoped for in London. In 1611 Lee agreed to make four silk knitting frames for Pierre de Caux, a silk knitter from Rouen, who had met Lee in London.[57]

The scale of production meant that the textile trade generated income from taxation in many countries. As a result, in 1450 Francesco Sforza, duke of Milan, declared his lands would be free of duties, so promoting trade from Genoa via Lombardy to the Alps as well as the export of cloth from Lombardy.[58] However, the international nature of the textile trade meant that it was also vulnerable to large-scale economic trends. For example, rising inflation in Europe during the sixteenth century had a significant impact on the Spanish wool trade. The price of Spanish wool had increased so much by the 1550s that sales dropped, and as a result by the 1560s the flocks had decreased by 20 percent.[59]

The ubiquity of textiles resulted in many governments wanting to ensure the quality of what was produced. These regulations could establish the length and width of specific fabrics, while the use of colored selvedges could denote the place of production. Seals were applied to show that the cloth had been checked against these criteria. For example, in 1483 the English government enacted that each broadcloth produced must be two yards wide, twenty-four yards long and have been watered.[60] Other forms of regulation were aimed at making certain textiles exclusive. For instance in 1574 only the weavers of the Topkapi saray in Istanbul were permitted to work with gold and silver thread, and their silks were reserved for the emperor.[61] The importance of the regulations was demonstrated when they were flouted. In 1630, an English East India Company factor based in Masulipatam complained that:

> The cloth of these parts is growne very deceitful, as wanting in both lengths and breadths, which will be very prejudiciall to the profit.[62]

Textile weaving relied upon a skilled workforce, particularly for silks. For a variety of religious and political reasons, this skilled workforce was also often a mobile one, resulting in a spread of knowledge. From the thirteenth century, Arab weavers, known as *mudéjares*, worked in Spain. After 1492 and the reunification of Spain by the Catholic monarchs, many of these weavers left Spain for North Africa and beyond.[63] In the sixteenth century Italian weavers came to Spain, bringing velvet weaving with them.[64] French and Dutch migrant weavers, many of whom were followers of the reformed religion, settled in London suburbs including Aldgate, Bishopsgate, Cripplegate, Shoreditch, Southwark, Spitalfields, Stepney, and Tower Hamlets.[65] In contrast, production of the raw materials often required a large but not necessarily skilled workforce. By the 1650s, several hundred slaves from Africa had been taken to the Caribbean, initially to grow tobacco but soon for growing cotton. From the 1680s onwards, numbers and the scale of production would increase rapidly.[66] (Figure 1.7.)

FIGURE 1.7: Chinese silk made into a coverlet, sixteenth to eighteenth century. © Victoria and Albert Museum, London.

The textile trade also had a strong link to urban development, often with positive consequences. For example, York developed as an entrepôt in the north of England as a market for leather and West-Riding cloth, along with Kendal.[67] By contrast, most of Exeter's sixteenth-century trade was with France. The city exported cloth from the West Country and imported canvas and linen. Their trade dipped in the early seventeenth century, reviving by the 1660s with the import of linen from the Low Countries, and the export of serge.[68] Norwich benefitted from the financial impact of the New Draperies and the migrants from the Low Countries between the 1580s and the 1620s.[69] Entrepreneurs such as William Stumpe, a cloth merchant, could build housing for their textile workers. He bought the site and buildings of Malmesbury Abbey "to make a street or two for clothiers in the back vacant ground of the abbey that is within the town walls."[70] However, the period also saw urban poverty and the textile and clothing trades were used to provide work and to teach skills. For example, on September 17, 1623 a proclamation issued in London declared that:

> many thousands of our poore subjects, both men, and women, and children, [were to be employed] in carding, basening, felting, dressing, pouncing, blocking and dying with certaine other feates concerning the working and making of Felts.[71]

Textile trade networks fell into two interlinked groups. First, there were the large-scale, national and international networks with routes by land and sea, with large cities and ports forming the key points in the system. The European voyages of discovery had a marked impact on the development of this, and Venice was ideally located to exploit all of these factors. The city had an extensive trade network ranging from London and Lisbon to Palermo, Constantinople, Alexandria, and Damascus. Venice emerged as a center of the woolen trade, producing 2,000 pieces of cloth in the 1510s which had risen to 28,729 in 1602.[72] Venetian merchants also bought wool and linen fabrics from western Europe in Augsburg and Nuremberg, while selling silk and spices brought in their great galleys from the east.[73] Second, there was regional or local selling based on inland and overland trade. This was facilitated by the development of road and river networks and coastal trade making it easier and cheaper to transport cloth for sale, even if it was of relatively low value.[74] The Southampton brokerage books record the volume, composition, and destinations of goods including textiles, dyes, and mordants, as well as teasels (a simple but effective tool for textile finishing), leaving the town by cart via the Bargate (the North gate) for a variety of places within Hampshire and beyond, including Bristol, Coventry, Kendal, and Salisbury.[75] As these examples demonstrate, the textile trade was complex, extensive and increasingly international.

DYES

The value placed on dyes, dyeing, and printing reflected the economic, social, and aesthetic significance of color in early modern society. Value was added to fabric by the dyeing process in two ways. First, the material gained color. Second, some colors (chiefly reds, purples, and black) were much more expensive than others, as demonstrated by the import duty in England charged at 8s on "Damask and caffa damask the yard" and at 13s 4d on "Damask and caffa damask crimson or purple in grain the yard."[76] Consequently, some colors were quite scarce and they were often restricted to the elite. As a result, cheaper dyestuffs could be substituted for more costly examples, and guilds were increasingly concerned to regulate the quality of dyes used and how fast they were to sunlight, to washing, spot cleaning techniques, and perspiration.[77] Most dyeing was undertaken in the yarn or the piece, but over-dyeing, and re-dyeing also took place.

Dyeing was a skilled occupation and the early modern period saw the continued specialization of dyers. For example, in Constance, Erfurt, Magdeburg, and Nuremburg the *Schönfärber* or luxury dyers worked with a single color, while the *Färber* or *Schwarzfärber*, the ordinary dyers, produced colors of middle quality that were either dark or dull.[78] As a result of being part of the skilled workforce, dyers migrated for economic and other reasons, including the hope for religious freedom, such as the woad dyers from Amiens who settled in London in Candlewick Street. Most textile dyeing was undertaken at a commercial level by dyers guilds, but by the late sixteenth and early seventeenth centuries recipes for home dyeing began to appear in receipt books.

The dye trade was national and international, and the natural sources from which dyes were derived were supplied from around the globe. Dyes can be divided in several ways. First, by their application method, into mordant dyes (dyes which are water soluble but will only bond with the fiber with the addition of a mordant, a soluble metal salt), vat dyes (dyes which are water insoluble and need converting into soluble form so that they can be applied to the fibers), and direct dyes (dyed which dissolve in water and do not need a mordant).[79] Second, by the color they produce: blue (woad, orchil, and indigo) (Figure 1.8), red (madder, cochineal, kermes, gain, chay or chaya), yellow (weld and dyers' broom), green (buckthorn berries, nettle leaves, until the sixteenth century when they started to mix woad or indigo with weld), and black (logwood).

FIGURE 1.8: A linen and cotton towel, dyed with either indigo or woad, Italian, 1400–1500. © Victoria and Albert Museum, London.

Blue was a popular color and it was achieved using two main dyes—woad and indigo. Woad (*Isatis tinctoria*) was grown in England (around Lincoln and Glastonbury) and Scotland. It was also imported from northern France from the twelfth century; merchants from Picardy had a warehouse in London from 1237.[80] By the fourteenth century, woad was grown in Sicily, Seville, Lombardy, Languedoc, and Thuringia, and it was exported to Byzantium and the Islamic world.[81] The spread of woad dyeing was reflected in its use for producing dyer's masterpieces (lengths of dyed cloth produced by an apprentice or journeyman wanting to become a master craftsman)—in Erfurt, Rouen, and Toulouse in the fourteenth century, in Milan in the fifteenth century, and in Paris and Nuremberg by the sixteenth century.[82] In contrast, indigo (*Indigofera tinctoria*) was imported into Marseilles from Baghdad in the Levant from the mid-thirteenth century. It was also grown round Agra and Ahmedabad in India.[83]

Moving to consider red, the Netherlands was the main European producer of madder (*Rubia tinctoria*) with large-scale production in the sixteenth century in Flanders and Zeeland. Magdeburg was the center of the German madder trade, especially with the Slavic nations.[84] Not surprisingly, English merchants were keen to encourage madder production in America, a new area of production and a new potential market. In April 1633, the government requested "that Mr Lane be afforded every facility for planting his madder."[85] Kermes or grain (*Kermes vermilio*) produced strong crimsons and scarlets.

Dyes new to Europe were discovered in the New World. For example, cochineal (*Dactylopius coccus*) came from Mexico and it was brought to Venice for the first time on February 9, 1543.[86] It was a very valuable red dye. In November 1608, 485 cases of cochineal worth 333,437 ducats were brought from the Indies to Seville.[87] Other new dyestuffs included logwood (*legno tauro*), a new black, and Brasilwood/Sappanwood (*Caesalpinia sapan*), a red dye derived from the bark of the Sappan tree from South America and the West and East Indies.

A range of additives, including potash (which was exported from the Baltic), were required for the dyeing processes to create the correct conditions in the dye bath. The most important additive, however, was alum, a sulfate of potassium and aluminium. It was mined in the area around the Black Sea and from the mines managed by the Genoese in Phocaea in the Gulf of Smyrna. When alum was discovered at Tolfa, near Civitavecchia, in the Papal States, it was exploited by Julius II, who leased its distribution to a number of Italian bankers, including the Medici of Florence and Agostino Chigi (c. 1465–1520) from Siena. In 1544–5 the Venetian Republic refused to honor the papal ban on Christians using alum from the Ottoman empire because "not only the goods of the infidel are brought to the lands of the Church, but the infidels themselves trade everywhere, and especially in Ancona."[88]

This period saw the publication of the first European text on dyeing, *Mariegola dell'arte de tentori*, in Venice in 1429.[89] However, one of the best-known books on dyeing—containing 108 recipes—was produced by Giovanventura Rosetti. Its full title was *Instructions in the art of the dyers which teaches the dyeing of woollen clothes, linens, cottons and silk by the great arts, as well as by the common*, but it was usually known as *The Plictho*. Practical developments in dyeing during this period included those undertaken by Dutchman Cornelis Drebbel (c. 1572–1633), who set up a dye works at Stratford-on-Bow in 1607. Drebel's scarlet was produced using cochineal with a tin and *aqua regia* (a mixture of hydrochloric and nitric acid) mordant, which gave a brighter hue.[90]

Color was significant in two ways. First, plain colors, especially when combined with the surface texture of the cloth, such as the sheen of satin or the contrasting weaves of a damask (Figure 1.9), could enhance the appeal of a fabric.

During the early modern period, the available color palette was increasingly linked to the connection between color and fashion. This was reflected in the fancy names the colors were given. The work of Giovan Andrea Corsuccio (1581) referred to variegated colors, including *fior di persica* (peach flower), *capo di picchio* (woodpecker's head), *fior di fava* (broad-bean flower), and *pel di gatto* (cat fur).[91] By the seventeenth century, Italian silks were available in lemon, lime green, salmon pink, turquoise, and olive green to name a few.[92]

Second, patterned textiles made increasing use of color. They could be monochrome damasks or voided velvets, or they could be polychrome using a growing repertoire of motifs and the size of the pattern repeat. From the 1430s, the pomegranate motif was increasingly popular on Italian silks.[93] By the mid-sixteenth century, an ogival lattice was important while the 1580s saw a new development: sprigged floral motifs.[94] By about 1630, flowers especially the chrysanthemum and peony, became much more natural, often on delicate stems with leaves.[95] In contrast, fifteenth-century silks from the Ottoman Empire often had designs of wavy lines or tiger stripes and three discs or leopard spots known as *chintamani*.[96] By the mid-sixteenth century these too had the ogival repeat, which may have been influenced by Chinese and Mamluk designs, along with carnations, palmettes, roses, and tulips.[97]

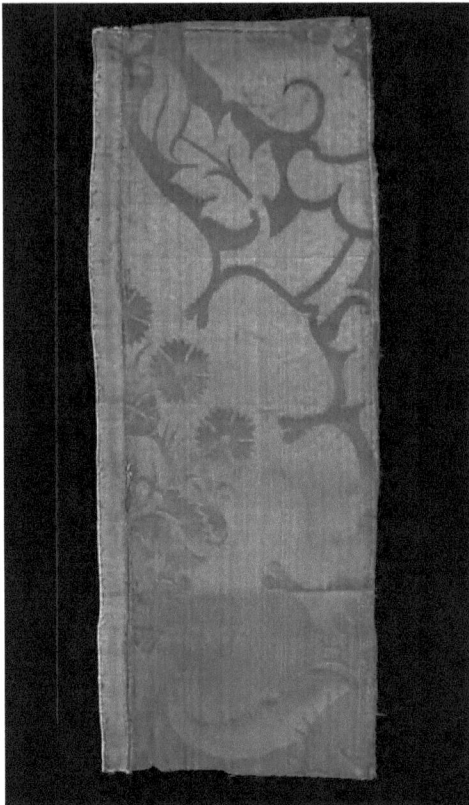

FIGURE 1.9: A piece of silk damask, Italian, second half of the fifteenth century. © Victoria and Albert Museum, London.

Dyeing was one way color could be applied to textiles; printing was another. Some block printing took place in Italy, the Netherlands, and northern Germany; the technique was described in Cennino Cennini's *Trattato della pittura* written c. 1400. The design was carved in relief on a wooden block but, compared with Indian printed textiles, the results were relatively unsophisticated in Europe until the 1650s onwards. By contrast, William Methwold described Coromandel cottons or calicos in his *Relations of the Kingdom of Golconda* (1626):

> The paintings of the Coast . . . are indeed the most exquisite that are seen, the best wrought all with pensil and with such durable colours that, not withstanding they bee often washed, the colours fade not whilst the cloth lasteth.[98]

Many of these were exceptional examples of printing and they were achieved using a paste (consisting of a dye and a thickener such as gum Arabic or starch) which was applied, then steamed and washed.[99]

Color thus became an increasingly important part of the early modern textile trade, adding financial and aesthetic value. However, the wish for color came at a price, which made dye production and dyeing the target of government legislation. For example, woad is a cruciferous plant that takes nutrients from the soil, leaving it unproductive for other crops. In sixteenth-century England, this became increasingly significant alongside the impact of poor weather on harvests, rising prices, and inflation. As a result, on October 14, 1585 a royal proclamation was issued prohibiting the sowing of woad "within 4 miles of any market town, or other town occupying the common trade of clothing."[100] On May 6, 1586 the sheriff of Southampton was ordered to arrest "one Cooper" for attempting to sow woad "contrary to her majesty's proclamation prohibiting the same."[101] The pollution produced by various textile and related trades also resulted in legislation restricting where they could be located. For instance, in 1533 Parisian dyers and leather workers came into conflict over access to clean water, as reflected in the city regulations which prevented:

> all furriers, tawers, and dyers to exercise their professions in their town or suburban homes; ordering them, when washing their wool cloths, to carry them or have them carried to the Seine below the Tuileries; . . . prohibiting them from emptying their tawing agents, dyes, or other such pollution into the river; permitting them to work outside of Paris near Chaillot at a distance of at least two bow shots from the suburbs under pain of confiscation of their goods and merchandise, and banishment from the kingdom.[102]

In a similar vein, the Wapping-based alum works polluted the Thames and the associated ponds and channels, resulting in poisoned fish and water that was unusable for brewing.[103] A century later, in 1694, Celia Fiennes' horse refused to go past a woad works near Hailes Abbey because of the unpleasant smell.[104]

CONCLUSION

Returning to the clothes given to John Williams, they provide an excellent overview of how and why textiles were significant in the early modern period. The list indicates that different fabrics were used to make different garments, while stressing the importance and value of wool and silk over linen (and cotton). The choice of black and tawny reflected two colors that were popular in the first half of the sixteenth century and linked to Williams's social position. In a hundred years' time, black would still be a sound selection but tawny would no longer be a fashionable shade. The wool cloth was possibly made in England but the silks, and probably the linen, were imports. While most of the goods supplied to the crown were sold by English men, many of these individuals had a network of trade links that extended across Europe and beyond. Indeed textile production and trade was truly international with traditional products thriving alongside innovative weaves and mixtures of fibers, new dyes and an evolving repertoire of decorative motifs.

CHAPTER TWO

Production and Distribution

SUSAN VINCENT

In 1583 English writer Philip Stubbes published *The anatomie of abuses*, a treatise that explored what he saw as the moral shortcomings of contemporary society. In it, he complains of "the Innumberable meryades of sundry fashions daily inuented."[1] This chapter explores how these myriad sundry fashions made it on to the backs of their wearers, the sorts of people Stubbes observed going about their daily business in clothes that he felt were both beyond their means and beyond moderation. Stubbes feared, among other things, the collapse of visual distinctions and a resulting social chaos, arguing against the "mingle mangle" of apparel that arose when any man could wear anything he could "get by any meanes."[2] But what were these means to which Stubbes alluded? How did an individual on the various rungs of the social ladder acquire his or her garments, and what did they then do with them? What kind of skills and knowledge did an early modern clothes consumer need, and what were the financial resources required? The chapter opens by looking at new clothes and their acquisition, whether garments made within the home, sourced from professional tailors, or purchased ready-made from a variety of suppliers. It goes on to consider strategies for shopping and the ongoing material value of clothing, before turning to the many facets of the second-hand market that facilitated the distribution of garments through a life cycle of repeated reuse.

ACQUIRING NEW GARMENTS

Although expressing his opinions more energetically than most, Philip Stubbes was in the majority in believing that apparel was important. This was a society in which clothes mattered in almost every conceivable way, and their acquisition was not undertaken lightly. As the other contributions to this volume make clear, dress intersected with religious and moral debates, was heavily implicated in understandings of social role and status, its ownership was the subject of regulatory laws and, as we will see, its economic importance loomed large in probably every Renaissance household. Most people owned relatively few garments, and getting hold of more took time, energy, and money.

Let's start by considering the underclothes, the linen shirt and smock (or shift). These can be considered as universal garments, put on daily by every man, woman, and child regardless of age, geography, or social position. In the process of dressing, everyone began here: drawing the garment over the head, the wearer's arms went through its sleeves which were long to the wrist, and its linen lengths fell uninterrupted to well down the legs. Being worn next to the skin like this, the shirt and smock kept the outer garments from being soiled by sweat and other secretions, and simultaneously made the heavier, often-woolen overgarments more comfortable. The underwear itself became quickly dirty, but, unlike the outer clothes, it was also easy to launder and bleach. In addition to such functional utility, personal linen—which also included head and neckwear, cuffs, and collars (bands)—was coupled with notions of decency and respectability: clean white linen, changed as often as personal circumstances allowed, was an outward manifestation of both housewifely skill and personal refinement. The different grades also materialized a sliding scale of moral, financial, and social worth: coarser types like a domestically produced variety were considered suitable for a laborer, while at the other end of the continuum, fine imported linens like cyprus or holland clothed wearers of rank and standing.

The making and care of household and personal linens was a particularly female preserve (Figure 2.1).[3] Buying the material from a linen draper, market, or pedlar (in rural areas there was also some domestic linen production), the woman cut the undergarment's panels from the linen piece and made them up. Straightforward in their construction they were generally sewn from rectangular panels or their triangular divisions, with shaping being achieved not by cutting but by stitching in tucks, darts, and gathers. A female

FIGURE 2.1: *Two sewing women*, by Geertruydt Roghman and Claes Jansz Visscher, Amsterdam, 1648–50. At the women's feet can be seen a basket with garments or fabric, a pair of shears, a yardstick for measuring, and a spool of thread. Rijksmuseum, Amsterdam.

workforce was also responsible for any embroidery or lacework on the garment, and in addition did all the laundering and starching required by a lifetime of wear (Figure 2.2).

Generally, but not always, all of these activities took place within the home. Constituting a flexible workforce primarily outside the guild system, such women might work solely for the needs of their families, on a professional basis, or somewhere between the two, either doing piecework or selling surplus production into the ready-made market. This variation in the organization of women's linen work can be illustrated by a few examples. In fifteenth- and sixteenth-century Rouen, the two linen drapers' guilds—the one selling new linen garments, the other second-hand—were exclusively female.[4] In Renaissance Florence, we know that many different women contributed piecework to the wider market, including women living in convents. The conventual needlewomen in particular were often from middling or high-status families.[5] We know too that with needlework being considered an essential female skill set, the making of shirts and smocks was also undertaken by women for themselves and for their families, including in the most elite of households. Until their divorce, Catherine of Aragon made shirts for Henry VIII; Princess Elizabeth sewed one for her two-year-old brother, the future Edward VI.[6] Likewise, gentlewoman Lady Brilliana Harley (bap. 1598–1643) made her son Edward's shirts. We learn of this from her letters, written to him at university: "I haue made 2 shirts for you till I make more. I purpos to send them this weake . . . I purpos, and pleas God, to send

FIGURE 2.2: Miniature from *Splendor Solis*, by Salomon Trismosin, fol. 32v, Germany, 1582. Women washing and bleaching linens. © British Library, London, MS Harley 3469.

FIGURE 2.3: Woodcut from Spanish tailoring book *Geometria y traca*, by Diego de Freyle, Seville, 1588. Tailors at work sewing, with another measuring a pattern or cloth preparatory to cutting out. Clothes hang from racks behind them. Folger Shakespeare Library, Washington DC.

you 4 more shirts as soune as I can . . . I haue sent you your linen." In another letter, Lady Brilliana asked Ned to send her an old shirt so she could take its measure—this being, in the absence of a pattern, a standard way of ensuring fit.[7]

Given their function as undergarments, their closeness to their owner—which included the bodily stains from years of wear—and a production that was frequently undertaken by loving and familiar hands, it is not surprising that there could be a profound intimacy to personal linens. By contrast, the constructionally more complicated outer wear was made by professional tailors, who were usually—although not exclusively—men (Figure 2.3).[8] It is unclear how much of the population were able to obtain their clothes bespoke. Certainly the elite used the professional services of a tailor, but the practice percolated a considerable way down the social scale. The account books of two early seventeenth-century Tuscan tailors, for instance, show their clients to have included barbers, cobblers, sailors, and builders.[9] With the main cost of a garment inhering in the cloth and trimmings rather than the labor of the tailor, it seems likely that everyone in a position to buy the fabric could afford to have it made up, at least on occasion. This accords with the numbers and distribution of tailors, whose shops were found in even small rural towns and whose services extended to the farther reaches of the countryside via itinerants. In larger towns such as York, by the late medieval period no one "could have been more than a stone's throw from a tailor";[10] in the European cities, clothing artisans occupied whole quarters and were a major guild and civic presence.

Given their ubiquity, it was lucky that tailors made good neighbors: their trade was quiet, required no special resources other than the cloth, and in contrast to many craft processes produced no foul waste. In setting up a business the overheads were low, the skill was easily portable, and the equipment required relatively cheap and simple: scissors and shears, pins, needles and thread, pressing irons, chalk, parchment strips for taking measure of clients, yardsticks for measuring out cloth.[11] However, although tailors were the most numerous, many more trades contributed to the production of a finished outfit. This "entire spectrum of providers" included hatters and hosiers, shoemakers, furriers, embroiderers, glovers, and potentially many other specialized artisans (Figure 2.4).[12] By

FIGURE 2.4: *The Shoemaker*, woodcut by Jost Amman illustrating Hartmann Schopper's *Panoplia omnium illiberalium mechanicarum* (*Book of Trades*), Frankfurt, 1568. A woman stops at the workshop's unshuttered window to inspect a pair of shoes. In the foreground, men sit sewing. Wikimedia Commons.

way of an illustration of the numbers that could be involved in clothing the well-to-do, in the ten-year period between 1569 and 1579, in outfitting his wardrobe the Florentine Niccolò di Luigi Capponi bought from sixty-seven different makers or sellers.[13] At the high end of the market particularly, in what has been called a "collaborative" process, many artisans might contribute to the construction of a just one single garment.[14] Most of these trades involved in the production of clothing were, in this period, organized into guilds, which oversaw the training of apprentices, the quality of the merchandise, the welfare of their members, and in addition participated in civic government. However, this official picture hides the informal layers of subcontracting and piecework that existed beneath the dominant guild structure, where poorer artisans and women provided a floating labor force for entrepreneurial and richer guild masters, or supplied domestically produced wares onto the market for sale by others.

When commissioning a new garment, the client customarily supplied the fabric and trimmings, which he or she would have purchased first from either a mercer or draper (the former typically dealing with more expensive textiles like silks and velvets, the latter with woolens), or at a local market (Figure 2.5). Taking this to the tailor with instructions

FIGURE 2.5: *Der Tuchhändler* (*The Draper*), miniature from Schachzabelbuch des Konrad von Ammenhausen, by Hans Schilling, 1467. A draper in his shop measures cloth for a customer. Stuttgart, Württembergische Landesbibliothek, Cod. poet. et phil. fol. 2, f. 244r.

for the finished garment, the completed item was ready in usually just a few days.[15] These seem like simple steps, but to be successfully achieved they required a particular set of competencies on the consumer's part. For a start, he or she needed to be able to judge the quality of the fabric, whether it would make up well into the finished garment, the reasonableness of the cost, and, given that its sale price was likely not fixed, be able to bargain with the retailer.[16] All of these skills are evident in a letter of 1534 sent to Lady Lisle (1493x5–1566) by a gentleman in her service, John Husee. First he tells her:

> [I] have bought xij yards of satin; I think there is no better worn: which cost viij^s and vj^d the yards. I have not yet delivered it to Mr. Skut [Scott, the tailor].

After reporting this simple transaction Husee goes on to consider the purchase of cloth of silver, an extremely expensive silk fabric interwoven with silver threads or strips, the procuring of which he was taking a great deal of care over.

And as for the cloth of silver, I have searched this town, as well strangers as others, but I can get none that liketh me with the price. I may have for xviij^s, xx^s, xxij^s, and so to xxviij^s the yards, but it is nothing to pass upon for your ladyship, for it shall never stand with your honour to wear it. I have found iij pieces, the musters [patterns] whereof I send herein closed; the plain muster will cost xl^s the yard; the violet wrought with knots of silver, xlvj^s viij^d; the other, branched, xl^s. Howbeit I like the plain cloth of silver best, and it sheweth best in the piece. And I saw this day Mr. Waring pay for xij yards of the same after xliij^s iiij^d the yard. I durst not meddle with it till in know your ladyship's pleasure . . . .[17]

Husee, then, had looked at many cheaper but inferior examples, before finally settling on a shortlist of three. While the final decision was Lady Lisle's, he advised her on which looked best in the bolt and by inference would show best in the made-up garment, and which although still costly, he was able to purchase for less than others had paid. Husee shows himself to have been an informed and discerning shopper.

After selecting his or her material, the customer had then to decide on how much to buy. Textiles were costly, and as the tailor kept the left-over remnants (Figure 2.6) after

FIGURE 2.6: *The Tailor*, woodcut by Jost Amman illustrating Hartmann Schopper's *Panoplia omnium illiberalium mechanicarum* (*Book of Trades*), Frankfurt, 1568. Depictions of tailors show great similarity across Europe. As well as the familiar tools and layout of the workshop, this illustration shows a box beneath the workbench for collecting fabric remnants. The men sew at the unglazed window to get the best light. Wikimedia Commons.

the garment had been cut out (which incidentally, the customer had to trust him to do as efficiently as possible), no one wished to buy any more than the minimum required. Individuals knew, therefore, how much fabric their garments would need.

Over and above these more functional competences, a customer also had to make decisions as regards a garment's design and fashionability, which in turn required a knowledge and scrutiny of current trends—the kind of trimmings for example, or perhaps the newest shaping of the sleeves. In the absence of fashion advertising, the streets and public spaces of Renaissance Europe were venues for observation, its inhabitants eyeing each other for new looks and new ideas.[18] Philip Gawdy's (1562–1617) London letters to his gentry family back home in Norfolk are filled with just such observations, ensuring the spread of fashion information from the city to the provinces. He assures his sister-in-law, for example, that he has seen both Queen Elizabeth and her gentlewomen at court wear the same style and cut of gown as the one he sent her (of tuff taffeta with an open wired sleeve), and that "it is now the newest fashion."[19] Letters might also work to relay taste over a wider reach, as the fashion conscious looked to trends in other European centers. In the midst of the English Civil War, Anne Lee wrote to the exiled Lady Mary Verney for news of what was in vogue abroad:

> Madam, I hear you ar at pares [Paris], you will be trim in all the new fashones, I will make no new cloues [clothes] till you direct mee . . . I hear thay ware [wear] now in Franc coulerd slefes and stomicheres [sleeves and stomachers].[20]

Those in courtly circles might in addition have their contacts abroad send them fashion dolls—miniature figures dressed in tiny illustrative versions of the latest style[21] (Figure 2.7).

FIGURE 2.7: Fashion doll, "Pandora," 1590s. Livrustkammaren/The Royal Armoury, Stockholm.

In the Renaissance then, an individual's responsibility for his or her dressed appearance was exercised more actively than in later societies characterized by a fashion press and mass production, in which the consumer's chief energies are spent on selection. The purchase of made-to-order clothing, particularly at the top end of the market, was an imaginative endeavor, and the most successful at it demonstrated both practical knowledge and design flair. As some saw it, the customer's creative input was greater than that of the tailor. In the Venetian Republic, for instance, one strand of commentary rated tailors as useful only for their skills in cutting and stitching, in all else accommodating themselves to the wishes of their customers, men and women who "are continually thinking up new and unusual fashions in dress."[22] This is an extreme articulation, and certain high-end artisans tailoring garments for elite customers were definitely pushing the boundaries of their trade and playing with new forms and design schemes.[23] However, the trade was an immensely varied one, encompassing master craftsmen working in luxury materials, to itinerant journeymen making a living sewing workaday clothes and doing repairs. In this kind of clothing market, the roles of consumer and producer were somewhat blurred, and the shopper buying a garment was cast also as a client buying practical expertise to help in the realization of his or her own ideas. It is certainly striking that when obtaining new clothes, individuals tended to speak as having created them themselves, discursively bypassing the input of the artisans who had been involved. As Anne Lee wrote in her letter to Mary Verney, she would *make* no new clothes until hearing what was newly fashionable in Paris; in her memoirs of her husband John (bap. 1615–54), Lucy Hutchinson wrote that he was "genteel in his habit, and had a very good fancy in making good clothes."[24]

Not all new garments, however, were made to order. There was a variety of ready-made items available from a range of sellers. Haberdashers and milliners stocked things like hats, jewelry, fans, feathers, gloves, and perfume, and also linen garments and embroidered items like women's waistcoats (jackets) and partlets (the fill-in piece to cover décolletage). Philip Gawdy looked for a ready-made hat for his brother (and he describes it in exactly these terms), but finding none he liked, had instead to "bespake it of purpose"—thus also giving us an early example of the "bespoke" designation for individually made-to-order garments (Figure 2.8).[25] Linen undergarments, neckwear, and nightcaps might also be sold by seamstresses from stalls or shops.[26] In *The French garden*, a French–English language-learning text published in 1605, one of the dialogues features a lady shopping for fabric and fashions. After bargaining over the price and purchase of some cambric, the shopkeeper tries to tempt the lady to more purchases:

> Will you buye no shirts, ruffes,
> Falling bandes, handkerchers, night-coyfes [coifs],
> Falles, sockes, edged lace,
> Boote-hosen wrought [embroidered],
> Or any other thing that we haue?[27]

Rural customers accessed this kind of merchandise from itinerant traders, the packmen and pedlars who carried household and personal items. Margaret Spufford has identified three main categories of ware carried by the traveling traders of seventeenth-century England: textiles (mostly linens), haberdashery (such as pins, needles and thread, hooks and eyes, ribbons, combs, pocket looking-glasses, and lace), and ready-made wearing items like stockings, gloves, coifs, caps, bands, and hoods.[28] The ready-made market was perhaps facilitated by the "assembled" nature of Renaissance dress, where component

FIGURE 2.8: *The Hatmaker*, woodcut by Jost Amman illustrating Hartmann Schopper's *Panoplia omnium illiberalium mechanicarum* (*Book of Trades*), Frankfurt, 1568. Wikimedia Commons

parts were laced and pinned into a complete ensemble. This meant that not only the ribbons and points that attached the components were bought separately, but so too could items like sleeves and partlets. Although appearing to be complete with the foundation garment, such articles might be bought and worn interchangeably.

We know tailors selling ready-mades existed in Tuscany, likewise hosiers in the cities in Italy sold made-up stockings, and in sixteenth-century Florence, Paris, and Venice, the dealers of second-hand clothing also carried stocks of new. Even in the small towns and villages of early sixteenth-century Bedfordshire, customers had access to "small wares," and possibly some made-up larger garments.[29] In the late sixteenth- and early seventeenth-century Low Countries, there was a thriving ready-made trade. Produced through subcontracting arrangements with small-scale artisans working for their richer, entrepreneurial fellows, ready-made garments included doublets, breeches, cloaks, and stockings. Although the prices of these items were cheaper than made-to-order clothing, they were still beyond the reach of the average laborer and the purchasers most probably came from the middle orders of society. The stock held by some of the dealers was large indeed: in 1604 one Antwerp hosier had over 2,000 pairs of stockings in keeping, with a delivery network supplying merchants and shopkeepers in towns throughout the region. Other dealers sent wares not only to rural customers via market stalls, but traded as far as German towns like Hamburg and Cologne.[30]

SHOPPING BY PROXY

As Philip Gawdy's letters home illustrate, shopping by proxy was a common strategy for acquiring apparel and textiles.[31] Simply put, this was the ordinary request that someone else obtain specific goods on another individual's behalf. The geographical mobility of relatives, friends, and agents were all routinely exploited in this way. One person's journey to, or residence in, a commercial center became an opportunity by which many could benefit.

Purchase by proxy involved the same range of competencies required for personal shopping, but these were exercised on another's behalf. Obviously, the individual making the request had to trust their proxy—their honesty, of course, but also their practical and their aesthetic judgment. Could they tell a bargain from an extravagance, or weigh up the differing merits of a range of textiles? Could they accurately assess quantities and size, or judge fashionability? The assumption was that this competency would be demonstrated by both men and women. Indeed, men's greater geographical mobility may have meant that they were the ones more often employed as proxies, acquiring personal items on behalf of both male and female contacts alike. Philip Gawdy supplied his father and brother with garments, but also his mother and sister-in-law, purchasing on their behalf a range of fabrics and finishings (such as damask, taffeta, gold thread, and buttons), and dress items (sleeves, gloves, a farthingale, pumps, and a hair caul). The activities of the male proxy thus run counter to the enduring inscription of fashion as feminized, and the buying of family clothing and fabrics as being a woman's occupation. These letters show the male shopper active in the purchase of textiles and garments, both making practical decisions and adjudicating on matters of taste. The male proxy did this for items in the male wardrobe and also for women's garments.

Shopping by proxy was by no means fool-proof though, and some of the letters tell us of some of the ways the process could go wrong. If the proxy did not feel adequately briefed or was uncertain what to purchase, he or she would apply for more detail, or refer the decision back to the party making the request, as John Husee did to Lady Lisle when sourcing cloth of silver for her. Contemporary letters also suggest that the proxy might be dilatory, and reminders become increasingly emphatic. Very often a topos of necessity was brought into play, the party requesting the item emphasizing their need for the garment, rather than that they merely wanted it.

Another feature of shopping by proxy was the number of links that could easily build in this chain of acquisition. At its simplest, only two parties were involved: the individual making the request and the person fulfilling it, who might also be personally responsible for delivering the items. Very often though, not only might the request be made on another's behalf, but the proxy themselves might seek help from a third or even a fourth party. Add to this the use of friends, the servants of friends, and professional carriers to transport the goods, and even the simplest of transactions could ripple outwards in an ever-widening circle of participation. Nor was the relationship between the party requesting and the party procuring the goods necessarily fixed. As circumstances changed so could roles, and proxy could become purchaser, and vice versa.

There is one more noteworthy thing about this method of obtaining dress. If clothing is an important aspect of an individual's identity—an articulation of subjectivity—then the acquisition of his or her garments by proxy is surely significant. If a person's sartorial choices tell us something about who they are, then what do we learn when those choices have been deputed to another? In these instances appearance is partly a product of self-fashioning—that Renaissance mantra[32]—but also to some degree the result of a co-creation. In situations, therefore, where shopping by proxy was common, perhaps what we might have seen was a blurring at the edges of identity. Dress may have staked out claims to individuality, but it also described networks of mutuality.

THE VALUE OF CLOTHING

The purchase of bespoke and ready-made garments, whether by the wearer or by someone working on his or her behalf, represents only the most visible strands of a much larger and more complex web of clothing acquisition and redistribution.[33] This diverse and restless circulation of garments was underpinned by the certainty of their value. Representing a major category of expenditure across all strata of society, for most individuals garments embodied a significant financial investment. In economies with few banking facilities and subject to coin shortage, clothing was an investment that could be realized if circumstances required. Garments were stored wealth and could, therefore, be turned back into cash, exchanged for credit, used to pay off debts, or used as payment for services rendered.[34] A striking example of apparel's potential to act as capital and to hold its value over even long periods of time comes from the archives in Florence. In 1490, a silk merchant called Marco Parenti sold his wife's kermes red wedding gown (the most expensive and fashionable dye of the time[35]) and separate gold-embroidered sleeves. His wife had not only been dead for many years, but the garments themselves, having been made for their marriage in 1447, were forty-three years old. Their age notwithstanding, Parenti sold them for fifty-seven florins, about the sum that for around a year would feed, clothe, and house a whole family.[36]

Another way of looking at the value of clothing is to consider livery. Meaning either the provision of cloth or garments, a sum of money for obtaining such items, or worn tokens of affiliation,[37] livery was a common part of work contracts, particularly in the context of apprenticeships and household service. John Dee (1527–1609), Queen Elizabeth's astrologer, noted the agreed conditions of payment when he took on new servants. At Michaelmas 1595, Dee employed Margery Stubble as a dry nurse. Her yearly wage was set at £3 and a gown of russet, while Edward Edwards, who joined the Dee household at the same time, was to have 10 shillings and a livery, the precise form of which was unspecified.[38] At about the same period, a young woman called Ellin was taken into service in the Conwy Valley in Wales. Over a period of about fifteen years as a maid in the household she was paid a significant number of garments but, it seems, little or no actual cash.[39]

The cost of apparel meant that its upkeep and care was a priority, preserving the garment but also protecting the investment it represented. This husbanding of resources

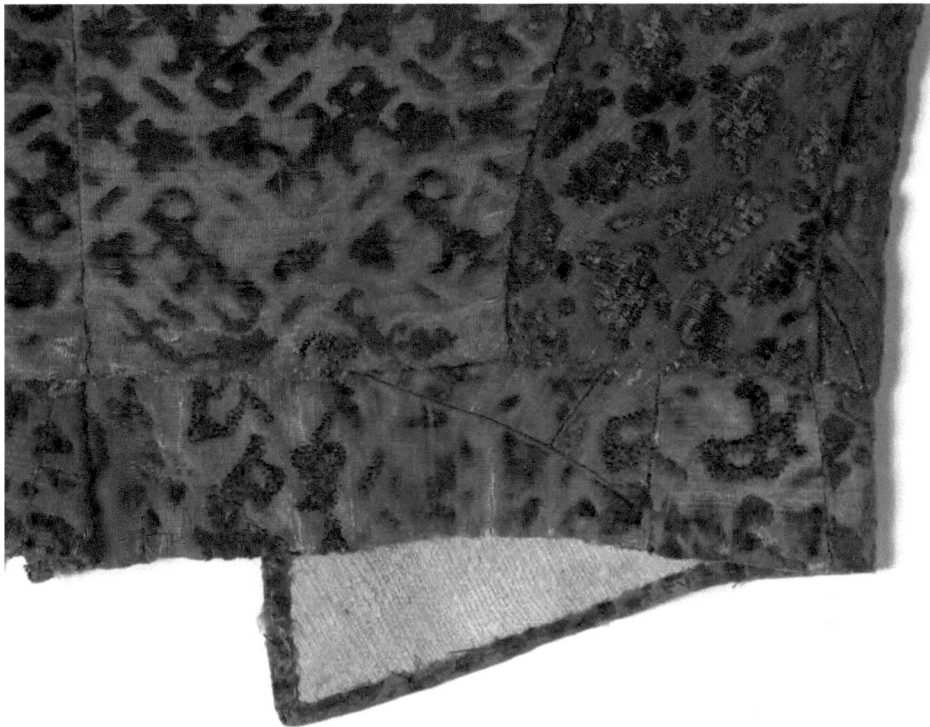

FIGURE 2.9: Early seventeenth-century doublet. This detail shows how the garment has been made with small scraps of differently patterned materials pieced together. © Manchester City Galleries.

extended to the decorative schema and making practices. Garments were cut from as small an amount of fabric as possible, and sometimes the pattern pieces themselves were pieced together from even smaller scraps (Figure 2.9). Combinations of fabrics were also used, so that the unseen sections of a garment were made with cheaper stuff, leaving the best for only that part of the item that would eventually show. Guards and borders—bands of ribbon or fabric applied as common decorative motifs—also served to protect the hems and edges of apparel, and could be easily replaced when refurbishment became necessary. Similarly, study of extant examples shows that the unpicking and turning of component pieces was a common way of extending the life, looks and value of a garment.[40] The quilted doublet in Figure 2.10 was not cut and sewn from new material, but carefully crafted from an existing item, most likely a bedcover.

The traces of such reuse and refurbishment also appear in the written record. In 1458, Agnes Paston (d. 1479) wrote herself a memorandum, a list of things to do. One of these was to see how many gowns her son Clement had, and those that were threadbare, to have their nap raised (a process of brushing with the spiky heads of teasels). She notes also that his short blue gown has already been raised once, and that it was itself remade from another longer gown.[41] Reuse was a way of life for everyone, even the very richest. The Earl of Dorset had clothing and caparisons remade as household furnishings; in 1619 he

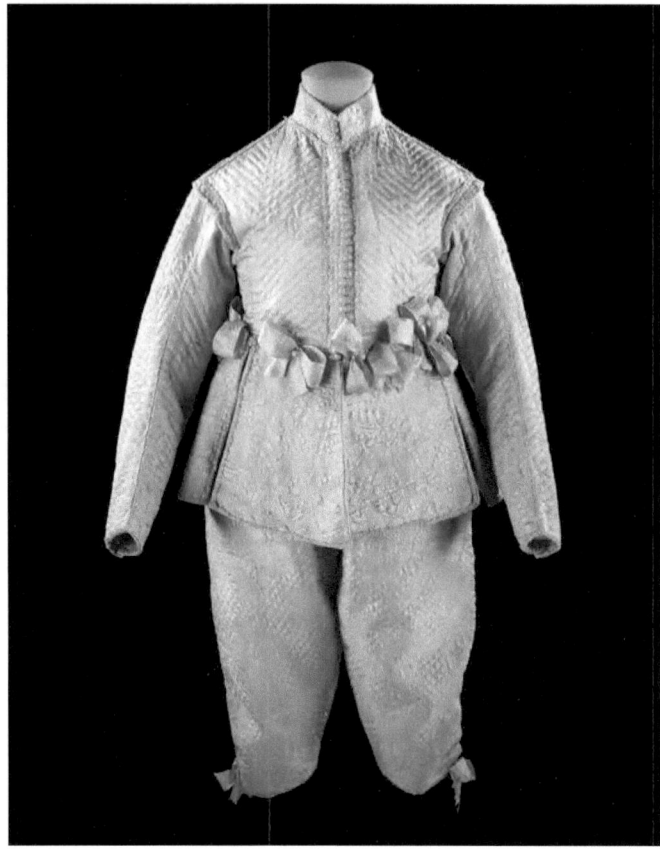

FIGURE 2.10: Suit made from quilted ivory satin from another source, with applied silk braid, England, 1635–40. © Victoria and Albert Museum, London.

gave his wife three of his old shirts for her to make cloutes [rags, nappies].[42]

An understanding of the cost of textiles and clothing, and the care taken to look after them, very helpfully contextualizes the contemporary fashion for slashing and pinking, those decorative cuts and frays so much a feature of elite Renaissance clothing (Figure 2.11). Such extravagant, wasteful use of luxury materials sets the benchmark of conspicuous consumption perilously high. Beautiful and bold design statements—"slashed, iagged, cut, carued, pinked"[43]—such fashions must also have been inflammatory to onlookers worried about the excess and moral dangers of sartorial display.

As a commodity, however, there was much more to apparel than either its utility or its monetary worth. Clothing was perhaps unique in the extent to which it worked also as a carrier of personal memory and meaning, and participated in the formation and articulation of social identities. Use value, exchange potential, aesthetic promise, personal significance, cultural meaning: clothing had it all. These layers of value meant that garments were guaranteed an ongoing life. Long after it was cut and sewn from new, wearing apparel entered into a whole world of reuse, passing through transformations and moving from owner to owner. It is to these second-hand circulations that we will now turn.

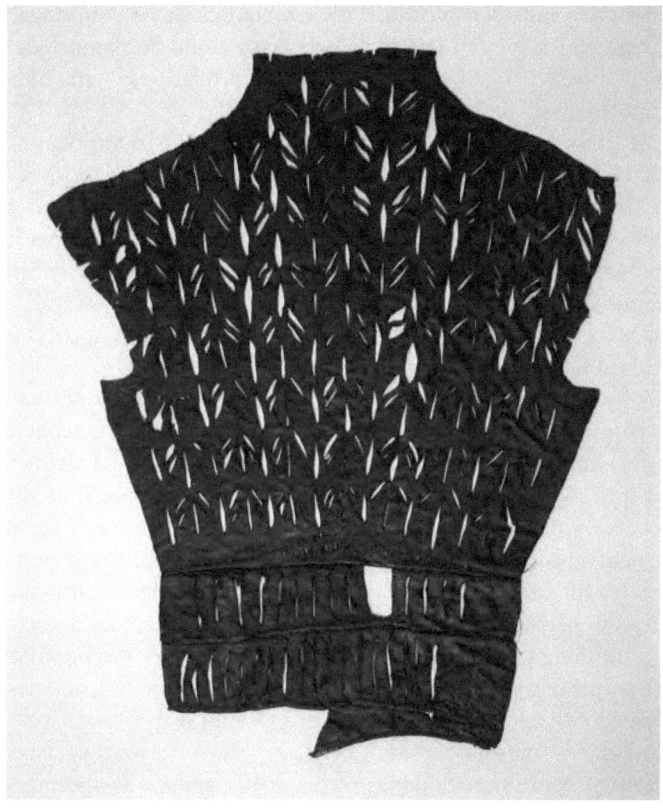

FIGURE 2.11: An elaborately slashed, sixteenth-century leather doublet, British. Metropolitan Museum of Art, New York. www.metmuseum.org

GIFTS OF APPAREL

Although the giving of new items was common in this period in many contexts—as tokens of affection for instance, or in the customary distribution of gloves to guests at weddings and funerals, or in those gifts made in a bid for preferential favor—we are concerned here with the handing-on of personal wearing apparel. Typically, such giving occurred in a downward direction through the social hierarchy, from superior to subordinate, a passage of goods that circulated both items of clothing and ideas about fashion. The monarch gave to his or her courtiers, masters to servants, and household heads to their dependants. We know that Henry VIII gave away large numbers of his and his family's garments—between 1516 and 1521 alone, there were ninety-one recipients (counted as individuals, pairs and small groups).[44] Although atypical in its largesse, Henry's giving was in itself conventional, it being commonplace for servants to receive the cast-off apparel from master and mistress. This kind of giving represented a more potent exchange than a simple grant of new apparel or the fulfillment of contractual obligations in the form of livery. Already-worn garments were imbued with the something of the identity and status of their owners—they were *personal*—and their gift signified favor and reward. In return—in accordance with the reciprocity that patterns all gift exchange—the garment's recipient owed service and allegiance. In a society configured by patronage, dress became a medium through which loyalty, goodwill, and favor could be channeled. The donation of garments helped weave together the fabric of social relations: "gifts of apparel were a constitutive gesture of social organization."[45]

The items of dress an individual received might be put to various uses. Obviously garments could be kept and worn. In 1540, Katharine Basset, Lady Lisle's daughter, was given by Lady Rutland a damask gown "of her own old wearyng." This gown went to enlarge Katharine's own wardrobe: she planned to effectively refurbish it by having it cheaply relined with buckram, but then edged with velvet.[46] When garments were the wrong size, sex, or status for their recipient, however, their value was realized in different ways, either by being cut up and their textiles employed in "new" apparel or furnishings, or by being sold on in the second-hand market.[47]

Another key feature of this gift economy was that the giver did not need to be alive. Testamentary bequests of clothing were very common, and extended the socially constitutive nature of the gift from beyond the grave.[48] Post-mortem giving in this context can be divided into two sorts: charitable and personal. The former usually consisted of the bequest to deserving poor of either cloth or clothing, or money for the same. The testator's personal apparel was seldom bequeathed. In return for such charity, the beneficiary was meant to pray for the deceased, and the ongoing use and wear of the clothing in question perpetuated the donor's post-mortem memory and social identity.[49] This method of clothing provision for some of the neediest in the population is evident throughout the whole of the late medieval and early modern period, and despite doctrinal and political fracture the practice survived the Reformation.

The majority of post-mortem clothing bequests, however, were of a personal nature, whereby the testator willed specific items of his or her apparel to specific people.[50] Even more than charitable giving, such donations perpetuated the donor's memory. They also materialized bonds of affection, potentially reinforcing the give and take of esteem, mutuality and obligation both between families and across generations. This is evident in the convoluted explanation Sir James Whitelocke (1570–1632) included in his family memoirs. A Mr. Croke had helped Thomas Pope, at this point a member of his household, into the king's service. "This mr. Croke," explains Whitelocke, "was my wife's great-grandfather." In recognition of the favor, in his will Thomas Pope left Mr Croke's son, Sir John, "sum of his best rayment, as a token of his love unto the house and familye."[51] The memorializing and constitutive nature of this particular bequest resonated down the years and across kin relations, to be recorded as part of his family's history by the recipient's granddaughter's husband.

Part of the legacy's importance to Whitelocke seems also to have been tied up in the qualitative estimation of the clothing—the bequest was some of Pope's "best" raiment. This is a common feature of bequests made in wills. Garments are often described by color, function and condition—"my best petticoat," "my worst hosen"[52]—and apportioned to individuals depending on the strength and nature of their relationship with the testator. In this way, clothing donations very clearly also materialized personal and affective hierarchies, matching commodity values with emotional and kinship bonds.

At its most basic level, of course, the testamentary gift of textiles and apparel was useful, and offered the recipient the choice of adding to his or her own wardrobe, reusing the legacy in some way, or realizing its financial potential through its sale or exchange. These various options were explored in 1633 by a woman called Elizabeth Busby, when willed a legacy of household and personal linens. She pawned a christening sheet, sold a waistcoat, and from a facecloth made an apron, and from a tablecloth made some smocks.

With two ruffs (garments whose concertinaed form incorporated substantial lengths of material) Elizabeth kept some of their fabric for herself, and sold the other part to a neighbor. From a biggin (child's cap, man's nightcap) she made a coif, and from another piece of linen a neckcloth, both of which she also sold.[53]

These few examples of the many ways in which clothing could be gifted reveal a once widespread practice. Although undoubtedly a common way of acquiring garments and textiles, they also show that the recipient did not necessarily keep such gifts for their own wearing. Elizabeth Busby, for one, transformed a part of her legacy to cash and to credit, which meant, of course, that the same linens were in turn passed on to yet new owners and more uses.

THE SECOND-HAND MARKET

The buying, selling, and pawning of clothes played an essential part in the distribution of apparel.[54] Studies reveal the second-hand market to have been a lively, fluid, and multidimensional enterprise, catering for all levels, and providing a stock of clothes from which a consumer might buy something from almost any price range. Through its workings, garments traveled in class and place, moving between different status groups and to different geographical locations. The gold-embroidered sleeves that we learnt Marco Parenti sold to a second-hand dealer in Florence, for example, might have ended up being worn as part of an outfit by an individual beyond whose means it would have been when either new, or if bought as an entire ensemble with its original gown. Fashions derived in an urban context might travel to a new rural home.

This breadth of reach is a striking characteristic of the second-hand business that marks it out from the operation of clothing resale and credit in later periods, in which such means of acquiring and capitalizing on garments were more limited to plebeian consumers. Under certain circumstances, in the Renaissance world almost anyone might sell or pawn their clothing. Multiple sources record the transactions that occurred right across the social spectrum, showing us that laborers and merchants, clerics and nuns, and patricians and royalty all participated in this alternative economic system.[55]

The men and women operating this system of credit and resale were as diverse as their customers. There were regional differences in its organization, but everywhere the market worked on a continuum of price and formality. At the top were the shop owners and guild members: in Florence and Bologna called *rigattieri*; in Venice they were known as *strazzaruoli*; in the Dutch-speaking Low Countries the term was *oudekleerkopers*; and in London, customers would visit an upholder or fripperer. The most successful at this level could, with entrepreneurial skill, become very well off. Beneath the shop dealers were the stall holders at markets, and then a range of unregulated itinerants, hawkers, and street sellers. This informal end of the trade was an easy one to join, requiring no equipment, artisanal skill or training, and although needing a shrewd eye for appraising a garment's value, having no overheads and being easy to combine with other activities. For these reasons, the lower end of the second-hand trade gave employment to women, migrants and newcomers. The trade also combined naturally with pawn-broking—clothing being by far and away the most frequently pawned commodity—and in practice it is rarely possible to tease out these two activities from one another, or to discern where one stopped and the other began.[56] If we turn back to Elizabeth Busby and her disposal of the linens willed to her in 1633, we find that her point of involvement with this market was at the most informal of levels, selling and pawning items directly to neighbors.[57]

Finally, the sources of the stock carried by these dealers were as varied as the dealers themselves. They were brought garments by individuals who wished to sell or pawn them, and in turn bought up unredeemed pledges pawned with others. Dealers might bid at public auctions of debtors' effects or the estates of the deceased, and some of the more entrepreneurial also sold ready-made items—piecework supplied by tailors, seamstresses, and other artisans in the clothing trades. And chronicler John Stowe (1524/5–1605)—himself a former tailor—in his survey of London points to yet another source of clothing stock. Stowe writes that he had read of a country man (by which many readers would have understood him to mean one naïve and inexperienced in the ways of the city, particularly those deceits practiced on the unwary) who lost his hood in Westminster Hall. Going to Cornhill—a quarter known for its vendors of second-hand clothing—he then found it hung out to be sold at a fripperer's stall, and was forced to buy it back.[58] Whether or not this story describes an actual event is neither known nor important, for what it does describe is an association between used clothing and shady practices that was very real indeed. The link between theft and resale was clear—the way, that is, a garment could disappear from its owner and reappear at the pawnbrokers or second-hand vendors—and led some authorities to seek to break the connection by imposing tighter restrictions on the used-clothes trade. Alarmed at the incidence of night-time theft, for example, in Bologna in 1454 the brokers and second-hand clothes dealers were required to close for business earlier, thus making the quick disposal of stolen goods more difficult.[59] It is to this darker side of the second-hand trade that we will now move.

STEALING CLOTHES

Clothing and textiles were the ideal things to steal. Useful, valuable, easy to filch and easy to carry, it is unsurprising to find that together they formed a major category of stolen goods. Given that in its turn theft represented the largest proportion of crimes committed, then the misappropriation of garments by one means or another must have been a possibility that always lurked and an actual experience for many. So frequent was the incidence of this type of theft that Thomas Harman, writer of a taxonomy of thieves and vagabonds, alleged its perpetrators belonged to a particular subspecies of criminal called "hookers" or "anglers," named after the long poles fitted with iron hooks they used to pluck garments through open windows and doors, and from where washing lay drying outside.[60]

Regardless of the status of such texts as evidence, this modus operandi was certainly real. And when we remember that the vast majority of ordinary houses at this time did not yet have window glass, using shutters to close against the night and the inclement weather, then having possessions lifted through the opening becomes more comprehensible. Dudley Carleton (1574–1632), English ambassador to Venice, described one such theft. In a letter to a friend, Carleton related that two visiting Englishmen had caroused themselves drunken to bed, whereof "one of them had all his clothes taken away or hooked out of the window . . . before he wakened."[61]

In 1641, the family of cloth merchant William Calley was hit: "on Saturday the 10th of this instant Aprill beteweene twelve and one of the Clocke at night wee lost eight payres of new Canvas [a coarse linen] sheetes layd in the garden to bee whited."[62] Unlike Thomas Harman's description of organized crime committed by professionals, William Calley suspected that those responsible for stealing their sheets were actually known to the family, and in this he was probably correct. Highway robbery aside, which frequently targeted apparel as well as cash and jewelry, most clothing theft was not organized but opportunistic—the casual pilfering of items left unattended. The contemporary social conditions that provided both knowledge and proximity were a definite incentive to such crime. With early modern rooms and beds being multi-occupancy, travelers thrown into proximity with shared sleeping arrangements, and neighbors mindful of each other's possessions and movements, there were many possible chances for pilfering.

Once stolen, clothing and textiles could be kept for personal use, or disposed of via the extensive and varied possibilities of resale and exchange. Whether passed on via a dealer, a neighbor, or a chance-met acquaintance, the ease with which stolen clothing could change owners meant that it played a significant part in the acquisition of apparel. While the garments may not have been worn by the thief personally, they would most certainly have been worn by someone else.

CONCLUSION

Let us end where we began, with Philip Stubbes and his fear of the promiscuous and proliferating mingle-mangle of apparel. Having spent a little time considering the multiple processes by which clothing might be acquired, it is now easier to look beyond the exaggerated tone of his complaints to appreciate the reality on which they were based. Just by walking down the street, Stubbes would have observed people dressed in all manner of garments, which they had obtained through a variety of mechanisms. Many clothes were certainly made to order—and this involved a particular expertise on the part of the customer—but this was just one aspect of a vast system of acquisition and loss, credit, gift, and exchange. Stubbes might see a passer-by dressed in his master's cast offs, or a housewife going to church wearing fine linen willed her by a friend or relative. Aging and second-hand garments could be spruced up with new linings and trimmings, or remade as an entirely different item. Apparel was bequeathed, sold, stolen, and even hired.[63] Any individual, moreover, could be involved at multiple points within this system, both selling and buying, being a recipient and in turn giving to others. Beneath this constant, restless passage of goods runs the solid fact of clothing's value and potency—the truth, in other words, of its fundamental importance to the world of the Renaissance.

CHAPTER THREE

The Body

ISABELLE PARESYS

From an anthropological perspective, in addition to their ornamental role, clothes have a fundamental part to play in maintaining decency and safeguarding the body against environmental factors such as cold and heat. In his *De Civilitate morum puerilium* (1530), the Dutch humanist Erasmus described clothing as "the body of the body." However, the dressed body is much more flexible than the body of flesh—its natural appearance can be easily reformulated. The Renaissance set a new sartorial precedent, with its artificial and often spectacular silhouette that substituted for the natural physical outline of the body. The dressed body is cultural, helping to express and shape the relationships Western peoples have with their physical body. The clothed body is also undoubtedly the primary visual identity-marker within any given society (signifying age, gender, job, and religion) and the sign of belonging to a given hierarchy, from princes down to paupers.[1] It is not surprising that during the Renaissance—often described as the time of the birth of the individual—portraiture became very popular among the elites, who were extremely attentive to their own image. Europeans were also keenly interested in the appearance of peoples across the world, encountered partly in the course of new explorations and colonization. Such proto-anthropological interest is testified by the large numbers of prints of contemporary clothing in costume books, atlases, and other kinds of maps.[2]

However, although we have many representations of fashionable bodies, mostly of the European social elites, few actual garments—the relics of wearers who vanished over 500 years ago—survive. Most of the rare, fragile examples we do have belonged to wealthy individuals because the everyday and much-used garments of people much further down the social scale were worn to rags. Nevertheless, these few remaining clothes are invaluable in showing us techniques of hand stitching and the levels of creativity employed, the latter particularly evident in the forms of underwear that reshaped the contemporary anatomy. Such garments are witnesses to the kind of ongoing wear made by the friction of gestures or the pleats of bodily movements. They can also give us an idea of their wearer's size or physical volume. All these factors evoke the presence of bodies that inhabited such garments over a period of time. This chapter will reconstruct the cultural history of that clothed body.

In the 1980s, Georges Vigarello and Philippe Perrot traced the connection between dress and wearer in their ground-breaking books on the history of the body.[3] Since the 1990s, influenced by cultural studies and social theory, many scholars have focused on the body in specific historical periods or from a more general perspective.[4] However, within the growing literature on fashion, very few publications directly address the body and clothing during the Renaissance.[5] Contemporary written sources can be equally unrevealing in this area, because although we have many Renaissance testimonials about fashion, either people were less insightful in describing the bodily experience of wearing fashionable items, or perhaps assumed that such a shared, common experience needed no articulation.

This chapter gives an overview of the significant aspects of the relationship between the body and dress between 1450 and 1650, and the developments that linked it to more modern cultures of dressing. The Renaissance was not only a cultural turning point but also an economic one, when much greater varieties and quantities of goods, such as textiles and items of apparel, were produced and consumed across the globe.[6] Many practices, including second-hand markets, renting, gift giving, theft, lotteries, auctions, or inheritances made goods accessible to broader sections of society outside the courts. Fashions changed more rapidly and spread across Europe. The growing court societies of the Renaissance were inventive places because of their dependence on a culture of display and distinction, which gave such prominence to self-presentation.[7] Specific relationships evolved between dress and the body and circulated through different societies all over Europe, dependent on the cultural, economic, or political influences of some leading countries (primarily Italy, Spain, and France during this 200-year period) and on the intensity of exchanges between them. This chapter will first present an overview of the most significant aspects of the dress system in relation to the body. It will proceed to focus on the ways clothing reshaped the body by emphasizing or tightening its natural forms. Finally, it will investigate attitudes towards skin and nudity, and issues relating to hygiene and the care and maintenance of dress.

THE OUTLINES OF THE DRESSED BODY

Clothes give a visible, social existence to the natural body. They conceal nudity, a manifestation of nature that it was felt must be controlled, and also display gender identities, embodying these through textiles and other forms of ornament. Since the fourteenth century, the evolution of fashion had deeply emphasized the differentiated outlines of male and female forms, which were reinforced even further during the late Renaissance. Bodies were concealed by clothes, therefore, in very different ways according to the sex of the wearer. The most striking distinctions concerned the lower half of the body. Male clothing throughout Europe shortened during the fourteenth century, with young aristocrats wearing doublets—a short and narrow garment that left their legs on display—instead of the long traditional gown that had given elite men a silhouette broadly similar to a female one. From the fifteenth century until the first part of the sixteenth century, the exaggerated breadth across the shoulders and the often impressive codpieces, both signs of virility, helped to distinguish male and female appearances (see Figure 3.1). Women's legs, in contrast, were not freely seen until the twentieth century. As if in a reverse process, during the sixteenth century the female gown abandoned the fluidity of the long, flowing fifteenth-century skirts that suggested the bodily contours beneath, in order to swell up using various complicated supporting structures (farthingales, padding, hoop-skirts) (see Figure 3.2). These hid exactly those parts of the female body that men ostentatiously displayed, accentuating the gulf between the sexes. By placing a bell shape over the female legs and hips, this early modern fashion created a striking anatomical disproportion between the upper and lower halves of the female body.

FIGURE 3.1: *Emperor Charles V and dog*, Jacob Seisenegger, 1532. Vienna, Kunsthistorisches museum. Inv. no. GG_A114. Photo: Imagno/Getty Images.

To summarize, the anatomy of dressed bodies underlined a clear sexual dimorphism: clothed female bodies were bottom-heavy, while clothed male bodies were top-heavy. Clothing thus reinforced Renaissance beliefs about physiognomy, a very enduring discipline inherited from Antiquity with the aim of interpreting the soul through physical appearance. One of the most influential works, Giambattista Della Porta's *De Humana Physiognomonia* (1586), explained how male and female body shapes were inverted through their temperamental differences. Women's lower body parts were larger because their cold natures pull them downwards; in contrast, men's natural heat pulled their bodies upwards.[8] The fundamental complementarity between men and women was thus reflected in their appropriately-dressed silhouettes.

A child's body also needed specific apparel to distinguish it from others. Considered to be malleable like wax, babies were swaddled to help their bodies develop correctly. When they emerged from this cocoon, both boys and girls wore the same unisex garments: long gowns, and linen caps that covered a child's ears and which were thought to prevent them from becoming too prominent (see Figure 3.3). Children remained in unisex clothing until six or seven years old, although in other ways, including in their education, they were treated very differently. The origins of this shared sartorial regime stemmed

FIGURE 3.2: French lady wearing a Renaissance farthingale with hoops, in the front of a map of Bourges. Georg Braun and Frans Hogenberg, *Civitates orbis terrarum, Coloniae Agrippinae*, typis T. Graminaei, 1593 [1st ed. 1572]. Villeneuve d'Ascq, Réserve commune de l'université de Lille, fonds Agache A–18. Cliché ANRT. Bibliothèque universitaire de Lille 3, fond patrimonial.

FIGURE 3.3: *The French Queen Anne of Austria with the Dauphin (future King Louis XIV)*, French school, before 1643. Versailles, Châteaux de Versailles et Trianon, MV7143. Photo: DEA/G. DAGLI ORTI/De Agostini/Getty Images.

yet again from the humoral medical beliefs of the sixteenth and seventeenth centuries. Before adulthood, both sexes were deemed to have the same bodily complexion characterized by heat and humidity. However, it was thought that children were dominated by their humid nature, making them soft, weak, unstable, and fragile, all features that made them similar to female nature with its humid complexion, while men were hot and dry.[9] The unisex gown worn by children did not express their biological difference but rather their infant femininity, as they shared the bodily complexion and character associated with women: humidity, weakness, fragility and lack of constancy. A boy's identity, therefore, was progressively developed through the abandonment of childhood dress. Born in 1601, the future French king Louis XIII wore his first hose at the age of four, as recorded in the diary of his personal physician Héroard; at five years old he exchanged his cap for a man's hat; at seven he wore doublet, breeches and sword like a miniature man.[10]

RENAISSANCE FASHIONS AS BODILY EXTENSIONS

Let us now focus on the major forms of bodily re-shaping in the Renaissance. These techniques, which played with different volumes and the extent to which clothing reflected the natural anatomy, helped to define the system of the fashionable body of the time, many aspects of which still endure in today's fashion world. Vertical and horizontal extensions were used to build a fashionable look for those who could afford to wear these sometimes spectacular, but also cumbersome and expensive garments. The performance of wearing clothes like this allowed members of Western social elites to display bodies that eloquently reflected their positions of power and cultural distinction.

Some of the most significant vertical extensions of the dressed body, which created an artificially elongated silhouette, were the Northern fashions culminating at the end of the fifteenth century. High headdresses were popular in the Low Countries and France up until the 1480s and 1490s: sugarloaf hats for men; women's hennins with gauze veils that echoed the long train of the V-neck gown with its large waistband (Figure 3.4). Although subsequent headdresses did not scale such heights, the sixteenth century continued to see women wearing substantial styles: hair nets with large feather-hats in Germany for example, as illustrated in Lucas Cranach's portraits; thick, round ornate hats in Northern Italy, including Florence and Mantua; English gable hoods with dark veils in England or more rounded French hoods. The 1580s to the 1610s saw a female Venetian fashion for wearing wire pads under hair to achieve the two-horned hairstyle as illustrated in this etching of a Venetian courtesan in a costume book by Bertelli (see Figure 3.5).

Vertical extensions also focused on the lower half of the body. Pointed shoes, known as *poulaines*, sometimes two-and-a-half times the natural length of the foot, were worn during the fifteenth century. These awkward shoes, which elongated and narrowed male and female outlines, fell into disuse around 1500. One vertical extreme in the realm of female footwear was the fashion for high platform shoes, with soles of cork or light wood, which first appeared in Spain (*chapines*) and Venice (*pianelle*) (see Figure 3.5). Derived perhaps from Turkish or Syrian high clogs, these chopines were also worn in late-sixteenth-century England and France, where Brantôme mocked courtiers who wore 65 centimeters-high platform shoes to look taller.[11] Only wealthy women could afford to have their mobility limited by such shoes that required them to "set their hands on the

FIGURE 3.4: *Portrait of a Lady*, Rogier Van der Weyden, c. 1460. National Gallery, London. Photo: Art Media/Print Collector/Getty Images.

FIGURE 3.5: Cortigiana Veneta, in Pietro Bertelli, *Diversarum nationum habitus*, Patavii, apud Alciatum Alcia et Petrum Bertellium, 1594–6. Photo: Hulton Archive/Getty Images.

heads of two matron-like servants or old women to support them[selves]", as the English diarist John Evelyn observed during his travels to Venice in 1645.[12]

The increase of natural bodily volumes, however, centered mainly around the hips, legs, shoulders, and neck. These textile superstructures extended the body's anatomy horizontally and, in its most extreme version, transformed clothing into an outer shell only tenuously related to the body beneath. The most prominent of these was the hooped skirt (farthingale, *vertugadin*, *reifrock*), which originated in late-fifteenth-century Spain. Held over a cage of hoops or a padded "bum roll," which took the full width of the skirt towards the feet, the first style was either rigid and conical, or bell-shaped (see Figure 3.2). The later, "French" version used a wheel or drum farthingale to increase the volume still further, giving the over-skirts a barrel-like appearance (see Figure 3.6).[13] The sheer volume of fabric—exceptionally expensive at that time—needed to achieve these shapes was striking, as demonstrated by the five meters of black satin used to make a c. 1615–20 petticoat analyzed by Janet Arnold.[14] In fact, although individual styles changed, from the Renaissance onwards the female dressed body embraced an artificially inflated silhouette. This was maintained in different forms until the late nineteenth century.

Men's dress was extended in different ways, emphasizing in turn shoulders, thighs, and crotch. Hips became a focal point of women's bodies and a sign of femininity, while for

FIGURE 3.6: *A Ball at the Valois Court* (detail), French school, c. 1580. Rennes, Musée des Beaux-Arts. Inv. INV794–1–135. Photo: DeAgostini/Getty Images.

men broad shoulders represented masculinity. An "athletic" shoulder breadth was a visual marker of manhood as seen in the Emperor Charles V's portrait by Jacob Seisenegger in 1532 (see Figure 3.1). However, by the middle of the sixteenth century, male fashions had evolved towards more slender shoulders, giving men a more vertical outline so that male bodies now seemed entirely composed of heads, arms, and legs. Historians have connected this elegant silhouette with a new literary ideal of beauty, influenced by Renaissance humanism, emphasizing grace over physical strength.[15] At the same time, the lower half of the male body was artificially extended around the hips, buttock, and thighs (see Figure 3.7). Breeches were inflated to varying degrees thanks to padding with horsehair. Featuring prominently at the center front of trunk hose, the codpiece, an over-developed sheath in the form of a penis case, remained an essential element in the display of virility up to the 1570s, before being replaced by less exaggerated and flatter-shaped breeches and trousers.[16]

But the most spectacular extensions of Renaissance fashions were certainly ruffs and large collars. These extensions reached a peak in Europe from the end of the sixteenth century until the 1630s. Relying on an abundance of linen and lace, many varied forms and highly skilled, decorative making techniques, these garments were used to extend the

FIGURE 3.7: *Richard Sackville, 3rd Earl of Dorset*, Isaac Oliver, 1616, portrait miniature. © Victoria and Albert Museum, London.

FIGURE 3.8: *Painter's Family*, Jacob Jordaens, c. 1621–2. Madrid, Museo del Prado. Photo: DEA PICTURE LIBRARY/Getty Images.

body shape beyond its natural limits. Emerging on male as well as female collars in the 1560s, ruffs, and later large collars, dramatically transformed the wearer's appearance.[17] Their whiteness and breadth, sometimes covering the full width of the shoulders, contrasted with dark or colored overgarments and inevitably drew an onlooker's gaze in towards the face (see Figure 3.8). These fashionable accessories emphasized the head, the noblest part of the body's high/low dichotomy, and particularly the face, which was the subject of a physiognomical literature that considered the face to be the "window of the soul," thought to reside within the head. The cultural impact of ruffs over time is such that in modern cinematic or theatrical representations, they continue to be a primary visual symbol of the late Renaissance.[18]

STIFFNESS AND CONSTRAINT

If enlargement and extension was the first principle of the fashionable Renaissance body, stiffness and constraint was the second. Clothing not only rearranged the physical body by concealing it or overemphasizing different aspects of it, it was also important to wear garments with the right degree of tension and tightness. All this required increasingly sophisticated tailoring techniques to create closely-fitting clothes, far removed from the simple cut of medieval tunics. This is probably one of the factors that gave rise to the first printed book of tailor's patterns. Written by Juan de Alcega, the *Practice of Tailoring, Measuring and Marking Out* (1580) was published when Spanish fashions dominated European dress.[19] Drawings and texts revealed tailoring tricks and the intimate links between this art and mathematics. A few years later, Francisco de la Rocha Burguen's pattern book (1618) invented the proportional-body system, based on an individual's stature, from neck to feet.[20]

During the second half of the sixteenth century, the male doublet evolved into a tight-fitting garment, reinforced with padding, using materials such as wool or horsehair, or boning. Stiff as drum skins, the male torso was shaped within a smooth carapace that articulated his anatomy as a sharp-edged form that was probably influenced by contemporary plate armor.[21] In the late 1550s, a slightly padded area, the peascod belly, appeared above the waistline of the doublet. But by the 1580s, its volume was increased to an overhanging paunch, making it more uncomfortable to wear (see Figure 3.6). Montaigne complained about its "heavy enlargement . . . [that] makes us entirely different from our natural selves, and awkward in arming ourselves."[22] He did not appreciate this courtly look that distended the natural body shape, testimony to the baroque taste for illusion and deceptive ornament that characterized the styles of the French and English courts.[23] The type of doublet that succeeded after the 1620s looked looser, but brought the male waist higher and was still reinforced and rigid.

Female torsos were even more affected by the desire for close-fitting garments. The first stays, or pair of "bodies" as they were called, appeared in the second half of the sixteenth century, influencing the outline and aesthetic of the female torso until the twentieth century. Bodies were a whalebone-reinforced undergarment, which compressed the lower chest and sharpened the waist with lacing. An additional wooden, bone, or ivory removable busk could be inserted at the center front to provide extra stiffening. The female chest, therefore, was sculpted into an inverted triangle whose inferior point could seem even narrower with the fashion for triangular-shaped stomachers. These were fastened to the front opening of the gown and rested with their point lying above the crotch. The voluminous skirts, enlarged with farthingales or hips rolls, helped to create an even narrower-looking waist through contrast (see Figure 3.6).

Even if stays were not worn,[24] the aesthetic of tightly-fitting body garments was a prerequisite for both men and women, and it was made possible by the use of ties and laces pulled to reach the desired silhouette.[25] Boys and girls wore less constrictive versions of adult garments, training them into the correct bodily alignment. Lastly, the emblematic Renaissance ruffs, as well as the wide, white, straight, and open collars that became fashionable from the 1580s, greatly helped to stiffen the bearing of the head. The stiffness of these structures, achieved by starching the fabric or by using a wire support (*supportasse*), helped the wearer hold his or her head straight in an upright and dignified posture.

All these fashionable garments created real constraints. To be dressed in such a way was a performance. The physical effort required is evident, especially if we take into account the weight of the clothes and hairstyles and their bulk. The bodies of monarchs and courtiers were certainly the most constrained because of the performative nature of appearances at court and because their social position required them to wear opulent fabrics. In 1571, for example, Marguerite de Valois, the French king's sister, participated in the Palm Sunday procession at Blois wearing a dress made from fifteen *aunes* (eighteen meters) of cloth of gold, "although it was extremely heavy." Brantôme, who admired her performance, tells us that only Marguerite's height enabled her to do it, otherwise "she would have collapsed under [its weight]."[26] Such clothing made the body inside almost inanimate, but these problems were obviously restricted to very small elite.

The stiffness, constraint, and upright postures accentuated by these garments were in fact iconic signs of individuals who did not have to use their bodies to labor in fields, on boats, at building sites, or as housemaids. This was the distinctive eloquence of the bodies of the social elite, whether noble or not, which were put on display in public ceremonies, court balls, or in portraits hung in the home (see Figure 3.8). This look cannot be explained, as traditional histories of costume usually do, as simply a European-wide vogue for Spanish fashions dictated by Habsburg political prestige. It was linked with cultural factors that were neither political nor Spanish, although the Spanish court was one of the first contexts to elaborate it. It was influenced by cultural requirements for bodily control, an integral part of education from childhood for members of the upper orders, using methods that constantly reiterated the discipline of the body, developing a "semiology of rectitude."[27] An upright posture, with no gesticulation, was vital at a time when appearances and bodily hexes, namely the combination of bodily attitudes including standing, walking and speaking, defined the social being. Castiglione, while promoting grace of countenance advised a courtier to "think about how he wishes to appear, and dress in a way which corresponds with the impression of himself he wishes to give, and see that his clothes help him to do so, even to people who cannot hear him speak or see him do something."[28] Numerous sixteenth-century conduct books, such as those by Erasmus, Castiglione, Della Casa, and their imitators in the following century, helped to promulgate throughout Europe an intensive concern with restraint and self-control as a body language. By 1580, the process was so well internalized among social elites that Montaigne, as a gentleman, could remark, "there is far more difference between the way I dress and that of a peasant in my country than between him and a man who is clothed only in his skin . . . I cannot stand being unbuttoned and shirtless, but our farmers would be hampered by working this way."[29]

CLOTHING, SKIN, AND BODY ON DISPLAY

Montaigne's pronouncement comparing the peasant to an unclothed man is profoundly interesting. It evokes the relationship between clothing and skin as well as clothing and nudity. For Montaigne, the peasant—a man less clothed than himself, who labored in a shirt in the fields to be able to move more easily—was quite naked. Montaigne was certainly thinking of the Native Americans, or Brazilians, "going naked," whom he also discussed in the same chapter of his *Essays*, and who so fascinated Renaissance people. Their figures became emblematic of non-clothed humanity in the printed costume books flourishing from the 1550s onwards.[30] Even though he described these native peoples as "all naked nations," travelers recorded that their skin was adorned with body-paintings, and their lips and cheeks sometimes pierced. Europeans often admired these ornaments, as well as their wearer's bodily health and physical perfection, as in the case of Jean de Léry describing the Brazilian Tupinambas.[31] But the most surprising aspect for European observers was that these peoples were not ashamed to expose their genitals "as they came from their mother's womb."[32] This "nudity" generated a debate because it contradicted the Biblical account of the Garden of Eden that explained human shame at nakedness through the idea of original sin, and thereby postulated a moral teleology for the necessity of covering the body. Encountering such a radically different body in the New World, some travelers and missionaries saw this as a form of innocence. Others thought that the lack of clothing was a sign that these people had been judged and abandoned by God. Comparisons with European habits led others to preach for simpler clothing that eschewed exaggerated display or expense, asserting that such excessive passion for dress had caused more ills than the nakedness of native peoples.[33] But the Christianization of peoples such as the Amerindians would finally force them to cover their skin, and the shirt would be their first sewn garment.

T-shaped shirts and smocks, made from hemp or linen, extended to cover the lower portion of the body were worn under outer garments (Figure 3.9). They were the most intimate kind of garment, acting as a second skin. So wearing only a shirt or a smock was regarded as being naked. This was the reason why they were only exposed in private relationships or when undergoing penitence or punishment. A French phrase used in a legal context, summed up the shirt's intimate connection with the linen and its symbolic assimilation with the nakedness. To be *nud en chemise* (to be naked wearing a shirt) was

FIGURE 3.9: Woman's smock, probably made in England from Dutch linen and Flemish lace, 1620–40. © Victoria and Albert Museum, London.

a punishment in which someone was condemned to make a public apology, carrying a heavy candle through the streets, in order to repair the damage of a crime. Considered to be a disgrace, the removal of clothing was inflicted during judicial torments. It was also used to humiliate people during inter-group conflicts such as the wars of religion. During the St. Bartholomew's Day massacre in Paris in 1572, the enforced stripping of Protestants by Catholics were acts of dehumanization intended to remove their victims' basic humanity: as heretics, they were no longer considered human.[34]

This is one of the reasons why, in this cultural context, the two naked pictures of Matthäus Schwarz are so touching. In July 1526, when he was twenty-nine years old, this wealthy German burgher from Augsburg commissioned two nude miniature paintings of his own body, back and front. There are among the 135 watercolor paintings showing the garments he wore over the course of his life, a topic he found so fascinating that he compiled pictures and text into an amazing private record, the *Klaidungsbüchlein* (*Book of Clothes*). His body is not portrayed within a religious context (as is the figure of Adam or depictions of the damned), or idealized according to the inherited Greco-Roman ideal, or pictured within an ethnographic frame (like the Amerindians). Instead, his naked self was replicated in a naturalistic mode, in maturity showing his downward sloping shoulders and portly belly.[35] He worried about gaining weight, which to him signaled aging and diminished attractiveness, and which was revealed when fashionable artifices were stripped away. In contemplating these nude pictures, maybe he recalled the first "clothing" introduced in his album, his mother's womb in her pregnant portrait, above the words: "I was there, hidden, in 1496."

Covering the skin was not only a matter of Christian ethics, or a means of gaining warmth, although this was especially significant during Europe's "little Ice Age" which began after a warmer period in the Middle Ages. The clothing carapace was also a key form of defense for vulnerable flesh. Galenic medical theories, current during the Renaissance, viewed the skin as permeable to external invading dangers.[36] At a broader level, the sartorial regime was very enveloping, focusing attention on areas that were revealed, such as the face, the hands and forearms, the neck or the chest. Indeed, during the Renaissance, when idealization of the human body coexisted with its concealment, clothing played with the body, hiding it while suggesting and defining its limits. According to changing fashions, some parts of the body could be partially revealed, inevitably provoking virulent criticisms from the conservatively minded of all dispositions, as with women's bared shoulders, low-cut necklines or the elbow-length sleeve of the 1630 and 1640s.[37] The boundaries, where areas of skin were visible, therefore became crucial. At the neck or the wrists, the second-skin shirt, ornamented by black, red, or golden embroidery, ruffs, or laces, symbolically revealed the body. Other tricks emphasized this game of hide-and-seek, including the fashion for slashing (see Figure 3.1) on outer garments for both sexes, thought to have originated in the clothes worn by Swiss and German soldiers for greater ease of movement, or the long Spanish-style slits separating strips of fabric.[38] These slashes revealed linings or shirts that touched the body.

Another fashion that played with the idea of revelation during the first two-thirds of the sixteenth century was the male codpiece, a protuberance that focused attention on the penis (see Figures 3.1 and 3.6). Under the influence of Swiss and German mercenaries, codpieces became rigidly upwardly curving. They were not real penis-holders, given that they were filled with wadding. Nevertheless, their transparently sexual role, alluding to vitality and fertility, implying sexual organs "three times as large as the original," as Montaigne complained, was evident. The symbolic function of the codpiece is reflected in contemporary belief in the magical practice of "tying the knot." This involved making a knot with string to represent the laces knotted through the eyelets of the codpiece and was thought to prevent erection and lead to impotency.[39] During the French wars of religion, Catholics mocked Huguenots as impotent *ébraguettés* (without virility) because they would not wear the prominent codpiece.[40] When painted on the bodies of princes by Clouet, Holbein, Titian, Moro, or Bronzino, codpieces gave special visibility to another dimension of power. Until their disuse in the 1570s, they stimulated French *bragardise*, a term which combined elegance and display with an exhibition of virility. More generally, the codpiece symbolized a masculine-centered triumphal humanism incarnated by the Rabelaisian "flying buttress," the huge codpiece of the famous giant Gargantua.[41]

BODILY CARE AND FASHIONABLE LOOKS

Given the vast array of cleaning and hygiene products on our modern-day supermarket shelves, we might be forgiven for wondering how Renaissance people took care of their body and clothing carapace. Outer garments were brushed or spot-cleaned but not laundered. Princely inventories, such as those of the sixteenth-century Valois, include many sticks and mud-scrappers. Most importantly, however, a special quarterly budget was provided for the king and queen's so-called *lavendiere de corps* (body-linens washing maid).[42] Undergarments were the only clothes that were really washed and bleached. Shirts, smocks, and drawers protected the wearer from outer garments, but they also absorbed the dirt and secretions of the body beneath. While men tucked their shirt-tails between their legs as drawers, we have very little evidence that Renaissance women wore drawers. This was one of the paradoxes of Western society, where the body was padlocked by clothing and where the female body was particularly supervised. Free buttocks and legs were well protected from the cold and sight—as required by decency and morality—but women's genitals were, in practice, easily accessible: "under the petticoat, fresh air; under the breeches, weapon at the ready."[43] A decent woman would not wear drawers, exceptions being when riding side-saddle, or the luxurious drawers inspired by men's breeches that were worn by some fashionable court ladies during the late sixteenth century.[44] These drawers, however, were mostly associated with Venetian courtesans—well represented in Italian costume books such as those by Pietro Bertelli (1589) (see Figure 3.5) or Cesare Vecellio (1590)—who wore *braghesse* (men's pants) under a masculine shirt or a gown as their professional sign.[45] It has been argued that this form of cross-dressing provided a frisson for the benefit of their clients, rather than functioning as a sign of modesty.

Owning shirts in the finest fabrics as well as several undergarments was a mark of refinement and etiquette, given the elite practice of changing daily or even more frequently. It was said that during a wedding ball in August 1572, the French king's brother, the duke of Anjou, fell desperately in love with the bride, Marie de Clèves, after wiping his face with her smock soaked with sweat that she just had changed before a new dance.[46] Even in more modest wardrobes, shirts—often more heavy and rough and woven in hemp—became increasingly common during the Renaissance. Historians have observed the growing propensity in this period for forms of "dry washing" of the body, consisting primarily of changing—or "shifting"—one's linen. This can be linked to a declining confidence in ablutions using water (thought to soften the body and to allow disease to penetrate the skin) and bathhouses (places of moral and public disorder).[47] Instead, especially in an age when water was difficult to provide in abundance, the cleanliness of linen signified the cleanliness of the body. The whiteness of shirts, ruffs, large collars, cuffs, and lace was considered a guarantee of social distinction. For centuries, cleanliness of the actual body was therefore essentially peripheral and limited to those parts that were visible—the head, neck, and hands.

The whiteness of these corporeal areas was not only a matter of bodily hygiene; it was also a fashionable standard of beauty that arose during the late Renaissance. The face, the female neckline and hands were especially regulated and cared for, with fashionable accessories and cosmetics used to maintain the milky whiteness expected among the wealthy. Gloves, for example, which protected against the roughening effects of exposure, became necessary accessories for both men and women, and continued to be so well into the twentieth century. Large hats could protect the face, but women sometimes wore masks or other full-face coverings to safeguard their pale complexions or even their identity outside the home (see Figure 3.2). As a form of coquetry, some women wore masks to attend theater performances in late-seventeenth-century England, although this was condemned by some not only as a feminine eccentricity but out of fear of the moral laxity that such anonymity might bring.[48] Hiding the face in public places was interpreted differently in Italy and Spain. In Venice, the noble *virgo* was expected to distinguish herself from the *matrona* (married woman) by wearing a *fazzuolo* when leaving the house, a veil that hid her face and chest. In Spain, patrician women wore a *mantó*, a kind of veil-mantle, described by Vecellio: "Like the Venetians, they surround their whole body with a coat but, with one hand, they skilfully make an opening for their eyes . . . so that it is difficult to see them."[49] In these cases, the protection of the skin was of secondary importance to the protection of the wearer's morals. Grounded in early Christian precepts articulated most famously by Saint Paul, women had to cover their head as a sign of submission to God and to men. The veil held men at a distance as it covered women's hair, regarded as an erotic area, and symbolized an intact hymen or the would-be-bride's chastity.[50]

"Dry washing" was not the only development in hygiene ushered in during the Renaissance. It was claimed that perfumes also had hygienic virtues in addition to their prophylactic properties, including their reputation for warding off the plague. The plague was latent in early modern Europe and doctors wore long-nosed masks, full of perfumed herbs that were supposed to protect them during the epidemic. The disease was thought to be spread through contact with pestilential air. Wearing perfumes made it possible to delay changing linens, and bodily cleanliness involved smell as well as vision. Clothes were scented with the heady and powerful fragrances from the latest innovations in perfumery which, in addition to European and Mediterranean plants (such as rose, violet, mint, lavender), used increasingly strong-smelling and costly animal or vegetal products coming from faraway lands in Asia or America (such as aloes, jasmine, clove, cinnamon, amber, musk, and civet).[51] Italian and Spanish perfumers were renowned throughout Europe. Small perfumed bags were placed in coffers or worn between linen undergarments and outer garments. In 1649, at the castle of Saint-Germain, when Queen Anne of Austria's coffers were unpacked by lackeys, the fragrance was so strong that the men were overcome or ran to escape.[52] Shirts, gloves, precious handkerchiefs, or muffs could be scented and were traditionally exchanged as gifts. Dry perfumes could be placed in hollow buttons, in rosary beads, or in little beads hanging on garters. Into the seventeenth century, some fine and elaborately decorated small balls of jewelry called pomanders, combined the functional with ornamental display (see Figure 3.10). Men and women hung them on their rosaries, chains, or girdles not just because of their aromatic virtues but also because of their presumed therapeutic (digestive, analgesic, astringent, purifying)

FIGURE 3.10: A six section silver pomander engraved with flowers, made in Western Europe, 1600–50. © Victoria and Albert Museum, London.

properties.[53] Other accoutrements relating to bodily hygiene could be worn decoratively over garments, such as small mirrors hung on women's girdles, or the golden toothpick and ear cleaner that the German banker Anton Fugger wore round his neck and over his black suit in his portrait by Hans Maler (c. 1525).[54] Such an accessory not only symbolized his concern with cleanliness but also his attention to his business and his moral health.[55]

CONCLUSION

During the Renaissance, the evolution of Western fashions contributed profoundly to the construction of what has been called "the old sartorial regime," with its rich, armor-like clothing. Some of its guiding principles, such as bodily extensions, the emphasis on volume, stiffness, and constraint, would have an influence on clothing silhouettes until the beginning of the twentieth century, particularly for women. Some Renaissance standards of bodily care, such as a white complexion, also continued to dominate the following centuries. The fashionable body and the bodily hexes it required arose from the habitus of elites, with its deeply embedded culture of distinction.[56]

The longevity of these fashions does not mean that they did not face criticisms. The number of publications dedicated especially to the denigration of fashion increased from the end of the sixteenth century and throughout the seventeenth. Clothing bore the brunt of satires by writers, diarists, and engravers. Ruffs, for example, were compared with millstones and wearers accused of wasting wheat to create these starched fabric sculptures, a particularly serious charge in years when harvests failed and starvation threatened the poor. Right at the end of the sixteenth century, Spanish writers mocked ruffs that had become so big that if they had been made of grass, a donkey could have grazed on them all day. Fashion became one of the symbols of the deadly sin of pride because it turned Christians away from modesty and the salvation of the soul. Few authors were concerned that clothing might impede bodily movement or cause health problems. Instead, people spoke out against the partial exposure of the body, such as the fashionable décolletage, or criticized anything that might make the body seem monstrous by transforming its natural God-given outline or by introducing confusion between male and female appearances. This idea of a monstrous body would be employed again by John Bulwer in 1650, in the title of one of the first comparative studies, dedicated to "all the native and nationall monstrosities that have appeared to disfigure the humane fabrick," including clothing and hair fashions.[57] Driven by a moral message or ethnological curiosity, all these writers expressed their fear of the transformation of the natural body by clothing and the dramatic fashions that the Renaissance brought. Although continuous reshaping of the body and the invention of further extravagant styles during the Age of Enlightenment strengthened the position of moralists, doctors and philosophers began to develop ideas that heralded a shift towards a more modern cultural representation of the human body.

CHAPTER FOUR

Belief

CORDELIA WARR

INTRODUCTION

Dress is inherently material. In the sense that it is physical, corporeal, and tangible, it seems to anchor the wearer to the secular world. The textiles that go to make up dress are subject to the economic processes of buying and selling. Yet precisely because clothing is a fundamental need it is also one which carries meaning in relation to belief. When dress, as a covering for the naked body, is considered within the context of Christianity, it is a post-lapsarian necessity, something imposed on mankind as a result of original sin. Against this background, dress provides a fertile ground for demonstrating belief and for focusing debates on moral and religious issues. The inherent tension between dress as material object and dress as conveyor of spiritual meaning is one which plays out in practices and disputes during the two centuries from 1450 to 1650, a period of significant religious upheaval encompassing the Protestant and Catholic Reformations.

VESTMENTS

Perhaps one of the most discussed areas where dress and belief intersected during this period was the issue of clerical vestments. For those in Catholic Europe, one of the ways in which they would have been aware of the status and religious authority of their priests was through the often sumptuous garments worn during the mass. The main garment worn for mass was the chasuble, a sleeveless vestment without fastenings. The cope, in effect a large cloak, was used as a processional garment with the dalmatic, a long wide-sleeved tunic, and tunicle, often a shorter version of the dalmatic, used by the deacon and sub-deacon respectively (Figure 4.1).

The symbolic meaning of the vestments used by the clergy had been laid out by William Durandus (d. 1296), Bishop of Mende, in the late thirteenth century.[1] Thomas Aquinas (d. 1274), in his *Summa Theologica*, supported the use of expensive vestments saying that: "Those constituted in positions of dignity, and the ministers of the altars more than others, are decked out in costly robes not for their own glory, but to signify the nobility of their office and of divine worship; therefore for them it is not wrongful."[2] A similar argument was used by Pius II (Aeneas Silvius Piccolomini) (d. 1464). In response to criticism such as that by Nicholas of Cusa (d. 1464), who had censured those who "appear now in red capes, now in golden ones" and claimed that the clergy should avoid luxury in their clothing,[3] Pius II noted that a priest who did not dress in a way that reflected the honor of his office would be the subject of ridicule.[4] His rationale points directly to one of the main stress points surrounding clothing used for religious purposes or to

FIGURE 4.1: Fifteenth-century dalmatic, silk with metal embroidery, Italian. Metropolitan Museum of Art, New York. www.metmuseum.org

demonstrate religious status: the use of "material things to depict spiritual truths."[5] Following scholars such as Aquinas, Pius II argued that the material expense of garments should reflect their spiritual importance. Appropriate colors, which changed with church feasts, were also prescribed. Innocent III (d. 1216) wrote instructions on liturgical colors before his election to the papacy in 1198.[6] These could vary according to national and local usage.[7] The colors were evident not only in the major vestments, such as the cope, but also, for example, in gloves worn by a bishop when celebrating a pontifical mass (Figure 4.2). The symbolic meaning of liturgical colors, although subject to change, could be very important. In 1495 Pope Alexander VI expressed his intention to wear white when taking part in a procession beseeching God to allay a storm that had left a number of casualties in Rome. His master of ceremonies pointed out that white was a color of joy and the pope wore violet instead.[8]

Although traditional mass vestments were used throughout the period in the Catholic Church, they were often the focus of internal debate. In Florence, at the end of the fifteenth century, the Dominican reformer Girolamo Savonarola (d. 1498) condemned the wearing of fine clothes in church, both for the laity and those who were members of a religious order or in holy orders. In his *De Simplicitate Christianae Vitae* (*On the Simplicity of the Christian Life*) (1496) he criticized monks and friars who wore expensive clothes made of soft wool. He further reprimanded those members of religious orders who rejoiced in being seen in front of the altar in vestments of gold and of silver, and of

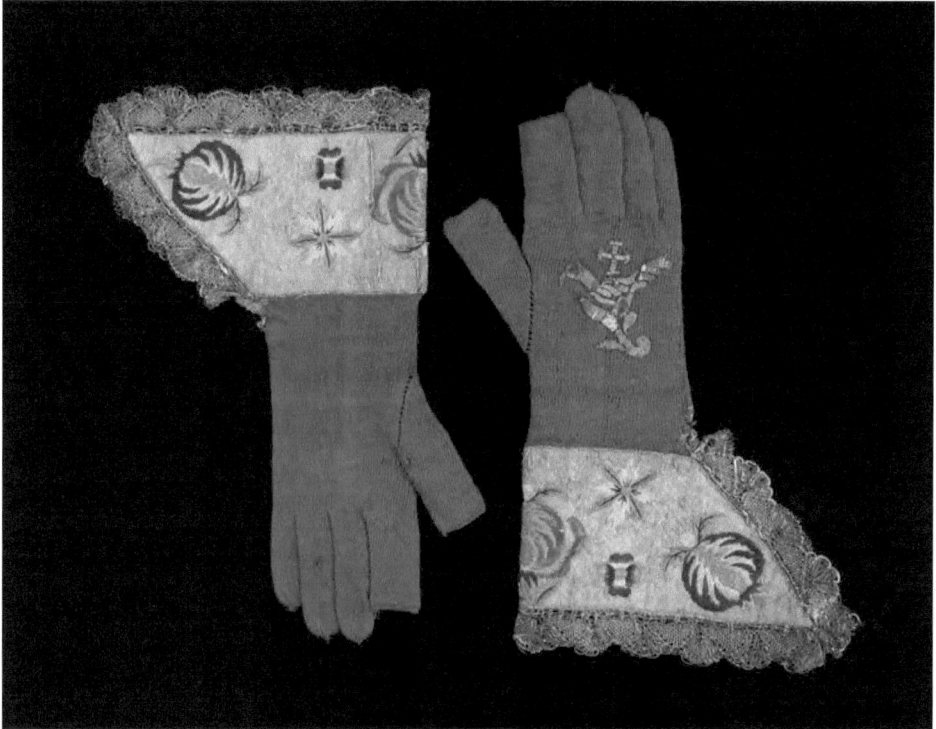

FIGURE 4.2: Bishop's gloves, first quarter of the seventeenth century, Spanish. Brooklyn Museum Costume Collection at The Metropolitan Museum of Art, New York. www.metmuseum.org

silk, going on to claim that "although they have made a vow of poverty, they run away from it as they would do if faced with a lioness or a bear whose young had been taken away from them."[9] Savonarola could have been referring to vestments such as those designed by Antonio del Pollaiuolo (d. 1498) in the 1460s for the Baptistery in Florence.[10] The twenty-seven extant scenes from the life of Saint John the Baptist were originally used on a cope, chasuble, dalmatic, and tunicle (Figure 4.3).

The magnificence of the vestments was a visible symbol of the "spiritual wealth" of the city.[11] Not only were the materials expensive—the seven embroiderers employed by the end of 1466 were working in or nué, which used a silk ground over which were placed horizontal lines of gilded silver wound around silk thread which were then stitched in place with vertical stitches of silk thread—but the difficult technique required skilled craftsmen and two of the embroiderers originated from the Netherlands. Furthermore, it appears that Antonio del Pollaiuolo was paid a considerable sum, 180 florins, for his work designing the scenes.[12] Embroidery, sewing, and spinning were accomplishments that were considered appropriate for women and in several Italian cities nuns made use of these skills. The nuns of Santa Brigida del Paradiso in Florence specialized in making church vestments and cloth furnishings, such as altar frontals, realizing the designs of painters such as Botticelli (d. 1510), Perugino (d. 1523), and Andrea del Sarto (d. 1530). Such work augmented convent income and, in the case of items destined for specific churches, could be seen as work which glorified God. However, these were still luxury items and, as such, could become the target of church reformers.[13]

FIGURE 4.3: *The Circumcision of John the Baptist*, designed by Antonio del Pollaiuolo, probably from the Baptistery cope, 1460s. Museo del Opera del Duomo, Florence. Photo: DeAgostini/Getty Images.

The retention of traditional vestments was discussed at the Council of Trent (1545–63), called by Pope Paul III (1534–49) to address some of the issues highlighted by the Protestant Reformation. During discussions in late August 1562 on the sacrifice of the mass, Cristoforus of Padua, the father general of the Augustinian Hermits, had commented on why vestments and other things such as music should be retained by the Catholic Church. On the issue of "[w]hether ceremonies, vestments, and external signs, which the Church uses in celebration, ought to be removed" Cristoforus argued that: "[I]t seems not, for they began in the time of the apostles . . . Outward signs arouse the people to devotion, just as song and sound incite to devotion in church."[14] For the Catholic Church, rich vestments reflected the glory of heaven.

PROTESTANT REFORM

Protestant reform during the sixteenth century precipitated a rethinking of what clothes were appropriate for those involved in the celebration of the mass. For many Protestant thinkers, the rich vestments used in the Catholic liturgy were evidence that the Church was mired in greed and corruption.[15] Reformers argued that the New Testament did not indicate that priests should wear special vestments for church services. However, some considered it necessary to demonstrate through an outward sign—clothing—that clergy held a particular place in society and corresponding obligations.[16] Martin Luther (d. 1546) argued that the wearing of distinctive clothing did not add to the authority of the clergy. Vestments were classified as *adiaphora*, things which were matters of indifference in religion. The Lutheran reformer John Bugenhagen (d.1558) wrote, on September 27, 1530:

> There is a twofold doctrine on chasubles ... one is the truth, namely, that chasubles can be used; this does not give scandal to those who are accustomed to hearing the gospel. The other is a Satanic lie out of the doctrines of devils, namely, that is it never lawful to use chasubles; this gives scandal to the people where they hear and believe such lies from ministers.[17]

Some protestant reformers, whilst admitting that vestments were "indifferent," argued that they should be kept. Many Lutherans did not completely abandon them and there was considerable difference in the clothing that Lutheran clerics used when celebrating mass.[18] Lutheran clergy in Brandenburg, for example, retained some vestments for the mass after the Reformation reached them in 1539–42, while those in Saxony and Hesse wore more modest clothing for services.[19] Other protestant groups maintained diverse attitudes towards the use of vestments. Anabaptists, Calvinists, and some followers of Zwingli rejected vestments completely: they were too closely associated with the perceived corruption of the Catholic Church. Anabaptists insisted on lay dress for those who conducted services, but other Protestant groups used a form of dress that ensured the person leading the service could be distinguished from the congregation.[20] During the second half of the sixteenth century there was a considerable variety of usage as debate continued over the appropriate dress for services, with some Lutherans using traditional Eucharistic vestments until the end of the century.[21]

VESTIARIAN CONTROVERSY

The English Church was to maintain vestments for use during church services only following considerable debate. The issues surrounding vestments during Elizabeth's reign gave rise to the so-called "Vestiarian controversy."[22] Henry VIII's (r. 1509–47) split from Rome did not trigger any great changes in religious observance. However, significant moves towards a Protestant church were made during the reign of Edward VI (r. 1547–53) and these included changes to vestments used during services. The Prayer Book of 1549 kept some vestments but when the new Prayer Book was published in 1552 instructions were given that "the minister at the time of the communion and all other times in his ministration, shall use neither alb, vestment, nor cope: but being archbishop or bishop, he shall have and wear a rochet; and being a priest or deacon, he shall have and wear a surplice only."[23] England returned to the Roman church during the reign of Mary Tudor (r. 1553–58) but Protestant reform was placed back on the agenda with the accession of Elizabeth I. Elizabeth's Act of Uniformity in 1559 essentially reintroduced the Prayer Book of 1552. However, the "ornaments rubric" allowed the vestments in use in the second year of the reign of Edward VI to be kept—the alb, and chasuble or cope—and worn for the Eucharist.[24] In 1563, however, the surplice, a white tunic, was stipulated as the vestment to be worn by the clergy at all services.[25] The retention of the surplice provoked some disobedience from those who wished to remove distinguishing vestments:

in December 1565, the fellows and scholars of St. John's College, Cambridge, protested by refusing to wear the surplice in chapel.[26] As can be seen from the earlier discussion, although the use of vestments was closely tied to the profession of religious belief it did not always allow a clear distinction between Catholic and Protestant.

MONASTIC DRESS

Religious dress was not confined to that worn by the clergy during mass or other liturgical occasions. As already noted, the clergy were expected to dress appropriately outside the context of church services. In Catholic Europe, there were also numerous religious orders, the members of which wore distinctive habits. The Counter Reformation saw the founding of new religious orders and the reform of some orders which already existed. Orders founded in the first half of the sixteenth century included the Society of Jesus, the Theatines, and the Barnabites. The Capuchins were formed as a group within the Franciscan Order and, despite resistance from other branches of the Order, were granted papal recognition in 1528. A number of female religious orders also had their origins during this period, such as the Ursulines, founded by Saint Angela Merici in Brescia in 1535. All of these orders had to address the question of what to wear. The habit not only identified the order to which the wearer belonged, it signified the spiritual commitment of the wearer. As such, it was an important bearer of meaning and some religious habits engendered significant debate.

AUGUSTINIANS

The debates on the form of dress used by members of the Augustinian orders demonstrate the issues at stake. The Augustinian Hermits, officially instituted by Pope Alexander IV in 1256, used the habit as a focal point through which to claim a direct link between their order and Augustine himself, who had died in 430. Their claim brought them into dispute with the Canons Regular of Saint Augustine. For the Hermits, the habit constituted a visual link to the saint whom they claimed as the founder of their order. The frescoes of the life of Saint Augustine in the church of Sant'Agostino in San Gimignano, painted by Benozzo Gozzoli between 1464 and 1465, include the scene of Augustine's baptism (Figure 4.4).

It is clear that immediately after the baptism Augustine will put on the habit of the friars who were later to take his name. Two bystanders carry the two main components of the habit—a white under-tunic and a black over-tunic—ready for the saint. In this way, the Augustinian Hermits of San Gimignano signified that they followed the type of Christian life first espoused by Augustine and, implicitly, relegated the Augustinian Canons to a position of lesser importance.[27] The tension between the Hermits and the Canons Regular was demonstrated in the dispute over the erection of a statue of Saint Augustine on Milan Cathedral when, in 1474, the decision of the Fabbrica del Duomo to have Augustine depicted in the habit of the Hermits was challenged by the Canons.[28] The Canons appealed to Gian Galeazzo Visconti but the duke rejected their case. The importance of Augustine as the "founder" of the two orders was such that the dispute quickly escalated and on May 13, 1484 Pope Sixtus IV (1471–84) had to intervene in the bull *Quia apostolos praecepit*. He attempted to calm the situation by ordering that there be no further debate on the subject but to no avail and the dispute continued after his death later that same year.[29]

FIGURE 4.4: *The Baptism of Saint Augustine*, Benozzo Gozzoli, 1464–5, fresco from the choir chapel, Sant'Agostino, San Gimignano. Photo: DeAgostini/Getty Images.

FRANCISCANS

The appeal to the habit worn by a founder as a mark of the religious observance of an order can also be seen in the case of the Franciscans. Differences in habit between branches of the Franciscan Order frequently centered on or emerged from the desire to return to the "primitive" way of life imputed to Francis of Assisi himself. Francis's rule of 1223 provided that each friar should have:

> [O]ne tunic with a hood, and if they wish it another without a hood. And those who are obliged by necessity may wear shoes. And let all the brothers be clothed in poor garments and they may patch them with pieces of sackcloth and other things, with the blessing of God.[30]

The patched nature of the tunic exemplified the poverty of the wearer and his adherence to the primitive Franciscan rule.[31] The Spiritual Franciscans of the early fourteenth century were recognized by their short, patched habits.[32] By the sixteenth and seventeenth centuries, the focus had shifted to the Capuchins as the true heirs of Saint Francis (d. 1226). The Capuchins had been formed after an Observant Franciscan, Matteo da Bascio, had declared his intention to return to the primitive rule of Saint Francis which, he claimed, was not currently being followed. Despite resistance from the Observant Franciscans, Matteo and his followers received papal approval in 1528 and were formed into a province, subject to the Minister General of the Conventual Franciscans. Their popular name stems from their hood (*cappuccio*). This aspect of their habit became a cipher through which the Capuchins' claims to have returned to the primitive life followed by Saint Francis was played out.

FIGURE 4.5: *Saint Francis in Meditation*, Francisco de Zurbarán, 1635–9, National Gallery, London. Photo: The Print Collector/Getty Images.

From the second half of the sixteenth century, Capuchins began to defend their form of habit. At some point after 1569, Fra Ruffino da Siena wrote a chronicle of the Capuchins, the first chapter of which focused exclusively on the habit and, in particular, the hood.[33] Fra Ruffino emphasized that Francis's habit had included a hood and cited the rule as evidence.[34] However, the question was not merely one of whether Francis and his first followers wore a hood but rather of the type or shape of the hood. The Capuchin hood is differentiated from that of the other branches of the Franciscan Order because of its pointed, four-cornered shape, and because it was sewn to the tunic.[35] Fra Ruffino claimed Saint Francis and the early friars had worn this pointed type of hood and cited as evidence the habit of Francis, in which he was believed to have received the stigmata, preserved at Florence, and that of Anthony of Padua preserved in the city where he died. Fra Ruffino also used visual art as evidence of the primitive shape of the hood and claimed that:

> Innumerable ancient paintings at Assisi, Rome and elsewhere, of the early friars bear out the testimony of the written word and show that the habit worn by the Capuchins is the same as that worn by Saint Francis and his companions. Not only the Franciscans but also all other religions wore the pointed hood over their heads up to the time of Pope John XXII, who ordered this to be changed for the rounded shape.[36]

For Fra Ruffino, the importance of the hood was such that he claimed that Giovanni da Cappella, a contemporary of Elia da Cortona (d. 1253) who succeeded Francis as minister general of the order, was the first to abandon the original form of the hood and wear it "thrown back over the shoulders ... but God punished him and he became a leper and ended most miserably by hanging himself."[37]

The habit patched with sackcloth envisaged in the rule of 1223 exemplified the belief, on the part of those Franciscans who insisted on a strict adherence to the rule of Saint Francis, that it was necessary to fully embrace poverty to follow Christ. In seventeenth-century Spain, artists such as El Greco (d. 1614) and Francisco de Zurbarán (d. 1664) depicted Francis meditating in a habit that was clearly patched (Figure 4.5).[38] The decree of the Council of Trent "On invocation, veneration and relics of the saints, and on sacred images" (Session 25, December 3–4, 1563) had specified that "great benefits flow from all sacred images ... because the miracles of God through the saints and their salutary examples is put before the eyes of the faithful, who can ... shape their own lives and conduct in imitation of the saints." Because of this it was especially important that images of the saints conformed to accepted knowledge about them.[39]

MODERATION IN DRESS

Although Catholic liturgical vestments were often marked by their cost and rich ornamentation, and the habits of the religious orders were sometimes marked by the appearance of poverty, much Reformation and Counter Reformation clothing was characterized by sobriety and moderation.[40] There was a considerable literature advising moderation in dress and often recommending black or dark clothing. The Jesuits (Society of Jesus), for example, did not have a prescribed habit and originally wore dress appropriate to the countries in which they worked.[41] In Rome, their dress was black, which was eventually to become the color worn by most of the order.[42] Black was commonly used for mourning dress during this period. In England black was the established mourning color by the fourteenth century although there continued to be some exceptions.[43] Mary Queen of Scots (d. 1587) wore *deuil blanc* (white mourning) after the early death of her first husband Francis II of France in 1560 (Figure 4.6). A widow was expected to put aside "all adornment and personal care," so signifying that the she was not looking for a new husband and was now focused on God.[44] For a widow, the wearing of modest mourning clothing signaled her religious beliefs, her pious attachment to her husband and her desire to dedicate herself to God after the death of her spouse. Some writers, including Cesare Vecellio in his *Degli Habiti Antichi e Moderni* (*Of Ancient and Modern Dress*) (Venice, 1590), compared the dress of widows to that of nuns.[45] Vecellio described the clothing of contemporary Venetian widows who "embrace the death of all vanity and bodily ornament" (Figure 4.7).[46]

Black was not solely the preserve of those in mourning. It was also worn in other circumstances and wearing it could emphasize particular moral attitudes. Alfonso the Magnanimous of Aragon, King of Naples (d. 1458), was reported by his biographer Vespasiano da Bisticci (d. 1498) to have made a habit of wearing black. Expensive black clothing distinguished the king, emphasized his sobriety and piety, and made ostentatious courtiers appear out of place.[47] Black clothing was widely used in European courts of the fifteenth and sixteenth centuries. Ercole d'Este, duke of Ferrara (d. 1505), educated at the court of Naples between 1445 and 1460, was in the habit of wearing black clothing when he returned to Ferrara, something which was noted by contemporaries.[48] The

FIGURE 4.6: *Mary Queen of Scots in white mourning*, after François Clouet, nineteenth century after an image of 1561, National Portrait Gallery of Scotland, Edinburgh. Photo: National Galleries of Scotland/Getty Images.

FIGURE 4.7: *De gli habit antichi e moderni di diverse parti del mondo*, Cesare Vecellio, Damiano Zenaro, Venice (1590). © University of Manchester.

fifteenth-century dukes of Burgundy favored black clothing.⁴⁹ The Holy Roman Emperor Charles V (d. 1558) and his son Philip II of Spain (d. 1598) also wore black. Both Charles and Philip saw the color not only as somber and befitting their rank but also as a color that emphasized their strong piety (Figure 4.8).⁵⁰

Although wearing black was a particular mark of sobriety and piety, sober dress was not limited to black. The Italian courtier and diplomat Baldassare Castiglione (d. 1529) encouraged restraint in dress in *The Courtier* and is shown in sober clothing in his portrait by Raphael (Figure 4.9).

During one of the conversations which form the book, Messer Federico advises that:

[F]or my part, I should prefer them [the clothes of the courtier] not to be extreme in any way, as the French as sometimes in being overample and the Germans in being overscanty . . . Moreover, I prefer them always to tend a little more toward the grave and sober rather than the foppish. Hence, I think that black is more pleasing in clothing than any other colour; and if not black, then at least some colour on the dark side. I mean this of ordinary attire . . . As for the rest, I would have our Courtier's dress show that sobriety which the Spanish nation so much observes, since external things often bear witness to inner things.⁵¹

FIGURE 4.8: *Philip II of Spain holding a rosary*, Alonso Sanchez Coello, 1573, Museo del Prado, Madrid. Photo: DeAgostini/Getty Images.

FIGURE 4.9: *Portrait of Baldassare Castiglione*, Raphael, 1514–15, Louvre, Paris. Photo: DeAgostini/Getty Images.

Messer Federico goes on to argue that a man's dress can give an indication of his character although clothing can also be misleading in this respect.[52] In fact, the courtier should "follow the custom of the majority."[53] He should not make himself conspicuous in any way. It was precisely because clothing was an indication of the inner person, their beliefs and morals, that it was so contested.

COSTUME BOOKS

Messer Federico's comments in *The Courtier* on the types of clothing worn by the inhabitants of various European countries demonstrate an understanding that clothing could indicate character traits associated with a particular area. Following the discovery of America, the opportunities for considering clothing and ornament within a geographical context were greatly expanded and the market for information about far flung lands led to the popularity of lavishly illustrated costume books in the second half of the sixteenth century.[54] Many of these books covered different regions of Europe and the known world in a specific order, and some laid claim to almost encyclopedic coverage. They also frequently included, to a greater or lesser extent, some moral commentary on the clothing of the people depicted with the illustrations accompanied by some explanatory text.⁵⁵ In the more elaborate texts, the author often makes some sort of moral judgment relating the person and their clothing.⁵⁶ Towards the end of the sixteenth century Jost Amman published a collection illustrating women's dress, the *Gynaeceum, sive, Theatrum Mulierum* (Frankfurt, 1586). The text accompanying the illustration of a Turkish prostitute makes a clear link between the attractiveness of her dress and her fallen status: "This is a prostitute, who sells her impure body for dirty money to a lover that pleases her. With the earnings of this sin she dresses herself prettily and beautifully, in order to attract the Turks even more easily with her false ornaments" (Figure 4.10).⁵⁷

François Deserps's *Receuil de la diversité des habits qui sont de present en usaige, tant es pays d'Europe, Asie, Affrique & Illes sauvages, le tout fait apres le naturel* (*A Collection of the various styles of clothing which are presently worn in countries of Europe, Asia, Africa, and the savage islands, all realistically depicted*) (Paris, 1562) is dedicated to Henry of Navarre, later Henry IV of France.⁵⁸ Each of the 121 woodcut illustrations is accompanied by a short verse. In the opening letter to the king, Deserps links excessive expense and display in clothing as something which leads to the sin of vanity and claims

FIGURE 4.10: Engraving from Jost Amman, *Gynaeceum, siue, Theatrum mulierum*, S. Feyrabend, Frankfurt (1586). © University of Manchester.

that his publication "can help us to retrench any overly sumptuous dress, which leads man to vanity: because as one recognizes a monk by his habit, the fool by his cap and the soldier by his arms, one recognizes in the same way the wise by his modest dress."[59] Despite Deserps' allusion to the well-known saying about the monk and his habit, it was generally recognized that clothing did not always serve to allow recognition of a particular type of person. Vecellio, in his *Degli Habiti Antichi e Moderni*, noted that Roman courtesans "dress in such fine style that few people can tell them apart from the noblewomen of that city."[60] Not all courtesans, who catered to a wealthy clientele, would have been able to dress as noblewomen but they probably did dress in line with the social status of their clients.[61] The way in which clothes give evidence of morals was not always as clear as commentators might have liked or claimed it to have been.

That dress and morals were closely linked is apparent in the etymology of the word: "costume" (Italian), "habit" (French), and "habit" (English) referred to both dress and the way in which one lived one's life or one's moral qualities.[62] This connection between the moral qualities of a person and their dress was also played out in comparisons between the fashions of European nations and the body decorations of those in the New World. One fashion that attracted particular ridicule in the late sixteenth century was that for excessive slashing, particularly slashed breeches. Breeches could be criticized because they were too short and did not provide enough coverage but also because they used excessive amounts of cloth. The fashion for commodious breeches was such that even those of the lower orders appear to have worn them. A man from Anglesey arrested in 1575 was wearing breeches into which he had stuffed stolen sheets.[63] Breeches were used in Elizabethan England as a means through which to discuss social status: the *Debate between Pride and Lowliness*, published in 1577, features a discussion between a pair of velvet breeches and a pair of cloth breeches.[64] Cut clothing had been fashionable since the late fourteenth century and had, along with other new types of clothing or perceived fashion excesses, attracted the ire of preachers.[65] It was one of the excesses of fashion at which John Bulwer took aim in his *Anthropometamorphosis: Man transformed: or, the artificial changling* (2nd edn 1653).[66] The woodcuts in Bulwer's work deliberately compared Europeans and the native of the Americas and other far flung lands.[67] Bulwer described the Brazilians as follows:

> The *Brasileans*, such as would be accounted manly and stout, cut great slashes in their breasts, arms and thighs, whereby they make the flesh to rise, which they cover with a certain powder, and make them looke blacke; which colour never goeth off during their lives, whereby, a far off, they seem to have cut leather Jerkins on their bodies, such as the *Switzers* use to weare.[68]

The description is accompanied by a woodcut of a Brasilian who, because of the cuts on his thighs, appears to be wearing slashed breeches (Figure 4.11).

The comparisons deliberately linked the body modification of "primitive" peoples with the excesses of fashion and, in doing so, attempted to persuade the reader that such fashions deformed and disfigured the body and demonstrated vanity in the wearer who should not seek to alter what was given by God.[69] In his Introduction (unpaginated) Bulwer argued that:

> The Spirit of God speaks admirably of the Body of man in Scripture, for, David faith, that his Body was curiously wrought in his Mother's womb as a piece of Embroidery or Needlework. Yet the blind impiety of some hath led them to such a height of

FIGURE 4.11: John Bulwer, *Anthropometamorphosis: man transformed: or, the artificial changeling*, William Hunt: London (1653, 2nd edn). © University of Manchester.

presumption, as to find fault with many parts of the curious Fabricke, and to question the wisdom of God in the contrivance thereof, upon such Blasphemous fancies men have taken upon them an audacious Art to forme and new shape themselves, altering the humane Figure, and moulding it according to their own will and arbitrement, varying it after a wonderful manner, almost every Nation having a particular whimzy as touching corporall fashions of their own invention. In which kinds of mutations, they do schematize or change the organicall parts of their bodied into diverse depraved figures.

Bulwer's Introduction highlights the perceived connection between man as a fabrication, "a piece of Embroidery or Needlework" and the fabrics worn on the body which alter the shape of that which had been formed by God.

DRESS AND MORALITY

Hardly any item of dress was immune from moralists' complaints. Long trains were one target. The courtier and poet Sir David Lindsay, in his *Ane Supplication to the kingis Grace in Contemptioun of Syde Taillis* (1530s), argued that long trains used by those who were not of sufficient social standing to wear them were a sign of pride.[70] He included both women and church clergy in his condemnation.[71]

The Puritan Philip Stubbes in his *The Anatomie of Abuses* (1583) singles out pride in dress as the worst type of that sin.[72] When Spudeus, a country yokel, asks the educated Philoponus, "How is pride of Apparell committed?" he receives the following answer:

> By wearing of Apparell more gorgeous, sumptuous, and precious than our state, calling, or condition of life requireth, whereby we are puffed up into pride, and induced to think of ourselves, more than we ought, being but vile earth and miserable sinners. And this sin of Apparell (as I have saide before) hurteth more than the other two, for the sin of the heart hurteth none but the Authour in whom it breedeth, so long as it bursteth not forth into outward show and appearance. And the pride of the mouth, though it be meere ungodly in it own nature, yet it is no so permanent . . . But this sin of the excess of Apparel, remaineth as an example of eveill before our eyes, & is a provocation to sin, as experience daily proveth.[73]

At the request of Spudeus, Philoponus then goes on to describe clothing in England to demonstrate the "sundrie abuses."[74] For Stubbes, social order as well as virtue are maintained through the appropriate use of clothing. Excess in clothing, or wearing clothing not befitting one's station in life, breaks down the social order and demonstrates the sin of pride in the wearer.[75] It was generally believed that pride and vanity were the sins which were most likely to result in excessive attention to and expenditure on appearance. Women were considered to be particularly vulnerable and there was a range of literature that advised on proper behavior and dress, and so aimed to help women avoid sinning through clothing. Juan Luis Vives (d. 1540), in his *De institutione foeminae christianae* (*The Education of a Christian Woman*), set out how women should behave and appear. For the unmarried young woman, Vives recommended that "[s]implicity has its own refinement, purer than that of luxury . . . She will not dress in silk but in wool; not in lace but ordinary linen; her dress will not be resplendent, neither will it be squalid."[76] A married woman was recommended to adhere to "the wishes and character of her husband,"[77] while a widow was advised that all personal adornment was to be avoided.[78] Vives' ideas about dress and decorum were widely dispersed.[79] His advice was founded on his moral and religious beliefs and he used Roman and early Christian writers such as Tertullian (d. ca. 225) and Cyprian (d. 258), to support his opinions. Members of religious orders, such as Savonarola, in his *De simplicitate christianae vitae* (1496), also advised women on their appearance, arguing that it should visibly demonstrate their Christian faith. Savonarola recommended simplicity in clothing and, like other writers on the subject, he distinguished between what was appropriate for women of different social ranks, since society had itself been ordained by God.[80]

SUMPTUARY LEGISLATION

The ability to differentiate between those of different status was also a concern of sumptuary legislation, which attempted to limit expenditure on conspicuous consumption. The relative importance of economic rationales and moral imperatives in sumptuary law has been much debated.[81] Statutes were often couched in terms of encouraging or ensuring financial stability or growth but there was also a strong moral and religious element to the reasons put forward for the enactment of sumptuary legislation. Many sumptuary laws specifically forbad certain types of clothing on the basis that they were an incitement to sin. The introduction to the passage dealing with clothing in the Basel ordinance of 1637 aimed to cut down on unnecessary expenditure but also identified excessive luxury in dress as offensive to God:

> ... [E]xperience shows us that when such useless, excessive ostentation and cost is not remedied and suppressed in good time, the Almighty God (to whom such a thing is most highly offensive and who punishes it every time, as we have examples enough in the holy scripture) will be still more violently angered and may bring upon us all heavier and harder punishments and distress ... Therefore let our beloved citizens hereby take warning so that everyone in his own household for himself, his wife, children and the servants entrusted to his care, put aside and refrain from great extravagant pride and conspicuous unnecessary cost, but rather use modesty and the honesty well-pleasing to God the Lord.[82]

Philip IV of Spain's pragmatic of 1639 forbad the *guardainfante*, a particularly large form of farthingale, to all except public prostitutes. Alonso Carranza had castigated it as "lascivious, dishonest, and causing sin, both to those who wear it, and to others because of it."[83] The exaggerated shaped of the *guardainfante* led to stories that women used it to hide lovers and pregnancies that arose outside marriage.[84] The Spanish legislation specifically associated it with sexual sin by limiting its use to prostitutes. Although there was a clear link between morality and dress the two were not always viewed in the same light in secular and religious contexts. In 1611, Philip III of Spain (d. 1621) promulgated a ban against veils, which ordered women not to cover their heads or faces, and to be accompanied by a male relative whenever they were in public. Such directives aimed to ensure that women could not damage the honor of the family. However, a number of churchmen, following Saint Paul (1 Corinthians 11: 12–16), believed that women should modestly cover their heads in public.[85]

DRESS AND THE AFTERLIFE

Clothing could indicate religious piety and virtue in this life, but it also had a place in the afterlife. The funeral ceremony marked the transition between this life and the next. Funerals for those with wealth or status were often public affairs involving processions with accompanying mourners. Some churches owned a specific set of vestments for funeral masses and these could have appropriate subject matter embroidered or stitched onto them. The chasuble of Robert Thornton, abbot of Jervaulx, Yorkshire (d. 1533) includes figures of the dead who rise from their graves (Figure 4.12).[86] A pair of black vestments "with white crosses rising out of the grave" was left to the church of Mells in 1527.[87] The subject matter of both expressed hope in the final resurrection on the day of judgment. The clothing of the deceased was a matter of public display and religious belief. In Renaissance Florence the deceased was often carried on an open bier.[88] For some, the clothing in which they were dressed for their cortège, funeral, and subsequent burial reflected their status in life. When Giuliano de'Medici's funeral was held in March 1516 the corpse was splendidly dressed in gold brocade and wearing full armor.[89] For others, burial clothing was an important means to demonstrate their piety. Saint Antoninus of Florence died on May 2, 1459 and was buried in the Dominican convent of San Marco. According to Tommaso Buoninsegni's account of the translation of his body in 1589, Antoninus was discovered to be wearing the habit of the Dominican order along with a small black hat. The only item that identified him as a bishop was the

FIGURE 4.12: Chasuble of Robert Thornton, early sixteenth century with later alterations. © Victoria and Albert Museum, London.

pallium.⁹⁰ Throughout the Renaissance, testators requested that they be buried in the habit of one of the religious orders. In sixteenth-century Madrid, the Franciscan habit was the most popular form of burial attire.⁹¹ Clothing allowed recognition in the afterlife. One legend which demonstrates this is that whereby Saint Francis of Assisi was said to be allowed to descend into purgatory each year on the anniversary of his death. Antonio Daza, in his *Historia de las Llagas de Nuestro Seráfico Padre San Francisco* (*The History of the Stigmata of Our Seraphic Father Saint Francis*), published in 1617, explained that on that day Francis was able to grant immediate salvation to some members of the Franciscan Order. Those associated with the Order were recognized through their habit.⁹²

Those about to die were sometimes covered with clothes that had been removed from statues of saints. This appears to have been the case at the shrine of Lluch in Majorca where, in 1565, the bishop allowed people to venerate a statue of the Virgin Mary covered with a cloak but forbad the removal of the cloak to cover the sick and faithful with it.⁹³ Such a practice may have come about as part of a need to comfort the dying with items which had a strong religious connection. The clothing and unclothing of statues seems to have been something most often enacted by women. In fifteenth-century Florence, for example, nuns often had statues of the baby Christ which they dressed.⁹⁴ The clothing and unclothing of the baby Christ was intimately bound up with the expression of their spirituality. Some statues were life-size and the clothes they wore may have served a dual purpose. A synodal constitution from Burgos in 1575 ordered that statues were to be covered only with dedicated clothing and not with anything that could also be worn by real women.[95] The clothing of the saints was important for the living as well as the dead. Relics, parts of a saint's body or items with which it had been in contact, could be clothing or textiles. After the death of Francesca Bussa de' Ponziani in Rome on March 9, 1440, her clothing was eagerly sought after by those seeking miraculous cures and many of those who came to venerate her body in Santa Maria Nova took away pieces of her garments.[96] Some of the witnesses in her subsequent canonization processes described the uses to which such relics were put. A woman named Donna Augustina reported that on the March 16, 1440 she had suffered so badly in one of her eyes that she could see nothing out of it but having placed some cloth that had been on top of Francesca's corpse on her eye, she was cured.[97]

CONCLUSION

Over the period from the mid-fifteenth to the mid-seventeenth century, concerns relating to clothing and belief reflected issues including the impact of the Catholic and Protestant Reformations in Europe as well as increasing knowledge of the New World. The former prompted a rethinking of the place of clothing within society, and particularly of the dress worn by church officials. Catholic religious orders founded during this period in some cases considered how clothing could help them in their aims, for example when working outside Europe, and in other cases deliberately sought out what they believed to be an early form of habit to demonstrate their strict adherence to a reformed religious life. Exploration of the New World stimulated new evaluations of the adornment of the body and the costume books published during this period express the diverse ways in which the geography of clothing could be used to further arguments about the morality of certain types of dress. However, these questions were, in many cases, ones which had been posed before, albeit in different guises and with diverse results. The Europe of the mid-fifteenth to mid-seventeenth centuries remained Christian, and religious and moral questions related to dress demonstrated this as they had done in the immediately preceding centuries. Dress continued to channel religious power through miraculous intervention and express religious authority through rich vestments. The embroidered decoration of silk vestments made manifest the riches of heaven on earth. Dress gave evidence of belief but it was also subject to interpretation in the light of that belief. Even among different branches of the same religious order the religious habit was a source of discussion and, sometimes, dispute, so important was it in defining the faith of the wearer. For most people dress continued to be an outward indicator of moral qualities and these were discussed in various types of publication, including those which advised on proper behavior. The meaning of dress was open to discussion: did rich clothing worn for the mass reflect the glory of God or was it merely a sign of corruption? Was excessively poor clothing a sign of humility or evidence of attention-seeking pride? In either case what was not in doubt was that dress and belief were inextricably linked and that matters relating to clothing were meaningful for just this reason. Dress impacted on the possibility of salvation. As such its importance could not have been more far reaching.

CHAPTER FIVE

Gender and Sexuality

ANN ROSALIND JONES

Remember how your Maker made for our first Parents coats—not one coat but a coat for the man and a coat for the woman—the man's coat fit for his labor, the woman's for her modesty.[1]

Or did He?

To understand the interplay of sex and gender in Renaissance clothing calls for a look at the ways in which social needs, fears, and pleasures shaped men and women's dress. This chapter explores how theories of sexed bodies and rules for gendered behavior in Europe from the fifteenth to seventeenth centuries were materialized—and resisted—in the wearing of clothes. The imagined instability of bodies, combined with the similarity of much apparel worn by both men and women, complicated and even upended strict gender oppositions. To show this uneasy complex in action, I will focus on some instances of gender panic that arose when people dressed in ways that challenged the categories prescribed by biological theory and normative gender. The evidence I use to support this claim is both visual and textual, drawn mainly from polemical, literary, and legal works whose writers attempted to manage practices and counter-practices in the gender turmoil that animated the order of worn things.

From head to toe, early modern male and female clothing was more similar than we might expect. Women and men's undergarments, collars, and shoes were constructed on the same patterns. Peasant men and women wore the same loose garments to work in; they put on the same straw hats to fend off the sun, they loosened or hiked up their main garments, they wore the same clogs and boots in bad weather, and they carried the same baskets to market.[2] The wealthy elite used accessories in styles shared by both sexes: hats, collars, lace, jewels, gloves, purses, handkerchiefs. The French beret, or "bonnet," was worn by both men and women in Germany, Italy and England.[3] In England in the first half of the sixteenth century, men and women of various ranks hung the same kinds of small bags and purses from their belts;[4] among other perfumed garments made and sold throughout Europe, gloves scented with musk, ambergris, and other substances were worn and given as presents by both men and women.[5] Historians of lace such as Doretta Davanzo Poli and Santina Levey illustrate collars, cuffs, and handkerchiefs made in the same styles for men and women.[6]

Both women and men wore shifts or chemises: full-cut, loose undergowns, made of linen or silk, and in the case of the poor, made of wool and worn as overgarments. Women's shifts might be longer than men's and the rich had theirs elegantly needle-worked, but they were basically the same garment with the same purpose: repeatedly

FIGURE 5.1: *Self-Portrait*, Albrecht Dürer, 1498, oil on panel, Prado Museum.
Photo: Imagno/Getty Images.

washable, they absorbed body oils and sweat. In Albrecht Dürer's self-portrait of 1498, he depicted himself in a sheer gathered linen chemise with gold trim (Figure 5.1). Two centuries later, Rembrandt painted the model he used for his Flora in a full, long-sleeved shift of heavier linen (Figure 5.2).

Shifts were designed for comfort. In contrast, structural underprops were used in both men and women's clothing to mold high- and middle-ranking bodies into fashionable shapes in rigorous ways. Women wore corsets stiffened with shafts of whalebone, ivory, and even iron under tight-laced outer bodices; men wore doublets with stiff fabric, boning, and padding that had the same effect of shaping the body.[7] Eugenia Paulicelli argues that the *corsaletto*, initially the snug upper body armor worn by soldiers, evolved into the woman's corset.[8]

Men, in fact, were often fashion leaders. In England, Henry VIII, in addition to having his clothing studded with pearls, was the first person to establish pearl earrings as a style.[9] Women, too, such as Frances Howard, Baroness Cobham, as seen in a portrait of about 1600, adopted the lavish use of pearls (Figure 5.3). But men would continue to wear

FIGURE 5.2: *Flora*, Rembrandt van Rijn, probably early 1650s, oil on canvas. Photo: Malcolm Varon. © The Metropolitan Museum of Art. Image source: Art Resource, NY.

FIGURE 5.3: *Portrait of a Lady in a Black Dress with Pearls*, English School, c. 1590. The Weiss Gallery, London.

them as earrings, as shown in portraits of noblemen such as Walter Raleigh (Figure 5.4), and, if the recent reassessment of a portrait owned by the Cobbe family is correct, Henry Wriothesley, third Earl of Southampton, Shakespeare's patron and lover.[10]

Early modern cultures, of course, imposed rules about how garments should conform to sexual identity. As toddlers, aristocratic boys wore the same dresses as girls, and when they were "breeched" it was a significant transition; pre-teen girls were put into stiff, tight bodices. In the early sixteenth century, the main silhouette for men was broad-shouldered and narrow-legged; for women, it was narrow-waisted and wide-skirted. Jane Ashelford, however, remarks that during the reign of Mary Tudor and Philip II of Spain, beginning in 1544, both sexes began to adopt the Spanish style of dress with its strong vertical lines and sober colors, especially black.[11] In Elizabethan England another male/female similarity arose: men's and women's dress alike was "subject to the same areas of exaggeration, namely the neck [ruffs], arms [full-cut sleeves] and hips [padded short breeches and robust farthingales]."[12] Men and women also resembled one another in their use of pinked and slashed fabrics, slit to reveal the chemise or colored lining underneath, and in the shape of their doublets or bodices, which lengthened and narrowed down to a point as the sixteenth century moved into the seventeenth.

FIGURE 5.4: *Portrait of Sir Walter Raleigh*, unknown English artist, oil on panel, 1588. © National Portrait Gallery, London.

But a surprising difference between men and women's clothing was that high-ranking men owned more of it than women. This is evident in inventories and wills from the French court in the late fifteenth century and in Henrician England, where men's wardrobes were much larger and more varied than women's.[13] Timothy McCall, writing about fifteenth-century Italy, demonstrates that noblemen's clothing, from courts to armies to political meetings, was intended to be highly visible. Dukes and princes in the public sphere were expected to dress "brilliantly," to wear shimmering and sparkling clothes and jewels. The same was expected of the many boys and young men who served them.[14] In contrast, the late fifteenth-century Frenchman Olivier de la Marche, in his *Parement des Dames*, emphasized the importance of much simpler garments for women: the chemise represented honesty, the girdle represented virtue and the purse represented generosity.[15] A richly dressed man was upholding the honor of his duchy or city or region, as were the women in his family. But an overdressed man or woman was likely to be seen as sexually suspect.

As angry writers witnessed, however, these rules could be flouted. When they were, various forms of subversion and erotic pleasure, as well as alarmed indignation, arose from the disordering of clothes as people saw, coveted, bought, borrowed, and wore them. One reason for the insistence on clearly gender-marked dress in this period was that the medical elite saw bodies as sexually unstable. In part, their thinking was based on a model elaborated by the second-century Roman physician Galen, who believed that men and women's sexual organs were the same: the penis and testes were worn outside the male body, homologous sexual organs were worn inside the woman's. This thinking underlay the remark of a student of the Italian physician Andreas Vesalius, Baldasar Heseler, who stated the shared-morphology thesis as follows: "If you turn the scrotum, the testicles, and the penis inside out, you will have all the genital organs of the female."[16]

Other threads of thought about sex and gender, focused especially on changeable fluids in the body, influenced medical practice in this period, derived from Galen and before him Hippocrates and Aristotle.[17] This system was based on four humors supposed to govern both the female and the male body; it was these fluids that produced sexual identity and gendered temperament. In men's bodies, hot and dry humors, choler and blood, predominated, leading to energetic and courageous action. In women's bodies, damp humors, black bile, and phlegm, predominated, making women cautious, patient, and affectionate. The social purposes of this binary are obvious: to keep conventional gender assignments in place. Yet the interplay of gender ideology and medical theories of sex was not one-dimensional. Food, drink, exercise, disease, intercourse, and strong emotion could shift the balance of humors, producing womanly men and manly women. The humoral body was susceptible to endless variation.

Another important solvent of absolute sexual difference was that women were understood to have semen as well as men. Though women's blood was colder, it could and needed to be heated up enough by sexual excitement to generate the seed that would share in conceiving a child.[18] An unbalanced mixture of humors meant that a woman with too much heat in her body could be as sexually aggressive as a man, a man with humors too cold might lactate, and a body in between destabilized gender difference completely by combining both sexes. In this world of bodies in process, mixed from the beginning and open to transformation, social order required some way to fix sexual identity, to enforce physical gender difference to link it to contrasting characters, capacities, and duties. Clothing was one way to do this. More than a visual shorthand for region and rank, dress incorporated its wearers into a manageable hierarchy of reproductive roles and political hierarchy. Clothes had to pin down what bodies themselves did not.

This is one way to understand how vehemently sartorial exceptions to the rules of gender were denounced. Such denunciations are historically useful not only on the level of ideology but on the level of material practice. They give a good idea of what people were actually wearing, legitimately or not.

In mid-sixteenth-century France, a detailed picture of wealthy women's dress was provided by the writer Artus Thomas (known as Thomas Artus until 1996) in his attack on the figure of the hermaphrodite, which historians have linked to the bisexual Henri III and his court of "les mignons du roi," male favorites.[19] Thomas's little book, *Les Hermaphrodites*, was written during the 1580s and published in Paris in 1605. On its title page is an engraving of a figure wearing a man's doublet and breeches but also a woman's high wig trimmed with bows and jewels; breasts are hinted at under the doublet (Figure 5.5).

FIGURE 5.5: Title page engraving, Artus Thomas, *Les Hermaphrodites* (Paris, 1605). Folger Shakespeare Library.

The book goes on to describe a fantastic island ruled by a king and his courtiers, all obsessed with clothing in blatantly unmanly ways. The narrator, an explorer blown off course in a storm, first observes the *levée* of the king of the island, who wakes up wearing face cream under a mask, a veil to protect his skin, and gloves to soften his hands. His servants wax his eyebrows, rouge his cheeks, curl his hair, and dye his beard, put him into padded hose decorated with laces, and stuff his big feet into tiny shoes. He is fitted into a tight doublet and lace collar, and his ruff, properly shaken into a full, flat wheel, is called the "dome of the rotunda" (65). After his servants hand him perfumed gloves and a huge vellum fan, they all bow down to this "demy-femme" (66). His hat, set on the top of his head so as not to disarrange his coiffure, is trimmed with a band decorated with jewels and pearls, resembling "the diadems that our women wore some time ago" (67).

This long passage is clearly satirical: Thomas uses the perspective of a naïve observer to mock men dressed in effeminate luxury. The accusation goes further than this, however. Clothing is political. To dress as the hermaphrodites do is to reverse the rules by which good kingdoms should be run. The topsy-turvy laws of the island order its inhabitants to dress "according to their fancy" and to embellish even well-tailored clothing with gold and silver embroidery, jewels, and pearls to avoid being seen as lowly, foolish wretches, "for in this island, the habit makes the monk, and not the other way around" (105). Women's dress is recommended for everyone; islanders of both sexes are enjoined to spend most of their time in conference with their tailors; and if they fail to change their fashions every month, they'll be seen as raggedy, uncivil misers. Reading this mock law code, we can see through the looking glass the sartorial virtues that Thomas is asserting: plain dress impervious to fashion, obedient to sumptuary laws, and above all, properly masculine or feminine.

Worst of all, the poem accompanying the title page figure of the hermaphrodite lightheartedly links his dress to the pleasures of bisexuality. The last thing that worries this clothes-crazed fop is who s/he is. Living in between brings erotic delight. Why worry? "I am neither male nor female/ Even so, I'm easy in my mind/ As to which of the two I should choose./ What does it matter who I resemble?/ Better to have them both at once./ That way double pleasure comes." Hermaphroditism on Thomas's island is not a physical anomaly but a chosen condition. It denaturalizes the system of gendered dress by exposing the artifice that governs it.[20]

An exaggerated fiction *The Hermaphrodites* may be, but it points to an important aspect of the social life of clothing, as previously mentioned, in this period: garments worn by both men and by women were imaginably transferable because they were nearly identical. A difference, however, arose in mid-fifteenth-century France between the extents to which men and women's clothes covered their bodies, occasioned by the rise of the doublet, a narrow man's jacket that grew increasingly shorter over the century.[21] In contrast to the long, loose gowns of medieval elites, doublets exposed more of men's bodies than women's styles did of theirs: "tightly sewn and shorter clothing for men brought different parts of the body separately into view for the first time."[22] As a result, men had to worry about revealing inappropriate parts of their anatomy. Alarm at this change underlies the description in the fourteenth-century French *Chroniques* of the new style worn by the French aristocracy: "Some wore their clothing so short that it barely covered their rumps, with the result that when they bent down to serve their lords they showed their underpants as well as what was inside them to those who stood behind."[23] In the 1590 costume book of the Venetian artist Cesare Vecellio, a woodcut of a French nobleman (Figure 5.6) shows his extremely brief breeches.

FIGURE 5.6: Cesare Vecellio, Nobile Francese, *Degli Habiti antichi e moderni di diverse parti del mondo* (Venice, 1590), 275. Private collection, Leverett, Massachusetts.

Vecellio remarks, with distaste, "They wear short *bracconi*, very tight on the thigh, which practically reveal the veins of their flesh."[24] The nobleman's bare knees don't improve the look.

The equivalent improper exposure of the body by women was the almost bare bosom with cleavage bolstered up by bodice stiffeners such as the metal, ivory, or wooden busk. This effect was far from universally admired. Thomas Nashe condemned it in his 1613 satire, *Christs's Teares over Jerusalem*: "Now come I to the Daughters of Pride [who] delight to go gorgeously. . . . Their breasts they embuske up on hie, and their round Roseate buds immodestly lay forth, to shew at their hands there is fruite to be hoped."[25] Critics also condemned women who wore veils for the sake of modesty but contravened the effect by baring their breasts. In the Brescian Giacomo Lanteri's dialogue *Della Economica* (Venice, 1560), the mother remarks that the pious founders of Venice decreed that "women, especially still unmarried women, would cover their faces completely with a black veil." But she goes on to say that they have invented a perverse variation on this convention:

Although women have kept their heads covered, little by little they have taken the liberty of wearing their gown so low as to expose so much cleavage that they show their entire breast. The result is that they appear to be much more lascivious than they would appear had they not worn the veil at all.[26]

About this time in France, Protestant authorities were likewise objecting to bared breasts, which they associated with other dissolute fashions. At La Rochelle in 1581, the Reformed synod recommended excluding from Communion women who showed off with "certain marked features of impudicity, . . . such as make-up, pleating, tufts of feathers, stitchings . . . and exposed bosoms."[27] Given how many women of different ranks wore low-cut gowns, from peasants, serving-women, women of the middling sort to aristocrats, such denunciations were obviously ignored. Décolletage brought pleasure to women and men alike. Dürer's loose-cut chemise in his self-portrait reveals the white skin of his chest, and Vecellio's woodcut of a Venetian prostitute, to which I will return, shows her in a doublet unbuttoned halfway down her torso—for the pleasure of her clients, and for her own profit, too (Figure 5.7).[28]

FIGURE 5.7: Cesare Vecellio, Meretrici publiche, *Degli Habiti antichi e moderni di diverse parti del mondo* (Venice, 1590), 145 verso. Private collection, Leverett, Massachusetts.

An item of men's dress that attracted similarly intense interest and disapproval was the codpiece. Patricia Simons offers a detailed history of this container for the "cods," or testicles, a hollow external prosthesis that both concealed and called attention to the organs inside. The codpiece—*braghetta* in Italian, *Latz*, meaning flap, in German, *braguette* in French—began as a device for easy access and unlacing for urination, and possibly as a guard against hanging accessories such as purses and swords. But as codpieces became more elaborate, taking on different forms from an upward curve to an ovoid bag or bulge, they may have got in the way of their practical function: "Their purpose, in other words, went beyond the utilitarian or the decorous."[29] Simons argues that this accessory signified a man's entire reproductive "package," including testicles, penis and accumulated semen, alluding to virility that went beyond the merely physical to encompass familial, political, misogynist and amorous assertion.[30]

A painting adduced in several discussions of the codpiece is Agnolo Bronzino's three-quarter-length portrait of Guidobaldo II della Rovere, painted between 1531 and 1532 (Figure 5.8). Against a dark background, the eighteen-year-old duke stands erect in

FIGURE 5.8: *Portrait of Guidobaldo II della Rovere, Duke of Urbino*. Painting by Bronzino (1531–32). Florence, Palazzo Pitti. Photo by DeAgostini/Getty Images.

a black suit of armor trimmed with gold and sharply nipped in at his waist. Above his snug red damask breeches, he wears a large codpiece of the same fabric, in the shape of a double circular roll. Konrad Eisenbichler interprets the bold stance of the young man in relation to the Greek inscription on a small piece of paper set above the brim of the helmet on which he rests his right hand: "It will certainly be as I have decided," referring to Guidobaldo's struggle with his father over whether he was to marry for love rather than dynastic profit.[31] In this context, the codpiece represents forceful filial aggression.

For some observers and thinkers, the codpiece was an embarrassment, or worse. As early as 1494 in his *Ship of Fools*, Sebastian Brant declared that short upper garments and codpieces were a "shame for the German nation."[32] In Montaigne's essays of 1575, he disdained the codpiece as indecent, setting it firmly into the French past and attributing it to present-day Swiss men instead: "What was the meaning of that ridiculous part of the breeches worn by our fathers, which is still seen on our Swiss?"[33] An anecdote about the women of the city of Ascoli recounts that they responded to a sumptuary law of 1553 prohibiting them from wearing the high-soled shoes called *pianelle* by pointing to the man's codpiece as much more indecent—"disonestissima."[34]

In other contexts, the codpiece was taken less seriously. Will Fisher quotes a seventeenth-century English writer describing the simple early codpiece, basically a soft flap of fabric tied to a man's hose with laces, or "points," at each side of the groin. The writer reminisces fondly about the capaciousness of this pouch: "this large and ample Codpiss supplied the want of pockets," because when its laces were undone, "they made way to the Linnen bags tied to the inside between the shirt and the Codpiss [and] these bags held everything they carried about with them."[35] The codpiece was a coin purse, lunch bag, letterbox, and handkerchief-holder all in one. This notion of abundance, outside and in, was a staple for comic writers such as Rabelais, who in his *Gargantua* of 1532 wrote a rapturous paean to his giant hero's enormous codpiece, which had a shape "like a bowed arch" and was trimmed with "rich diamonds, precious rubies, rare turquoises, magnificent emeralds and Persian pearls ... like one of those grand Horns of Plenty that you see on Roman monuments."[36] He adds that the promise of male genital power made by the size and decoration of the codpiece was truthfully based on Gargantua's real body: "On one point I will inform you now, however, that not only was it long and capacious, but well furnished within and well victualled, having no resemblance to the fraudulent codpieces of so many young gentlemen which contain nothing but wind, to the great disappointment of the female sex."

But codpieces became a highly alarming topic when women were accused of wearing them. Fisher quotes the Welsh poet William Gamage, whose collection of epigrams, *Linsi-Woolsie* (1613), included a poem entitled "On the feminine Supremacie," about a site of imagined sexual reversal rather like the island inhabited by Thomas's hermaphrodites: "I often heard, but never read till now,/ That Women-kinde the Codpeeces did weare;/ But in those Iles, the men to women bow."[37] Worn by the wrong sex, codpieces and breeches signaled sexual danger. Breeches certainly were worn by Italian prostitutes. The Roman city police arrested "about fourteen prostitutes between 1594 and 1606 for wearing men's clothing, usually a beret and a cloak, sometimes breeches as well."[38] Many more women probably dressed this way, undiscovered, in order to move about the city freely after curfew. Legislators saw the problem as broader than nocturnal disguise: they prohibited prostitutes during Carnival from appearing "In windows or in public dressed as men ... nor may they wear cloaks."[39]

Female/male cross-dressing was also practiced by prostitutes in other cities. In the late fourteenth century, Florence openly welcomed prostitutes in the hope that they could attract homosexual men back to heterosexuality. But, as Richard Trexler shows, this plan backfired because prostitutes who dressed like men attracted gay men, and they performed acts "against Nature," such as anal and oral sex, the same as those their customers engaged in with one another.[40] This was no way to return men to their wives and families. Another objection to cross-dressed prostitutes was that some wore men's capes, gowns, and hats to help their customers conceal their depravity. Or, on the contrary, they wore their clients' clothes—hats, for example—to reveal who was using their services.[41] In 1502, the city outlawed transvestism, as it had done in 1206, but court cases up through the first decades of the sixteenth century show that prostitutes had not given it up. Between 1441 and 1523, over half the prostitutes who appeared in the Florentine court that oversaw offenses against public morality were accused of wearing men's clothes.[42]

In Venice, a 1578 edict prohibited the same thing: "Courtesans and prostitutes of Venice in recent times, in order to take and tempt young men ... have found this new method ... of dressing themselves in men's clothing, wearing *ninfe* [ruffs], doublets and other clothes."[43] Such laws in Venice have been interpreted as a response to the homoerotic message cross-dressing sent—but not an entirely negative response. As in Florence, Venetian authorities in part tolerated prostitutes' use of the style in the hope that that women dressed in men's clothing would be able to draw the city's homosexuals away from bonds with men.[44]

To return to Vecellio's print of the Venetian prostitute (Figure 5.7,), he gives a detailed description of her bi-gendered dress:

> all of them have an outfit tending toward men's clothing: they wear a doublet of silk or linen ... padded with cotton, exactly as young men wear. ... Next to their skin they wear a man's shirt, made with as much delicacy and elegance as they can afford. ... Many wear short breeches like men.[45]

The woodcut, in fact, shows less than the comment says: the *Meretrice Publica* wears her hair in the style of the *corno*, with tightly curled peaks at each side of her forehead; she carries a fashionable paper fan; and she holds up her skirt to reveal her high-soled shoes. What makes the image so disturbing is that these are women's fashions. On the surface, this prostitute is not disguised as a man. More startlingly, Vecellio tell us, she is layering an ensemble of garments signaling femininity above another that signifies masculinity: beneath the coiffure, skirt, and platform shoes lie the breeches and hose of the opposite sex. Images of the time rose to the challenge of confirming that prostitutes did indeed wear this combination of men's doublets and narrow, short breeches under their skirts. Pietro Bertelli's titillating peek-a-boo engraving of a Courtesan and Blind Cupid, published in Padua in 1578, gives two views of such a woman: womanly on top, manly underneath. First we see her in her fashionable long gown but then we can lift up a flap to reveal her breeches—masculine—and her *pianelle*—feminine. Figures 5.9a and 5.9b. The effect is comic but also disturbing. The lower part of the woman's long bodice, now truncated at her waist by the lifted flap, appears unnervingly similar in form to a codpiece.

In the early seventeenth century in London, visible gender cross-dressing by women briefly became a fashionable style, arousing the fury of preachers, moralists, and pamphleteers who castigated women for wearing men's hats and doublets, and having their hair cut short. Evidence for this is that King James commanded the ministers of London to denounce the style from their pulpits on a certain Sunday, and to order the

GENDER AND SEXUALITY

FIGURES 5.9a & 5.9b: *Venetian Courtesan*, *Le vere imagini et descritioni delle piv nobilli citta del mondo*, Donato Bertelli (Venice, 1578), plate 28. © The Metropolitan Museum of Art. Image source: Art Resource, NY.

husbands of London to keep their wives from wearing such clothing, if necessary by depriving them of the money to acquire it.[46]

In two states of an engraving of the time, Simon van de Passe depicted the noblewoman Frances Howard, first wearing an exaggerated bouffant coiffure of blond hair with a small feather attached at its back. Figure 5.10a. In the second state of the engraving, she is wearing a man's hat with a large decorative plume and hair cut short to just below her ears. Figure 5.10b.

FIGURES 5.10a & 5.10b: *Frances Howard, Countess of Somerset*, Simon van de Passe, engraving (Hollstein, vol. XVI, no. 115), state I and state II. Rosenwald Collection, courtesy National Gallery of Art, Washington DC.

The second engraving would have been credible at the time: the countess was the subject of horrified gossip because she had been accused of poisoning Thomas Overbury, an enemy of her husband Thomas Carr, the Duke of Somerset. In 1615 and 1616, another woman too, had been accused of the murder: the seamstress Anne Turner, known for having brought the style of yellow starch for ruffs from France to England, who confessed to providing poison for the murder. Howard herself was said to have ordered the whole affair. Turner was hanged; Howard was freed because of the bond her husband shared with the king. In the second version of Van de Passe's print, the shock effect of Howard's short hair and her man's hat with its ostrich feather is intensified by her very low-cut gown, which sets aggressively naked femininity against masculine headgear in what was obviously intended to be a disturbing combination. The exposure of a woman's breasts here, far from being a sign of femininity, is a mark of sexual aggression, a usurpation of male prerogative.[47]

This disturbance of properly gendered dress is the theme of two pamphlets published in London in 1620, *Hic Mulier (The Manly Woman)* and *Haec Vir (The Womanly Man)*. The writer of *Hic Mulier* denounces manly women as imitators of the two criminals in the Overbury murder: "From the first you got the false armoury of yellow Starch. From the other, you have taken the monstrousnesse of your deformitie in apparrell."[48] He links this monstrousness to blasphemy via a misinterpretation of Genesis: "Remember how your Maker made for our first Parents coats—not one coat but a coat for the man and a coat for the woman—the man's coat fit for his labor, the woman's for her modesty."[49] In fact, neither Biblical account of the sartorial effects of the Fall specifies that God gave different garments to Adam and to Eve, and each account says that after the Fall, they were banished from Eden both wearing the skins of animals.

In addition to mishandling Scripture, the writer takes a literary turn: he personifies particular items of dress to animate them as signs of women's immorality. As Susan Vincent points out, the target here is not that women are becoming men; rather, this new style shockingly exposes parts of their bodies that are distinctly female.[50] In contrast to the virtuous garments they should be wearing, neat headdresses and gowns suited to their sex, they are participating in a parade of unruly sartorial creatures, "exchanging the modest attire of the comely Hood, Cowl Coif, . . . or Kerchief to the cloudy Ruffianly broad-brimmed Hat and wanton Feather, the modest upper parts of a concealing straight gown to the loose, lascivious embracement of a French doublet."[51] Chic cross-dressing, says the writer, is clear evidence of sexual sin in other contexts:

> Not only such as will not work to get bread will find time to weave herself points [laces] to truss her loose Breeches; and she that hath pawned her credit to get a Hat will sell her Smock to buy a Feather; she that hath given kisses to have her hair shorn will give her honesty to have her upper parts put into a French doublet (269).

The writer rises to his highest pitch of indignation in a passage in which, like Thomas in *The Hermaphrodites*, he links cross-dressing to political reversals of the most horrific kind, through which uncivilized and violent hordes could take over the states of Europe: "If this be not barbarous, make the rude Scythian, the untamed Moor, the naked Indian, or the wild Irish Lords and Rulers of well-governed Cities" (269).

John Trundle, the publisher of this pamphlet, commissioned a title page illustrated with a woman having herself dressed in this style. Figure 5.11.

On the left a barber holds a comb and raises up the shears with which he has cut the woman's hair to above-the-shoulder length; at the right a tiny tailor adjusts the laces that

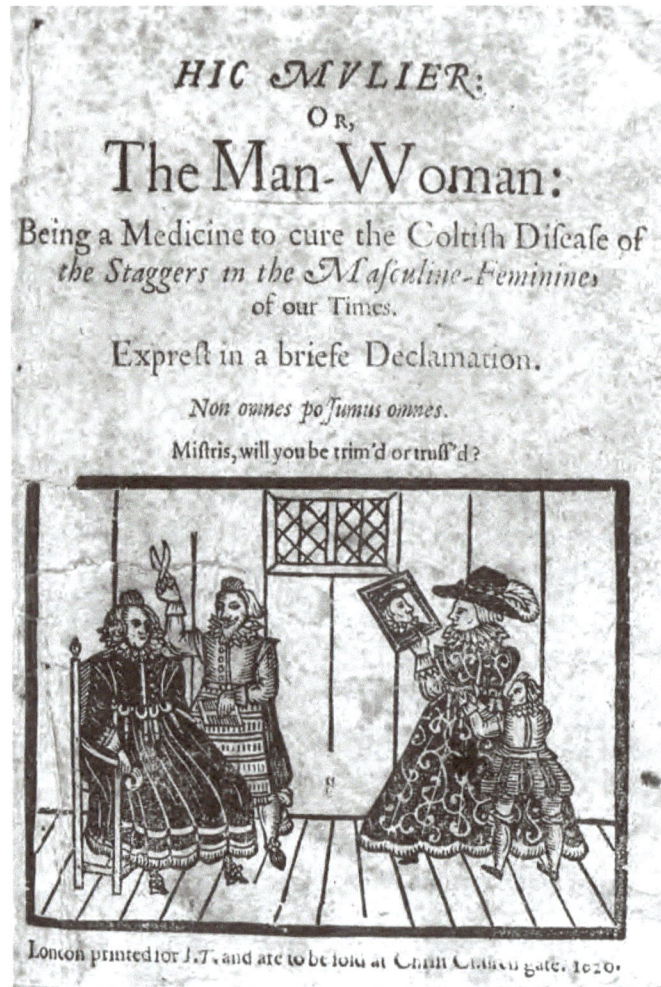

FIGURE 5.11: Title page, "Hic Mulier: or, The man-woman," (London, 1620). RB61256, The Huntington Library, San Marino, California.

attach his short-haired customer's patterned doublet to the breeches she presumably wears under her skirt, as she gazes into a mirror to admire her broad-brimmed, ostrich-feathered hat, and her short-cropped hair. The women loom large; they dwarf the purveyors of the gender-bending look.

In the same year, after *Hic Mulier* had gone through a second printing, Trundle brought out another pamphlet, *Haec Vir, or The Womanish-Man* (Figure 5.12). In this title page, the cross-dressed woman is not only wearing the "ruffianly hat" and the "lascivious" doublet: more dangerously, she is carrying a revolver in one hand, wearing a sword whose pommel we see at the right side of her skirt, and stepping along in boots with spurs attached. The Womanly Man, a diminutive figure compared to Haec Vir, is dressed in padded, paneled trousers trimmed with extravagantly long ties at the bottom to hold up his hose. He carries a badminton racket and three shuttlecocks, belonging to a sport that Hic Mulier insists is a woman's game.

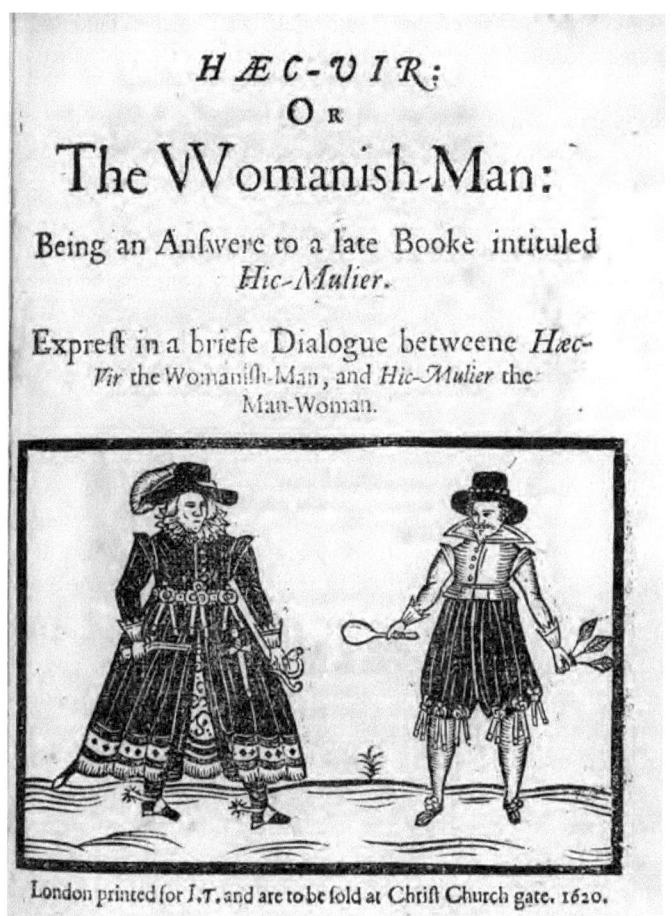

FIGURE 5.12: Title page, "Haec Vir: or, the Womanish-Man," (London, 1620). RB61267, Huntington Library, San Marino, California.

Haec Vir opens with each character's comic misrecognition of the sex of the other. Their dialogue then allows the writer to create an eloquent and persuasive persona for Hic Mulier. When Haec Vir repeats the first pamphlet's claim that women in men's clothes are slaves to fashion, he provokes her high-spirited, culturally relativist rebuttal.[52] Her defense against Haec Vir's charge (repeating the earlier pamphlet) that women who dress as men are submitting to foolish novelty is to offer a survey of diversity and change in dress throughout time and place: Greek and Roman widows mourned in white rather than the black of their time; for men to go without moustaches, as they do in England, is thought "unmanly" elsewhere; to ride sidesaddle, as women including Catherine de Medici and Elizabeth I had recently done, was once thought "abominable pride."[53] Local habits of dress and behavior vary so much that they are clear evidence of the "thousand things that onely Custome and not Reason hath approved." At Hic Mulier's suggestion, each debater returns to conventionally gendered clothing and behavior, but not as proof that they have rediscovered fixed essences. Rather, the dénouement implies that equal collaborators can redistribute gender habits and items of dress by choice. If Hic Mulier and Haec Vir can bargain to return to traditional social roles as signaled by their dress, their pact demonstrates, as Hic Mulier has claimed, that such modes are man-made, not divinely given.

Moralists throughout Europe were also alarmed by class cross-dressing: people wearing clothes above their station. Writing about sumptuary law in England and France, Peter Goodrich sums it up as "both an express and tacit legislation of the licit objects of desire."[54]

Related to the prohibition of idolatry and to military and legal hierarchies of honor, dress codes throughout Europe were obsessively complex, enumerating in detail what rank and income were required for wearing particular fabrics, jewels and accessories. In France up to the fifteenth century, sumptuary laws were few and far between, but by the 1450s the king's councilors were intoning a complaint heard all over Europe for centuries:

> among all the inhabited regions of the earth none [is] so deformed, variable, outrageous, excessive and inconstant in its garments and dress as [our] nation; . . . one cannot tell people's estates or occupations, be they princes, noblemen, citizens, merchants or craftsmen, because everyone, man or woman is allowed to dress as they please in cloth or gold or silver, silk or wool regardless of their origins, estate or occupation.[55]

Henry VIII of England promulgated four Acts of Apparel from 1510 to 1533, including the fines that people wearing clothes above their station had to pay.[56] Women were exempted from these laws, on the assumption that they had no need to identify their rank in public as men did, and that husbands controlled and paid for their wives' clothes. Later in England, however, and throughout Europe, laws focused sharply on women. In Genoa, the laws imposed sobriety of dress. A regulation of 1571 limited the fabric of ruffs only to linen, excluding silk and lace trim; the use of blue powder in the starch of ruffs may have been a way to embellish the required fabric.[57] In an edict of 1582, married women and widows were ordered to wear black gowns from October 15 to May 15; their cloaks were to be made only of plain wool or a wool and silk blend.[58]

In Venice, the sumptuary laws were infringed so often, Maria Giuseppina Muzzarelli argues, because they were made to be broken. The fines exacted from transgressors acted as an indirect tax on the rich:

> Taking advantage of the wealthy's passion for ostentation . . . sumptuary laws indicate a deliberate will on the part of lawmakers to redistribute some of a city's economic resources . . . legislators used the legal system to aid the less privileged and the city in general.[59]

This view of sumptuary law as a form of indirect taxation of the rich is now widely accepted. Patricia Fortini Brown remarks on "the futility of . . . attempts to legislate conspicuous consumption."[60] When the *Provedditori alle Pompe*, whom we might call the fashion police, outlawed wearing more than one necklace of pearls, Venetian women obeyed but promptly ordered single necklaces long enough to reach their waists. Courtesans were forbidden to wear pearls, but they did.[61] They also wore the best false pearls they could buy.

The dress of prostitutes disguising themselves to fool foreign men who came to the city in search of sex was an abiding concern of the ruling bodies in Venice. Their fear was that the reputation of the city's virtuous women was being damaged by prostitutes who dressed as the wealthiest noblewomen did. The preliminary explanation for a 1548 edict against this practice targeted the pimps, male and female, who drew young women into the trade by promising them elegant clothing:

> They persuade them in all sorts of wily ways that they will dress them up and turn them into noblewomen, and as soon as they have fallen into the hands of such procuresses, they take away the shifts, caps, stockings, shoes, ornaments, sashes, gowns, and capes that they have only rented for them, and because of the cost of these rentals, the girls fall into debt to these procuresses, who then live on their earnings. They can never free themselves and are forced by necessity to commit terrible sins, and they become accustomed to the vices of prostitution.[62]

Brothel keepers in London used the same device of dressing their whores in up-market finery, though trial records and stage plays suggest that there was less trickery involved: pleasure could come from pretending rather than believing that a whore was a lady. In a fascinating analysis of sixteenth- and seventeenth-century trial records from the Bridewell Court, Christine Varholy quotes from the transcript of a case in which a prostitute acting as a witness against two women accused of being bawds described in intricate detail the clothing one of them lent her:

> Mistress Miller caused . . . [her] to putt on a crimson damask petticote of white and redd and a great farthingale covered over with yellow cotton and a rough velvett gowne with a payre of satten sleeves cutt with a trayne and a rabata [a fashionable standing collar] imbrodered with white flowers of needlework with a border of gold buttons with a white zer [a type of hat] uppon her head.

At this point, the prostitute says, she had sexual relations with one of the Lord Chamberlain's men and Mistress Miller received half of her payment. The prostitute added that she earned from four to ten shillings for such a performance, a price range that suggests such disguises could be very profitable. Varholy's research leads to the conclusion that the circulation of second-hand clothing in London produced a "crisis of interpretation": a woman could artfully use opulent borrowed garments to offer the pleasure of class transgression to men paying for sex with a woman of higher rank[63]— "making most solemne love to a petticote."[64]

Varholy then turns to plays of the period, pointing out that they worked differently from the costumed performances of prostitutes in that the audience was aware of the actual social status of the characters. As an example, she gives Ben Jonson's *The New Inn*, in which "cross-class erotic role-play" is carried out by a tailor, Nick Stuff, and his wife Pinnacia, who have sex while she is wearing a gown he has made for the noblewoman Lady Frampul. They run into trouble when they take this game public by going to a ball: Lady Frampul recognizes the gown she has been waiting for, which she orders to be cut up because it has been corrupted. The tailor loses his payment. But the plot is richly comic, and its success suggests that its audience, rather than being shocked by the illicit circulation of the lady's gown, was as titillated by cross-class eroticism as were its characters.

The practice of dressing like a lady and being paid accordingly was also a topic of English poetry during this period. In Thomas Nashe's "The Choise of Valentines," the mistress of a brothel speaks directly to Tomalin, the hero, who has come to London to find his country sweetheart Francis, now a prostitute. He will not be able to see her, he is told, unless he can pay for the privilege of sex with the "lady" she resembles by wearing elegant clothes:

As yow desire, so shall yow swive with hir,
   But think your purse-strings shall abye-it deare;
For, he that will eate equaile's must lavish croune's;
   And mistris Francis in her velvet goune's,
And ruffs, and periwigs as fresh as Maye
   Can not be kept with half a croune a day. (61–66)[65]

I will conclude this chapter with a third text about early modern gender-mixing: the trial record of a person accused of transvestism in seventeenth-century America. The story begins in the settlement of Warrosquyoacke, Virginia 1629, when a servant reported that a recent immigrant, Thomas Hall, had "layen with a mayd of Mister William Bennetts."[66] According to English law, this would have been a simple case of fornication, but several married women in the town who had heard stories about Hall's ambiguous sexual identity set off an alarm that ended in a case adjudicated across the river in the colony's General Court at Jamestown. This was not an easy case, or one that could be settled in the court alone. Kathleen Brown points out:

> The location of Hall's case in a recently settled English colony may account in part for the extraordinary historical visibility and heterogeneity of the community's response to Hall. In addition to its distance from the structures of metropolitan [London] scientific and legal authority, Warrosquyoacke lacked both a parish church and a local court. As in most settlements in Virginia in the 1620s, such formal local institutions of authority simply did not exist. In their absence, the responsibility for producing and maintaining gender distinction fell almost entirely to laypeople.[67]

The judges needed imagination and flexibility to deal with the diverse opinions of the settlers who had confronted Hall.

Thomas/Thomasine Hall told the court that he had performed as both a man and a woman during his life, unapologetically describing how he had changed clothes to take the opportunity of better-paid jobs—the military, household service in the New World—available to men. Work, not sexual deviousness, had been his motive. He explained that he dressed as a woman now only "to get a bitt for my Catt" (172)—presumably because a woman asking for leftovers for her pet would be more sympathetically treated than a man. But the colonists were unwilling to tolerate his shifts between men and women's clothes. The issue came to a head when he was asked whether he was a man or a woman: he answered "both."

This response was intolerable. It provoked a series of intrusive physical investigations: women and men repeatedly examined his body. He was found, as he had said, to be a hermaphrodite—as we would say, an intersex person: he had a very small penis and an undeveloped vagina. The three women first decided that he was a male, his master considered him a female, the women changed their minds, and the governor of the colony finally declared him a man. However inconclusive the results, a decision had to be made.

Hall was lucky. In medical and legal practice at the time, hermaphrodites were normally told to choose the sex they preferred and stay with it, but transvestism on the European continent was a capital crime. Although the English subscribed to the Old Testament prohibition of cross-dressing—"the woman shall not wear that which pertaineth unto a man, neither shall a man put on a woman's garment, for all that do so are abominable unto the Lord thy God" (Deut. 22:5)—their laws did not condemn cross-dressers to death. If they were punished, it was for using clothes as a disguise in order to cohabit with lovers or spouses of the same sex.

The problem the colonists faced was that "the transvestite undermined society's ability to use clothes to stabilize distinct sexual identities."[68] The court's decision focused precisely on this issue. The verdict was that Hall should keep the name and wear the dress of a man, given his history as a soldier and manservant. But he was also sentenced to wear two accessories belonging to women, one on his head and one over his breeches: "a Coyfe and Croscloth [a cloth worn across the forehead] with an Apron before him." Bi-gendered clothing, that is, had to define who he was. The headgear and apron signaled his gender-switching past and broadcast a warning that he was not entitled to the sexual or legal identity of a man. But to make this point, the verdict imposed another form of cross-dressing upon him—not prohibited, but rearticulated by juxtaposing at the same time the two kinds of apparel he had worn at different times in his previous life.

No gender normalcy was affirmed in this decision. Hall's history, rather than any part of his body or its sexual essence, explained who he was and determined his strangely complicated sentence. He had used clothing to create useful identities for himself because clothing displayed a social, not an innate self. Confronted with this complexity, the Virginia judges acknowledged what contemporary moralists denied: dress was evidence not of sexual difference but of social differentiation.

The micro-history of Thomasine/Thomas Hall sums up the social anxieties analyzed in this chapter regarding physiologically ambiguous bodies, secret versus public sexual identities, and above all, the refusal of simply gendered garments—fiercely condemned, but in certain cases, officially sanctioned. The outer garments of the Renaissance elite might distinguish the two sexes, but the shaping of bodies required by fashion and the accessories used by men and women alike blurred such distinctions, as did modish cross-dressing. Further down the class scale, and especially in the world of sex workers, vestimentary disguise was frequently the norm, in spite of laws to the contrary—laws that could be suspended for pragmatic social reasons. In the view of medical practitioners, sexuality was too labile to produce one-dimensionally gendered men and women; even though such ambiguity was subject to official prohibitions, people used clothing in ingenious ways to circumvent them. Clothed as women, clothed as men, clothed as both: the Renaissance body evaded fixation in any single category of gender or single regime of dress.

CHAPTER SIX

Status

CATHERINE RICHARDSON

lay searche for a young fellowe named Peter William Peare . . . his apparel is a black cloth doblet black round hose laid on with statute lace a payre of white fryce slopes . . . laid on with red lace and copper wyer.[1]

This memorandum, recorded by John Fisher, Town Clerk of Warwick in the English West Midlands in 1571, is full of information about the social status of the "young fellowe named Peter William Peare." The lace on his garment suggests an interest in fashionable display: it is showy but not necessarily expensive—red lace with copper wire provided a cheap imitation of the gold lace worn by the elite, catching the light but not costing a fortune. His "statute lace," probably woven according to the 1571 statute and therefore made locally rather than imported, indicates that he was below the level of the gentry, an impression reinforced by the cloth and frieze (a coarse woolen cloth) of his doublet and hose, fabrics permitted under the dress legislation for servingmen, yeomen, and husbandmen—those nearer the bottom of the social scale. But this is not, primarily, a description of Peare's status; it is an aid to seeking him out. Whereas modern police forces issue photofit images of individuals' faces, early modern authorities provided information about their clothing, which suggests the complex interplay between the way exteriors advertised a person's socio-economic position and presented their individuality. Legislation insisted that the dress of whole groups should be recognizably the same; people perceived a close relationship between clothing and identity.

This chapter offers new documentary evidence which helps us to explore how individuals' dress was shaped by their social position—whether the similarities and differences were of form or just of scale. It considers the impact of the relationship between London and provincial centers on the provisioning of dress, arguing that we may have understood sumptuary legislation in the past, but we have not seen how clothing was financed, purchased and worn across the social scale, and that doing so helps us better to understand early modern social relations.[2]

SUMPTUARY LEGISLATION

Sumptuary legislation was in force across Europe throughout the period of this volume—it finally tailed off in the eighteenth century. These laws were a feature of a wide range of European political systems, from highly centralized nation states to relatively democratic cities and, on the level of duration and quality at least, it has been argued that there was little difference between Catholic Italian cities and the Protestant towns of Switzerland and England. While the most enthusiastic period of regulation in the majority of Europe was the seventeenth century—volumes of legislation peaked then in Florence, Venice, and France, for instance—in England the focus was in the sixteenth century.[3]

Edward III had begun 267 years of English sumptuary legislation with the first "act of apparel" of 1337, a run of eighteen laws and numerous additional statutes that ended just after James I's accession in 1603.[4] From the later fourteenth century onwards, close and increasingly complex links were made between social status, income, the type and amount of fabric that might be worn in particular garments, and the accessories with which they might be accompanied. The details of this legislation suggest a particularly sensitive contemporary visual awareness of the way appearance should reflect social distinctions, but while they divide society into small sections, their primary concern is to distinguish the elite from the non-elite.

Henry VIII's 1533 act, for instance, reserved for himself and his family the color purple and the fur of the sable. Going down its long and complex list of ranks suggests the links it forged between dress and status: no one below the rank of duke and marquess, for example, was permitted cloth of gold or tissue; below a baron's son or a knight (or anyone able to expend £200 after all charges), chains or other ornaments of gold weighing more than an ounce, velvet in his garments, leopard fur, or gold embroidery. Then, lower down still came satins, silks, taffetas, and damasks, lesser imported furs, imported linens, other colors such as scarlet or crimson, and finally smaller jewelry and expensive fabrics used sparingly: for sleeves, caps, or purses. At the bottom, although servingmen, journeymen, yeomen, and husbandmen were all permitted to wear "cloth" (probably meaning a plain woven woolen) in their hose, distinctions were made in relation to its value, and therefore its quality: servants in husbandry and journeymen's cloth was limited to a cost of 16d per yard, whereas husbandmen, yeomen, and other kinds of servants could use cloth costing 2s a yard. The latter could also have their hose guarded and add local lamb or coney [rabbit] fur, although their shirts and headgear must not be embroidered or trimmed with silk, gold, or silver. In other words, while the higher groups were distinguished by type of fabric, the lower were divided by the quality of their cloth and the embellishment and accessories that they might add to it, indicating a society that could readily gage by eye the type, weight, and finish of a variety of different materials.

Many exceptions were also listed, primarily relating to two groups: those whose clothing reflected royal magnificence, such as members of the royal household and the recipients of presents from the royal family (in other words, the extensions of elite power), and those whose authority made the nation function, like the clergy, or civic officials such as mayors, aldermen, and bailiffs.[5] This essay will return at the end to these latter difficult groups, whose power stood somewhat outside the social hierarchy.

The legislation also reveals a potent mix of economic and moral imperatives. It aimed to keep the balance of payments in check by preventing excessive purchase of foreign goods, and to support local industry.[6] But a tension is clear here too, between the mention of foreign wares that threatened the national economy, and debt that endangered personal finances. Moral concerns link the latter threat to the breakdown of society. In her final proclamation in 1597, Elizabeth I noted "the great inconvenience that hath grown and daily doth increase within this her relm by the inordinate excess in apparel," hoping once more for a "reformation," and identifying the results of such abuses as the decay of the socially-binding performance of hospitality as money was bled out on less worthy things, an increase in crime as a result of penury and, of course, the "confusion of degrees, where the meanest are as richly dressed as their betters." Together, these concerns show dress at the center of methods of demarcating status, underpinning the way individuals related to one another socially, morally, and economically. On one man's purchase of silk lace made outside the country for his bonnet, the legislation suggests, rests the stability of the realm.

THE TOP OF SOCIETY

Given that we have a wider range of information about elite dress than for any other social group, this essay begins with their sartorial practices in order to set the terms by which we might make comparison between the processes and functions of dress at each social level. Within the bald descriptive outlines of fabric types offered by the sumptuary legislation, what did the elite actually wear, how might they have regarded their clothing, and how might others have regarded it—what was its impact? A short story about a visit Robert Dudley, Earl of Leicester, paid to Warwick suggests partial answers to those questions. It was written by John Fisher, who made the note about the "young fellow" with which this chapter began. The Earl had come to celebrate the French chivalric Order of St. Michael at St. Mary's church in the town, an event that necessitated a formal civic procession that displayed prominently the connections between social hierarchy and dress:

> [T]he commoners in Gownes should goo foremost two and two together; then next after the Comoners 4 Constables to go on a Rank with little white sticks in their handes, then next after them should follow the 12 principall Burgesses two and two in order the youngest going foremost; then after the principal Burgesses followed such of my Lords Gentlemen, and Gentlemen of the Shire as that day waytid uppon him; then after the Gentlemen, cam the Serjant bering his Mace, then next after the Serjant followed the Bailief alone in a Gowne of Skarlet . . .

The fullest description, however, is reserved for the image that the Earl himself created. It very clearly articulates the writer's sense of his fundamental difference from all the others in the procession, in ways that are analogous to the description with which this chapter began by suggesting that his dress defined both his status and his personal identity:

> then cam my said Lord thearle of Leycester by himself apparelled all in white, his shoes of velvet, his stocks of hose knit silk, his upper stoks of white velvet lined with cloth of silver, his Dow[b]let of silver, his jerkin white velvet [drawn] with silver, beawtified with gold and precious stones, his girdle and skabard white velvet, his Roobe white Satten embrowdered with Gold a foot broade very curiously, his cap black velvit with a white fether, his Color of Gold besett with precious Stones, and his Garter about his legg of S. George's Order, a sight worthie the beholding.[7]

The account goes on to praise Leicester's gestures, stature, and proportions, concluding that "in the eies of this writer, he seemed the only goodliest personage Male in England." The Earl's apparel is summarized as "costly and curious"—its value is obvious from the enumeration of fabrics familiar from the sumptuary legislation, and its workmanship is skilful and elaborate, but also intricate and delicate, current meanings of "curious": time and ingenuity have been expended upon it. In this example, we see the visual impact of social distinctions as the sumptuary legislation's dry divisions are transformed into the impression which noble clothing might make on those of lower social status (even though their status might have been considerable within their own communities) and hence the way it created and sustained the authority that came with rank.

The Earl's outfit, which is described in strikingly similar terms to the one in which he was painted in the portrait in Figure 6.1, is a typical courtly mixture of high fashion and enduring forms worn in procession. His garter of St. George showed his membership of an order limited to twenty-six individuals, including his queen and members of other European royal families.[8] His robe of white satin and gold embroidery, symbol of the principal French chivalric order, was granted him by Charles IX as a compliment to the queen, who was unable to wear one herself as the order was a male military one.[9] These robes and accoutrements had a stability of form that symbolized the continuity of dynasties, and they were available only to the monarch and the top of the nobility. They were tied to specific occasions—keyed into their own moments of wearing. In a similar way, Henry VIII wore his robes of estate, his parliament robes, his crown, and other regalia in a series of courtly rituals which embellished the major liturgical feast days,

FIGURE 6.1: *Robert Dudley, Earl of Leicester*, Anglo-Netherlandish School, c. 1564, oil on panel, Waddesdon, The Rothschild Collection (Rothschild Family Trust), acc. no. 14.1996. © The National Trust, Waddesdon Manor.

respecting "days of estate, crown-wearing days, the days for wearing purple and scarlet and days of mourning." At processions on feast days, the king walked under a cloth of estate, framing the visual impact of his clothing, and he wore his crown on important religious festivals such as the eve of Twelfth Night and Epiphany, and purple or red velvet on "Christmas day, Easter, Whitsunday and All Saints." His scarlet parliament robes, valued at £200, were worn to its opening, in procession, "accompanied by the peers spiritual and temporal in their robes."[10] The year was shaped and patterned, colored by changing courtly dress.

This was also complex and intriguing clothing. On New Year's Day 1574, for instance, three years after his progress through Warwick, the Earl of Leicester gave the queen "a fanne of white fethers, sett in a handle of golde . . . on each syde a white bear and twoe perles hanging, a lyon ramping with a white moseled[muzzled] beare at his foote."[11] The interplay between his armorial identity (the bear, his emblem, as in Figure 6.2) and the personal nature of the gift; the erotic charge of its message and the public arena in which it might have been used, show something of the ritualized, mannered nature of dress, and its engagement with the politics of the realm. This kind of dress had to be carefully read by those in the know; it was part of the cerebral enterprise of elite identity.

Such complex identities were also offered in reflected form in the liveries of elite households. The 1,500 men who comprised Henry's household included not only his close personal servants, but his hunt servants, the master of his barge and the watermen, sailors on the *Mary Rose*, and a whole host of other minor officials. In addition, livery *en*

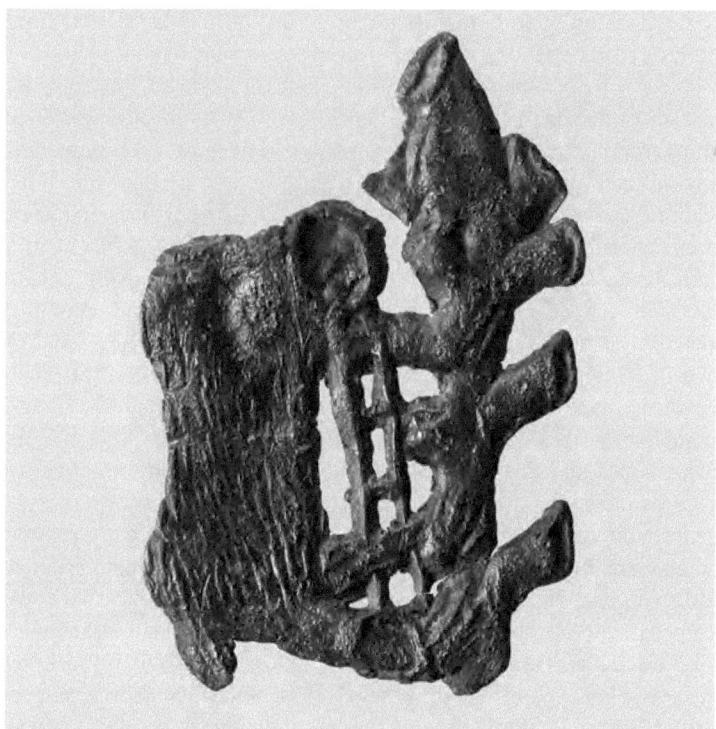

FIGURE 6.2: Lead alloy livery badge, chained bear and ragged staff of Earls of Warwick, British Museum, Museum number 1904, 0720.23. © Trustees of the British Museum.

masse would be provided in red for coronations, and black for funerals: at Henry and Catherine's coronation a total bill of £4,750 included £1,307 spent on 1,641 yards of livery cloth.[12] In contrast, a bill for livery cloth the Earl of Leicester received in the 1560s lists over 260 individuals including a parfumier, trumpeter, jerkin-maker, and dwarf.[13] These individuals were marked out as a group by wearing the same cloth. Livery made them a part of the social image of their superiors, giving the elite's identity a wider reach.[14] The livery badge in Figure 6.2 shows the bold heraldic language of lineage which told others who one's lord was, spreading his authority throughout his areas of influence.

In addition to such static ways of marking identity, these noble wardrobes also demonstrated the movement of fashion (more sophisticated than the mere display of wealth) as a crucial part of political supremacy. Whereas those below them might spend a great deal more on dress in some years than others, the court had to ensure an annual display of their magnificence. The singularity of Henry's clothing communicated his sovereignty through its sumptuous European fabric—he granted licenses to foreign cloth merchants on the understanding that he had first sight and choice of their wares[15]—and through its scale: few members of the nobility could rival his expenditure on his wardrobe.[16] In addition, the range of the wardrobe was augmented by garments and accessories given as gifts, especially at new year.[17] Previous years' garments were recycled or given away to other members of the royal household to make space for new ones, leading to a regular renewal of wardrobe stock. These reciprocal processes of gifting in and out of the royal wardrobe ensured that the monarch's taste was a subject of great interest to courtiers, and that their sartorial superiority was repeatedly underlined as they wore the best clothing first before handing it on. While legislation aimed at fixed representation of cloth, spending power ensured endless variety of style.

Fashion partly reflected national identities, and the style of European courtly dress became a marker of political allegiance. Adoption of, for instance, Hispanic court fashion following the dominance of Emperor Charles V could be read as a statement of allegiance to the empire—Eleonore d'Autriche, Queen of France, and Eleonora di Toledo, Duchess of Florence, both "gave clear messages of imperial allegiance by wearing Spanish attire in their adopted countries long after their marriages."[18] In addition to letters and ambassadorial visits, fashion dolls were sent as diplomatic gifts—in 1515 the King of France requested a doll dressed like Isabella d'Este, including "shirts, sleeves, undergarments, outer garments, dresses, headdresses, and hairstyles," and Queen Juana of Spain died in possession of two in dresses and outer garments.[19] Elizabeth I's tailors similarly produced buckram *toiles* "with samples of arrangements of braid and decorative pinking" to aid her choice. This was fashion on a truly European scale, closely keyed into international markets and taking advantage of various information networks to transfer styles between countries.

Outside court circles, we can explore the clothing of the lower sections of the elite through the account books of two provincial knightly families who went on shopping trips to London in 1620. Sir Thomas Puckering of The Priory in Warwick was the son of the Lord Keeper of the Great Seal, a Privy Councillor who had risen through the ranks as a lawyer. Sir Thomas was admitted to the Middle Temple in 1605 and Lincoln's Inn in 1621, but he was a landed gentleman rather than an ambitious lawyer, and spent most of his time in the Midlands.[20] A member of the middling gentry group of Warwickshire, he had an income estimated at over £2,000 per annum in lands.[21] The year 1620, the only surviving year of his account book, was the start of what turned out to be a modest parliamentary career as MP for Tamworth in Staffordshire, in which office he spent two extended periods of time in London.

Sir Hamon and Lady Alice Le Strange of Hunstanton were part of one of Norfolk's oldest gentry families. Sir Hamon was knighted for riding to Scotland to inform James of Queen Elizabeth's death, but he preferred to stay in Norfolk rather than joining the court. His wife Alice was also a native of the county, and his cousin. After a difficult period of debt when Hamon first inherited,[22] the Le Stranges increased their spending with their income, from below £1,000 a year in the 1610s to over £2,000 in the 1620s, matching the Puckerings' in this period, and textiles and clothing were their most significant expense after food. Their accounts show, however, large annual variations in the amount they spent on dress, from £256 in 1620 to £53 in 1613 (10.1 percent and 30.3 percent of total expenditure respectively).[23] Puckering's bills for just over £56 in 1620 are on the modest side. The contrast with annual monarchical expenditure is instructive—Henry VIII's nearly a century earlier in 1542–3, for instance, was £7,263 13s 6½d.[24]

Both families made the most of the opportunities that London afforded for buying goods unavailable in the provinces. It was becoming a more popular destination for shopping in the early seventeenth century as its status as an entertainment capital grew—the "season" ran between autumn and the end of spring, drawing in wealthy landed gentry from the provinces—and new purchasing opportunities were opening up with the "exchanges," the first shopping centers. Here, shopping brought together the court and the city "in a new social formation."[25] This dominance of one capital city contrasted sharply with the situation in other places in Europe. In Italy, for instance, "diversity and competition" between the towns of the relatively more urbanized area of the northern and central peninsula meant distinct fashions and therefore rivalry for market share.[26] London, in contrast, became the concentrated national arena for fashion, and Puckering made around three quarters (by number) of his clothing purchases there, spending £54 6s 3½d as opposed to the £2 1s 5d he paid out in Warwick. He engaged especially in clothing "projects" in the capital, for instance an important suit of scarlet, comprising doublet, hose, and cloak, for which he planned the purchases of fabric and trimmings carefully.[27] These were by and large made in just over a week: first the trimmings and then £15 for five yards of scarlet at the considerable cost of £3 per yard, "to make a dublet, and hose, and a cloke with." He paid an additional 51s for 4¼ yards of scarlet baize to line a relatively full cloak, and the next day bought two dozen crimson buttons and loops for the cloak and one long button and loop suitable for its neck for 9s 6d. The doublet was faced, and its narrow skirts lined, with a quarter of an ell of crimson taffeta, and five dozen buttons bought, presumably for center front and wrists. Both suit and cloak were "laid on" with 5½ ounces of crimson silk galloon (or ribbon) lace, and the outfit was finished off with a pair of crimson taffeta garters and shoe roses edged with silk lace. It was laced together with three dozen crimson silk and gold ribbon points (prominently displayed on the outside of the suit) and hung at the waist with a girdle of crimson satin embroidered and fringed with musk color silk (a dark reddish-brown). In addition, Puckering purchased a musk color felt hat with a crimson and musk band. The effect must have been overwhelming! Some sense of its impact is provided by the image of a contemporary doublet belonging to Gustav Adolphus of Sweden, shown in Figure 6.3.

Comparing the Puckerings to the Le Stranges emphasizes the particular nature of London as a market: they too spent more in the capital than in the provinces, although this was in the form of shorter visits, rather than extended stays: "On average, someone

FIGURE 6.3: Scarlet doublet belonging to Gustav Adolphus of Sweden, Livrustkammaren, Stockholm, 1620s. Photo: Göran Schmidt/The Royal Armoury, Stockholm.

from the household visited London twice a year, Norwich four times a year, and King's Lynn six times." Unlike Puckering, they did not always concentrate on outerwear. Their most expensive trip was in 1628, when they bought new dresses for their fourteen-year-old daughter costing over £20, but on their 1620 trip around 120 purchases were made, including a new black bed for over £50, and "£5 worth of books, and gloves, hats, stockings, lace, boots, spurs, cloth, earthenware, brass and ironware, silverware and a new upholstered couch" at a total cost for the visit, including accommodation, of £185 5s 6d.[28] Families like the Puckerings and the Le Stranges, then, used several different strategies to acquire dress appropriate to their status in a variety of markets, but with a clear sense of London's fashionable supremacy.

However diverse the elite might have been as a group, however wide the variety in their purchasing power over cloth, outside the court their clothing differentiated them more clearly from their peers than from one another. The delicacy of their fabrics, the intricacy of their embellishment, the unity of their style (they could buy complete outfits at once rather than individual garments), the complexity of the processes of their dressing (demanding servant help),[29] and the livery they gave to ensure those servants reflected their status, all advertised the elite's power and authority by showing them to be fundamentally different to the rest of society. This group were the most obviously influenced by the growing availability of foreign fabrics as a result of the opening up of new markets in the early modern period, a change that grew in pace towards the end of the period considered in this volume: in London, for instance, the Levant Company imported raw silk in vast quantities from Europe and, after the Restoration, from the Middle East.[30] The events at which they could use dress to advertise their status were infinitely larger in number and greater in audience, and the eye-catching nature of the clothes was designed to exploit that: the detail encourages careful and lengthy looking.

THE BOTTOM OF SOCIETY

The sumptuary legislation, as we have seen, paid considerably less detailed attention to the lower portion of the social scale—the yeomen, husbandmen, and servants—where the social stratification was less precise. These groups (almost by definition of their inclusion in the legislation) were not poor, but they are the lowest that the historian can reach through the kind of probate materials most likely to specify individuals' dress. Margaret Spufford puts their wealth in moveable goods (all their possessions) at under £50 for laborers, less substantial husbandmen, and artisans; between £50 and £149 for husbandmen and lesser yeomen; and above £150 for yeomen, prosperous craftsmen, and minor gentlemen.[31] There was, of course, potentially a direct relationship between these individuals and the poor (as defined by their need for relief from their neighbors), as personal circumstance or the frequently hard economic conditions of the period meant that these lower groups could easily slide into poverty. Such definitions highlight the transitory nature of this group—servants might be "poor" because, as young men and women, they owned little but their clothing; artisans might become prosperous craftsmen in the course of a successful trading life, or might descend into the need for relief if their businesses did not thrive.

Danae Tankard offers some individual vignettes of lower-status wardrobes: Jane Smith, a spinster, with four old petticoats and two waistcoats valued at 14s 6d, her wearing linen including aprons at 5s, and a felt hat with a cypress band at 2s; Joan Hawkins, widow, dying in possession of two petticoats (one 10s and a russet one for 12d), a gown (2s), safeguard (6d), and hat (2s), with various linens, aprons, and stockings worth 4s. Unlike the fabrics of the elite, these clothes would have been made of locally-produced cloth, possibly woven at home. With apparel worth £1 1s 6d and 19s 6d respectively, these women were reasonably well provided for.[32] Their poverty at the time at which their possessions were itemized is indicated by the fact that so much of their capital was in dress—they had very little else to their name.

The lower end of the social scale was defined against the upper by this broad group's status as *working* people. Whereas the king had clothes for every occasion, they had just one change: probate materials offer evidence of the significance of the contemporary distinction between "working" and "holiday" clothes—for instance in 1580, James Marsh of St. Margaret's Westminster bequeathed to his servant Alice Gall "newe and double apparrell meete for her bodye aswell lynnen as woollen (viz) for the holie daie and workinge daie as becommeth a servaunte to have."[33] Performed only weekly, this action of changing clothes must have been one of the key conceptual distinctions between the lower sort and the poor, who had only one set of outer clothes; for the former, the rhythm of contrast between the working week and leisure time structured their dress both practically (holiday clothes were kept for best until demoted) and symbolically (changing clothes signified a change of pace and activity and, for the godly, a shift from focusing on this world to engaging with the next).

In a series of probate accounts filed after the death of a parent, Spufford identifies what constituted a child's outfit: a coat, a jerkin or doublet, and breeches for a boy; a waistcoat and petticoat for a girl, and perhaps a coat too. Gowns she considers too upmarket to belong to individuals of this lower status. In addition, there would be headwear, shirts, or smocks, stockings, and shoes. Before 1610, she calculates the average price of a new outfit at 15s 10d for boys, and 12s 4d for girls, rising to £1 3s 3d and 14s 9d respectively in the period between 1610 and 1660. While there were variations in price for individual items (jerkins for between 1s and 12s, for instance), in accordance with the sumptuary legislation's narrow range of fabrics the same cloths were used.[34]

The differences in value between outfits, then, were a result of differences in quality of cloth, and the addition of trimmings. Children whose fathers had owned moveable goods worth over £150 "were far more likely to have [lace] bought to trim their clothes often"—in other words the very top of the working group may well have been more clearly set apart from the rest visually. Tankard's research also indicates the importance of colored ribbons used as apron and shoe strings, of hat bands, and neckwear fastenings, and other work has shown the significance of these accessories in the process of romance and their close links to individuals' perceptions of their attractiveness to others.[35] Rather than the type of fabric from which garments were made, which distinguished between the levels of elite status, the quality of the material used and the wide variety of trimmings with which clothes could be embellished made the distinctions among the meaner sort manifest to their neighbors. Even small gifts had the potential to change visual appearance, and style, status, and identity were shaped through small and precious pieces of cloth.

We get some sense of how significant an aspect of the lower-status economy dress was when we see the part it played in the incomes of servants as "livery"—the allowance of cloth for the year's clothing. A wages assessment from the Borough of Colchester in 1583 assesses "a bailiff of husbandry" at 53s 4d in wages, with a livery of 10s. A common servant of husbandry aged over twenty was assessed at 33s 4d with a livery of 6s 8d, and a women servant "of the best, being a cook and taking charge of a household or a dairy," over eighteen, at 20s with a livery of 10s. The liveries of journeymen (apprentices who had served their term) similarly varied from 6s 8d to 10s, suggesting a fairly uniform sense of appropriate amounts of fabric. Comparing it, admittedly very roughly, with the costs of children's outfits determined by Spufford, suggests that around a half of adult clothing might be expected to be renewed each year. Evidence from wills indicates the kind of cloth this might have been: Stephen Cannon of Foulness willed, in 1573, "that my brother John shall receive of John Edwards my master . . . two yards of homemade cloth which he oweth me for my quarter's service." In some cases, the cloth explicitly allowed for variation: in 1575 "Aaron Yonge of Waltham Abbey, tailor," took as his apprentice John Ethyn, aged seventeen, for seven years, "giving him at the end of his term 5s and a double apparel convenient for workday and holyday." Alternatively, Sir John Petre of Thorndon Hall gave his servants an allowance of "summer and winter liveries of cloth," which indicates the next stage in increasing variety of dress.[36] Clothing was a part of the payment servants of all kinds received, partly because it was essential to their ability to perform their work, and partly because the appearance it gave them shaped the honor and credit of the household they served.³⁷

If these people constituted the bottom of the sumptuary hierarchy, then the poor beneath them were defined by the act of receiving charity. Throughout the period considered here, the definition was a moralized one, visually dividing the "idle" from the "deserving" poor. Although we are perhaps more familiar with the structured systems of relief following the introduction of the Poor Law in 1601, work on medieval charity has shown some interventions in the material culture of poverty. Analyzing the role of clothing in post-mortem charitable gift giving, Sheila Sweetinburgh has considered how donors employed clothing in their "pursuit of salvation," binding the beneficiary to pray for them. Medieval benefactors clearly thought explicitly about their actions in terms of the seven corporal acts of mercy, which placed clothing the naked alongside feeding the hungry, giving drink to the thirsty and hospitality to the stranger, visiting the sick, ransoming prisoners, and burying the dead. However, the naked were not by any means their primary concern: of those who gave to the poor at all, only 9 percent of women and 6 percent of men gave such items. Examples include Juliana Lucas of St. John's parish in Thanet who bequeathed, in 1520 "her working clothes to the twelve poor women who were to bear her to her grave," a gift of appropriate status and encouraging industriousness, in which a woman used dress to mark out a sense of solidarity with her female neighbors by increasing their stocks of clothing. Fourteen years later, Thomas Aldy of Sandwich, in contrast, asked his executors to provide four poor men with a black gown each, which they were to wear at his burial, month's mind, and twelve month's mind (masses held at intervals after an individual's death), while they held the funeral torches over his bier.³⁸ The provision of new clothing and the explicit attention paid to the events at which it was to be worn aimed to co-opt the poor in the definition of their wealthier neighbors.

Some private charity remained after the Reformation. In Warwick, the inmates of Leicester's hospital were, for instance, "to have Liveries (viz. Gowns of blew cloth, with a Ragged Staff embroidered on the left sleeve) and not to go into the Town without them."³⁹ Thomas Puckering paid £6 to the bailiff to fulfil the conditions of his mother's will to provide gowns for the poor women of Warwick at Christmas. In the 1630s, Thomas himself founded a hospital there for eight poor women, whose later accounts record as receiving "clothing for two years in *December*" as well as "xxxiiiiˢviiiᵈ payable among them by even portions (once a quarter)."⁴⁰ The connection between the clothing of the poor and the wider social identity of the rich could be strong within the latter's geographical sphere of influence.

By and large, those personal relationships between giver and receiver which used clothing's communal visibility in the creation of mutual responsibilities of care and prayer diminished across Europe in the sixteenth century, however. Beginning in Germany in the early 1520s, poor laws were also being enacted in the Low Countries, France, northern Italy, Scandinavia, and England a decade later. Catholic and Protestant cities and those with mixed populations adopted such legislation, although some in more moderate form, and "revenues destined for the poor ... [were] ... channelled and dispensed" through citizen- and clergy-run agencies.⁴¹ Personal donation became public apportionment, and the definition of the poor by their richer neighbors shifted from an individual to a communal act. As a result, the records of provision move from personal testamentary documents to civic and parochial archives. For instance, London parishes often dealt with their foundling children by paying foster parents outside the capital to keep them. In an especially detailed example, St. John Zachary paid, in 1650/1, "for keeping of the child which was left att Goldsmiths hall before it went to Nursse, 2s., for a Coate, two Neckcloaths . . . two Shirtts, two Aprons and a black quaife and two Crostcloaths for itt, 3s. 10d.; for two payre of Stockins & a wastocat, 2s. 2d.; for a paire of shews 8d, & an underpetticoat and a barrow, 2s.; for pins & sope &carrieing of itt Downe, 2s. 6d."[42] Later on in these children's lives, the parishes were responsible for apprenticing them, at which point they provided both an indenture fee and a further suit of clothing.

Such records do also indicate connections to the ritualized nature of Christian provision of clothing alms seen in the medieval performance of the Acts of Mercy. The church wardens' accounts of St. Giles Cripplegate, London, for instance, record provision for their paupers at All Souls and on Good Friday. In 1649/50, at All Souls, they paid out for gowns to be made for thirty men and women and coats for twenty-two children, plus stockings and shoes, and a breakfast for the male tailors and the women who made up seventy-two shirts and smocks. Some sense of the communal nature of the enterprise is given by the breakfasts, and the symbolism of newly-clothed poor families appearing at church on these two liturgically significant days must have been visually very potent. Such events are interestingly close to the courtly marking of the liturgy through dress.

We can see quite literally with the example of the inmates of Leicester's hospital, how the poor's acceptance of charity gave them an identity that linked them to their benefactor by wearing his/her badge. Furthermore, it seems likely that all these specially-made outfits for the poor would have been recognizably similar: cutting garments from the same fabric and making them at one time would result in uniform outfits,[43] worn on occasions that drew attention to their provenance. Their reliance upon livery as a model that extends the glory of their wealthy benefactors, be it lord or town, is striking. Early modern clothing worked as a system that did not only divide social groups but held them in a clear hierarchical relationship to one another.

THE MIDDLE OF SOCIETY

Disrupting the binding of poor and servants to the rich—to the dependency of clothing relationships—was the growing middle of the social order.[44] Alongside the formal divisions of the sumptuary legislation, in practice people described the social structure of early modern England in "much cruder, less precise and perhaps more effective terms" such as the "language of sorts." These pragmatic ways of dividing the world have a great deal to tell us about the points where the two large social sections described earlier might have met—the bottom of the top and the top of the bottom. By the 1640s there were recognized "better," "meaner," and "middling sorts," but in the earlier sixteenth century the dynamic between the top and bottom was often expressed in pejorative, political terms "pregnant with actual or potential *conflict*." In local communities, day-to-day interaction was not with the elite, but between the meaner and their betters, as the latter defined themselves! The "better sort" in Warwick in 1628, for example, were defined as "men of estate and generally best affected to religion and of the discreetest sort of inhabitants," in contrast to the easily corruptible "meaner sort" of the town. Here and elsewhere, they were local rulers—not those studied in the first section of this chapter, nor the general population represented in the second. They described themselves as the "'principal,' 'substantial,' or 'chief' inhabitants of a parish, or as 'the best men'."[45] The middle of the social order was increasingly vocal about its status in documentary and sartorial terms.

Returning now to the procession that accompanied the Earl of Leicester to Warwick church, it is possible to see representatives of this group and their sense of their own self-importance in relation to men who considered themselves their social betters. Warwick's elite are all wearing gowns as symbols of their civic power; the constables with "little white sticks in their hands" and the sergeant with his mace show their puissant jurisdiction over the town. The common councilors are first, then after the constables come the principal burgesses ordered from youngest to oldest (least to most venerable), then the Lord's gentlemen, then the sergeant, then the bailiff "alone in a Gowne of Skarlet." If this is a procession organized by rank, then the Lord's supporting retinue of gentlemen are firmly sandwiched between the burgesses and the sergeant, and some way before the self-consciously resplendent and isolated bailiff in the scarlet belonging to his highest urban office. The ordering of the procession implicitly suggests, in other words, that the status of Warwick's rulers, most of whom we would now see as members of the middling sort, was superior to that of the "Gentlemen of the Shire," at least at this event. The exceptions the sumptuary legislation made for these urban rulers indicate some of these tensions around local as opposed to national authority.

As a group, the middling sort is notoriously diverse in economic and social terms. They have been defined as those belonging to "independent trading households" who had to work for their income, either with their hands or with professional skills.[46] For this group in particular, social mobility (in one direction or another) was an expectation, a prospect that must have shaped their attitudes towards their dress. We can follow such a man's possible career trajectory through many of the clothing states outlined earlier, from apprentice to journeyman to small trader, "followed by gradual advancement within a trade guild or other body, according to experience and seniority."[47] As a successful older man, he might expect to hold office within his guild or his local community, as an urban administrator such as a common councilor, poor law official, or churchwarden. In this way, the middling sort provided a point of contact and communication between the two groups considered so far, and their dress clearly signaled their purchase on the social ladder and their direction of travel. While we know a good deal about the way the mercantile elites of Italy and Germany used clothing to signal their growing economic and political power, we know very little indeed about this more diverse English social grouping.[48]

Like the elite, as successful older men with established businesses of their own, members of the middling sort might expect to own both fashionable and ceremonial clothes, having to invest in the kind of civic dress described by the Town Clerk of Warwick. The scarlet gowns of mayors, bailiffs, or aldermen of England's towns functioned in a similar way to robes of state but on a smaller scale, communicating authority and stability by visually stressing tradition and continuity for their corporation and office, rather than themselves. When the queen visited Canterbury just after Leicester's visit to Warwick, for instance, it was decreed that the mayor and aldermen would "Ryde in the Scarlett gownes with foote clothes to mete the queens majestie," whereas the common councilors were "to be a foote in their best apparall in decent gownes."[49] These scarlet aldermanic gowns were also very valuable items—always the most expensive piece of clothing owned, usually among the most valuable possessions of the town's leaders.[50] Having one's portrait painted in such a gown, as the mayor of Totnes did in the painting in Figure 6.4, was an

FIGURE 6.4: Christopher Wise (c. 1566–1628), Mayor of Totnes (1605 and 1621), Nicholas Hilliard, oil on canvas, Totnes Elizabethan House Museum, acc. no. TOTEH1963.128.

important aspect of marking urban livery's "symbolic power to transform the layman into the civic official" and the status of both town and individual.[51]

We can analyze the different purchasing practices of such men's investment in fashionable dress through account books kept by two individuals from rather different urban backgrounds, which have received little if any scholarly attention. Thomas Cocks was the auditor and Chapter Clerk of Canterbury Cathedral in the early seventeenth century. Between 1607 and 1610 he kept a book of accounts in which he recorded purchases for himself, his sons, and his wife who boarded with a local family because she was "distracted of her wits."[52] A member of a minor gentry family from just outside Sandwich in Kent, he appears to have sold his family property shortly after coming of age and moved to the town. John Hayne the younger, on the other hand, was a second-generation cloth merchant from Exeter whose accounts cover the years 1631–43. He held parochial office as churchwarden of St. Mary Arches and collector for the poor, for whose maintenance he himself paid 6s a year.[53]

Both men's account books are full of details about the nature, quantity, and frequency of their clothing purchases. Taking as an example the number of transactions Thomas Cocks made in 1607, apparel came third, after entertainment (mainly gambling) and drink. Seventy-nine separate clothing-related entries were made, or one-and-a-half a week, covering the purchase of new items, cloth, and tailor's bills, or the mending or translation of old ones.[54] As for the elite then, the provision and maintenance of dress took up a considerable amount of the middling sort's time.[55]

The ways in which the middling went about its purchase were rather different to the practices of their betters, however. With cash scarce, most early modern purchases were made on credit of some kind. However, the middling urban trading household in particular was part of a network of producers who were also consumers, meaning that they could engage in a form of barter, rather than simply credit with a final reckoning.[56] On January 21, 1635–6, John Hayne records that Philip Foxwell, a silkman, "oweth me v^{li} for 20 o^z of golde & silver lace (silke weight) [delivered] him this day; which I am to take out in Comodities of him, allowing him a penny on a shilling of it, as per his Note 5li."[57] These mutual exchanges are a key part of middling status, where active trade or professional activity gives individuals a purchase on the market—a stock of goods or services to be exchanged with neighbors and a set of trusted contacts. In addition, in the opposite direction, the relatively large amounts of the same kind of garment that they owned meant that they could pawn clothing if times became hard, or exchange it if fashions changed.[58]

For smaller items and for mending, both men used the services of grocers (the "general stores" of the period),[59] and the various purchases made at one time offer important information about the relationship between clothing needs and the structures of early modern urban commerce. Cocks' servant paid, for instance, "for 1li candle 4d, for sealing wax 1d, for muscadel 3d, for soalling a pair of stockings 6d, for mithridate 4d." The maintenance of dress and small readymade items could be dealt with as part of the purchase of daily necessities. In addition, Cocks names several tailors whom he used for different types of larger purchase. This strategy shows his sense of the distinctions between principal and lesser clothing, and also his understanding of his position within the social networks of middling commercial identity within the town—he divides purchases between smaller concerns and those with social and political authority.

Despite this investment in the local economy, however, both men also bought from further afield although, unlike their elite counterparts, shopping was not part of their leisure activities. Hayne spent 7s on "14 black points bought in Rouen," for instance, a personal purchase facilitated by his mercantile activities and connections, but he also obtained goods from London. Cocks was a more tentative shopper in the capital, perhaps because he was less confident in his commercial links there. He sent Pike, the Canterbury footpost, on his behalf, to "buye me furre & skynes at London" and stockings, and his servant Chilman was reimbursed "for my nightecappe by him [paid] 3s 10d" when the latter returned from the town. Unlike the elite, these men purchased most goods locally and only occasionally dipped a toe in the waters of London fashion.

Hayne's account book in particular offers evidence for the function of clothing in life cycle events at this social level. Preparations for his wedding include "watchet and silver ribban for favors" and the kid gloves for his maid servants, purchases that underline the role of accessories in marking out the households of the middling, mediating between the strictures of the sumptuary legislation around type of cloth and the need to state personal style and ambition.[60] It is a pattern that is seen in lower-status evidence too, but is more pronounced, elaborate and expensive here. When Hayne senior died in November 1639, his son's various funeral payments included "2 black taffeta hoods for Susan & Sarah my daughters," ribbon for girdles and black coats for them, and "2 yards ½ black Sifers for my Nurse & 2 servants to weare about their necks."[61] The involvement of the whole household in a fitting expression of mourning was clearly important to Hayne's sense of propriety for his first-generation cloth merchant father, underlining the scale of his own successful commercial enterprise by dressing his servants as well as his family.

Accessories in particular were also significant as gifts between the sexes. Cocks had a close relationship (type unclear) with his wife's nurse, and often bought her small gifts: "a girdle 3s 10d and 2 yards quarter of cipers 5s 6d" for "my valentine," as he calls her, for instance. Hayne's accounts also cover the period of his courtship of Susan Henly, during which he bestowed on her gifts including several knives with ribbons, two purses (one embroidered), two pairs of gloves, two needle cases, a ring and a "paire of posie bracelets." The "590 pearle & 590 currall" of which the bracelets were made, costing £4 18s, would advertise both the strength of Hayne's sentiment and the prosperousness of his business.[62] Analysis of urban inventories shows that Hayne's kind of prominent middling sort were the only ones to wear precious jewelry, its presence making a show within the streets of the town and, we might suppose, intended to connect them with their social betters.[63]

Hayne, as might already have become apparent, was a man more concerned with style than Cocks. Whereas the latter had clothes mended, the former had his possessions translated into the latest fashion. He was younger, on his way up the social ladder, and he lived in Exeter, which had a rich material culture in every sense of the word, shaped by its status as a significant port. Its merchants dominated its government,[64] and they were personally very wealthy men, with average estates of £1,900 (although this pales into insignificance next to the average wealth of their London equivalents, at £8,000). As Jonathan Barry and Christopher Brooks point out, "notoriously, merchants, professional men . . . might earn more than many gentlemen, but were often adjudged non-gentle on grounds of occupation, birth, life-style and possibly lack of power."[65] Hayne's purchases of accessories and embroidered goods put him on a par with his social superiors—unlike Peare, he does not necessarily need to use fake gold lace. He is just the kind of man who, Alan Hunt claims, spurred on the sumptuary endeavor across Europe—not a legal response to stable social relations, but a "product of circumstances in which a hieratic social order has come under internal pressure."[66]

CONCLUSION

While it is hard to calculate annual incomes and compare individuals' spending on dress at all points on the social scale, this essay has shown that, in every case, clothing represented a considerable percentage of an individual's worth and a great deal of time and effort went into acquiring it. It is also possible to make some material comparisons. We can put alongside one another Henry VIII's pair of gloves "enbrauderd with neyldewerke" listed in his Wardrobe in the inventory of 1521; the two large pairs bought for the Earl of Leicester by his groom of the Chamber in 1584 "perfumed and trymed with black silke and goulde" for 24s; the pair "laced with black silk and sliver" that Sir Hamon Le Strange purchased for £1 2s in the 1610s; and those for which John Hayne paid 10s to Mrs Ledgingham, wife of his regular glover, in the mid-1630s: "a pairs tawnie & glode embroderd."[67] We can see connections between the showy work on all these pairs, advertising the elevated rank and authority and the aesthetic fluency of their wearers within a specific arena. The example in Figure 6.5 from the Metropolitan Museum of Arts collection demonstrates the visual effect of the embellishment, especially the light-catching precious metals. By the time of Hayne's purchase in the second quarter of the seventeenth century, we might see individuals of all these ranks as part of a coherent market for high-status goods.[68] This analysis of the relationship between clothing and social status has also found shared sartorial practice in basic structural patterns that shaped ways of expressing social relations through dress across the scale, such as the complex interplay between traditional and fashionable clothing on which the elite and the middling built their authority, or livery as a connection between social groups which,

FIGURE 6.5: Pair of leather gloves, British, 1600–25, Gift of Irwin Untermyer, 1964, 64.101.1246 & 1247, The Metropolitan Museum of Art, New York. www.metmuseum.org

with the downwards diffusion of used clothing—from courtier to gentleman or from testator to pauper—tied social groups together even as it separated them. Active choice of embellishment allowed all but the needy poor to shape their visual identities, suggesting a coherent clothing system that connected individuals and their practices across the social scale—one that allowed the Earl of Leicester's clothing to be read by the inhabitants of Warwick.

Moving between the strictures of the legislation and the day-to-day interactions of particular communities—from prescription to practice—has revealed a shift in focus from the fixed language of status to the more mobile discourse of sorts: from national definitions to local and regional differences worked out face-to-face. It is in these direct interactions where dress "shows"—where it nuances the way individuals interact with one another's clothed image. Clothing knowledge and purchases followed, and themselves shaped, complex social interactions that related ranks to one another as they distinguished between them. The range of interactions of those in the middle in particular was very broad indeed—they walked with Earls *and* administered charity to the poor. Dress was one of the key strategies at their disposal with which to articulate their perception of a social position that grew in prominence across a couple of generations, and the quality of

FIGURE 6.6: Sir Henry Unton by unknown artist, oil on panel, c. 1596. © National Portrait Gallery, London.

the lace on their gloves perhaps played a more significant role in the making of the middle classes than historians have previously realized. Following these social relations has shown the complexities of the interrelations of dress as an expression of status and its role in articulating individual and familial identity.

The position of dress in the marking of various kinds of timescale and moment in the lifecycle was significant in different ways for all these groups—there were the courtly and mayoral processions and the poor's performance of their charity in new clothes on key liturgical festivals; there was the significance of augmented clothing at marriages and funerals. In Figure 6.6, the striking narrative of the whole life of Sir Henry Unton shows how such events were perceived to shape an individual identity, which became the sum of appropriately-clothed rites of passage of various kinds. At these moments, the social orders might come together, and their dress expressed both distances and proximities. In these formal situations, but also in the urban street, elements of different social groups were clearly viscerally aware of one another's presence and the way their relative status was expressed in what they were wearing.

CHAPTER SEVEN

Ethnicity

EMİNEGÜL KARABABA

INTRODUCTION

Geographically extending from Crimea to Sudan, from Bosnia to the Persian Gulf, from the Caucasus to Morocco, Ottoman society was made up of many populations.[1] Hungarians, Serbians, Croatians, Bosnians, Albanians, Romanians, Bulgarians, Greeks, Turks, Arabs, Jews, Berbers, Kurds, Laz people, Armenians, and Georgians are some examples of these different groups.[2] A multiplicity of ethnicities, languages, religions, and sects, as well as institutions and even administrative systems, existed in this vast territory. Ottoman society was multicultural.[3] On the one hand, each group had its own shared histories, customs, belief systems, and everyday practices that differentiated them from the others and gave them an identity. On the other hand, interactions between groups in the region resulted in similarities between groups or hybridities. The ways that people adorned their bodies, their dress, and their accessories were symbols representing group identities. This chapter examines how representations of ethnic dress in Ottoman society constructed ethnicities.

Ethnicity is a relatively new concept.[4] After the emergence of nation states, groups living within the borders of a nation were homogenized by national identities.[5] In the meantime, the notion of ethnicity emerged in order to identify different communities within a larger nation state. Ethnicity was developed as an alternative term to race, a fundamentally essentialist and politically loaded concept associated with the biological roots of a group. In contemporary social theory, an ethnic group is understood as a subgroup within a broader society; its members see themselves as distinct, and they claim kinship and common history, and share symbols representing the group identity.[6] However, when this concept is applied to the early modern context, religion is more significant than the claims of kinship, culture, or common history in defining ethnicity.[7] Throughout my analysis in this chapter, therefore, ethnicity and religion operate hand-in-hand in identifying the boundaries of groups.

Ethnic identity is always in flux; that is, it is an identity that is continuously shaped by group members and others whom they encounter. Internal and external definitions of ethnicity are continuously constructed.[8] Ethnic identities are assigned to the group and also defined, accepted, resisted, redefined, rejected, or defended by the group members.[9] In other words, groups continuously make assumptions based on the categories of "us" and "them."[10] Symbolism expressed through dress is a way of representing the categories of "us" and "them" and their characteristics. This chapter looks at how ethnicities in Ottoman society were continuously defined through the symbolism of dress.

This research covers the period of the sixteenth and seventeenth centuries and uses travelers' notes and their drawings, costume albums, and Sultans' decrees as data sources. Travelers' notes and visual data are useful for identifying the dress of different ethnic and religious groups, and how interactions with outsiders construct external definitions of an ethnicity. Sultans' decrees, in the form of sartorial codes enforcing how different groups should adorn their bodies, aimed to externally define ethnicities and religious identities through dress. Peoples' circumvention of such codes demonstrates resistance to the state's attempts for defining their ethnicity. During the early modern period clothing marked prescribed identities—gender, age, marital status, rank, and locality—and to maintain the social order sumptuary laws attempted to enforce specific clothing styles for different communities.[11] However, ethnic identities were not static because people who were outsiders to the group interpreted ethnic clothing in various ways and individuals belonging to ethnic communities resisted these state-enforced sartorial regimes. Each interaction with "the Other," either at the individual or institutional level, created a new definition of ethnicity in the Ottoman context and the boundaries of the ethnic identities were continuously constructed.

The study necessarily has some limitations. Firstly, Turkish clothing styles are not included because the term "Turk" was used not only for an ethnic group but also to refer to the Muslim community in general. Also, Muslim men working in different posts had different uniforms signifying their occupations. Therefore, it is hard to define a Turkish ethnic dress in such circumstances. Secondly, I have not discussed how ethnic communities constructed and communicated themselves internally through dress. This topic has to be left to future research, at a time when textual and visual sources produced by the community members themselves have been identified and examined.

In the rest of the chapter, I first delineate how interactions with the Other yielded continuous constructions of ethnic identity through representations of style, color, and clothing materials. Clothing of Bulgarian, Serbian, Greek, Jewish, and Armenian ethnicities living in the Ottoman lands and their interpretations by western travelers are presented. Next, I show the legislative ordering of ethnic/religious identities and try to interpret how these codes attempted to enforce clothing specific to religious and ethnic groups. In sum, I aim to demonstrate that styles, colors, and materials of dress did not represent static ethnic identities but rather reconstructed them continually, responding to a variety of tensions such as class, religion, and ethnic status games.

BULGARIAN CLOTHING

Most European travelers who went to Istanbul visited the Balkans on their way, and some of them depicted the clothing styles of ethnic groups in the Balkan region and constructed ethnic identities through representations of the ethnic dress. Bulgarians and Serbians are the groups mentioned most frequently in these travelers' notes. Hans Dernschwam,[12] a German traveler in the convoy of the ambassador for the Habsburg Empire, Ogier Ghiselin de Busbecq, visited a village close to the river Nishava[13] where he encountered Bulgarian women. Dernschwam's depictions of Bulgarian villager women are very similar to their depictions in an album prepared in the sixteenth century (see Figure 7.1). Austrian ambassador, Bartolemeo von Pezzen, who lived in Istanbul from 1586 to 1591, ordered this album from an unknown painter to record the scenes and characters in the Ottoman lands. In Figure 7.1, four Bulgarian women are standing on bare ground in different poses, pictured with domestic objects. The note in Old German below the figure states

FIGURE 7.1: Bulgarian village women, Codex Vindobonensis 8626. Österreichische Nationalbibliothek.

that the Bulgarian women are selling food and drink to passers-by. The engraving provides different views of their clothing. Three of them are depicted from the front, and the fourth is seen from the back, showing the viewer her long braids. They also represent the industrious life of village women, contrasting with the leisurely life[14] of townswomen, especially those of the higher ranks. The first woman in the figure is holding a cup and a jug, the second a loaf of bread and a bowl, the third a bowl of eggs, a loaf of bread, and a jug, and the last is spinning with a distaff and spindle.

All of the women in this illustration have similar dresses, fastened with a belt in the same color as the dress. Under their colorful long dresses, the first and third women from the left wear white trousers, which are called *don* in Ottoman Turkish. Most of the Muslim women recorded in probate inventories of the period wore trousers and shirts under their dresses, like the Bulgarian women pictured here.[15] The material, styles, and ornamentations might differ from the Turkish, however, while Dernschwam found the *don* of Bulgarian women similar to those of Hungarians.[16] That is, regional exchanges between different groups existed in dress styles, and similarities were also used to make sense of ethnic groups and wider regional characteristics.

The women depicted in Figure 7.1 wear white shirts with loose sleeves, embroidered with red and black on the sleeves and at the neck. While in South Bulgaria, Stephan Gerlach—a German priest traveling in the envoy of the Holy Roman Emperor Maximilian II, on a mission to renew a peace treaty with the Ottoman Empire—saw Bulgarian women with red embroidery on their shirts.[17] During his visit to Sophia, the ambassador Busbecq also saw Bulgarian townswomen wearing a single dress or a shirt made of coarse linen.[18] Busbecq considered the embroidery on the shirts to be very indelicate, and interpreted them as tasteless and comic.[19] During his encounter with these women, Busbecq felt that they were astonished by the modest and plain style of the clothing worn by himself and his friend.

A Bulgarian identity was constructed through the interaction of Bulgarian townswomen and travelers. In Busbecq's interpretive framework, colorful, cheap, shiny, indelicate, and coarse materials represented a tasteless/unaesthetic, comic/inappropriate style, and low status. As an outsider, when making meaning he refers to his own cultural background as a Protestant, well-educated diplomat with high status. Busbecq compared Bulgarian embroidery and the material quality of Bulgarian shirts with the ones in his culture in order to construct an external definition of Bulgarian ethnic identity as lowbrow and tasteless.[20]

The German priest Gerlach noted, too, Bulgarian women with rings, coin earrings, and necklaces with blue beads and coins similar to those worn by the women in Figure 7.1, who have blue-colored accessories: bracelets, large and long necklaces, and very large circular earrings.[21] Dernschwam and Solomon Schweigger, a fellow member of the diplomatic entourage, also mentioned that Bulgarian village women had necklaces made of mussel shells, shiny worthless stones, beads, bones, and even coins.[22] Young girls had copper and silver earrings made by Gypsy craftsmen and they also wore copper or bronze rings.[23]

Dernschwam was astonished by Bulgarian women's headwear and drew a simple figure of it like a truncated cone. "We saw a novel type of women's clothing at our new stopover. Unlike village women of other countries, they [Bulgarian women] do not cover their faces and wore an outer garment covering them from head to toe. Their headdress looks as if they wore an upside-down bowl. The bottom part of it is as wide as will fit the head, the upper part is narrower."[24] It was hard for Dernschwam to construct a meaning for this ambiguous object, the Bulgarian-style hat. For him, such a style was very similar to pearl-decorated crowns wore by aristocrats in Bohemia and Hungary. To create an interpretive framework, he was forced to associate the style of hat with a different object belonging to another culture and to compare the two. However, the decorations on the hats of poor Bulgarians were made of worthless beads just like their accessories. Although in his interpretive framework the style of the headdress corresponded to high social status, the cheap material of the Bulgarian headdress communicated Bulgarian identity as poor and low status.

Busbecq also found the hats of the Bulgarian townswomen in Sophia awkward and impractical, with their larger tops, which would hold rainwater rather than let it flow over. He also pointed out that anything shiny, such as small coins, pictures, and colored glass, was used to decorate these hats, making women look taller but limiting their ability to move. He implied that Bulgarian people were primitive in the sense that they were not rational enough to use a functional style.[25]

Gerlach described pieces of silver or feathers being used as finials, *sorguç*, on Bulgarian women's headwear.[26] In Figure 7.1, three women have these feather finials as decorations.

Two of the figures have long hair braided with blue- and red-colored bands and blue balls hang from the ends of their plaits. This hair accessory was called *saçbağı*, and its silver and gold versions have been identified in an analysis of Bursa[27] probate inventories as a luxury novelty in the seventeenth century.[28] In a village close to Plovdiv, Dernschwam witnessed young Bulgarian girls with many long braids. Some of them gathered these braids up on their ears like the third woman from the left in Figure 7.1.[29] Again the hairstyle, which was novel to Dernschwam, appeared very complex and he interpreted it as being made of horsehair rather than being created from human hair. This ambiguous hairstyle did not exist in his interpretive framework and therefore he failed to construct a Bulgarian ethnic character relating to it.

SERBIAN CLOTHING

On their journeys through the Balkan region, travelers encountered Serbian villagers as well. To differentiate Serbians from the others, they compared their clothing with other groups such as Bulgarians, Turks, Croatians, and Gypsies living in the region. For example, Gerlach compared the Turkish and Serbian women living in Nish and used clothing to create contrasting identities. Turkish women on the streets of Nish were fully covered and the ends of their scarves hung down their backs (Figure 7.2). Gerlach found this style

FIGURE 7.2: Jost Amman, a picture of a wealthy Turkish woman appearing in public with her children, German woodcut, 1577. © Victoria and Albert Museum, London.

similar to that of nuns in his culture and therefore interpreted it as orderly and respectable. In contrast, he identified Serbian women's dress as attractive and seductive. They wrapped their breasts and hips with shawls and wore silver or lead accessories on their ears. Comparisons with Turks and their covered look, representing respectable women, created their opposite in Serbian women, whose appearance was interpreted as liberated and seductive, but less respectable.[30]

The simple style of Serbian shirts, ugly headscarves, and home woven coarse clothes represented for Western commentators the primitive character of Serbian dress. Consequently, in travelers' depictions a primitive character for Serbian identity is implied as well. Gerlach saw Serbian women wearing very simple shirts, fastened by a belt with ends that hung down the front.[31] Rather than wearing woolen dresses, they wore coarse linen fabric that they themselves had woven.[32] Dernshwam states that Serbian women wore ugly headscarves similar to those worn by Croatians. Their veils and scarves, which were made of plain linen, were also similar to the scarves of Gypsies who were living in the region. Girls generally did not cover their hair but had finials made of braids that to Dernschwam looked very awkward, just like the Bulgarians. In other words, finials could not represent an ethnic character due to their ambiguity for the outsider.

GREEK CLOTHING

Greek communities living in different geographical locations in the Empire had different dress styles, which were used as symbolic resources by outsiders in constructing Greek ethnic identities. Travelers of the period frequently mentioned clothing and accessories of Greek women living in the Pera district of Istanbul and Greek villager women living around the region. Greek women's ostentatious clothing and accessories and their liberated style were often emphasized in travelers' discourse.[33] By depicting extravagance and highlighting female sexuality, travelers were interpreting Greek women as both full of pomp and liberated compared with other women in Ottoman society.

Nicolas de Nicolay, the French geographer, visited Ottoman lands and the Middle East in 1551 in the envoy of the French ambassador to the Ottoman Empire. In 1567–8, he published his observations in a book titled *Quartre Premiers Livres des Navigations et Pérégrinations*. The book also contains sixty sketches drawn by Nicolas and engraved by Lyon Davent. For example, a Greek girl from the Pera district of Istanbul in an extravagant house dress is described and depicted in the book (see Figure 7.3).[34] As Nicolay mentions in his text, young Greek girls or newly married women wore dark red hats, which were made of satin patterned fabric, sometimes woven with metal threads and wrapped around with bands two inches wide, ornamented with pearls and precious stones.[35] The girl in his account wears this type of hat, with cords made of silk and gold wrapped over her head (Figure 7.3).[36] The accessory attached to her headdress is a *sorguç*, or finial, which can also be seen in portrayals of wealthy high-class Muslim women in numerous images produced during the period.[37]

In travelers' discourse Greek women—regardless of their economic and social backgrounds—are all presented as sumptuous, with dresses made of expensive materials such as velvet, damask, and satin.[38] Their shirts were made of taffeta or other silk cloths and were embroidered with gold threads.[39] Cesare Vecellio, an Italian artist, in 1590 published a book about the clothing of Renaissance Europe, Asia, and Africa. In it, he also claims that Greek women living in the Pera district at this time wore fabrics made in Bursa.[40] Although some of these fabrics seemed to be luxury items, Muslim women of

FIGURE 7.3: *A Greek Girl Living in Pera, Constantinople*. Engraving provided by Ayşe Yetişkin Kubilay.

middling ranks living in Bursa consumed these fabrics, and they even spread to lower-status groups between the mid-sixteenth and mid-seventeenth centuries.[41]

Greek dresses made of fabrics woven with gold, silver, or silk threads, embroidered with flower motifs in gold threads, or ornamented with buttons were frequently mentioned.[42] These extravagant fabrics that travelers saw must have been consumed by the affluent factions of the Greek community. Probate inventories of the townswomen living in Bursa demonstrate that high-status Muslim women also wore similarly luxurious materials made of gold and silk in their everyday lives, while ordinary townswomen contented themselves with cheaper lower-quality versions.[43]

This ostentatious style of the Greek women was favored not only by women living in large cities such as Istanbul, but also by those living in villages. The trickling down of styles from cities to villages and the consumption of cheaper versions is probable. For example, Antoine Galland, a French scholar who visited Istanbul in the seventeenth century in the envoy of the French ambassador, witnessed Greek villagers around rural Edirne[44] displaying the same extravagance.[45] In his notes, Galland described knitted woolen outer garments decorated with fur, embroidered headwear, silver belts, and satin jackets as being typical of rural Greek women's dress.

Both Nicolay and German travel writer and poet Michael Heberer interpreted this extravagance in dress styles as reflecting the arrogance and haughty attitude of the Greek woman.[46] These drawings and texts attribute a moral significance to the dress styles and appearances of people.[47] The style and extravagance representing these attitudes was used to identify and differentiate Greek women from the others in different communities that travelers encountered throughout their lives. An external ethnicity was in the making. The interpretive frame of a traveler, an outsider's perspective, constructs the fluid Greek female ethnic identity. Each interaction with the Other redefines ethnic identities.

It was not only the expensive fabrics but also the jewelry and precious accessories worn by Greek women that drew the attention of travelers.[48] These women braided their hair with gold cords, decorated their foreheads with precious gems and their chests and necks with gold or silver chains, and wore gold bracelets and silver slippers.[49] At a wedding ceremony, Gerlach saw that they had crowns on their heads that were made of precious gems such as rubies or turquoise, and they wore gold chains around their necks, gold earrings, gold bracelets, and rings (see Figure 7.3 and Figure 7.4). Most of the guests at the ceremony wore silver shoes, or *nalin* in Turkish.

In situating Greeks as a separate ethnic group, Gerlach compares them with Turks. Both Turks and Greeks wore crowns made of gold, or silver plated with gold, and decorated with precious stones.[50] Gerlach argues that the value of these crowns varied around 5,000 to 6,000 ducats. This must be an exaggerated estimate since 5,000–6,000

FIGURE 7.4: Greek women, Codex Vindobonensis 8626. Österreichische Nationalbibliothek.

ducats corresponds to 350,000–400,000 *akçe* (the Ottoman currency); during the mid-sixteenth century,[51] this would have been extremely expensive, even for gold jewelry. For example, wealthy women living in Bursa in the mid-sixteenth century typically possessed around 8000 *akçe*'s worth of jewelry in their probate records.[52] Nevertheless Gerlach's discourse and exaggerations emphasize this sumptuous Greek identity. In his costume book, Cesare Vecellio also argues that the Greek women of the Pera district wore clothing very similar to that of Turkish women.[53] Similarities in style identified Greek women as part of the greater Ottoman community, but their ostentation and liberated appearances differentiated them from the rest of the society.

Greek women also used gold wires when braiding their hair, which hung down their backs.[54] The gold and silver cords used in hair braiding were fashionable items of the period among Muslims as well.[55] Sometimes Greek women used twenty to thirty ducats' worth of hairnets, probably like the ones depicted in Figure 7.4. The Greek women in this image have black hair, which can be seen under their crowns, and have gold hairnets flowing over their shoulders. Gerlach wrote that they wore gold chains on their ankles and gold rings on their toes. Their slippers were decorated with silver spangles and precious stones. Jewelry was not only used as a status marker and to represent rank, it also aestheticized female body parts such as the arms, ears, and hair.

Various elements of the drawing in Figure 7.3 aim to focus the viewer's attention on the body, connoting female beauty and sexual attractiveness: the wavy, semi-loose, long hair of the Greek girl flowing over her wide shoulders and bosom; the glittering pearl earring emphasizing her uncovered neck and chest, which are also decorated with gold chains and necklaces; and her arms, which although hidden under the shirt of a striped thin fabric, have their form clearly outlined, and the bracelets on their wrists carefully detailed. Nicolay's view of the Greek girl's beauty was in line with sixteenth-century depictions of the ideal female physical form. That is, under the dress a muscular and massive body is concealed.[56]

One way of establishing Greek identity in sartorial terms was the way in which it was contrasted with the appearance of Ottoman Muslim women—that is, the former were seen to boldly adopt clothing styles that displayed specific parts of their bodies. Greek women never covered their faces and even sought to attract attention by displaying their necks and partly their breasts.[57] They wore white shawls that covered only their shoulders and back, but not the chest or neck. Sixteenth-century travelers Philippe du Fresne-Cenaye and Heberer stated that even in public Greek women did not veil their faces.[58] Displaying parts of the body by not covering them, and even decorating them to attract attention, represented a means of differentiating Greek women as more liberated but also as more frivolous than others in society.

JEWISH CLOTHING

The Jewish people were perhaps the most interesting in terms of establishing ethnic identities, given that representations of Jewishness through dress were greatly influenced by the wider societies in which the Jewish subjects of these representations lived.[59] Jews not only spoke the language of the broader community in which they were settled, but they also wore the same style of clothing as that community. Therefore, it was possible to see Jewish people wearing long clothing like the kaftans of Italian, Turkish, or Greek people. They fastened their kaftans with belts and wore silk clothing underneath them. Recalling Dernschwam's description, the appearance of two Jewish physicians in a costume album executed by Lambert de Vos, an artist with the Habsburg embassy who visited Istanbul in the sixteenth century (see Figure 7.5), resembles Turkish clothing styles. Both of the men depicted wear blue robes with a red lining and a red belt. On top they have black gowns and black or blue shoes. These similarities with Turkish dress must have created ambiguities in terms of ethnic identity. That is, by resembling members of the Ottoman Muslim community, members of the Jewish community constructed ambiguities in defining the boundaries of Jewish ethnicity through their clothing consumption. Therefore their dress styles do not communicate a distinct Jewish identity but instead seek to establish their sense of belonging within the wider community. Internal definition of ethnicity allows symbolism of the other; these styles represented a specific Ottoman Jewishness that simultaneously marked their place within a larger group.

On the other hand, headwear styles and clothing colors were used to differentiate ethnic identity as separate from the wider community. Turks and Jewish men differentiated themselves by wearing white and yellow turbans respectively.[60] Depending on their occupational or social backgrounds, Jewish men also wore different types of headgear. For example, it was possible to see a Jewish man wearing an Italian-style black beret or a Jewish physician wearing a red conical hat.[61] Figure 7.5 shows two Jewish physicians: one

FIGURE 7.5: Two Jewish physicians from the album of Lambert de Vos (1574). Der Staats-und Universitätsbibliothek, Bremen.

with a red conical cap and the other with a yellow turban. In Jerusalem, the yellow turban had been a symbol of the Jewish people from ancient times onwards.[62] Nicolay also informs us that Jewish people living in Chios were forced to wear a yellow headdress and the ones living in Thessaloniki had yellow turbans.[63] Therefore, certain styles, such as conical caps, or colors, such as yellow, were symbols used to represent Jewish ethnic identity. Hybrid styles came to represent negotiations in terms of representing Jewish ethnicity, and sometimes institutional practices such as legal enforcements were influential in these processes.

Accessories and different styles of dress were also used to denote female Jewish ethnic identity. For example, MelchisédechThévenot, a French scholar and traveler, reported that Jewish women attached pieces of platinum or tin to their hair and covered their hair with gold or silver embroidered scarves.[64] They generally tied a handkerchief around this scarf as well. During the late seventeenth century, the Dutch artist and traveler Cornelis De Bruyn observed that Jewish women in Istanbul wore their hair in a bun on their neck, which was put in a colored silk pouch, and wore pearl necklaces made of many strings.[65] That is, members of an ethnic community negotiated different symbolisms through style, color, and qualities of material, to draw the boundaries of being simultaneously an Ottoman subject and a Jewish individual.

Within the Jewish community itself, there were factions that differentiated themselves from other Jews through types of dress. For example, Karaite Jews, both men and women, were known for their fine silk damask dresses.[66] Rather than style or color, the quality of the fabric represented the hierarchy of different groups within the community. Karaite Jews constituted a small population within the Jewish whole, around fifty to one hundred households in Istanbul during the sixteenth century.[67] However, it seems that they had higher economic and social status within the community, which was represented through their flamboyant clothing.

When he encountered the Jewish people in Istanbul, Dernschwam constructed a definition of Jewish ethnicity through comparisons with the community to which he himself belonged.[68] For Dernschwam, the luxurious style of Jewish women's dress surpassed even that of the European aristocracy. They wore satin, damask, and velvet dresses and had gold-embroidered shirts and skirts. Most of the Jewish women had gold necklaces and bracelets. He expressed the view that a Jewish woman without a gold necklace must be a very poor one. That is, the luxuriousness of the material of their dresses and their accessories represented the affluence of the ethnic community as a characteristic constructed through comparison of the categories of "us" and "them."

In addition, the state apparatus tried to use sartorial legislation to enforce specific dress styles, colors, or qualities of material in order to differentiate Jewish from Muslim identity. For example, Thévenot stated that Jews were ordered to wear purple dresses and headwear, jackets, and shoes.[69] Gerlach noted that legislation concerning the clothing styles of non-Muslim people had been issued over and over again.[70] Attempts were made to force them to wear cheap clothing made of coarse materials rather than fine fabrics, but these enforcements were circumvented. Gerlach argued that the reason for such bans was excessive public displays of clothing and accessories by Jewish women and men. He gave the example of a Jewish woman wearing a necklace worth 40,000 ducats and walking around the streets of Istanbul, or of a few Jewish men who were seen out and about in velvet or silk clothing.[71] Although 40,000 ducats seems to be an exaggeration, Nicolas de Nicolay's engraving of a Jewish woman from Adrianople (current day Edirne) in Figure 7.6 has her wearing a large necklace that matches Stephen Gerlach's description.

FIGURE 7.6: Jewish woman from Adrianople (current day Edirne). Folger Shakespeare Library, Washington DC.

Non-Muslim subjects of the Empire were forbidden to wear clothing made of silk or fine fabrics. They had to wear clothing made of coarse fabrics. Instead of elegant shoes, they had to wear coarse cheap shoes and coarse turbans. Instead of long trousers, they were only allowed to wear stockings and leggings. If officers caught a non-Muslim wearing a silk belt, the law demanded its confiscation.[72] Although travelers' notes and repetitive issuing of codes demonstrate that these legislative enforcements were not always successful, it shows that institutions also had a role in defining an ethnic identity through dress.

ARMENIAN CLOTHING

In the sixteenth century, Gerlach found the dress of Armenians living in Istanbul very similar to that of Turks, wearing loose trousers and shirts.[73] English traveler Peter Mundy visited Istanbul in 1618 and ordered a costume album in which an Armenian lady was also portrayed (see Figure 7.7).

FIGURE 7.7: *Portrait of an Armenian Woman*, 1618. © The Trustees of the British Museum.

The clothing of the Armenian women in the figure fits very well with Gerlach's description. She has a white scarf that covers her finial and shoulders, leaving some parts of her black hair uncovered. She wears a black robe, buttoned down the front from the neck to the waist. The robe has a blue lining, seen at the sleeves and from the opening of the robe at the skirt. She has a large belt fastened over the robe. Loose white trousers and a pair of yellow shoes can be seen under the robe, even though the clothing codes officially only allowed Muslims to be dressed in such footwear.[74] Thus the depiction of an Armenian woman with yellow shoes, coupled with the continuous reissuance of sartorial codes, demonstrate that Armenian women were active in constructing their ethnicities in public by disobeying sartorial regulations.

The woman in Peter Mundy's album also wears a *sakalduruk*, an accessory attached to her headwear that surrounds her face. Gerlach witnessed Armenian women with veils similar to those of Turkish women,[75] although the Armenian veils were white, not black. As a status symbol, Armenian women from the upper classes had black veils but they were woven with gold threads so as to differentiate their look from that of the Turks'. Also unlike the Turks, the backs of these scarves featured gold embroidery that cost around ten to fifteen ducats. Gerlach stated that Armenian women had jewelry under their scarves, around their foreheads, necks, and ears, but he considered Greek women to be more conspicuous in their dress.[76] That is, Armenian ethnic identity was constructed by comparisons between Armenians, Turks, and Greeks, and they were ranked in terms of ostentation.

In addition to continuous reproduction of ethnic identity through cultural interactions, a non-Muslim identity was also communicated through clothing. Ottoman sartorial codes were particularly aimed at separating the appearance of Muslims and non-Muslims by ordering different styles, colors, and materials for these different religious groups. Sometimes the codes also differentiated between non-Muslim ethnicities.

ORDERING SOCIETY: SARTORIAL CODES AND ETHNICITY

During the sixteenth and seventeenth centuries, Ottoman social order was challenged by different dynamics. There was high mobility among social classes; transitions between religious groups (especially from Christianity to Islam); and migration from rural areas to the small towns.[77] For example, in the sixteenth century, Gelibolu'lu Mustafa Ali, an Ottoman bureaucrat, and in the seventeenth century Koçu Bey, an Ottoman scholar, complained about the difficulties of maintaining social order due to social mobility and migration.[78] The Ottoman administrative class insisted that people from different ranks, occupations, or religious backgrounds had to display specific signs so as to easily differentiate the groups to which they belonged.[79] The rationale behind this was to prevent excessive consumption of luxury items and to establish a status hierarchy.

For more than two centuries, sumptuary laws were regularly reissued in an attempt to maintain order and identify social groups through their clothes.[80] Styles, colors, and fabrics were used as signs to identify different groups in the social order.[81] However, the reissuance of these laws also demonstrates that they were circumvented, and that in spite of the concerns of the administration to maintain "unambiguous signs of difference,"[82] Ottoman subjects attempted to create ambiguity and disorder in this process of identification, especially in the cities.

From the fifteenth century onwards, sartorial codes were issued over and over again, and applied in and around Istanbul, the capital of the Empire.[83] These clothing rules both prescribed, and limited access to, certain materials, styles, and colors to identify Jewish and Christian people. To maintain the hierarchy between the Muslim and non-Muslim communities, non-Muslim men were supposed to wear very modest, dark-colored clothing, and were supposed not to attract attention.[84] Muslims, by contrast, were allowed to wear bright and light-colored clothing—including green, a hue that represented this religious community regardless of an individual's ethnicity—and also white turbans and, as mentioned earlier, yellow shoes. For example, a decree issued in 1571 banned non-Muslims living in Diyarbakır (a city in South-East Asia Minor) from wearing green *çağşır* (a kind of trouser that becomes tighter at the knees), green *başmak* and *papuç* (shoe styles), and white turbans. Also, in the same decree, non-Muslim women were banned from wearing veils and white *makrama* (large shawls), which were signs adopted by Muslim women.[85]

In the fifteenth century, after the conquest of Macedonia, a decree was issued: Christians were ordered to wear blue headwear and long dresses, and Jews were ordered to wear yellow ones.[86] This rule continued in force, and even later in the sixteenth century Turks and Jewish people were differentiated by the color of their headwear, as mentioned earlier. Turks wore white, Jewish men wore yellow turbans, and Jewish surgeons were allowed to wear red conical hats.[87]

It was not just colors but also textiles and garment types that were regulated in order to represent different ethno-religious communities. In 1568, fine quality kerseys (*çuka*), robes (*kaftans*) made of satin, *kutnu* (a fabric made of silk and cotton), and other quality fabrics, and *çağşırs* made of fine quality cloth were banned to Jews and Christians. In other words, an attempt was made to establish a hierarchy of status between Muslims and non-Muslims through the signification of material quality. In addition, there was a ban on non-Muslim access to clothing styles, such as cavalry-type turbans made of fine muslins and *içediks* (soft slippers worn inside shoes).

Later that same year, the Jewish people's disobedience of these laws resulted in the reissuance of another decree.[88] In this second ruling, the requirements were more detailed. Quality of material, style, and color were all combined as signs to identify ethno-religious communities. For example, Jewish people and Christians were ordered to wear brown cloaks (*feraces*), dark grey kerseys, linings made of *bogası* (coarse cotton cloth) without stitches, and black shoes (*başmak*) without a lining and flat on top. Also, they were limited to using belts made of half-cotton and half-silk cloth, which was not to exceed a value of thirty to forty *akçes*. *İçediks* could be made from thick black and brown sheepskin leather (*meşin*), but not from *sahtiyan* (fine quality leather, generally red or yellow, made from goatskin). Non-Muslim subjects were restricted to apparel of modest quality; fine, expensive, and colorful materials were markers of high status, and were limited to Muslims. The enforcement of such signification was used as a way of creating visible differentiation between social groups, and was seen as a way of maintaining the social order.

In this same decree, non-Muslim female clothing was clearly defined by referring to pre-existing legislation. Such women were banned from wearing *feraces* and *arakiye* (a small cap), as these two styles were associated with Muslims. They were also prohibited from wearing collars made of *seraser* (an expensive silk cloth), which an etiquette book of the period identifies as appropriate cloth for higher status people.[89] Non-Muslim women were restricted to wearing trousers only in blue. They were allowed only relatively modest materials, such as dresses made of *kutnu* (a fabric made of cotton and silk) and certain shoe styles. However, depictions by travelers demonstrate that the consumption of extravagant cloth and precious jewelry by non-Muslims was very common. Furthermore, the repetition of these sumptuary laws shows that restrictions on style and color were not being obeyed by non-Muslim groups. In other words, there was resistance to the assigned representations. External definition of ethnicity by the state and internal definitions and redefinitions of ethnicities were negotiated.

Such sartorial legislation not only considered non-Muslims as a single community, it differentiated among them according to their ethnicities. In one code, Armenians were specifically mentioned.[90] They were allowed to wear clothing similar to that of the Jewish people, but had to wrap a small multi-colored (*alaca*) sash around their heads as a sign of Armenian identity. Armenian women were allowed to wear *fahir* (fine) dresses and *terlik*,[91] which was a dress made of a very thin transparent fabric worn over a kaftan.

Nine years following this, another decree was issued, referring to non-Muslims' disobedience of sartorial codes. In it they were banned from wearing kerseys (*çuka*), imported kerseys (*iskarlat*), satin, silk brocade (*kemha*), or silk robes (*kaftans*). Although *ferace* as a style had been banned before, in the new decree non-Muslims were only banned from wearing silk *feraces*. All of the permitted clothing was to be made of coarse cotton fabric and they were restricted from using very fine muslins.[92] These changes in the requirements also show that representations of ethnicities in Ottoman society were in flux; over time, groups and the administration continuously negotiated these representations, leading—in terms of signification—to some social ambiguities and to disorder.

CONCLUSION

This chapter has presented the dress of different ethnic communities living in the Ottoman Empire in the sixteenth and seventeenth centuries. Concepts of ethnicity were developed through interactions between the ethnic group and the Other, whether that Other was an individual or an institution. In processes where an individual interacts with the community, the individual makes sense of the ethnic group through the style, color, and quality of its adornment. In this meaning creation process, if the qualities of the adornment encountered by the individual were ambiguous or did not exist within his or her interpretive framework,[93] that individual generally attempted to make sense of it by finding the best fit. Thus, for example, the German Hans Dernschwam compared the headwear of Bulgarian village women with the crowns worn by the Bohemian aristocracy.

If the adornment was familiar, then the viewing Other compared both the object and its meaning with the one existing in his or her interpretive framework. The three dimensions of materiality (style, color, and quality) were made use of in this comparison process and their symbolism used to interpret not only the clothing, but also the character of the ethnic identity in question. For example, the Habsburg ambassador Busbecq interpreted the red embroidery on the shirts of Bulgarian women as indelicate. These interpretations not only described the meaning of the clothing, but also communicated for him the nature of the women wearing it—that is, the garments communicated or defined their ethnicity as, in this case, a tasteless or less sophisticated people. In such a context, each interaction actually resulted in a different interpretation, depending on who the viewing Other was; the culture and background from which the person came created a new understanding of the ethnic group. That is, ethnicity was always in flux, even in an early modern context.

Comparison between different ethnicities living in the same region was another process of ethnic identification. Interactions between groups did not always create distinctive styles, but sometimes formed similarities or hybridities. For example, Jewish people generally mixed their styles with those of the society in which they lived, and Armenians were described as looking similar to Turks in their clothing. In a society, ethnic groups not only encounter people from other cultural backgrounds, but they also interact with institutions. In the Ottoman case, just as in any other early modern state, the administration aimed to maintain clear differences between different groups—especially along religious lines—but sometimes among ethnic groups as well. The administration also used colors, styles, and materials as symbolic resources to identify ethno-religious communities. However, communities did not always accept these assigned symbols: they were sometimes resisted or rejected. Both the continuous reissuing of the clothing codes and the ostentatious styles of the Greek people as described by travelers provide evidence of such resistance. In such cases there is room for ambiguity, and the association of the object (dress style, color, and quality) with a specific community becomes blurred, thus challenging the social order.

Although the focus here has been on the Ottoman Empire, the processes described in this chapter, whereby ethnicities were defined and negotiated through vestimentary signals, were common throughout early modern Europe. The mutual construction of ethnic identities across the divide of sartorial difference was a feature of the growing number of travel accounts in the period, whether they recorded journeys taken between different European polities, or further afield to the boundaries of the known world being ever expanded in this age of exploration and nascent colonization. From Augsburg to Zealand, Venice to the Virginias, travelers noted with interest how inhabitants were dressed and—crucially—made sense of these observations by reference to familiar paradigms. Extrapolating outwards from known frames of reference, observers thus incorporated the strange and unusual into their own schema and imputed moral and behavioral qualities accordingly. Such observations fitted, too, with the proto-anthropological stance that was a feature of the period. As in Cesare Vecellio's *Habiti Antichi et Moderni*, or the other costume books that were produced at this time, the drive was to record, understand, and find a place for the cultural relativities being encountered in the Renaissance world. Likewise, the sumptuary laws discussed here that prescribed and restricted clothing fabrics and forms were echoed throughout Europe. Although the latter generally sought to codify rank and wealth differences (see Chapter 6), there were sometimes provisions to fix the appearance of minority ethnic and religious groups.

In sum, although group identities are often assumed to have been static and prescribed in the early modern period, a variety of individual- and institutional-level interactions with the community resulted in a continuous co-creation of ethnic identities through clothing as a symbolic resource. In the Ottoman Empire, as elsewhere, the way people dressed was potent, enabling the endless flux of inclusion and separation, similarity and difference, that underscored the identity of the self and the Other.

CHAPTER EIGHT

Visual Representations

ANNA REYNOLDS

INTRODUCTION

The explosion of visual imagery accompanying the widespread cultural changes we now associate with the Renaissance provides an unprecedented insight into how people attired themselves during the period. The relative scarcity of surviving Renaissance garments, accessories, and jewelry, tested by hundreds of years of changing tastes and damaging atmospheric conditions, makes the examination of visual representations a vital component in understanding and interpreting the clothing of this period. The wide range of visual material produced encompasses both flat and three-dimensional art. However, as this chapter will demonstrate, the kind of information about dress provided by each type of object is highly variable, and comes with its own particular limitations and caveats to interpretation of which the modern viewer must be aware.

Strictly speaking, to describe clothing of the period as *Renaissance* is in many ways inaccurate, as unlike other forms of visual material produced during this period (most notably paintings, sculpture, and architecture), the clothing forms themselves did not take inspiration from classical antiquity. The term is therefore instead used here to describe a broad and approximate date range rather than a consistent stylistic feature. The first part of this chapter will discuss the relevance of, and limitations to, Renaissance visual source material. After this, each of the main visual media will be described and its particular value examined. In other words, we will consider *where* images of dress appear; *why* the artists, makers, and patrons chose such depictions; and finally, *what* such representations can tell us about how the men and women of the Renaissance were actually clothed.

THE IMPORTANCE OF VISUAL SOURCES

Partly due to important technological advances, we have far more visual material for the fifteenth century—most notably paintings and illuminated manuscripts—than for preceding ones. Alongside this, the growing secularization of art meant that the range of figures portrayed (and the clothing worn) broadened and increasingly tended to reflect the contemporary reality of the society in which the artists were working. Like clothing, the different survival rates for various types of visual media are affected by war, changing religious ideologies, taste, and fragility, giving us a biased view of their importance during the fifteenth and sixteenth centuries.

The young sitter in Figure 8.1 was one of the daughters of Joris Vekemans, a prominent Antwerp silk merchant, either Cornelia or her older sister Elisabeth.[1] This life-size,

FIGURE 8.1: *Elisabeth or Cornelia Vekemans*, Cornelis de Vos, c. 1625, Museum Mayer van den Bergh. © Museum Mayer van den Bergh, Antwerpen.

full-length portrait demonstrates a number of advantages that visual imagery holds over extant garments, which typically survive in isolation without the rest of an outfit. Images can reveal unexpected color combinations—here the sage green hanging sleeves and skirt open to reveal coral silk garments beneath, enlivened with blue ribbons. In general, the greater permanence of pigments used in painting compared with the dyes used for fabrics means that portraits can be useful indicators of the original colors of clothing, although later this chapter will also discuss how changes in the appearance of paint may also occur. The level of completion of a painting should also be considered—this portrait is unfinished, probably because the sitter's father died in 1625, so consequently, the final intended appearance of the clothing may have been slightly different.

Through portraits of this type, the viewer is also able to understand how various garments were worn together and how they were accessorized. Here the young girl wears a standing collar of pleated translucent linen edged with lace, along with a matching tucker filling the square neckline of the bodice. Plain linen and lace cuffs decorate the wrists, blue ribbon rosettes feature on the bodice, the sitter carries a folding fan, and wears gold bracelets on each wrist. Portraits also show how different elements of clothing actually looked on a body, and can indicate how or where they were supported or padded. In this case, the play of light across the green fabric of the bodice clearly shows that it was stiffened—it does not crumple at the waist as the wearer sits—unlike the fabric of the matching skirt, which falls into natural pleats beneath her left arm.

As this example demonstrates, clothing in a Renaissance portrait usually occupies a significant proportion of the surface area and is frequently the most eye-catching and colorful part, standing out against a background that is often dark. When examined in conjunction with the biography of the sitter and the broader context of the commission, visual images can help us understand *why* something was worn, rather than simply allowing us to identify the component features of an outfit. Here for example, the particular attention with which the girl's clothing has been chosen by her parents and then rendered in paint by the artist will surely have been a conscious decision and will have served as a reminder of her father's silk trading business to anyone visiting the family home, demonstrating both the range of colors and high quality of the fabrics to which he had access, as well as his own personal wealth and social status.

THE LIMITATION OF VISUAL SOURCES

The documentary value of an image must always be considered in light of the artist's original intentions, just as a literary source is prone to bias, so too is visual material. Portraits, for example, were often not a simple and literal representation of the clothing worn, but were intended to be "read" and interpreted according to complex visual codes that could provide information about the sitter's social status, wealth, age, gender, marital status, reputation, personal history, nationality, religion and so on. It is important to recognize that such cultural interpretations can be highly sophisticated and multi-layered, and may radically differ from modern perceptions.

Catherine Carey, Countess of Nottingham of c. 1597 by Robert Peake (Figure 8.2) demonstrates the potential complexity of such visual messages. As First Lady of the Bedchamber and Mistress of the Robes, the sitter occupied a highly privileged position at the court of Queen Elizabeth I.[2] Her clothing is both highly fashionable and incredibly ornate, consisting of an embroidered bodice with a low pointed waistline, a skirt pinned into pleats over a wide wheel-shaped farthingale, an open ruff, and a long decorative veil attached to a tall headdress. Catherine Carey's outfit will have indicated to the sixteenth-century viewer both her fashionability and her esteemed status, a status that meant she had servants to help her don such complicated attire. The bodice and skirt are embroidered with a huge variety of plants including roses, lilies, strawberries, pansies, vine leaves, grapes, sweet peas, honeysuckle, and hazelnuts, each of which will have held a particular symbolic meaning during the Renaissance, meanings that were laid out in contemporary botanical herbals and emblem books. Roses and pansies in particular were associated with Elizabeth I herself, and may have been intended here in homage to the sitter's mistress. In addition to this botanical inspiration, the embroidery also includes obelisks (representing Protestantism), snakes (symbolic of prudence or wisdom), and the Fermesse, a stylized S, which represented fidelity. The dress may possibly have originally belonged to Queen Elizabeth I, and been given to Catherine Carey as a perquisite of her position. Regardless,

FIGURE 8.2: *Catherine Carey, Countess of Nottingham*, Robert Peake, c. 1597, private collection, courtesy of The Weiss Gallery.

her appearance wearing this dress in such a prestigious portrait will have held deliberate and multi-faceted meanings, linking her to the Elizabethan court.

An artist working during the Renaissance had to balance realism—producing a recognizable image—with idealization—to produce a beautiful work of art. Artists selected and emphasized those elements of dress that best suited their motivations. This idealization based on contemporary notions of beauty applies both to the clothing worn and to the body beneath—the attenuated, narrow-waisted figures seen in early Renaissance medieval manuscripts for example, whose draped clothing falls in perfect International Gothic curves, were a construction of the illustrator. In the same way that a portraitist may smooth over pock-marked skin in a painted portrayal, the clothing depicted often does not show signs of wear. Stains are ignored despite the fact that during the period the majority of outer layers of clothing were impossible to wash. Similarly, some artists give a misleading impression of how fabric reacts to the human body beneath, with creases effortlessly smoothed in a painted version.

Visual representations can also be misleading on construction, ignoring fastenings and seams altogether, or giving the impression of a fabric pattern continuing across a join which in reality was expensive (since it used more fabric) and complicated. Medieval illuminated manuscripts often include some figures wearing fashionable outfits, while others in the same scene wear invented fantastic or historical clothing. These differences were based on established conventions about what type of clothing different figures should wear, so that the story would be easy to interpret for the reader. So biblical and religious figures were shown in tunics and mantles, pagans in large jewels and turbans, while ordinary people wore contemporary clothing of the period.[3] Similarly, certain colors or shapes held particular meanings—the color green, associated with hope, might therefore be deliberately chosen for a young couple in love, while dagging (zig-zag edging to fabric) was used to indicate someone involved in inappropriate sexual activity. In portraits, too, clothing can be a creation of the artist, and the sitter did not necessarily own or wear the attire in which they are represented. Hiring clothing for a portrait was an option, as was drawing from an artist's own inventory of props or designs.[4] A more likely explanation for the same distinctive cloth of gold fabric appearing in three portraits by Hans Holbein is that the artist used a pattern design rather than that the three different sitters owned clothing made from the same fabric.[5] As Emilie Gordenker has shown, some seventeenth-century Dutch artists (most notably Van Dyck) deliberately mixed fantasy and reality to create clothing for their sitters that was meant to appear classical, literary, or pastoral.[6]

Likewise, commissions sometimes took several years to complete and a date inscribed by the artist may refer to either the year of commencement or completion. New fashions were rarely portrayed as soon as they were invented—sometimes a documentary source can provide a more accurate dating of a new fashion. Round-toed shoes, for example, were remarked on as a fad in 1480, yet were first portrayed in illuminated manuscripts only three years later.[7] Fashions also took time to spread from an urban center to a provincial region, so a dated portrait of a member of the rural gentry can give an inaccurate representation of how long a fashion remained in style among the metropolitan elite. Similarly, older people tended to retain styles popular from their youth long after they had passed from the repertoire of the more fashionable members of society.

Portraits from this period overwhelmingly tend to portray the rich—the influential but restricted circle of people who could afford to commission an expensive work of art. They usually show people wearing their best clothing, perhaps even purchased specifically for the purpose of the portrait, rather than more usual everyday wear, which would generally be of a similar cut and style, but with less expensive fabrics and simpler trimmings. As a result, portraits can give a misleading sense of the richness of clothing, even for members of the aristocracy. Formal clothing, as chosen for a portrait, can also be more old-fashioned than more informal styles that change more frequently.

PAINTINGS

Until the modern period, the majority of western painting was figurative, with different hierarchies of subject matter: history painting (religious and mythological scenes), portraiture, genre painting (showing daily life), landscapes, animal painting, and still life. During the medieval period, religious imagery was most prevalent, while the sixteenth century saw the rising importance of secular history painting including mythological scenes, along with portraiture. During the seventeenth century, landscapes, everyday scenes, animals, and still life became increasingly popular subjects for artists, particularly in Protestant countries, where overtly religious subjects (such as portraits of the Virgin and Child) had largely fallen out of favor (although religious themes could instead be implied through symbolism). When looking at dress, portraiture is obviously of particular importance, although clues about clothing can be found in other genres too.

The depiction of dress in painting was also influenced by the materials used. In the Renaissance paints consisted of a colored pigment mixed with a binding medium. During the fourteenth and fifteenth century, pigments were combined with egg yolk to produce tempera paints. The introduction of oil as a carrier medium resulted in paints that were slower to dry, allowing artists more flexibility and also giving them the opportunity to blend smoothly from one color to the next, enabling them to model form, light, and shade. The earliest use of oil painting is recorded by artists working in Northern Europe, where the medium is associated with the ability to represent fabrics and jewelry with meticulous jewel-like accuracy. Ann Jones and Peter Stallybrass point out how the final painting—and its price—depended on the pigments used, which in turn were graded and selected for the different elements in a composition, with the most expensive often reserved for fabrics and jewelry.[8] The pigments themselves, derived from colored mineral, earth, plant, and animal sources, can change significantly over time. This can, as we will see, give a misleading effect of the color of the clothing portrayed.

Portraits

Portraits can be single, double, or group, and are most frequently found in bust-length, half-length, or full-length formats—the size affected the cost of the commission. The full-length life-size portrait of *Gian Gerolamo Grumelli* by Moroni (Figure. 8.3), which was painted in Bergamo near Venice c. 1560 will have been an expensive and time-consuming undertaking.

The painting has become known as the "Man in Pink", reflecting the distinctive nature of its dominant color and the unity of the sitter's outfit, although a close look reveals how skillfully the artist has represented the subtle variations in texture and decoration across the different components. Grumelli's sleeveless jerkin is constructed from pink silk velvet, embroidered with a delicate silver foliate design and worn over a matching long-sleeved doublet. The canions extending over his thighs from the bottom of the paned trunk hose are made from the same shimmering fabric. Grumelli's hose, held up at the knee by pink garters decorated with white tassels, are of knitted silk while his shoes, decorated with long slashes, are apparently made from velvet. The only items of attire that are not pink are the black sword suspended from a black leather sword belt, a black hat accessorized with pink and white feathers, and a white linen shirt decorated with red embroidery at the collar and cuffs. The distinctive pink pigment presumably represents a real outfit, yet its use is also typical of artists working in the area around Venice, whose use of a broad variety of brilliant pigments reflects the region's importance as a center of trade for exotic materials used in a variety of industries.

Portraitists were the first group of painters to become specialized in one particular genre. From the seventeenth century, the role of the specialist drapery painter also developed. In a busy studio working on a number of commissions simultaneously, the drapery painter was responsible for completing areas of fabric after the subject's face had been completed by the signature artist. This meant that dress took on an even more focal

FIGURE 8.3: *Man in Pink (Gian Gerolamo Grumelli)*, Giovanni Battista Moroni, c. 1560, Fondazione Museo di Palazzo Moroni. Photo: DeAgostini/Getty Images.

role. The Renaissance also saw the development of specific rooms in palaces or country houses dedicated to displaying portraiture.

The development of painted votive portraits, which feature the image of a patron kneeling in devotion within a religious image, was also new during the Renaissance. These usually show the donor in fashionable contemporary dress alongside religious figures attired in classical draperies or the robes of their orders. The *Moreel Triptych*, dated 1484 and painted by Hans Memling (Figure 8.4), is a fine example. This painting is also thought to be the first family group portrait produced in the Netherlands that still survives today. Intended for St. James's Church in Bruges, the triptych was commissioned by Willem Moreel, a local merchant, businessman, and dignitary who held a number of official positions in the city. The central panel portrays St. Christopher carrying the Christ child, flanked by Sts Maurus and Giles (to whom the church was dedicated). The outer panels show, on the left, Willem Moreel with his five sons, and on the right his wife Barbara van Vlaenderberch with eleven of their eventual thirteen daughters, six of whom were painted after the landscape had already been completed.[9] The matriarch and patriarch are guided by their name saints—St. Barbara, identifiable by the tower on

FIGURE 8.4: *Moreel Triptych*, Hans Memling, 1484, Groeninge Museum, Bruges. Photo: Fine Art Images/Heritage Images/Getty Images.

her right arm, and St. William of Maleval, wearing a black Benedictine habit over his soldier's armor.

Barbara van Vlaenderberch wears a black damask gown with a deep U-shaped collar over a black gorget with a rectangular neck, with a white partlet filling the décolletage. A wide red belt and truncated cone headdress over which a fine linen veil is suspended complete her outfit, which is overall relatively restrained.[10] Her eldest daughter, kneeling immediately behind, wears the habit of a Dominican nun, while the second eldest, on the right, wears an adult gown like that of her mother. The younger daughters wear simpler cotes with piped edges and gold frontlets on their heads. One daughter has her name, Maria, printed on her headband.[11] Willem Moreel wears a red tabard lined with fur, and his sons wear gowns lined with fur over high-necked black or red doublets. The donors are easily distinguished from the sacred figures by their dress, which is evidently expensive and fashionable, although not overly ostentatious—entirely appropriate for an altarpiece commissioned by a wealthy and important local family.

Genre Paintings

Although portraits provide a large amount of visual information about dress, they have a number of limitations, some of which can be supplemented with other sources. The standard composition of a portrait showing the figure from the front, often at a slight angle, hides the back of an outfit from view, while the popular bust-length format excludes anything worn below the chest. Genre scenes and topographical views can prove particularly useful in this respect, by showing figures from a variety of angles, as well as the clothing worn by people of a different status, many of whom would not have been able to afford a portrait commission. Genre scenes including figures from different social groups can highlight hierarchical differences in clothing. They also occasionally include figures in the process of dressing or undressing, or doing other activities requiring the removal of clothing, thus giving an insight into the layers worn beneath which are usually hidden in portraits. Moreover, genre scenes can also provide an insight into contemporary practices, social customs, and manners surrounding dress, such as what was worn to bed or how clothing was stored. A number of Dutch landscapes show how linens were laid out to be bleached in the sun, while other scenes show processes involved in textile manufacture, such as lacemaking. A series of paintings by the Leiden artist Isaac Claesz. Van Swanenburg shows the various stages in the wool making process in his home town, including *Het ploten en kammen* (shearing and combing) and *Het vollen en verven* (fulling and dyeing).[12] Landscapes too are sometimes populated with small figures, whose silhouette can be particularly interesting. They can also be a useful means for dating landscape or architectural scenes that contain few other clues.

The Peasant Wedding by Pieter Bruegel the Elder (Figure 8.5) illustrates some of the ways that dress can enhance our understanding of a genre painting and the cultural context that it depicts. A rustic barn serves as the location for a wedding feast in Brabant. The bride is seated at a table beneath a green canopy. She is distinguished by her green clothing, her loose hair with its halo-like headdress, and her demeanor. As custom dictated, she does not eat but instead sits still, eyes cast down, hands clasped. The rest of the figures are shown in action—eating, carrying, pouring, piping—and represent a cross-section of society. On the far right, a wealthy landowner is shown in conversation with a monk who has perhaps just conducted the wedding ceremony. The landowner is recognizable by the sword at his waist (the mark of a gentlemen) and his fashionably cut doublet made of expensive patterned black silk, unlike the plain wool and linen garments worn by the other attendees. The difference in clothing between the peasants and the outsiders (the monk and the landowner) is echoed in their different behaviors. The latter are engaged in eager conversation while the former are focused on the food, with few interpersonal interactions. Dress and body language in conjunction lead the viewer to consider a contrast between the different social manners and priorities of the figures.[13]

FIGURE 8.5: *The Peasant Wedding*, Pieter Bruegel the Elder, 1567, Vienna Kunsthistorisches Museum. Photo: Fine Art Images/Heritage Images/Getty Images.

Apart from the bride, all the women wear unadorned plain linen veils that completely conceal their hair and either hang behind their head or are folded back up to the crown. The men wear a variety of different types of headwear, which suggests that the imaginative appropriation of ordinary dress forms was a common strategy. The cap worn by the piper is decorated with three silver coins, while the young child in the foreground has been given an expensive peacock feather to adorn his oversized hat. One of the figures carrying the makeshift platter of bowls has tied a bunch of white ribbon aglets to his red cap, while his companion uses the upturned brim of his green bonnet to carry his wooden spoon.

The figures are shown from all angles, and the artist has portrayed details about how the clothing was constructed, for example, seams running up the back of the men's hose, and the eyelet holes around the bottom of their doublets through which the garments were laced together. The bagpiper in red and white was originally portrayed with a large codpiece that was painted out sometime after 1622, since it appears in a copy produced by the artist's son in that year. Although there is anecdotal evidence that Pieter Brueghel attended events like that shown here, despite its apparent verisimilitude it is unlikely to represent a particular wedding and will not have been an exact representation of what was worn. As with a portrait, it will have been sanitized and carefully composed by the artist.

Portrait Miniatures

Another specific type of painting, the portrait miniature, was first established during the 1520s at the English and French Renaissance courts. The technique of painting a portrait in miniature developed out of manuscript illumination and the etymology of the name "miniature" is not based on size, but technique (being derived from the Latin *miniare*, to color with red lead —the technique originally used for capital letters in manuscripts).

While their small size and deliberate concentration on facial likeness naturally limits the amount of information about fashion that a miniature can contain (they only rarely show a figure in full-length), an examination of the details of jewelry and neckwear is often revealing. Miniatures were frequently given as private gifts, either as a love token or as a mark of favor from the monarch to his or her subjects. Some were also used as diplomatic gifts from one ruler to another, or to convey a likeness during marriage negotiations. Miniatures were easily transportable and wearable, and were often set into jeweled lockets or elaborate cases. Although some were copies of larger paintings, the majority were painted from life, and their intimate nature—viewed in private and serving as a prompt to the memory of a person in their absence—possibly means that the facial likeness was subject to less idealization and the clothing to less contrivance than a formal portrait intended for public consumption.

Furthermore, occasionally portrait miniatures show people in clothing that might not have been deemed suitable for a full-length portrait. It is probably no coincidence that the two portraits showing English queens in masque dress are both in miniature format.[14] Isaac Oliver's miniature of Anne of Denmark of c. 1610 shows the queen with her hair worn half-loose in curling tendrils over her shoulders, the rest in a complicated arrangement of plaits, pearls, gemstones—quite unlike the formal hairstyle set over pads seen in her other portraits.[15] She wears the mantle over one shoulder which was a common feature of masque dress but which never appears in full-length images of the queen. Similarly, John Hoskins' miniature of Henrietta Maria shows the queen dressed as "Divine Beauty and the Stars" in *Tempe Restor'd*, performed at Whitehall in 1632. Again her hairstyle and feather headdress are unusual departures from contemporary fashions, as are the numerous silver stars decorating her bodice.[16]

Frescoes

Fresco painting had been employed since antiquity, but it enjoyed a revival in the fifteenth century as part of the renewed interest in the classical world, and was used to decorate the walls and ceilings of churches, public buildings, and private homes. In Italy in particular, the significant fresco cycles in both secular and religious buildings provide a wealth of information about fifteenth- and sixteenth-century dress. The church of Santa Maria Novella in Florence contains numerous frescoes designed by leading Renaissance artists in collaboration with important patrons. Among the most celebrated and well preserved are the two cycles by Domenico Ghirlandaio and his team of assistants decorating the Tornabuoni Chapel, the main chancel in the church. Completed between 1485 and 1490, they depict scenes from the life of the Virgin Mary and the life of St John the Baptist, while also incorporating numerous portraits of members of the wealthy Tornabuoni family and their acquaintances, whose patriarch, the banker Giovanni Tornabuoni, was responsible for commissioning the cycles. These members of the Florentine elite appear in contemporary fifteenth-century fashions alongside the biblical figures in the sacred narrative, whose clothing is simpler and more akin to classical drapery. Here the former are presented as detached observers rather than active participants in the scene, and their appearance brings the story into the present, emphasizing the reality of the sacred events.[17]

In *The Birth of the Virgin Mary* (Figure 8.6), clothing is used as a narrative device to instruct the congregation by differentiating between the different characters in the story.

FIGURE 8.6: *The Birth of the Virgin Mary*, Domenico Ghirlandaio, 1486–90, Santa Maria Novella, Florence. Photo: Peter Barritt/Getty Images.

It takes place inside an opulent room decorated with a classical bas-relief frieze of playing putti and intarsia paneling, which the central figures in contemporary dress must have endowed with greater immediacy and relevance. On the right, St. Anne reclines in bed, watching the midwife prepare to bathe her newborn daughter, Mary. On the left, a procession of five young women arrives to congratulate the new mother. The figure leading this group, who stands out because of her elegant dress and her position closest to the central axis of the composition, is the patron's only daughter Lodovica Tornabuoni, who was only fourteen in 1490 when the cycle was completed. Lodovica's dress clearly highlights her importance. Her brocaded gown (*cioppa*) is of the most fashionable cut, with a tight front-laced bodice, square neckline and skirt pleated from the waist, and is constructed of an extremely expensive silk brocaded with gold thread woven with flying eagles and suns with rays.[18] The way in which this garment falls stiffly to the ground, in contrast to the fluttering skirts of the young girl pouring water, reveals the different weights of the fabrics from which they are constructed.[19] Ludovica's trumpet-shaped sleeves are slashed at the elbow and open at the shoulder seam to reveal her white shirt (*camicia*) worn beneath, which is arranged into puffs. The fifteenth-century custom for a married woman to cover her hair in public was not strictly observed in the warmer Italian climate, although Lodovica's youth is suggested here by the absence of a veil. She was married in 1491 and is shown here wearing a distinctive *crocettina* (cross surrounded by pearls) pendant that formed part of her dowry.[20]

Changes in the Physical Appearance of Paintings

One important consideration when interpreting the clothing in a painted representation is how the physical appearance of the picture surface might have changed over the centuries. Certain pigments have a tendency to change appearance and the impact can be accelerated by climatic conditions, particularly exposure to light, moisture, and atmospheric pollution. Moreover, the discoloration may disproportionately affect the different pigments across the paint surface, giving a particularly misleading impression of an artist's intentions, both in terms of the hue of a fabric for example, but also in terms of spatial regression and three-dimensionality.

Organic pigments derived from plants and animals tend to discolor most, in particular red lakes, yellow lakes, and indigo. The effect is clearly seen in the *Portrait of the St. Adrian Civic Guard* c. 1630 (Figure 8.7).[21] The Netherlandish *schutterij* or civic guard were voluntary defensive organizations whose membership consisted of wealthy citizens appointed by the magistrates. Militia group portraits of this type (known as *schuttersstukken*) were commissioned when the membership changed—each officer contributed to the artist's fee and is clearly individualized to commemorate his prestigious role. The officers shown here had just completed their three-year tenure. The figures are shown descending the staircase of their meeting hall, the St. Adrian Gallery in Haarlem, led by the Colonel of the troop, Pieter Jacobsz Olycan, who can be identified by his orange sash. The Ensign (flag bearer) was always a young bachelor, usually shown more extravagantly dressed than the other figures. Here Ensign Saloman Colterman appears on the right, wearing a white silk doublet patterned with flowers (in November of 1630 he married and had to resign from the post).

The very pale greyish-blue sashes worn by several other officers were painted with indigo, a pigment that is particularly prone to fading on exposure to light. A small section of one of the sashes that was covered by the frame reveals that originally the paint was a

FIGURE 8.7: *Portrait of the St. Adrian Civic Guard*, Hendrick Gerritsz Pot, c. 1630, Frans Hals Museum, Haarlem. Photo: Margareta Svensson.

much brighter shade of blue. This has an impact on the aesthetics of the painting (the sashes do not stand out as they once would have, and show shallower three-dimensional modeling), but also on its meaning, since it is now not immediately obvious that the colors worn correspond closely to those of the state flag—dark orange, white, and blue.[22] The blue sashes are better preserved on the left side of the painting than on the right, probably due to the fact that during the eighteenth century the painting hung to the left of a large window in the hall of the St. Adrian civic guard. In other militia group portraits, for example *The Banquet of the Officers of the St. Adrian Militia Company in 1627* by Frans Hals, the blue sashes show a better level of preservation, probably due to a combination of factors including thickness of the paint layer and exposure to light. Interestingly, when used as a textile dye, indigo does not display such fugitive properties as when used in paintings.

Other changes to pigments over time can also distort the visual impact of a painting today. For example, tiny touches of silver, often used to recreate the shine of pearls in miniature paintings, have a tendency to oxidize, giving the impression of dark beads making up a necklace instead of the creamy white lustrous pearls originally intended. The oil used as a carrier medium can become discolored and yellow, turning blues green. Likewise, the varnish used to cover the finished painting and make the surface shine can also discolor over the years and lend a painting an excessively brown hue. These changes are accidental. Sometimes, however, the clothing in a painting is deliberately retouched, occasionally by the original artist but more usually by subsequent generations so that the styles fit the current prevailing aesthetic. Furthermore, nineteenth-century restoration and cleaning with strong abrasives and solvents has sometimes removed subtleties, leading to a distorted visual appearance in the surface textures of fabrics. All changes, whether deliberate or accidental, must be borne in mind when interpreting a painting as visual evidence for historical dress.

ILLUMINATED MANUSCRIPTS

The fourteenth and fifteenth centuries saw the peak production of illuminated books, with the main centers being firstly located in Paris and, by the mid-fifteenth century, Flanders. The earliest were religious (Bibles and Books of Hours), although the emphasis became increasingly secular in the fifteenth century, with new translations of classical texts, romances, and historical accounts. The invention of the printing press and moveable type stimulated the decline in manuscript production by the mid-sixteenth century. However, large numbers of manuscripts survive from the fifteenth century and provide a wealth of information about fashions from the period. Their colors are particularly brilliant, having been protected from light damage within the closed pages. They often show many different types of people, both rich and poor, dressed for numerous different situations and climates. However, they also frequently combine figures in fashionable dress alongside others wearing (sometimes inaccurate) historicizing or invented clothing. Sometimes historical events are placed within the context of contemporary society.

An illumination of *Philosophy Presenting the Seven Liberal Arts to Boethius*, attributed to the Coëtivy Master, which dates from c. 1460–70 (Figure 8.8), is typical in depicting classical and allegorical figures in clothing familiar to an elite Renaissance readership. The original text, *The Consolation of Philosophy* by the Roman philosopher and statesman Boethius (c. 480–524), was written in prison c. 524 while he was awaiting trial for treason, and was one of the most widely read works during the Middle Ages and Renaissance. Here Boethius is shown on the left speaking to Philosophy, who presents him with the personification of the seven liberal arts, each of whom is shown with their attribute: Grammar (book), Rhetoric (scroll), Logic (patterned wheel), Music (musical notation),

FIGURE 8.8: *Philosophy Presenting the Seven Liberal Arts to Boethius*, Coëtivy Master (Henri de Vulcop?), c. 1460–70. The J. Paul Getty Museum, Los Angeles.

Geometry (set square and measure), Arithmetic (scroll with symbols), and Astronomy (armillary sphere). Despite representing a late Roman text, the illustrator shows the female figures dressed in various different styles of clothing and headwear popular at the Burgundian court in the late fifteenth century. Astronomy wears a steeple-shaped hat draped with a fine transparent veil, Music is shown in a small gold pillbox-type padded hat known as a *bourrelet*, while Geometry wears a rather unusual tall folded *bourrelet*. Grammar and Rhetoric have chosen simple veils of thick linen to cover their hair and are also dressed in the most basic styles of clothing—a simple cloak and gown. As befits her senior rank, Philosophy as leader of the group wears the tallest, most complicated headdress—an M-shaped kite-like *hennin* constructed on shaped wires, evidently heavily starched, and worn over a gold steeple-shaped cap. As Margaret Scott notes, this also fits with Boethius's description of her as seeming to touch the sky.[23] While some of the women are dressed in simple gowns others are more ornate. Geometry, for instance, wears a V-necked green gown trimmed with gold at the neckline and hem, with a wide black belt encircling the high waistline. One side of the gown is tucked up to stop it trailing along the ground as she walks. Boethius wears a floor-length pink gown trimmed with fur at the hem and wrists, and a red cap. Again, he is not shown as a fifth-century Roman but in a traditional style of clothing worn by older men during the second half of the fifteenth century, which vaguely recalls academic dress.[24]

DRAWINGS

The increasing focus on naturalism and direct observation of the world, which was such a key feature of the Renaissance, resulted in the flourishing of drawing as a medium. Technology too had an impact—an increased supply of paper during the fifteenth century provided an alternative to costly parchment derived from animal skin, while print-making techniques provided a means by which works on paper could be easily replicated and disseminated. Renaissance drawings served numerous purposes, from allowing an artist to work up early ideas for a composition, to capturing the transitory appearance of a loved one, or the form of a sculpture or building. Some drawings were intended only for the artist's eyes. Others, known as *modelli*, were shown to patrons for appraisal, whose increasing involvement in the development of large fresco or painting commissions during the Renaissance, together with a greater emphasis placed on originality and creativity in design from the artist, necessitated regular discussions about both concept and composition.[25] In this way drawings served as visual aids to be adjusted and refined as necessary. Some costume designs by Inigo Jones in England and Bernardo Buontalenti in Italy were evidently produced to be shown to the patron of a theatrical production for approval, occasionally providing them with options from which to choose.[26]

Many artists made studies of figures, which were then incorporated into a final painting or print, sometimes serving as standard patterns to be reused as many times as necessary. Albrecht Dürer was evidently fascinated by the intricacies of dress, both male and female. His drawings of Irish peasants and soldiers show that this interest straddled social classes and nationalities.[27] A series of pen and ink drawings shows the women of Nuremberg attired for various occasions. *Nuremberg Lady Dressed for the Home* (Figure 8.9) is thought to date from c. 1500 and was probably modeled by Dürer's wife Agnes.[28] The woman's bodice has long sleeves covering her wrists and a neckline concealed by a cape-like collar (*Gollar*) probably of wool, decorated with black braid or embroidery,

FIGURE 8.9: *A Woman of Nuremberg Dressed for the Home*, Albrecht Dürer, c. 1500, Veneranda Biblioteca Ambrosiana. Photo: DEA/G. CIGOLINI/VENERANDA BIBLIOTECA AMBROSIANA/De Agostini/Getty Images.

trimmed (and possibly also lined) with white fur, and fastened with a brooch.[29] Over her skirt she wears a finely pleated linen apron and a pouch purse hangs from the leather girdle around her waist. Her hair is completely covered by a fine linen veil or *Steuchlein*, which was standard attire for married German women of all classes, and is tied at the nape of the neck. It is worn over a large padded support cap beneath known as a *Wulsthaube*. She carries a handkerchief in her left hand. This drawing reveals interesting details about clothing construction, for example, that the pleated apron continues above the girdle and is apparently suspended from the neck. It also shows features of everyday dress, like the leather pouch, which might not necessarily have been included in a formal painted portrait.

PRINTS

Prints allow the reproduction of multiple images from a single matrix, and the rapid growth in the print-making market during the Renaissance was the key means by which visual information was spread throughout Europe. Prints were used to convey the appearance of a work of art, the facial likeness of a person, or a fashionable style of foreign clothing. They often contain particularly revealing details about dress, as line becomes more important in the absence of color. However, although many prints are dated, using this as evidence for the date of the clothing portrayed can be problematic. Prints were often republished at a later point, sometimes with changes which resulted in the production of various different versions or "states," and the date inscribed may represent either the original or the later year. Prints were also sometimes based on paintings dating from much earlier, so the date on a print may suggest that a fashion persisted for much longer than was actually the case.

Prints by Abraham Bosse are particularly invaluable resources, given that they invariably show bourgeois figures in the contemporary fashions and surroundings of seventeenth-century France, even when the subject matter is traditional or biblical. *La Galerie du Palais* by Bosse (Figure 8.10) represents three of the small arcaded shops found in the Palais de Justice on the Ile de la Cité in Paris in the 1630s.

Based on a play by Corneille entitled *La Galerie* of 1632, Bosse shows the elegantly dressed men and women browsing the items on offer.[30] On the right the seamstress's shop includes standing bands, falling bands, tuckers, pinners, and cuffs, which are pinned on display and contained within stacked boxes. The mercer's stall in the center offers gloves, ribbons, masks, muffs, and fans. Three of Bosse's own designs for fans still exist and the seller selects a box marked *"eventails de Bosse."*[31] Such prints do not simply show what was worn—they also show how fashion was integrated with the behavior and manners of

FIGURE 8.10: *The Gallery of the Palace of Justice (La Galerie du Palais)*, Abraham Bosse, c. 1638. The Metropolitan Museum of Art, New York: www.metmuseum.org.

daily life. Bosse's depiction of shopping both as a spectacle and a social activity—and as a new sphere of public life in which women were active participants—is echoed in a growing number of literary and visual sources from the seventeenth century onwards, including Ben Jonson's *Epicoene or the Silent Woman* of 1609–10.[32]

Although the fashionable clothing represented in this print matches that in other visual and literary sources, some satirical prints use exaggeration to highlight elements of dress subject to contemporary social comment. The pitfalls of a search for fashionability are a recurring theme of ridicule. While a deliberate casual negligence in dress was highly fashionable during the 1630s, the extreme to which it is taken in some of Bosse's disheveled and undone cavaliers suggest an element of theatricality and mockery which must be acknowledged. Satires can, however, be a particularly useful aid in gaging social reactions to fashionable styles, which were evidently deemed noteworthy enough to parody.

The sixteenth century saw the introduction of the first costume books, which were illustrated with prints.[33] These can be considered the precursors to the true fashion plates which first appeared in France in the late seventeenth century, and demonstrate the fascination with exploration and classification that was a broader feature of the Renaissance. The most well-known early costume books were those by Abraham De Bruyn (Antwerp 1581), Jean Jacques Boissard (Paris 1581), and Vecellio (Venice 1590 and 1598). Systematically and hierarchically organized, they show figures from a variety of nationalities, cities, and social positions, and were a source of inspiration for fashionable men and women, costume designers and artists, while also circulating styles of dress internationally. The documentary value of the portrayals, however, must always be tempered with an understanding that they often propagated stereotypical conceptions of the clothing worn in each country, and that the artist may sometimes have been working on verbal descriptions rather than direct observation. By his own admission in his opening "Discorso" to Book II, Vecellio says that his representations of dress in Asia and Africa are based on second-hand reports rather than evidence of his own eyes or dependable testimony.[34]

TAPESTRIES

This chapter has so far focused on the traditional flat arts—painting on canvas, panel, plaster or parchment, and drawing or printing onto paper. However, what are now often described as the decorative arts, a category into which dress itself falls, frequently depicted a variety of clothing forms. Tapestries reached an extraordinary level of detail and skill in the fifteenth century, and were far more highly valued during the Renaissance than paintings. Like paintings, they often incorporated figures in contemporary dress, even when portraying historical subjects. The key centers for tapestry production in the period were France and the Low Countries, in particular Arras and Tournai. Woven on a loom, tapestries were often copied from a full-scale cartoon that was hung behind the warps. Cartoons themselves are rare survivals, as they were usually created on paper and reused multiple times, or cut into pieces to make the transfer of the design more manageable. Tapestries, too, are subject to particular pressures, the dyes used for the threads often being even more prone to fading than in paintings, and the wool in particular being affected by mold and insect damage.

The Unicorn is Found is the second tapestry from The Unicorn Tapestries series in New York (Figure 8.11). Analysis of the clothing of the figures has been important in establishing

FIGURE 8.11: *The Unicorn is Found (from The Unicorn Tapestries)*, 1495–1505. The Metropolitan Museum of Art, New York: www.metmuseum.org.

a date range for the tapestries (c. 1495–1505)—in particular the shape of the round-toed shoes worn by the men and the hairstyles. Dress also provides clues to the identity and roles of the various figures in the hunting party, and so is an aid to the narrative. Here the lord of the hunt appears in the top right wearing a red hat decorated with a large plume, a doublet made of cloth of gold woven with a pomegranate design, and a gold chain around his neck. The lymerer appears in the left foreground—he is responsible for questing the game and holds his specially-trained scenting dog on a lead while pointing to the unicorn. He wears protective knee-high leather leggings over his blue hose, as recommended in the popular hunting guide, *La Livre de la Chasse (Book of the Hunt)* by Gaston Phébus of 1387, to guard against brambles and thorns.[35] The level of detail contained within the tapestries is extraordinary and indicates many intricate features of clothing construction, including seams up the back of hose, ribbon points fastening codpieces, and ornate knots on the leather straps of the hunting horns. Nevertheless, despite this detailed rendition of the clothing worn in a Renaissance hunt, the styles are likely to have been idealized. The men wear a huge range of different doublets, hose, hats, and footwear, which lend variety and interest to the composition, but whose variations are likely to have been exaggerated for visual effect.

SCULPTURE

Unlike the two-dimensional visual sources discussed so far, sculpture modeled in the round allows a three-dimensional representation of a clothed figure. Many new sculptural forms were developed in this period, including the revival of the classical portrait bust, which became popular in the fifteenth century and was produced in a wide range of materials including marble, polychromed wood, wax, terracotta, and bronze. Dating from 1453, Figure 8.12 is the earliest securely dated Renaissance marble bust.[36]

It represents Piero de Medici and was originally placed in a niche above a door in the Palazzo Medici. The sitter is shown wearing a sleeveless tunic over a velvet doublet woven in a pomegranate design in a number of different piles. The border of the tunic is decorated with diamond rings, a Medici device symbolizing strength and fidelity. While the individualized nature of this marble bust is influenced by antique sculpture, truncating the figure horizontally across the arms and including such fine details of clothing are new innovations.[37] Unlike antique examples, most fifteenth-century male portrait busts are inscribed beneath on a *cartellino* bearing the name of the sitter, artist, and date which is useful when interpreting the dress portrayed. One limitation of much Renaissance sculpture, however, is that it often shows men clothed in classically-inspired armor, as seen in the bust of Piero de Medici's younger brother Giovanni, rather than the contemporary fashions worn by Piero.[38]

FIGURE 8.12: *Piero de Medici*, Mino da Fiesole, 1453–4, marble, Museo Nazionale del Bargello, Florence. Photo:y DeAgostini/Getty Images.

CONCLUSION

Technical innovations, coupled with cultural changes associated with the Renaissance, meant that a wider variety of visual material was produced in Europe than ever before. Growing interest in individualization evidenced in the rise of portraiture as a genre was reflected both in the facial features of a subject, and also the details of his or her attire. Given the scarcity of surviving clothing examples from the period, these visual sources are of huge value. While this chapter has focused on the most significant sources, others such as ceramics, stained glass, mosaics, and embroidery can also prove revealing.

Visual sources do not, however, replace the value of extant garments. Nor should they be considered in isolation, but are best compared alongside literary and documentary sources, including accounts of household spending, letters, memoirs, contemporary publications and social commentary. Very occasionally, the literary and visual sources can be aligned, as in the case of the clothing worn in a miniature by Isaac Oliver of 1616, *Richard Sackville, 3rd Earl of Dorset* (Figure 3.7). The Sackville inventory of 1617 clearly describes some elements of this outfit in detail, including the trunk hose: "Item one paire of Bullen hose of Scarlett and blew velvet the panes of Scarlett laced all over with watchett silk silver and gold lace and the puffs of blew velvett embroidered all over with sonnes Moones and stares of gold." However, in the inventory, the suit consists of only five matching items (hose, gloves, stockings, hatband, and boothose) and does not include the doublet, shoe roses, girdle, and sword hanger seen in the miniature.[39] The discrepancy is perhaps explained by the fact that at this date, the Earl was heavily in debt and had sold many of his possessions.

Just as many of the artistic forms explored in this chapter showed an interest in depicting earlier styles of dress, particularly classical ones, so this impulse continued well after this period. Types of clothing worn during the fifteenth, sixteenth, and seventeenth centuries were of interest to later generations of artists such as Gainsborough, whose sitters in "Vandyke" dress wore clothing based on the styles of the 1630s.[40] However, nineteenth- and twentieth-century "redrawings," in costume books and encyclopedias, can produce a very inaccurate, distorted, and sentimentalized view of Renaissance clothing. Women in such illustrations, for example, sometimes display the sloping shoulders revealed by ogee necklines and low pinched waistlines deemed attractive during the mid-Victorian period, which completely change the fit of a Tudor bodice.[41] The dress historian must always be certain therefore that they are looking at a true Renaissance source, not a later interpretation, one which imposes the aesthetics of its own period in terms of construction, color or even body type onto those of the past.

CHAPTER NINE

Literary Representations

GERRY MILLIGAN

Roland Barthes famously explained that fashion was a language that had a material vocabulary and grammar, but he also insisted that fashion acquired its meaning through the written language found in magazines, newspapers, and advertisements.[1] In the Italian Renaissance, certain texts described dress in ways that Barthes might have also recognized as fashion literature. These works included costume books such as Cesare Vecellio's *Clothing of the Ancients and Moderns* (1590, revised 1598) and Giacomo Franco's *Clothing of Venetian Women* (1610), both of which contained images and narratives that defined the dress of numerous social categories and professions of people. There were also more didactic texts that were concerned with dress, and of these, the most influential was Baldesare Castiglione's *Book of the Courtier* (1528). This widely translated work about the ideal courtier was also a revolutionary book in fashion history. It offered an insightful analysis of dress and behavior, and it identified a phenomenon of dress that closely resembles what we know today as fashion. Indeed, Eugenia Paulicelli argues that the first modern conceptualization of fashion was established in Italy around the time of and principally via Castiglione.[2] The Italian fashion system was thus well established by the time the word *moda* made its first appearance in Agostino Lampugnani's treatise *The Rented Carriage or of clothing and fashionable habits* (1648).[3]

What we know about dress and fashion in the Italian Renaissance is principally thanks to the work of art and material historians, who have explored how clothing was produced, worn, and regulated, as well as how individuals and communities crafted identities through economies of clothing. Scholars of Italian literature have also contributed to this discourse, and thanks to a select number of studies, we are able to locate the masterpieces of the Renaissance as coordinates on the map of the modern fashion system.[4] To varying degrees, such historians and literary scholars have concerned themselves with what texts (literary and otherwise) can tell us about clothing in the Renaissance. The hermeneutics of dress in the Italian context has instead been left to a number of dispersed articles, and it awaits a more systematic study. As an attempt to synthesize certain elements of dress across Renaissance Italian literature, the current chapter will look not only at texts that overtly discuss dress but also at those that use dress as a meta-narrative device for reading and writing, and particularly for crafting the politics of identity. We begin by addressing the hermeneutics of literary metaphors of dress and in particular the role of the veil as both metaphor and material sign of literary identity construction. The second half of the chapter will then turn to the phenomenon of sartorial and identity transformation.

DRESS AND THE HERMENEUTICAL PROCESS

When Petrarch translated the famous tale of Griselda, the last novella in Boccaccio's *Decameron*, he wrote to Boccaccio to tell him that he had "changed the garment of the Italian" by clothing the story in Latin.[5] The metaphor of literature as clothing was not new to Petrarch. He had already explored the relationship in *Canzoniere* 125 and 126 where he addressed his texts as women who needed to be properly attired to go in public. In the last verses of poem 126 he states, "If you were to have the ornaments you desire, you could boldly leave this wood and go among people" (126, vv. 66–8).[6] In these early beginnings of humanism, Petrarch claimed that the Latin language and the craft of poetry were the clothing and jewels of literature, and thus we might consider him as a literary tailor, one who dressed his text for public view. Not only do his metaphors in both the novella and poem speak to the notion that women were to be clothed by men for public view, they also suggest that texts—and by implication people—were also fundamentally changed by ornament and dress. Clothing, like literature, had the potential not only to be transformed but to transform.

Two centuries later, the poet Ludovico Ariosto described not his choice of Latin but his narrative technique of weaving plot lines as that of crafting a *gran tela* (great cloth) (13.81).[7] Ariosto called his poem, the *Orlando furioso*, a "cloth" not a "tapestry" as it is so often translated, and the distinction is important, for cloth, unlike a tapestry, is implicitly a material to be fashioned and refashioned.[8] In contrast to Petrarch, Ariosto challenges himself, the characters, and the reader to fashion and design this cloth into meaning.

This process is exemplified in Canto 26, when a knight battles for possession of the woman, Marfisa. In this episode, the female knight Marfisa wears feminine dress instead of her usual armor. An enemy knight sees Marfisa and makes the assumption that she is a woman who can be won by defeating her male companions. After unhorsing the men in Marfisa's company, he proceeds to claim Marfisa as his possession, since, in his assessment, it is his right as both male and victor. Marfisa, still dressed in feminine clothing, then explains that such actions would typically be permissible, but she is not the lady that her dress might imply (26.79). After her speech, Marfisa removes her dress and prepares to put on her armor. Ariosto interrupts the sartorial transformation and tells us that when clothed in only a doublet, Marfisa's identity was already changed: "her handsome, well-proportioned body, all but her face, took on a likeness to Mars" (26.80).[9] The narrator describes a hybrid body determined by clothing, and it is telling that Marfisa's gendered identity is for a second time projected onto her by a gazing male other.

In this episode, Ariosto comments on the struggle between dress, social identity, and agency. The scene is unlike typical literary transvestism since in this case, the viewer did not mistake Marfisa's gendered identity. When the knight came upon her, Marfisa was a woman who was in a sense masquerading in women's clothing. The discontinuity between Marfisa and her feminine dress underscores her difference from social norms. Indeed, when she boldly refuses to be a passive participant in the economy where women are traded between men, her first act of defiance is the removal of her feminine dress. What is unclear, however, is whether feminine dress is the sign of women's vulnerability or the means by which women become vulnerable. In episodes such as this, Ariosto prompts the reader to also consider his or her own role in the process of identity construction. Does the author clothe and transform identity (as in Petrarch), or does the reader create meaning by projecting desires onto individuals so that identity might fit into social categories (imperfect as they may be)? To what extent might individuals resist such categories or merely exchange one costume for another? It is to this tension among author, reader, desire, identity, and dress that we will now turn.

THE VEIL

Perhaps the most problematic of garments in Renaissance literature was the veil. The veil was not only a ubiquitous object in the early Italian literary tradition, it was also the item of dress that was most frequently used as a metaphor to signify the self-reflexive acts of writing and reading.[10] The veil appears in texts as a material garment as well as a metaphor, and as a metaphor it could be understood theologically as the corporeal veil of the soul or in more straightforward cases as Christian piety. Moreover, the veil could also signify the obfuscation of truth, and for Dante, this item of dress was also a metaphor for the text itself. In a memorable moment in the *Comedy*, Dante addresses the reader to perceive truth beneath his veil of poetry: "Look now and see the meaning that is hidden/beneath the veil of my strange verses" (*Inf.* 9.62–3).[11]

Petrarch, more than Dante, appropriated the metaphor of the veil to represent the antitheses of opacity and transparency, secular and sacred. Writers and visual artists after Petrarch drew on his characterization of the veil as a sign of human contradiction. Agnolo Bronzino's portrait of the poet Laura Battiferri, who wears a transparent veil and holds a book of Petrarch's sonnets is but one example of how the veil can be read in oppositional (i.e. erotic and chaste) ways (Figure 9.1).

FIGURE 9.1: *Portrait of Laura Battiferri*, Agnolo Bronzino, c. 1555, oil on canvas, Palazzo Vecchio, Florence. Photo: DeAgostini/Getty Images.

FIGURE 9.2: *Diana and Actaeon*, Titian, 1556–9, oil on canvas, The National Gallery London/ The National Galleries of Scotland. Photo: National Galleries of Scotland/Getty Images.

Petrarch's poetic veil also laid the foundation for the innovative conceptions of the veil that we find in Leon Battista Alberti's explanation of optics. For Alberti, a veil not only obscured truth, it could clarify it. In his treatise *On Painting*, Alberti instructs the would-be artist to view through a veil any object he wished to reproduce. Nothing, Alberti insists, is "more convenient than that veil" to make imitation possible since one can see the contours and outlines best when perceived through its fibers.[12] Alberti's material veil might at first seem to share nothing with Dante's veil of poetry that must be lifted or Petrarch's veil of contradictions, but they do indeed provoke the same function. All of these veils beckon the reader to gaze—perhaps to read—for these veils must be read for one to conceptualize if not the truth at least the artistic representation of the truth.

With regards to Petrarch's poetry, Margaret Brose has argued that as we move from Dante to Petrarch, the veil as article of dress transitions from allegory to fetish, and it becomes the "rematerialized site of desire" compensating for the loss of the transcendental body.[13] It is an eroticization of the veil of chastity, an early example of the shift that Paulicelli has pointed out as occurring in the Cinquecento, as the veil moved from symbol of the sacred to a secular accessory.[14] Throughout Petrarch's *Canzoniere*, the veil is fetishized and comes to substitute the woman entirely. This process is particularly evident in poem 52, the famous madrigal of Actaeon and Diana. In the myth as told by Ovid, Actaeon happens on the virgin goddess Diana with her nymphs bathing in a pool. Angered by his gaze, Diana changes Actaeon into a stag, and he, unable to speak, is subsequently devoured by his hounds. Petrarch revises the Ovidian myth so that his beloved does not bathe her body but instead washes her veil. The gazing poet fixates not on a naked woman but on the cloth between her hands:

> Diana never pleased her lover more,
> when just by chance all of her naked body
> he saw bathing within the chilly waters,
> than did the simple mountain shepherdess
> please me, the while she bathed the pretty veil
> that holds her lovely blonde hair in the breeze. (52.1–6)[15]

The veil of Diana and the fetishized veil in general continued to feature in art and literature after Petrarch. In a particularly Petrarchan mode, Titian's painting of this same Ovidian myth, *Diana and Actaeon* (1556–9), multiplies the veil from one to many, a concept that is emphasized by the reflection of Diana's veil in water (Figure 9.2).[16]

Moreover, the painting plays with the various viewpoints of the male subject: Actaeon and a presumably male viewer. While Acteon handily swipes away a red veil-like fabric, and while he is positioned so that he sees Diana directly before him, the viewer of the painting instead finds Diana's body in the moment of turning away. Thus the viewer, perhaps more than Actaeon, is likened to Petrarch; he is compelled to see the veil, indeed multiple veils (and multiple women) as the fetishized sign of Diana's naked body.

The Veil in Tasso's Aminta

The significance of the veil in literature reaches an apex in Torquato Tasso's hugely influential pastoral play, *Aminta* (performed 1573). The veil signifies female chastity and sexuality, the instability of identity, and the human limitations of discerning truth. Laden with such meaning, Tasso's veil is much like the handkerchief of Shakespeare's *Othello*, the "ocular proof" of Desdemona's infidelity, a proof that in Shakespeare is ultimately and tragically unreliable.[17] In Tasso as in Shakespeare, when identity is metaphorically woven into cloth, it provides the catalyst for real and even violent events.

The plot of *Aminta* revolves around the love of the play's namesake for the chaste nymph, Silvia. She disdains the love of all men, and her veil, as in Petrarch, is the crucial cloth that separates her body from men or quite literally from the gaze of men. Jane Tylus has noted the centrality of the veil to the play, and her argument centers on Tasso's presentation of the veil as a symbol for dissimulation and as a modern invention.[18] The Golden Age of unveiled pleasure is continually contrasted to the impenetrable modern age, and the veil becomes both symbol and instrument for the internalization, dissimulation, and restraint of desire, the hallmarks of Tasso's vision of the modern era.[19] The chorus sings that in the Golden Age, "the nude, young virgin would display her fresh roses that now a veil conceals" (I. chorus. 598–601).[20]

Silvia's own innocent use of the veil is called into question by the more cynical nymph, Daphne, who claims that Silvia embellished her veil while gazing in a pool to attract men's attention: "She bent, and it appeared as though she was in love with herself, and sought counsel from the water as to how she should arrange her hair, and above her hair her veil, and above her veil her flowers" (II.ii.134–40).[21] If Tasso complicates women's use of the veil by suggesting that it both obstructed and attracted lovers, he also extends this ambivalence to men.

Aminta, though a seemingly naive lover, once feigned a bee sting on his lip to receive a kiss of pity from Silvia. His history of deception places his naiveté in doubt, and it becomes difficult to determine if Aminta is indeed innocent or continuing his proven method of seducing Silvia through pity. This uncertainty comes to the fore during the play's most eventful moment, when we hear that Aminta and his friend Tirsi discover Silvia in the woods, where she is being held and tied naked to a tree by a Satyr. Silvia is a vulnerable, naked and shackled woman, and much is made of the fact that Aminta diverts his eyes while untying her. Tylus has argued that his behavior reflects an internalized code of restraint that veils the otherwise naked woman.[22] This is the "veil" of civility that modern society had imposed on the court. It is perhaps even more effective than the actual diaphanous material cloth, for this restraint is much like the veil "honor" that is decried in the chorus of Act I: "You, honor, first veiled the fountains of delight . . . teaching beautiful eyes to gaze downward" (I.chorus.603–11).

After Silvia is untied and flees into the woods, it is her actual veil that enacts a central plot shift. A nymph claims that Silvia must have been killed by wolves, and as proof she shows the torn veil to the characters and spectators of the play: "Here is her veil!" This moment is one of the very few actions in this narrative play, and it is highlighted in the engraving in the Aldine edition of 1583 (Figure 9.3). In the woodcut, Silvia's body tied to a tree (a scene not actually staged) is shown in the foreground, but in the center of the image, in the background, is the messenger holding the torn veil. The image highlights how

FIGURE 9.3: *Aminta*, 1573, Satyr trying to rape Silvia, act III, engraving, Torquato Tasso, Aldine edition, 1583. Photo: DEA PICTURE LIBRARY/De Agostini/Getty Images.

Aminta takes possession of the veil, a cloth that in Tasso, as in Petrarch, stands in for Silvia's body. Suggestively, the veil is one of the few props in the play, and the material stability of this sign is countered by the ever-shifting meaning of what it signifies. Of course, it is also a sign that has been misread, for Silvia is alive.

In his misery, Aminta attempts what may or may not be a sincere attempt at suicide, and the play ends with Silvia finally conceding to Aminta out of pity. The message of the play and more specifically of the veil is left in intentional ambiguity. We question whether Aminta had believed Silvia's veil to truly be impenetrable or whether he had dissimulated his strategy of seduction. It was, after all, his use of a veil that ultimately won him the prize of Silvia. We cannot know if Aminta was the innocent shepherd who diverted his eyes to cover Silvia with a "veil" of honor or whether he had become a modern lover, dissimulating desire under a veil of feigned respect. Perhaps for Tasso, these two veils had become indistinguishable.

As we reflect on the veil in Tasso, we can see why this accessory became so popular in literary texts. The veil lent itself as material metaphor for the uncertainty and ambiguity of the human condition. The veil could be worn to signify feigned innocence or feigned authenticity. This deception was not necessarily negative, but rather, it was a generative mediator of fictions. The veil was a tool that allowed characters to claim innocence while operating in the realm of modern and courtly dissimulation. In effect, the veil was the remaining vestige of innocence—or at least sign of innocence—that could exist in a world of dissimulation.

The Veil and Identity: Prostitutes and Nuns

Even the material veil took on metaphorical and antithetical meanings. Following custom as well as sumptuary regulations, widows, nuns, prostitutes, and unmarried virgins were identified by their veils. According to Giacomo Lanteri's *Della Economica* (1560), a Venetian law required unmarried women to wear veils so that "men could distance themselves from lasciviousness and therefore not become effeminate and soft, but would be virile and robust with their souls and bodies."[23] Lanteri claims women would cover their faces with veils but, contrary to the intentions of the lawmakers, they would also pull their dresses down to show so much cleavage that "they appear to be more lascivious than they would appear had they not worn the veil at all."[24] According to Lanteri, instead of marking the chastity of unmarried women, the veil signified women's sexual availability.

For very different reasons, laws were also regularly passed that imposed veils on prostitutes. These regulations were meant to provide visual distinctions between noblewomen and courtesans, who had amassed considerable wealth and wardrobes. It was not uncommon for prostitutes to be required to wear yellow veils, a color that had been used to mark marginalized groups since the Middle Ages.[25] The difficulty of distinguishing prostitutes from "ladies" was noted in several texts, including Vecellio's *Clothing, Ancient and Modern, of Various parts of the World* (1590, revised 1598): "Modern Roman courtesans dress in such fine style that few people can tell them apart from the noblewomen of the city."[26]

Vecellio's narrative and images of courtesans expose how desire and anxiety over dress might be related. Indeed, the visual similarity of the courtesan and noblewoman was both a cause for unease and erotic pleasure. Such ambivalence is suggested in Vecellio's discussion of Venetian women. Vecellio shows that Venetian courtesans look much like widows, both wearing veils of considerable length. In his depictions of the two types of

FIGURE 9.4: *Habiti antichi: overo raccolta di figure delineate dal gran Titiano, e da Cesare Vecellio suo fratello, diligentemente intagliate, conforme alle nationi del mondo*. Cesare Vecellio (Venice, Combi and la Noù, appresso capo Francesco Bodio, 1664). Image courtesy Hathi Trust.

women, however, it is action not clothing that distinguishes them. The courtesans are shown peeking out from their veil as well as slightly lifting their skirt[27] (Figure 9.4).

The similar appearance of prostitutes to widows could also imply a shared status of independence (Figure 9.5). Widows were a category of women, like prostitutes, who could navigate the world in a somewhat autonomous fashion, outside the control of husband or father. The anxiety and/or erotic impulse that was caused by the proximity of the widow's appearance to a prostitute was suggestive enough to inspire artists to frequently depict the image of the prostitute peeking out from a widow's garments.

This ambivalence of sexual promiscuity and devout widowhood was reflected in literary texts beyond costume books as well. Giovanni Boccaccio's *Corbaccio* (c. 1355) tells of a widow who would go to church and lift her veil in the presence of men since she knew that her white face would look beautiful against black cloth.[28] On the other hand, Stefano Guazzo's *Civil Conversation* (1574) claimed that veiled widows were simply the targets of infamy regardless of their actions: "the most wise and honest widows are a continual target of stinging tongues, and it seems that the more these unfortunate women cover their heads and cover their eyes with their black veils, the more the desire flames up

LITERARY REPRESENTATIONS 183

FIGURE 9.5: *Théâtre de tous les peuples et nations de la terre avec leurs habits et ornemens divers, tant anciens que modernes, diligemment depeints au naturel par Luc Dheere peintre et sculpteur Gantois* (manuscript), Lucas d'Heere (1534–84). Image courtesy Universiteitsbibliotheek, Gent Library.

in the spirits of others to try and find some fault in them."[29] The veil, it seemed, could not guarantee a woman the identity of modesty it was meant to signal.

The most obvious category of women associated with the veil was nuns; indeed the phrase "to take the veil" signified becoming a nun in the sixteenth century just as it does today. However, as the writer and nun Arcangela Tarabotti (1604–52) reminds us, many young women were forced to take the veil against their wishes. In Tarabotti's summation, the ritualistic vestments were not only a costume; they made a mockery of religious conviction. She states that in the past, girls who were unhappy with being a nun could leave the convent, but in her own day, she tells us, this was no longer the practice:

> As long as they take the veil "everything's all right." No matter how much they protest, their prayers are in vain. So they go through the rites in appearance only; they embrace Jesus, their bridegroom, feigning the ceremony; they offer Him their hearts mouthing the words, in fact belonging still in the world.[30]

Regardless of the woman's religious beliefs or life ambitions, the nun's veil was what created and signified an identity, perhaps even against her wishes.

DRESSING IDENTITY

In our earlier discussion, we addressed the way that identity was crafted through the use of the veil as both metaphor and material garment. The balance of this chapter will address the ways that the phenomenon of sartorial transformations signaled transformations

FIGURE 9.6: *Esther before King Ahasuerus*, Caspar van den Hoecke, seventeenth century, oil on canvas, Kunsthistorisches Museum, Vienna, Austria. Photo: Imagno/Getty Images.

of identity. We begin with two Renaissance retellings of Biblical stories as they exemplify how dress transformations differed from metamorphosis or religious conversion because they always retained a characteristic of reversal; clothing proved to be the perfect instrument to communicate unstable identities.

Two of the best-known Biblical women to be depicted as transformed by clothing were Esther and Judith. Both were active agents in their transformations, and both were dangerous to bad men. Esther transformed herself from a modest wife who hid her Jewish identity into a be-jeweled and bold queen. Her transformed self allowed her to reveal her identity, negotiate with her husband king, and convince him to not massacre the entire Jewish people. Judith, on the other hand, begins her biblical tale as a penitent widow dressed in simple clothes, but when her city is under siege by an attacking army, she dresses in fine clothing and adorns "herself with all her ornaments" (Judith 10:3) so that she might attract the attention of the attacking general. As the biblical stories explain, Esther succeeds in convincing her husband to not only spare the Jews but kill all of those who had spoken against them. Judith of course cuts off the head of the general Holofernes. Both texts offer ambivalent messages about dissimulation and the role of clothing in women's deception of men and as such became popular in visual representations across Europe (Figures 9.6 and 9.7).

The danger (to men) of seductive female dress and cosmetics was a central topic of Renaissance literature, but when these tools were used for divine good, the message was problematic at best. Jerome, translator of the Bible and writer on proper dress for Christian women, was particularly uneasy around the Judith story.[31] Not only did

FIGURE 9.7: *Judith with the Head of Holofernes*, Lucas Cranach, c. 1530, oil on wood, Kunsthistorisches Museum, Vienna, Austria. Photo: Getty Images.

he announce that the book was apocryphal, he added commentary in his translation to explain that her beauty and dress had divine not erotic origin: "the Lord increased her beauty ... because all this dressing up was one that did not proceed from sensuality, but from virtue."[32] It is no wonder that in Renaissance artistic representations, Judith is depicted in a broad spectrum of dress: from simple to ornate, from armed to naked.[33]

In her literary versifications of the Judith and Esther stories, Lucrezia Tornabuoni (1425–82) focused particularly on the clothing of her heroines to explain how they were able to insert themselves in the world of powerful men. When Esther approached her husband, to reveal her Jewish identity, she dressed so that she appeared "in every inch a queen."[34] Additionally, she wore a large jewel around her neck, whose value, the author tells us, was "priceless." This singular jewel is presumably intended to remind the reader of the counter-dowry pendants that were given as gifts to fifteenth-century Florentine brides, like the one depicted in a bridal portrait thought to be of Ginevra d'Antonio Lupari Gozzadini[35] (Figure 9.8).

It is thus suggestive that a literary text written by Tornabuoni, the wife of a Medici ruler, depicts a queen as using a visual language of dress to negotiate with her husband. This fits with what Adrian W.B. Randolph has explained was the Florentine impulse to make brides "legible" through the wearing of the bridal pendant or brooch.[36] In this case,

FIGURE 9.8: *Portrait of a Woman, possibly Ginevra d'Antonio Lupari Gozzadini*, attributed to the Maestro delle Storie del Pane, c. 1485–90, Metropolitan Museum of Art, New York. Robert Lehman Collection, 1975, www.metmuseum.org

Esther wears around her neck a symbol of her pre-marital virginity, a gift whose value is elided with the priceless worth of the jewel.

In Tornabuoni's telling of the Judith story, we find that the author takes a different approach to ornamentation, likely seeking to mitigate the moral question of an unmarried woman seducing a foreign enemy. The fifteenth-century poem, unlike other depictions of the story, does not describe Judith as seductive, nor does it describe her dress as erotic or particularly luxurious. Instead, after Judith's transformation into fine clothes, Tornabuoni repeatedly describes her as so "clean" that she seems "a little angel ... descended from paradise."[37] Additionally, the enemy general Holofernes, is also transformed. Struck by the sight of Judith, his "ferocious heart became human."[38] Moreover, he attempts to attract Judith by changing clothes. He puts on a short fitting doublet and brushes his beard and runs about his tent in good humor awaiting her arrival. If this new lover reminds us of the canonical Italian literary tradition in which a man is elevated by the love of a woman, surely Tornabuoni is commenting on this when Judith slays Holofernes out of divine righteousness. In Tornabuoni's reworking of this story, she emphasizes a morality beyond that of the courtly amorous tradition. A sartorial transformation of clothing or even a softening of heart for the love of a woman does not stand in for conversion or reconciliation with God.

Gender Identity

In many texts, clothing could transform if not the sex of a person, at least the public recognition of the person's sex. Such transformations were presented as standard cases of transvestism, where the subject intentionally wished for his or her gender to be misrecognized, or as a gender transformation caused by the corrupting power of clothing. In Ariosto's *Orlando furioso*, the relationship between gender and clothing is put on the line in Canto 32 when Bradamante arrives dressed in armor at Tristan's castle.[39] Outside Tristan's castle, the virago Bradamante defeats several knights and is thus granted entry. In the eyes of the observers, she then transforms from male to female when she removes her helmet to show long locks of blond hair. It is an incomplete transformation, however; she continues to wear her armor, the costume that had *made* her male (in the eyes of others) in the first place. Her sex presents a problem because Tristan's castle has different rules for men and women to gain entry: men fight, and women compete in a beauty contest. Bradamante, however, responds to her host by challenging the alignment of gender, clothing, and sex.

> There are plenty of others who have long
> hair, like me, and that doesn't make them
> women. Whether I gained entrance as a knight
> or as a woman is clear: Why then do you wish to
> call me a woman, if my every gesture is
> that of a man? . . . (XXXII)[40]

Bradamante states that her host has judged her to be a woman based on her hair just as he had earlier judged her to be a male knight because she was dressed in armor. Because her actions were those of a knight, she asks why her hair would trump the clothing and actions of earlier. Significantly, Bradamante claims that she may assume the gender she wishes, but the irony is that her gender is a performance both limited and enabled by the clothing she wears. Deanna Shemek has smartly pointed to the armor or "metal border" that separates the identities that Bradamante must reconcile.[41] But this border is also strikingly malleable, for Bradamante can fashion her armor to create a gender ambiguity. Through dress she is betwixt and between genders; she creates a "supplementary" identity, one that is perhaps neither man nor woman but knight.[42] If she is not to be disrobed, she then asks, how can one know that she is female:

> I neither came here as a woman, nor do I wish
> that as a woman my advantage should be judged.
> Who shall say, short of me disrobing,
> that I am or am not that which she is?
> What is not known should not be told (XXXII.3–8)[43]

Bradamante implies that to disrobe would end her game of ambiguity, and not only are we uncertain what one might find beneath the armor, we are made aware that such a discovery would be unwelcomed by Bradamante. With her blond hair lying upon her armor, Bradamante chooses to display an overlapping of genders that is different from the character Marfisa, a warrior woman who claimed her virago identity as inaccurately represented by women's clothing. Bradamante instead uses dress as her weapon. She wields more power from this interstitial space than would be possible from the putative binaries of male and female.[44]

Situations in which men are transformed by clothing are somewhat different. Though there are occasional theatrical plots (e.g. *The Deceived* (1532)) that involve male characters who are mistaken for women, the more interesting transformations of men into women are found in texts that are critical of masculinity.[45] In many works, clothing is what instigates a sex change, while in other texts clothing is merely the sign of an already changed and effeminized man. Thus clothing can signify effeminacy just as it can be an effeminizing force.

Like the ancient Hercules, heroes of Ariosto's and Tasso's epic poems are seduced by a woman and are transformed from "manly" warriors into "effeminate" lovers. In Canto 7 of the *Furioso*, Ruggiero is described as having been fundamentally altered by the love of the sorceress, Alcina. While previous lovers of Alcina were changed into various *flora*, Ruggiero's transformation by Alcina is more mundane and is marked by clothing: "The delicious softness of his dress suggested sloth and sensuality" (7.53). He is adorned in gems and necklaces, and even his body is subject to effeminization: "his two arms, hitherto so virile, were now each clasped by a lustrous bangle" (7.54). This gendered change was also a moral one, as the narrator explains: "all about him was sickly, all but his name; the rest was but corruption and decay" (7.55). So, too, does Tasso describe the condition of the hero Rinaldo, in love with the fair Armida. When Rinaldo is discovered by his comrade knights, he, like Ruggiero, is cloaked in jewels and fine clothes rather than arms. When he gazes at himself in a shield, Rinaldo is ashamed of his appearance, and in particular, he notes that his sword was "effeminized" by luxury and had become a "useless ornament" rather than a "military instrument" (16.30). He undoes his transformation, returning to a "virtuous" identity of warrior, by the suggestive action of destroying his clothing as if destroying the garment would also erase the temporarily assumed identity: "ripping to shreds his vain fashions and those unworthy luxuries, signs of miserable servitude" (16.34).

The association of male dress with a gendered identity was central to didactic and moralizing texts as well. The tension that was implicitly debated by such works was whether dress itself was corrupting men or was only the symptom of a corrupt society. In her work on adolescence in Renaissance Italy, Ilaria Taddei explains that in the fifteenth century, ornaments were feared to corrupt boys, and thus various sumptuary legislations regulated the use of clothing by boys below fourteen or eighteen years of age (Figure 9.9).[46]

Laws such as the Florentine ruling of 1497 prohibited the wearing of gold, silk, and embroidery for boys below the age of fourteen because adolescence was targeted as a precarious moment when proper masculine development was at risk of being corrupted by clothing. Similarly, the medical professor Francesco Pontano (fl. 1428–35) in his treatise "On the Whole and Perfect State of Maidens" warned that vanities and ornament debased men (who were meant to be near the angels) to a status "below pigs." These *scelleratissimi maschi* (most defiled men) whitened their cheeks and necks, removed body hair, and cut and lightened their hair and it changed them to a status "neither of men nor of women" (13–30).[47]

Pontano's treatise is hardly unique. There were any number of writers of the Quattro and Cinquecento who located much of the world's ills in men's hairstyles, shaven faces,

FIGURE 9.9: Finely dressed young men in a detail from *Miracles of St. Bernardino*, 1473, by Pietro Vannucci, known as il Perugino (c. 1450–1523), tempera on panel, Galleria Nazionale dell'Umbria. Photo: DeAgostini/Getty Images.

and ornate clothing, and these writers were particularly concerned with young men since being masculine was seen as a developmental process.[48] Adolescence was considered a most precarious age, even *pericolosissima* (most dangerous) as the writer Silvio Antoniano described in his *Three books on the Christian education of sons* (1584).[49] The danger came from a lack of discipline, particularly regarding adolescent males' sexual instincts, and one of the best ways to control these boys was to regulate their hairstyles and wardrobes, eliminating anything that might have them appear in public as *una vezzosa femminetta* (an affected girl) (1.2).[50] Most moralists expressed rancor about men's dress simply because it threatened what they believed to be proper masculinity, but many authors also suggested real-world implications to clothing choices. The colloquial and candid work *The Marbles* by Anton Francesco Doni (1513–74) explains quite clearly that if the world had taken a "bad path" it was because men had become women, and that this transformation was dangerous since men had exchanged the sword for a spool. In the following passage, we see that men's proper clothes are those meant for ruling and defending the republic; effeminate clothing was not merely the effect of, but the powerful cause for, the loss of Italian sovereignty:

let me vent the anger I have with men who have become women . . . For heaven's sake, you circle about me with brooches, little medallions, plumes, little hats, small dress-swords, perfumed gloves, and distorted buttons, tiny necklaces, and slashes and supersized slashes. Oh you look like young beautiful women! The clothes of a man are the helmet and the toga, as well as the leading, the governing, the acquiring, and the defending of the republic.[51]

The Performance of Dress

If clothing could transform paupers into nobles, widows into seductive lovers, and men into women, it was not only because dress made exterior a personal interior but because public appearance had the potential of subsuming subjective identity.[52] This meant that not only what a person wore but how he or she wore clothing was of the utmost importance. In the concluding section we will look at Castiglione's writings on the performance of dress to consider how he emphasizes not so much material clothing but the manner in which it is worn. For Castiglione, it was not changing dress but performing dress that transformed an individual.

In the sixteenth century, the appropriateness of dress became privileged over its lavishness.[53] Moreover, beauty became ever more associated with what we might call the performed act of concealed exhibition. Alberti already described this sort of performance in his fifteenth-century *Vita*, where he explained how one should take the utmost care in behavior so that walking, riding, and speaking seem natural. To achieve this, he tells us, one must add "art to art to make the result seem free of artifice."[54] Almost a century later, Baldesare Castiglione's best seller, *The Book of the Courtier*, codified this behavior and called it *sprezzatura*: "(To pronounce a new word perhaps), to practice in all things a certain *sprezzatura*, so as to conceal all art and make whatever is done or said appear to be without effort and almost without any thought about it."[55] The opposite of this *sprezzatura* was "affectation," a quality that was to be avoided for it debased the individual in public opinion partly because it was less beautiful. Indeed, in Castiglione one could argue that the manipulation of dress was privileged over dress itself.

One speaker points to the complex notion of manipulating dress in an observation of daily life:

> Have you ever noticed when a woman, in passing along the street to church or elsewhere, unwittingly happens (in play or through whatever cause) to raise just enough of her dress to show her foot and often a little of her leg? Does this not strike you as something full of grace, if she is seen in that moment, charmingly feminine, dressed in velvet shoes and dainty stockings? (I, XL)[56]

This brief passage effectively and simply communicates the tension between authenticity and artifice, between affectation and *sprezzatura*. The speaker is not so much fascinated by the velvet shoes and dress that frame a woman's leg but rather by the performance of the woman, whose skirt has lifted perhaps by her own intent and perhaps not. Although the woman's leg could have been revealed through natural consequence, it is far more impressive, even desirable, if the woman were able to intentionally perform this act without the observer knowing her role. This *sprezzatura*, with its attention to public surveillance and performance of the "natural" is still part of modern day parlance in the world of fashion, where fashion blogs discuss what is "sprezzy" and what is not.[57]

Although the notion of *sprezzatura* may seem at first glance quite easily mastered, what becomes quickly evident is that society might judge one's artful behavior to be a failure. The speakers, all gathered at the court of Urbino, provide examples of successful and failed performances. Their critique presents at least two challenges: it is difficult to know the rules of taste, and it is nearly impossible to identify the arbiters of social performance. Castiglione's speakers, all well-placed men at the court of Urbino, dispense judgment with self-proclaimed status of expertise as might a fashion commentator at a red carpet event, but there is no clear way to discern who might be a fashion judge. Such power is not, for example, limited to the prince. All eyes of the court are potential critics. These judges who codify the rules of appearance—rules that negotiate self-expression alongside societal and commercial forces—make Castiglione's book a fundamental text in the history of fashion.

This social choreography of clothed bodies also included, at least for women, the performance of cosmetics.[58] Castiglione incorporates cosmetics into his theory of *sprezzatura*, and thus he obfuscates the rules of beauty unlike moralists such as Alberti, who condemned them outright as damaging to the integrity and value (financial as well as moral) of the female body.[59] Castiglione states that women are "bound" to care more about beauty than men, and therefore they can take measures to alter their natural appearance (III.9), but when he addresses cosmetics specifically, the rules become quickly muddied. One speaker suggests that cosmetics are used in an attempt to "seem" beautiful, but that it is only beautiful if the viewer is uncertain if a woman wears them (I.40). After praising such invisible cosmetics, the speaker goes on to say that true beauty is when a woman does not paint her face at all. It is a cliché that actually catches women in an impossible bind as well as masks the fundamental point of the entire *Book of the Courtier*. If a woman were to exert true *sprezzatura* in her cosmetics, a viewer would not be able to discern whether such color were natural or not. A woman can thus never claim true natural beauty for there will always be a suspicion of artifice.

If women are challenged to find the right balance between nature and affectation, men are charged with a different balance, the demonstration of elegance and masculinity, style and political alliance—and Castiglione dedicates three chapters to discussing this (II, 26–8). In an attempt to generalize all men's dress, the speaker Federico Fregoso states that men should simply dress as they please as long as they follow custom. The statement is disingenuous, however, for not only must a man determine and imitate the custom of others, he must successfully perform his class without risking vanity, effeminacy, and even political alliance. Clothing was political as it was associated with the influx of foreign (Spanish, French, English, Turkish) fashions, and as Amedeo Quondam and others have noted, Castiglione draws the important connection between Italian dress and contemporary politics when he states that fashion is homologous to the subjugated Italian condition.[60] As Federico states:

> But I do not know by what fate it happens that Italy does not have, as she used to have, a manner of dress recognized to be Italian: for although the introduction of these new fashions makes the former ones seem very crude, still the older were perhaps a sign of freedom, even as the new ones have proved to be an augury of servitude, which I think is now most evidently fulfilled. (II, 26)

As there is no Italian fashion, Federico attempts to forge one, a fashion he calls a *giusto mezzo* a "middle ground" between foreign extremes. He states, for example, that men should avoid excess in dress and wear only dark colors unless it is a festive occasion.

However, this performance of the *giusto mezzo* can easily misfire, as Federico explains. If the courtier errs on the side of restraint, he risks being drab; if he leans too far towards extravagance, he risks being effeminate (II, 27).

Effeminacy was a label given by society's judges to indicate a failure of male dress. However, any performance of dress, be it wearing a Spanish hat or surreptitiously lifting one's skirt hem or plucking one's eyebrows, was more than a successful or failed fashion attempt. It was also a means of exerting agency through appearances as well as demonstrating personal desire while aware of the gaze of others. If we circle back to our original discussion of the veil—an article of dress that the beloved could manipulate to control the lover's gaze—we find that this very dialectic expands into a social and more regimented arena of gazing in sixteenth-century literature. Not just the lover but the entire court (and in some circumstances all the eyes of the piazza) gazed on each other's dress with scrutiny. Aware of that gaze, people modulated their dress to suit the desires of one group or another, or perhaps like the fictional Marfisa and Bradamante, they chose to resist the social categories that were demarcated by dress. In all cases, literature gave meaning to these garments but it also obscured meaning, and ultimately it guided people through the swiftly changing material world.

NOTES

Introduction

1. John Nevinson, "The Dress of the Citizens of London," in *Collectanea Londiniensia: Studies in London Archaeology and History*, eds Joanna Bird, Hugh Chapman, John Clark (London and Middlesex Archaeological Society, 1978), 265.
2. Desiderius Erasmus, *Collected Works of Erasmus: Colloquies*, vol. 1, trans. and annotated by Craig R. Thompson (Toronto: University of Toronto Press, 1997), 18.
3. William Harrison, *Description of England* (Folger Shakespeare Library, Washington, 1994), 145–6.
4. David Hillman and Carla Mazzio (eds), *The Body in Parts* (London: Routledge, 1997), vi–xxix.
5. Kristen Ina Grimes, "Dressing the World: Costume Books and Ornamental Cartography in the Age of Exploration," in *A Well-Fashioned Image: Clothing and Costume in European Art, 1500–1850*, eds Elizabeth Rodini and Elissa B. Weaver (Chicago: University of Chicago Press, 2002), 13–22.
6. Elizabeth Sutton, *Early Modern Dutch Prints of Africa* (Aldershot: Ashgate, 2012), 7.
7. Scott Manning Stevens, "New World Contacts and the Trope of the 'Naked Savage,'" in *Sensible Flesh: On Touch in Early Modern Culture*, ed. Elizabeth D. Harvey (University of Pennsylvania Press, 2003), 132–3.
8. Stephen Greenblatt, "Mutilation and Meaning," in Hillman and Mazio (1997), 236. See also Will Fisher, "Had it a codpiece, 'twere a man indeed," in *Ornamentalism: The Art of Renaissance Accessories*, ed. B. Mirabella (Ann Abor: University of Michigan Press, 2011), 103 & 108–9.
9. Greenblatt (1997), 531.
10. Dinah Eastop, "Textiles as Multiple and Competing Histories," in *Textiles Revealed*, ed. Mary M. Brooks (London: Archetype Publications, 2000), p. 17.
11. Ann R. Jones and Peter Stallybrass, *Renaissance Clothing and the Materials of Memory* (Cambridge: Cambridge University Press, 2000), 32.
12. Chiara Buss, "Silk, Gold, Crimson," in *Silk, Gold, Crimson: Secrets and Technology at the Visconti and Sforza Courts* (Milan: Silvana Editoriale, 2009), 54–5; F. Magaluzzi Valeri, *La corte di Ludovico il Moro*, vol. 1 (Milano, 1929), 374, cited in *Women in Italy, 1350–1650: Ideals and Realities*, eds M. Rogers and P. Tinagli (Manchester: Manchester University Press, 2005), 249.
13. Cordula Van Wyhe, "Piety, Play and Power: Constructing the Ideal Sovereign Body in Early Portraits of Isabel Clara Eugenia (1568–1603)," in *Isabel Clara Eugenia: Female Sovereignty at the Courts of Madrid and Brussels*, ed. Cordula van Wyhe (Madrid and London: Centro de Estudios Europa Hispánica and Paul Holberton Publishing, 2012), 122.
14. Martha C. Howell, *Commerce Before Capitalism* (Cambridge: Cambridge University Press, 2010), 208.
15. Craig Clunas, *Superfluous Things: Material Culture and Social Status in Early Modern China* (Honolulu: University of Hawai'i Press, 2004), 150–1.
16. Catherine Kovesi Killerby, *Sumptuary Law in Italy, 1200–1500* (Oxford: Clarendon Press, 2002), 33–4.

17. Carmen Bernis, *Indumentaria española en tiempos de Carlos V* (Madrid: Instituto Diego Velázquez, 1962), 31.
18. Amanda Bailey, "'Monstrous Manner': Style and the Early Modern Theater," *Criticism*, vol. 43, no. 3, Summer 2001: 259.
19. Nicholas Davidson, "Theology, Nature and the Law," in *Crime, Society and the Law in Renaissance Italy*, eds Trevor Dean and K.J.P. Lowe (Cambridge: Cambridge University Press, 1994), 92. On the laws for young women in Genoa, see Diane Owen Hughes, "Sumptuary Law and Social Relations in Renaissance Italy," in *Disputes and Settlements: Law and Human Relations in the West*, ed. John Bossy (Cambridge University Press, 1983), 93–4.
20. Maria Hayward *Rich Apparel: Clothing and the Law in Henry VIII's England* (Aldershot: Ashgate, 2009), 41–60.
21. Emilie Gordenker, *Van Dyck (1599–1641) and the Representation of Dress in Seventeenth-Century Portraiture* (Turnhout: Brepols, 2001), 71.
22. See S.A.M. Adshead, *Material Culture in Europe and China 1400–1800* (Basingstoke: Macmillan, 1997), 27–8.
23. Quoted in Marieke de Winkel, *Fashion and Fancy: Dress and Meaning in Rembrandt's Paintings* (Amsterdam: Amsterdam University Press, 2014), 43.
24. For further discussion of dress, disguise, and identity see Susan J. Vincent, *Dressing the Elite* (Oxford: Berg, 2003), Chapter 5, 153–88.
25. Stefano Guazzo, *La civil conversazione*, vol. 1, ed. A. Quondam (Modena: Panini, 1993), 140.
26. Quoted in Karen Newman, *Fashioning Femininity and English Renaissance Drama* (Chicago: University of Chicago Press, 1991), 119.
27. Cesare Vecellio, *De gli habit antichi e moderni di diverse parti del mondo* (Damiano Zenaro: Venice, 1590), 140.
28. William Brenchley Rye, *England as seen by Foreigners in the days of Elizabeth and James I* (New York: B. Bloom, 1967), 71.
29. See J.L. Colomer and A. Descalzo, eds, *Spanish Fashion at the Courts of Early Modern Europe*, vols. I & II (London: Paul Holberton, 2014).
30. Vecellio (1590), 233.
31. Melanie Schuessler, "French Hoods: Development of a Sixteenth-Century Court Fashion," in *Medieval Clothing and Textiles,* vol. 5, eds R. Netherton and G.R. Owen-Crocker (Woodbridge: Boydell & Brewer, 2009), 129–60.
32. Yassana Y. Croizat, "'Living Dolls': François Ier Dresses His Women," *Renaissance Quarterly* 60 (2007): 94–130.
33. Catherine Mann, "Clothing Bodies, Dressing Rooms: Fashioning Fecundity in The Lisle Letters," *Parergon*, vol. 22, no. 1, January 2005: 137–157.
34. Thomas Middleton, *Anything for a Quiet Life*, Act I, Scene I in *Thomas Middleton: The Collected Works*, eds Gary Taylor and John Lavagnino (Oxford: Oxford University Press, 2007), 1602.
35. Karen Newman (1991), 120.
36. Ulinka Rublack, *Dressing Up: Cultural Identity in Renaissance Europe* (Oxford: Oxford University Press, 2010), 4.
37. Karen Newman, *Cultural Capitals: Early Modern London and Paris* (Princeton University Press, 2007), 2.
38. Margaret F. Rosenthal, "Clothing, Fashion, Dress, and Costume in Venice (c. 1450–1650)," in *A Companion to Venetian History, 1400–1797*, ed. E.R. Dursteler (Leiden and Boston: Brill, 2013): 889–928; Ilja Van Damme, "Middlemen and the Creation of a 'Fashion Revolution': The Experience of Antwerp in the Late Seventeenth and Eighteenth Centuries," in ed. Beverly Lemire, *The Force of Fashion in Politics and Society* (Aldershot: Ashgate, 2010), 21–40.
39. David Gilbert, "Urban Outfitting: The City and the Spaces of Fashion Culture," in *Fashion Cultures: Theories, Explanations and Analysis*, eds S. Bruzzi and P. Church-Gibson (London: Routledge, 2000), 17.

40. Erasmus (1997), 371–2.
41. Howell (2010), 232.
42. John Evelyn, *Memoirs of John Evelyn*, ed. William Bray (London: Frederick Warne & Co, 1897), 160.
43. Fabrizio Nevola, "'Più honorati et suntuosi ala Republica': botteghe and luxury retail along Siena's Strada Romana," in *Buyers and Sellers, Retail Circuits and Practices in Medieval and Early Modern Europe*, eds B. Blondé, P. Stabel, J. Stobart, I. Van Damme (Turnhout: Brepols, 2006), 68–9.
44. Ronald M. Berger, *The Most Necessary Luxuries: The Mercers' Company of Coventry, 1550–1680* (University Park: Penn State Press, 1993), 17.
45. Jane Whittle and Elizabeth Griffiths, *Consumption and Gender in the Early Seventeenth-Century Household: the World of Alice Le Strange* (Oxford: Oxford University Press, 2012), 56.
46. Carlo Marco Belfanti and Fabio Giusberti, "Clothing and Social Inequality in Early Modern Europe: Introductory Remarks," *Continuity and Change* 15.3 (2000): 359–65.
47. Richard Goldthwaite, *The Economy of Renaissance Florence* (Baltimore: John Hopkins University Press, 2009), 607.
48. Paolo Malanima, *Il Lusso dei Contadini, consumi e industrie nelle campagne toscane del sei e settecento* (Bologna: Il Mulino Ricerca, 1990), 24.
49. D. Davanzo Poli, *Il sarto*, in *Storia d'Italia: La Moda*, eds C. Marco Belfanti and F. Giusberti (Turin: Einaudi, 2003), 541–3; Eugenia Paulicelli, *Writing Fashion in Early Modern Italy* (Aldershot: Ashgate, 2014), 5–7.
50. See Elisabeth Salter, "Reworked Material: Discourses of Clothing Culture in Early Sixteenth-Century Greenwich," in *Clothing Culture 1350–1650*, ed. C. Richardson (Aldershot: Ashgate, 2004), 179–91.
51. Joan Thirsk, "The fantastical folly of fashion: the English stocking knitting industry, 1500–1700," in *Textile History and Economic History: Essays in Honour of Miss Julia de Lacy Mann*, eds N.B. Harte and K.G. Ponting (Manchester: Manchester University Press, 1973), 50–73.
52. Rublack (2010), 247–8. See also E. Welch, "New, Old and Second hand Culture: the Case of the Renaissance Sleeve," in *Revaluing Renaissance Art*, eds G. Neher and R. Shepherd (Aldershot: Ashgate, 2000), 101–19.
53. M.G. Muzzarelli, "Seta posseduta e seta consentita: dalle aspirazioni individuali alle norme suntuarie nel basso Medioevo," in *La seta in Italia dal Medioevo al Seicento*, eds L. Molà, R.C. Mueller and C. Zanier (Venice: Marsilio, 2000), 218–27.
54. G. Baldissin Molli, *Fioravante, Nicolò e altri artigiani del lusso nell'età di Mantegna* (Saonora: Il Prato, 2006), 111 and 131–49.
55. Fred Davis, *Fashion, Culture and Identity* (Chicago: University of Chicago Press, 1992), 24–5.
56. Diane Owen Hughes, "Distinguishing Signs: Earrings, Jews, and Franciscan Rhetoric in the Italian Renaissance City," *Past and Present* (1986), 112 (1): 20–1.
57. Castiglione, B. *Il Libro del Cortegiano* (Venice: Aldo Manuzio, 1528), Book II, xxvii.
58. Stephen Greenblatt, *Renaissance Self-Fashioning: From More to Shakespeare* (Chicago: University of Chicago Press, 1980), 162–3.
59. Peter Burke, "Representations of the Self from Petrarch to Descartes," in *Re-writing the Self*, ed. Roy Porter (London and New York: Routledge, 1996), 18.
60. Howell (2010), 251.
61. Rosenthal (2013), 897–8.
62. See Stallybrass and Jones (2000), 57.
63. Quoted in Marieke de Winkel, *Fashion and Fancy: Dress and Meaning in Rembrandt's Paintings* (Amsterdam: Amsterdam University Press, 2006), 128.
64. Harry Berger, *The Absence of Grace: Sprezzatura and Suspicion* (Stanford: Stanford University Press, 2000), 24.

65. Laura R. Bass, *The Drama of the Portrait* (University Park: Penn State Press, 2008), 45.
66. Ellen Chirelstein, "Emblem and Reckless Presence: The Drury Portrait at Yale," in *Albion's Classicism: The Visual Arts in Britain, 1550–1660*, ed. L. Gent (New Haven and London: Yale University Press, 1995), 287–311.
67. R.C. Bald, *Donne and the Drurys* (Westport CT: Greenwood Press, 1986), 13–15.
68. Daniela Costa, "La Raffaella di Alessandro Piccolomini: un'armonia nella disarmonia?" in *Disarmonia, bruttezza e bizzarria nel Rinascimento*, ed. L. Rotondi Secchi Tarugi (Florence: F. Cesati, 1998), 148.
69. A. Di Benedetto (ed.), *Prose di Giovanni Della Casa e altri trattatisti cinquecenteschi di comportamento* (Turin: Utet, 1991), 499.
70. See Fredrika Jacobs, "Sexual Variations: Playing with (Dis)similitude," in *A Cultural History of Sexuality in the Renaissance*, ed. B. Talvacchia (London: Bloomsbury, 2012), 78–9 and Tessa Storey, "Clothing courtesans: fabric, signals and experiences," in *Clothing Culture 1350–1650*, ed. C. Richardson (Aldershot: Ashgate, 2004), 95–108.
71. See Amanda Wunder, "Seventeenth-Century Spain: The Rise and Fall of the *Guardainfante*," *Renaissance Quarterly*, vol. 68, no. 1, Spring 2015, and Stanley Chojnacki, "La Posizione della Donna a Venezia nel Cinquecento," in *Tiziano e Venezia*, eds M. Gemin and G. Paladini (Vicenza: Neri Pozza, 1980), 67–8.
72. Cited in E. Tosi Brandi, *Introduzione a Cesena* in *La Legislazione Suntuaria Secoli XIII–XVI, Emilia Romagna*, ed. M.G. Muzzarelli (Rome: Ministero per i beni e le attività culturali, 2002), 345, note 11.
73. Laura Levine, *Men in Women's Clothing: Anti-Theatricality and Effeminization, 1579–1642* (Cambridge: Cambridge University Press, 1994), 20–21.
74. See, for example, Laura R. Bass and Amanda Wunder, "The Veiled Ladies of the Early Modern Spanish World," *Hispanic Review*, vol. 77, no. 1, Winter 2009: 97–144, and Benjamin B. Roberts, *Sex and Drugs before Rock 'n' Roll: Youth Culture during Holland's Golden Age* (Chicago: University of Chicago Press, 2012), 45–74.
75. See Peter Burke, *The Historical Anthropology of Early Modern Italy* (Cambridge: Cambridge University Press, 1987), 165 and Bass (2008), 28.
76. James R. Farr, "Cultural Analysis and Early Modern Artisans," in *The Artisan and the European Town 1500–1900*, ed. G. Crossick (Aldershot: Scolar Press, 1997), 63–9, and James R. Farr, *Artisans in Europe, 1300–1914* (Cambridge: Cambridge University Press, 2000), 114–16.
77. John Cherry, "Healing through Faith: The Continuation of Medieval Attitudes to Jewellery into the Renaissance," *Renaissance Studies*, vol. 15, no. 2 (2001): 154–71. See www.concealedgarments.org
78. Sandra Cavallo and Tessa Storey, *Healthy Living in Late Renaissance Italy* (Oxford: Oxford University Press, 2013), 103–6.
79. Karen Raber, "Chains of Pearls: Gender, Property, Identity," in *Ornamentalism*, ed. Mirabella (2011), 168.
80. Harrison (1994), 148.
81. Carlo Carnesecchi, *Cosimo I e la legge suntuaria del 1562* (Florence: Stabilimento Pellas, 1902), 14, fn 1.
82. Roze Hentschell, *The Culture of Cloth in Early Modern England* (Aldershot: Ashgate, 2008), especially chapter 4, 103–28.
83. Marta Ajmar-Wollheim and Luca Molà, "The Global Renaissance: Cross-Cultural Material Culture," in *Global Design History*, eds G. Adamson, G. Riello and S. Teasley (London: Taylor & Francis, 2011), 13–14.
84. Ulinka Rublack, "Matter in the Material Renaissance," *Past and Present*, no. 219 (May 2013): 67–76.
85. See, for example, Jones and Stallybrass (2000), 134–71.
86. Quoted in Larissa Taylor, "Dangerous Vocations," in *Preachers and People in the Reformations and Early Modern Period*, ed. Larissa Taylor (Leiden and Boston: Brill, 2001), 93.

87. Andrea Caracausi, "Beaten Children and Women's Work in Early Modern Italy," *Past and Present*, no. 222 (February 2014): 101.

Chapter 1

1. T. Dekker, *The Seven Deadly Sinnes of London* (London, 1606), 32.
2. The National Archive, Kew, E101/417/4, f. 6v; M.A. Hayward (ed.), *The Great Wardrobe Accounts of Henry VII and Henry VIII*, London Record Society, 47 (Woodbridge: Boydell & Brewer, 2012), 78.
3. K.J. Allison, "Flock management in the sixteenth and seventeenth centuries," *Economic History Review*, 2nd series, 11 (1958): 98–112.
4. R. Lockyer, *Habsburg and Bourbon Europe 1470–1720* (Harlow: Longman, 1974), 11 and 62; P. Spufford, *Power and Profit: The Merchant in Medieval Europe* (London: Thames & Hudson, 2002), 226.
5. Lockyer, *Habsburg and Bourbon Europe 1470–1720*, 61–2.
6. E. Kerridge, *Textile Manufactures in Early Modern England* (Manchester: Manchester University Press, 1985), 73.
7. N. Canny, *The Oxford History of the British Empire: Volume 1 The Origins of Empire, British Overseas Enterprise to the Close of the Seventeenth Century* (Oxford: Oxford University Press, 1998), 279.
8. F. Braudel, *The Structure of Everyday Life: Civilization and Capitalism 15th to 18th Century*, vol. 1 (London: Harper Collins, 1981), 326.
9. Ibid., 327.
10. F. Morrison, *Itinerary*, vol. 1 (London, 1617), 45.
11. L. Clarkson, "The linen industry in early modern Europe," in *The Cambridge History of Western Textiles*, vol. 1, ed. D. Jenkins (Cambridge: Cambridge University Press, 2003), 476–7.
12. SR 24 Hen VIII, c. 41. It was repeated in 1563 (SR 5 Eliz I, c. 5) although the emphasis was on providing yarn for fishing nets.
13. M. Channing Linthicum, *Costume in the Drama of Shakespeare and his Contemporaries* (Oxford: Clarendon Press, 1936), 102.
14. G. Riello, *Cotton: The Fabric that Made the Modern World* (Cambridge: Cambridge University Press, 2013), 90.
15. A. Seiler-Baldinger, *Textiles: A Classification of Techniques* (Bathurst: Crawford House Press, 1994), 3.
16. Ibid., 85–6.
17. J.L. Bolton, *The Medieval English Economy 1150–1500* (London: J.M. Dent Ltd, 1980), 155.
18. Spufford, *Power and Profit*, 250. Also see R.A. Goldthwaite, *The Economy of Renaissance Florence*, (Baltimore: Johns Hopkins University Press, 2009), esp. ch. 4, and L. Monnas, *Merchants, Princes and Painters: Silk Fabrics in Italian and Northern Paintings 1300–1550* (New Haven and London: Yale, 2008), 6–8.
19. J. Harris (ed.), *Textiles: 5000 Years* (London: Harry N. Abrams, 1993), 169.
20. L. Mola, *The Silk Industry of Renaissance Venice* (Baltimore and London: Johns Hopkins University Press, 2000), 60–1.
21. Harris, *Textiles: 5000 Years*, 86.
22. J.M. Rogers and R.M. Ward, *Süleyman the Magnificent* (London: British Museum Press, 1988), 164.
23. Harris, *Textiles: 5000 Years*, 86.
24. J. Guy, *Woven Cargoes: Indian Textiles in the East* (London: Thames and Hudson, 1998), 26.
25. Ibid., 26.
26. M. King and D. King (eds), *European Textiles in the Kerr Collection 400 BC to 1800 AD* (London and Boston: Faber & Faber, 1990), 134–5.

27. L. Monnas, "New documents for the vestments of Henry VII at Stonyhurst College," *Burlington Magazine*, 131 (1989): 345–9.
28. A. Sutton, *The Mercery of London: Trade, Goods and People, 1130–1578* (Aldershot: Ashgate, 2005), 298.
29. Ibid., 298.
30. Spufford, *Power and Profit*, 253.
31. T.S. Willan, *A Tudor Book of Rates* (Manchester: Manchester University Press, 1962), 19.
32. W.D. Smith, *Consumption and the Making of Respectability, 1600–1800* (New York and London: Routledge, 2002), 47.
33. B. Lemire, "Fashioning cottons: Asian trade, domestic industry and consumer demand, 1660–1780", in *Cambridge History of Western Textiles*, 1, ed. Jenkins, 493.
34. Herman van der Wee, (in collaboration with John Munro), "The western European woollen industries, 1500–1750", in *Cambridge History of Western Textiles*, 1, ed. Jenkins, p. 434.
35. Mola, *Silk Industry*, 172.
36. TNA E101/417/4, ff. 7v–8r; Hayward, *Great Wardrobe Accounts*, 81–3.
37. See J. Cherry, "Leather," in *English Medieval Industries: Craftsmen, Techniques, Products*, eds J. Blair and N. Ramsey (London: A.&C. Black, 1991), 295–318, and R. Thomson, "Leather manufacture in the post-medieval period with special reference to Northamptonshire," *Post Medieval Archaeology*, 15, (1981): 161–75; J.M. Cronin, *The Elements of Archaeological Conservation* (London: Routledge, 1990), 265.
38. For example, six fragments of a leather high-necked jerkin, c. 1530–c. 1570, ABO92 <2835>, [406]; G. Egan, *Material Culture in London in an Age of Transition: Tudor and Stuart Period Finds c. 1450–c.1700 from Excavations at Riverside Sites in Southwark*, MoLAS Monograph 19 (London: Museum of London, 2005): no. 2, 18–20.
39. See J. Swann, *History of Footwear in Norway, Sweden and Finland* (Stockholm: The Royal Academy of Letters, History and Antiquities, 2001), 81–100.
40. E. Veale, *The English Fur Trade in the Later Middle Ages*, London Record Society (Woodbridge: Boydell & Brewer, 2003); Cronin, *Elements*, 265.
41. T. Sherrill, "Fleas, fur and fashion: Zibellini as luxury accessories of the Renaissance," *Medieval Clothing and Textiles*, 2 (London: Boydell Press, 2006), 121–50.
42. E. Veale, "From sable to mink," in *The 1547 Inventory of King Henry VIII: volume 2 Textiles and Dress*, eds M.A. Hayward and P. Ward (London: Harvey Miller for the Society of Antiquaries, 2012), 341.
43. W.G. Mullins, *Felt* (Oxford and New York: Berg, 2009), 16.
44. Ibid., 103, 107.
45. Ibid., 105.
46. P.E. Cunnington, *Costume of Household Servants* (London: A & C Black, 1974), 64.
47. J. Arnold, *Patterns of Fashion: The Cut and Construction of Clothes for Men and Women c. 1560–1620*, (London and Basingstoke: Macmillan), 46, ill. 329–30.
48. Horse hair was used as padding in a pair of trunk hose, c. 1615–20, Museo Parmigianino, Reggio Emilia; Arnold, *Patterns of Fashion*, no. 23b, 90–1.
49. Egan, *Material Culture*, nos. 178–219, 48–51.
50. Ibid., no. 220, 51.
51. Sutton, *Mercery*, 118–19.
52. S. Levey, "Lace in the early modern period, c. 1500–1780," in *Cambridge History of Western Textiles*, 1, ed. Jenkins, 585.
53. For the definitive text on lace, see S. Levey, *Lace: a history* (Leeds: Maney, 1990).
54. L. Levey Peck, *Consuming Splendour: Society and Culture in Seventeenth Century England*, (Cambridge: Cambridge University Press, 2005), 91, 99, 106–7. And in Virginia, ibid, 99–103.
55. N. Geffe, *The Perfect Use of Silk-Wormes and their Benefit* (London, 1607), 13.
56. J. Thirsk, "Knitting and knitware c. 1500–1780," in *Cambridge History of Western Textiles*, 1, ed. Jenkins, 565–6.

57. Ibid., 573–6. Also J. Thirsk, "The fantastical folly of fashion: the English stocking knitting industry, 1500–1700," in *Textile History and Economic History: Essays in Honour of Miss Julia de Lacy Mann*, eds N.B. Harte and K.G. Ponting eds (Manchester: Manchester University Press, 1973), 70.
58. Spufford, *Power and Profit*, 226.
59. Lockyer, *Habsburg and Bourbon*, 62.
60. SR RIII, c. 8.
61. Harris, *Textiles*, 86.
62. Guy, *Woven Cargoes*, 32.
63. Harris, *Textiles*, 176.
64. Ibid., 176.
65. Kerridge, *Textile Manufactures*, 24.
66. Canny, *Origins of Empire*, 179.
67. P. Clark and P. Slack, *English Towns in Transition 1500–1700* (Oxford: Oxford University Press, 1976), 48.
68. Ibid., 50–1.
69. Ibid., 53.
70. W.G. Hoskins, *The Age of Plunder: The England of Henry VIII 1500–1547* (London: Longman, 1976), 120.
71. J.F. Larkin and P.L. Hughes (ed.), *Stuart Royal Proclamations: Royal Proclamations of King James I, 1603–1625*, vol. 1 (Oxford: Clarendon Press, 1973), 581.
72. D. Sella, "The rise and fall of the Venetian woollen industry," in *Crisis and Change in the Venetian Economy in the 16th and 17th Centuries*, ed. B. Pullan (London: Methuen and Co, 1968), 109.
73. Lockyer, *Habsburg and Bourbon*, 94.
74. Spufford, *Power and Profit*, 227.
75. See the website of the Overland Trade Project led by Professor Michael Hicks of the University of Winchester, www.overlandtrade.org
76. Willan, *Tudor Book of Rates*, 21.
77. E.P.G. Gohl and L.D. Vilensky, *Textile Science: An Explanation of Fibre Properties* (Melbourne: Longman Cheshire, 1980), 130–1.
78. M. Pastoureau, *Blue: The History of a Colour* (Princeton: Princeton University Press, 2001), 72.
79. J.H. Hofenk de Graaff, *The Colourful Past: Origins, Chemistry and Identification of Natural Dyestuffs*, (Berne: Abegg-Stiftung Foundation, 2004), 15.
80. Bolton, *Medieval Economy*, 155.
81. Pastoureau, *Blue*, 63–4.
82. Ibid., 66.
83. Guy, *Woven Cargoes*, 19.
84. Pastoureau, *Blue*, 64.
85. W.N. Salisbury (ed.), *Calendar of State Papers, Colonial America and West Indies*, I, 1574–1660, (London: HMSO, 1860), 162.
86. Mola, *Silk Industry*, 122.
87. H.F. Brown, (ed.), *Calendar of State Papers Venetian, vol. 2, 1607–1610* (London: HMSO, 1894), 186.
88. Mola, *Silk Industry*, 70.
89. Channing Linthicum, *Costume*, 1.
90. A. Butler Greenfield, *A Prefect Red: Empire, Espionage and the Quest for the Colour of Desire*, (London: Doubleday, 2005), 137–40.
91. Mola, *Silk Industry*, 133.
92. Harris, *Textiles*, 174.
93. Ibid., 172.

94. Ibid., 172.
95. Ibid., 173.
96. Ibid., 86.
97. Ibid., 87.
98. Guy, *Woven Cargoes*, 30.
99. Gohl and Vilensky, *Textile Science*, 130–1.
100. J.F. Larkin and P.L. Hughes (eds), *Tudor Royal Proclamations: The Later Tudors 1553–1587*, vol. II, (Oxford: Clarendon Press, 1969), 516, no. 678.
101. J. R. Dasent (ed.), *Acts of the Privy Council of England*, 1586–87, vol. 14 (London: HMSO, 1897), 91. With thanks to Louise Fairbrother for this reference.
102. Pastoureau, *Blue*, 69.
103. See E. Cockayne, *Hubbub: Filth, Noise and Stench in England, 1600–1770* (New Haven and London: Yale University Press, 2007), 211. With thanks to Jemima Matthews for this reference.
104. Quoted in D. de Marly, *Working Dress: A History of Occupational Clothing* (London: B.T. Batsford Ltd, 1986), 30.

Chapter 2

1. Phillip Stubbes, *The anatomie of abuses* (London: Richard Iohnes, at the sign of the Rose and Crowne, 1595), 24, sig. [D4v].
2. Ibid., 11, sig. C2r.
3. On personal linens and their manufacture, Janet Arnold, *Patterns of Fashion 4: The Cut and Construction of Linen Shirts, Smocks, Neckwear, Headwear and Accessories for Men and Women, c.1540–1660*, completed by Jenny Tiramani and Santina Levey (London: Macmillan, 2008); Susan North and Jenny Tiramani (eds), *Seventeenth-Century Women's Dress Patterns: Book One* (London: V&A Publishing, 2011), 9, 12–13, 110–35.
4. Susan Broomhall, "Women, Work, and Power in Female Guilds of Rouen," in *Practices of Gender in Late Medieval and Early Modern Europe*, eds Megan Cassidy-Welch and Peter Sherlock (Turnhout: Brepols, 2008), 199–213.
5. Carole Collier Frick, *Dressing Renaissance Florence* (Baltimore: John Hopkins University Press, 2002), 39–44, and Carole Collier Frick, "The Florentine 'Rigattieri': Second Hand Clothing Dealers and the Circulation of Goods in the Renaissance," in *Old Clothes, New Looks: Second-Hand Fashion*, eds Alexandra Palmer and Hazel Clark (Oxford: Berg, 2004), 15, 20–25.
6. Arnold, *Patterns of Fashion 4*, 9.
7. *Letters of the Lady Brilliana Harley*, ed. Thomas Taylor Lewis, Camden Society 58 (1854), 153, 158, 192, 95.
8. On the craft of the early modern tailor, Janet Arnold, *Patterns of Fashion: The Cut and Construction of Clothes for Men and Women c 1560–1620* (London: Macmillan, 1985); and North and Tiramani (eds), *Women's Dress Patterns*, 9–11.
9. Monica Cerri, "Sarti toscani nel seicento: attività e clientela," in *Le Trame della moda*, eds Anna Giulia Cavagna and Grazietta Butazzi (Rome: Bulzoni, 1995), 421–35. My thanks to Dr. Elizabeth Currie for this reference.
10. Heather Swanson, *Medieval Artisans: An Urban Class in Late Medieval England* (Oxford: Basil Blackwell, 1989), 45.
11. Matthew Davies and Ann Saunders, *The History of the Merchant Taylors' Company* (Leeds: Maney, 2004), 58, 59.
12. Collier Frick, *Dressing Renaissance Florence*, 31.
13. Elizabeth Currie, "Fashion Networks: Consumer Demand and the Clothing Trade in Florence from the mid-Sixteenth to Early Seventeenth Century," *Journal of Medieval and Early Modern Studies* 39 (2009): 485–6.
14. Currie, "Fashion Networks," 493.

15. Jane Ashelford, *The Art of Dress: Clothes and Society 1500–1914* (London: National Trust, 1996), 51.
16. For a discussion of contemporary consumer culture: Evelyn Welch, *Shopping in the Renaissance* (New Haven and London: Yale University Press, 2005).
17. *The Lisle Letters*, ed. Muriel St. Clare Byrne, 6 vols. (Chicago and London: University of Chicago Press, 1981), II, 210.
18. On the importance of appearances, Ulinka Rublack, *Dressing Up: Cultural Identity in Renaissance Europe* (Oxford: Oxford University Press, 2010).
19. *Letters of Philip Gawdy*, ed. Isaac Herbert Jeayes (London: J.B. Nichols and Sons, 1906), 28.
20. Frances Parthenope Verney, *Memoirs of the Verney Family During the Civil War*, 4 vols. (London: Longmans, 1892), II, 235. Stomacher: triangular insert worn at the bodice front.
21. Janet Arnold, *Queen Elizabeth's Wardrobe Unlock'd* (Leeds: Maney, 1988), 157–8; Yassana Croizat, "'Living Dolls': François Ier Dresses His Women," *Renaissance Quarterly* 60 (2007): 94–130.
22. T. Garzoni, *La Piazza Universaledi tutte le professioni del mondo* (1585), quoted in Grazietta Butazzi, "'The Scandalous Licentiousness of Tailors and Seamstresses': Considerations on the Profession of the Tailor in the Republic of Venice," in *I Mestieri della Moda a Venezia: The Arts and Crafts of Fashion in Venice, from the 13th to the 18th Century*, Exhibition Catalogue, rev. edn. (1997), 46.
23. Elizabeth Currie, "Diversity and Design in the Florentine Tailoring Trade, 1550–1620," in *The Material Renaissance*, eds Michelle O'Malley and Evelyn Welch (Manchester: Manchester University Press, 2007), 154–73.
24. Lucy Hutchinson, *Memoirs of the Life of Colonel Hutchinson*, ed. N.H. Keeble (London: Dent, 1995), 19.
25. *Letters of Philip Gawdy*, ed. Jeayes, 141.
26. Jane Ashelford, *Dress in the Age of Elizabeth* (London: Batsford, 1988), 79–84.
27. Pierre Erondelle, *The French garden* (London: Edward White, 1605), sig. Kv.
28. Margaret Spufford, *The Great Reclothing of Rural England: Petty Chapmen and their Wares in the Seventeenth Century* (London: Hambledon Press, 1984), 90–102.
29. Harald Deceulaer, "Entrepreneurs in the Guilds: Ready-to-wear Clothing and Subcontracting in Late Sixteenth- and Early Seventeenth-Century Antwerp," *Textile History* 31 (2000): 133–49, with reference to the European-wide phenomenon, 145. Anne Buck, "Clothing and Textiles in Bedfordshire Inventories, 1617–1620," *Costume* 34 (2000): 35.
30. Deceulaer, "Entrepreneurs in the Guilds."
31. For a survey of the subject, Claire Walsh, "The Social Relations of Shopping in Early Modern England," in *Buyers and Sellers: Retail Circuits and Practices in Medieval and Early Modern Europe*, eds Bruno Blondé, Peter Stabel, Jon Stobart, and Ilja Van Damme (Turnhout: Brepols, 2006), 331–51.
32. Stephen Greenblatt, *Renaissance Self-Fashioning: From More to Shakespeare* (Chicago: University of Chicago Press, 1980).
33. On the importance of this flow of goods—particularly clothing—outside formal retail channels, Beverly Lemire, "Plebeian Commercial Circuits and Everyday Material Exchange in England, c. 1600–1900," in *Buyers and Sellers*, eds Blondé et al., 245–66.
34. E.g. Ann Matchette, "Credit and Credibility: Used Goods and Social Relationships in Sixteenth-Century Florence," in *The Material Renaissance*, eds O'Malley and Welch, 225–41.
35. Susan Kay-Williams, *The Story of Colour in Textiles* (London: Bloomsbury, 2013), 47–9.
36. Collier Frick, "The Florentine Rigattieri," 17.
37. Joanna Crawford, "Clothing Distributions and Social Relations c. 1350–1500," in *Clothing Culture 1350–1650*, ed. Catherine Richardson (Aldershot: Ashgate, 2004), 156. Also on livery, Ann Rosalind Jones and Peter Stallybrass, *Renaissance Clothing and the Materials of Memory* (Cambridge: Cambridge University Press, 2000), 17–21.

38. *The Private Diary of Dr. John Dee*, ed. James Orchard Halliwell, Camden Society, o.s. 19 (1842), 53–4.
39. Ilid Anthony, "Clothing Given to a Servant of the Late Sixteenth Century in Wales," *Costume* 14 (1980): 32–40.
40. On making and maintenance, Ninya Mikhaila and Jane Malcolm-Davies, *The Tudor Tailor: Reconstructing Sixteenth-Century Dress* (London: Batsford, 2006), 42, 45. For a detailed look at the alterations to an early seventeenth-century waistcoat, North and Tiramani, (eds), *Women's Dress Patterns*, 34–47.
41. *The Paston Letters: A Selection in Modern Spelling*, ed. Norman Davies (Oxford: Oxford University Press, 1983), 46.
42. Peter Mactaggart and Ann Mactaggart, "The Rich Wearing Apparel of Richard, 3rd Earl of Dorset," *Costume* 14 (1980): 41–55; *The Diaries of Lady Anne Clifford*, ed. D.J.H. Clifford (Stroud: Sutton, 1990), 81.
43. Stubbes, *Anatomie of apparel*, 29, sig. E3r.
44. Maria Hayward, "Fashion, Finance, Foreign Politics and the Wardrobe of Henry VIII," in *Clothing Culture*, ed. Richardson, 173–8.
45. Jones and Stallybrass, *Renaissance Clothing*, 19.
46. *Lisle Letters*, VI, 25.
47. Hayward, "Fashion, Finance, Foreign Politics," 177. On gifts of clothing to and from Elizabeth, Arnold, *Queen Elizabeth's Wardrobe*, 93–103.
48. See Kathleen Ashley, "Material and Symbolic Gift-Giving: Clothes in English and French Wills," in *Medieval Fabrications: Dress, Textiles, Cloth Work, and Other Cultural Imaginings*, ed. E. Jane Burns (New York: Palgrave Macmillan, 2004), 137–46.
49. See Sheila Sweetinburgh, "Clothing the Naked in Late Medieval East Kent," in *Clothing Culture*, ed. Richardson, 109–21; Dolly MacKinnon, "Charitable Bodies: Clothing as Charity in Early-Modern Rural England," in *Practices of Gender in Late Medieval and Early Modern Europe*, eds Megan Cassidy-Welch and Peter Sherlock (Turnhout: Brepols, 2008), 235–59.
50. See Elisabeth Salter, "Reworked Material: Discourses of Clothing Culture in Early Sixteenth-Century Greenwich," in *Clothing Culture*, ed. Richardson, 179–91; Kristen M. Burkholder, "Threads Bared: Dress and Textiles in Late Medieval English Wills," in *Medieval Clothing and Textiles* 1, eds Robin Netherton and Gale Owen-Crocker (Woodbridge: Boydell Press, 2005), 133–53. For an extensive study using wills as primary source material, Maria Hayward, *Rich Apparel: Clothing and the Law in Henry VIII's England* (Farnham: Ashgate, 2009).
51. *Liber Famelicus of Sir James Whitelocke*, ed. John Bruce, Camden Society 70 (1858), 24.
52. Jane E. Huggett, "Rural Costume in Elizabethan Essex: A Study Based on the Evidence of Wills," *Costume* 33 (1999): 74–88; discussion of garment descriptions and quotes, 75–6.
53. Sara Mendelson and Patricia Crawford, *Women in Early Modern England 1530–1720* (Oxford: Clarendon Press, 1998), 222.
54. See for this area: Collier Frick, "The Florentine Rigattieri"; Patricia Allerston, "Reconstructing the Second-Hand Clothes Trade in Sixteenth- and Seventeenth-Century Venice," *Costume* 33 (1999): 46–56; Patricia Allerston, "Clothing and Early Modern Venetian Society," in *The Fashion History Reader: Global Perspectives*, eds Giorgio Riello and Peter McNeil (London and New York: Routledge, 2010), 93–110 (an earlier version published in *Continuity and Change* 15 (2000): 367–90); Kate Kelsey Staples, "Fripperers and the Used Clothing Trade in Late Medieval London," in *Medieval Clothing and Textiles* 6, eds Robin Netherton and Gale Owen-Crocker (Woodbridge: Boydell Press, 2010), 151–71; Harald Deceulaer, "Second-Hand Dealers in the Early Modern Low Countries: Institutions, Markets and Practices," in *Alternative Exchanges: Second-Hand Circulations from the Sixteenth Century to the Present*, ed. Laurence Fontaine (New York and Oxford: Berghahn Books, 2008), 13–42; Deceulaer, "Entrepreneurs in the Guilds"; Beverley Lemire, "Shifting Currency: The Culture and

Economy of the Second Hand Trade in England, c. 1600–1850," in *Old Clothes, New Looks*, eds Palmer and Clark, 29–47.
55. Jones and Stallybrass, *Renaissance Clothing*, 26–32; Matchette, "Credit and Credibility."
56. Matchette, "Credit and Credibility," 227; Jones and Stallybrass, *Renaissance Clothing*, 30, 184. Also on the frequency of clothing pledges, Lemire, "Plebeian Commercial Circuits," 251–2, albeit with statistics mostly for a later period, and "Shifting Currency."
57. Mendelson and Crawford, *Women in Early Modern England*, 222.
58. John Stowe, *The Survey of London*, orig. pub. 1598 and 1603 (London: Nicholas Bourn, 1633), 215–16.
59. Trevor Dean, *Crime in Medieval Europe 1200–1550* (Harlow and London: Longman, 2001), 19.
60. Thomas Harman, *A caueat for common cursetors vvlgarely called uagaboes* (London: Wylliam Gryffith, 1567), sig. B4v–C1r.
61. *Dudley Carleton to John Chamberlain 1603–1624: Jacobean Letters*, ed. Maurice Lee (New Brunswick: Rutgers University Press, 1972), 153.
62. Public Record Office, State Papers Domestic, Charles I, SP16/479/78.
63. A phenomenon particularly common it seems in Italian cities: e.g. Allerston, "Clothing and Early Modern Venetian Society," 100.

Chapter 3

1. Isabelle Paresys, "The Dressed Body: the Moulding of Identities in Sixteenth Century France," in *Cultural Exchange in Early Modern Europe*, vol. 4; *Forging European Identities, 1400–1700*, ed. H. Roodenburg (Cambridge: Cambridge University Press–European Science Foundation, 2007), 227–257; Ulinka Rublack, *Dressing Up: Cultural Identity in Renaissance Europe* (Oxford: Oxford University Press, 2010).
2. Ulrike Ilg, "The Cultural Significance of Costume Books in Sixteenth-Century Europe," in *Clothing Culture, 1350–1650*, ed. C. Richardson (Aldershot: Ashgate, 2003), 29–47.
3. Georges Vigarello, *Le corps redressé. Histoire d'un pouvoir pédagogique* (Paris: Delarge, 1978) and Philippe Perrot, *Les dessus et le dessous de la bourgeoisie, une histoire du vêtement au XIXe s* (Paris: Fayard, 1981).
4. E.g. Odile Blanc, *Parades et parures. L'invention du corps de mode à la fin du Moyen Age* (Paris: Gallimard, 1997); Joanne Entwistle, *The Fashioned Body. Fashion, Dress and Modern Social Theory* (Cambridge: Polity, 2000); Susan J. Vincent, *The Anatomy of Fashion: Dressing the Body from the Renaissance to Today* (Oxford: Berg, 2009).
5. See Susan Vincent, "From the cradle to the grave. Clothing the early modern body," in *The Routledge History of Sex and the Body, 1500 to the Present*, eds Sarah Toulalan and Kate Fisher (London and New York: Routledge, 2013), 163–76.
6. Evelyn Welch, *Shopping in the Renaissance: Consumer Cultures in Italy 1400–1600* (Yale: Yale University Press, 2005).
7. Erving Goffman, *The Presentation of Self in Everyday Life* (New York: Anchor Books, 1959).
8. Sylvie Steinberg, *La Confusion des sexes. Le travestissement de la Renaissance à la Révolution* (Paris: Fayard, 2001), 180–94.
9. Ibid., 103–8.
10. From Philippe Ariès, *L'Enfant et la vie familiale* (Paris: Seuil, 1975), 79.
11. Brantôme, *Recueil des Dames* (Paris: Gallimard, 1991), II, III: "Sur la beauté de la jambe, et la vertu qu'elle a," 451–2.
12. Quoted by Giorgio Riello, "From Renaissance Platforms to Modern High Heels: Disequilibrium of gait," in *A Feast for the Eyes! Spectacular Fashions*, eds A.C. Laronde, S. Boucher and I. Paresys (Milano: Silvana Editoriale, 2012), 115–17.
13. This style was also adopted in England and the Low Countries, but not in Spain or in Italy: Janet Arnold, *Patterns of Fashion: The cut and construction of clothes for men and women c. 1560–1620* (London: Macmillan, 1985), 49.

14. Ibid.
15. Gabriel André Perouse, "La Renaissance et la beauté masculine," in *Le Corps à la Renaissance. Actes du XXXe colloque de Tours 1987*, eds J. Céard et alii (Paris: Amateurs de Livres, 1990), 60–76.
16. Thomas Lüttenberg, "The Cod-piece. A Renaissance Fashion between Sign and Artefact," *The Medieval History Journal*, vol. 8, no. 1 (2005): 49–81.
17. See various examples in Janet Arnold and Jenny Tiramani, *Patterns of Fashion 4: The cut and construction of linen shirts, smocks, neckwear, headwear and accessories for men and women c. 1540–1660* (London: Macmillan, 2008).
18. Paresys, "A profusion of ruffs," in *A Feast for the Eyes*, 100–3.
19. Juan de Alcega, *Libro de geometria, práctica y traça, el cual trata de lo tocante al officio del sastre* (Madrid: Guillermo Drouy, 1580).
20. Francisco de la Rocha Burguen, *Geometria y Traça perteneciente al officio de Sastres* (Valencia, Pedro Patricio Mey, 1618). See Doretta Davanzo Poli, "Il sarto," *Storia d'Italia, Annali 19, La moda*, eds M. Belfanti and F. Giusberti (Torino: Einaudi, 2003), 539.
21. Vincent, *Dressing the Elite*, 48–9.
22. Montaigne, *Essais*, in *Oeuvres complètes* (Paris: Gallimard, 1962), Bk. I, chapter XLIII.
23. Jacqueline Boucher, *Société et mentalités autour de Henri III* (Lille: Atelier de reproduction des thèses, 1981), 1138.
24. Not all fashionable ladies were followers of such a constrictive system. In sixteenth-century Italy, for example, some women espoused an alternative silhouette. A Venetian ambassador visiting Paris in 1577 thought that women were "even more elegant . . . and more slender" (than his country women) because of their soft waist and *vertugadin*. But a French traveler in Italy, just a few years later, marveled at the "overly loose waists" of Roman women, which "made them seem pregnant," a statement apparently not intended as a compliment, see "Voyage de J. Lippomano, ambassadeur de Venise en France en 1577," in *Le Voyage en France. Anthologie des voyageurs européens en France, du Moyen Age à la fin de l'Empire* eds J.-M. Goulemot et al. (Paris: Laffont, 1995), 126–7; Montaigne, *Journal de voyage en Italie*, in *Oeuvres complètes*, 1217.
25. Jenny Tiramani, "Pins and Aglets," in *Everyday Objets: Medieval and Early Modern Material Culture and its Meanings*, eds T. Hamlin and C. Richardson (Aldershot: Ashgate, 2010), 92.
26. Brantôme, *Recueil des Dames*, 129.
27. Vigarello, *Le Corps redressé*, chapter 1.
28. Baldassare Castiglione, *Il Libro del Cortegiano* (Venezia: Aldo Manuzio, 1528), Bk. II, chapter 27.
29. Montaigne, *Essais*, Bk. I, chapter XXXVI, 223.
30. E.g. François Deserpz (Desprez), *Receuil des la diversité des habits, qui sont de present en usage, tant es pays d'Europe, Asie, Affrique & Isles sauvages* (Paris: Richard Breton, 1562).
31. Jean de Léry, *History of a voyage to the land of Brazil, otherwise called America* (1578), ed. J. Whatley (Berkeley: University of California Press, 1990).
32. Franck Lestringant (ed.), *Le Brésil d'André Thévet. Les singularités de la France Antarticque (1557)*, (Paris: Chandeigne, 1997), 126.
33. Christian Marouby, *Utopie et primitivisme. Essai sur l'imaginaire anthropologique à l'âge classique* (Paris: Seuil, 1990), 126–37; Murdoch Graeme, "Dress, Nudity and Calvinist Culture in Sixteenth-Century France," in *Clothing Culture*, ed. Richardson, 123–36.
34. Denis Crouzet, "Imaginaire du corps et violence au temps des troubles de Religion" in *Le corps à la Renaissance, Actes du colloque de Tours, 1987*, eds J. Céard et el. (Paris: Amateurs de livres, 1990), 115–27.
35. *Un banquier mis à nu. Autobiographie de Matthäus Schwarz, bourgeois d'Augsbourg*, ed. Ph. Braunstein (Paris: Gallimard, 1992); Rublack, *Dressing Up*, chapter 2.
36. Georges Vigarello, *Concepts of Cleanliness: changing attitudes in France since the Middle Age* (Cambridge: Cambridge University Press, 1988); Vincent, *The Anatomy of Fashion*, chapter 5.

37. Ibid., 146–8.
38. Christine Aribaud, "Les taillades dans le vêtement de la Renaissance: l'art des nobles écritures," in *Paraître et se vêtir* (Sainte-Etienne: PU Sainte-Etienne), 143–58.
39. Montaigne, *Essais*, Bk. III, chapter V, 70.
40. Béroalde de Verville, *Le Moyen de parvenir (1617)*, (Albi: éd. du Passage, 2002), 57.
41. Jeffrey C. Persels, "Brageta Humanistica, or Humanism's Codpiece," *Sixteenth-Century Journal* 28 (1997): 79–99; Rabelais, *Gargantua* (Paris: Garnier-Flammarion, 1968), 70.
42. Paresys, "Vêtir les souverains français à la Renaissance: les garde-robes d'Henri II et de Catherine de Médicis en 1556 et 1557," in *Se vêtir à la cour en Europe (1400–1815)*, eds I. Paresys and N. Coquery (Villeneuve d'Ascq: Centre de recherche du château de Versailles-IRHiS-CEGES Lille 3, 2011), 133–57.
43. Daniel Roche, *The Culture of Clothing: Dress and Fashion in the Ancien Régime* (Cambridge: Cambridge University Press, 1996), 182.
44. Roberta Orsi Landini and Bruna Niccoli, *Moda a Firenze 1540–1580: lo stile di Eleonora di Toledo e la sua influenza* (Florence: Polistampa, 2005), 133.
45. Pietro Bertelli, *Diversarum Nationum Habitus Gentum* (Padua: Alci, 1589), and Vecellio, *Habiti antichi et moderni di tutto il mondo* (Venezia: Zenaro, 1590).
46. Quoted in *Essais historiques sur les modes et la toilette française par le chevalier de****, tome premier (Paris: Librairie universelle Pierre Mongie, 1824), 142–3.
47. Vigarello, *Concepts of cleanliness*, part 1, chapter 1.
48. Vincent, *Anatomy of Fashion*, 141.
49. Vecellio, *Habiti antichi et moderni*: Citella Spagnuola, fig. 621–2.
50. Rosine Lambin, *Le voile des femmes. Un inventaire historique, social et psychologique* (Bern: Peter Lang, 1999).
51. Annick le Guérer, *Le parfum des origines à nos jours* (Paris: Odile Jacob, 2005).
52. Vigarello, *Concepts of Cleanliness*, part 2, chapter 3.
53. *Le bain et le miroir: soins du corps et cosmétique de l'Antiquité à la Renaissance*, eds I. Bardiès-Fronty and M. Bimbenet-Privat (Paris: Gallimard, 2009), 329.
54. Hans Maler, *Portrait of Anton Fugger*, c. 1525. Paris, musée du Louvre, inv.: RF2002–28.
55. Bardiès-Fronty and Bimbenet-Privat, *Le bain et le miroir:* p. 315.
56. On the corporal hexes and the habitus, see Marcel Mauss, "Les techniques du corps," *Journal de Psychologie*, XXXII, mars–avril 1936: 363–86; Pierre Bourdieu, *La distinction, Critique sociale du jugement* (Paris: Minuit, 1979).
57. John Bulwer, *Anthropometamorphosis* (London: J. Hardesty, 1650).

Chapter 4

1. Willliam Durand, *On the Clergy and their Vestments*, trans. and intro. Timothy M. Thibodeau (Chicago: University of Scranton Press, 2010).
2. Quoted in Ulinka Rublack, *Dressing Up: Cultural Identity in Renaissance Europe* (Oxford: Oxford University Press, 2010), 82.
3. Thomas M. Izbicki, "Forbidden Colors in the Regulation of Clerical Dress from the Fourth Lateran Council (1215) to the Time of Nicholas of Cusa (d. 1464)," *Medieval Dress and Textiles* 1 (2005): 105.
4. Rublack, *Dressing Up*, 85.
5. Andrea Denny-Brown, "Old Habits Die Hard: Vestimentary Change in William Durandus' *Rationale Divinorum Officiorum*," *Journal of Medieval and Early Modern Studies* 39/3 (2009): 547.
6. Innocent III, *De sacro altaris mysterio* (Sylvae-Ducum: Verhoeven, 1846), 86–92.
7. J. Wickham Legg, *Notes on the History of the Liturgical Colours* (London: John S. Leslie, 1882).
8. John Gage, *Colour and Culture* (London: Thames & Hudson, 1993), 84.

9. Girolamo Savonarola, *De simplicitate christianae vitae*, ed. Pier Giorgio Ricci (Rome: Angelo Belardetti Editore, 1959), 100–1 (liber IV, conclusio VIII): "et cum votum paupertatis emiserint, fugiunt eam quasi leaenam et ursam captis filiis."
10. Alison Wright, *The Pollaiuolo Brothers: The Arts of Florence and Rome* (New Haven and London: Yale University Press, 2005), 257–86.
11. Ibid., 260.
12. Ibid., 261.
13. Sharon Strocchia, *Nuns and Nunneries in Renaissance Florence* (Baltimore: Johns Hopkins University Press, 2009), 126–44.
14. Craig A. Monson, "The Council of Trent Revisited," *Journal of the American Musicological Society* 55/1 (2002): 10.
15. Graeme Murdock, "Dressed to Repress? Protestant Clerical Dress and the Regulation of Morality in Early Modern Europe," *Fashion Theory: The Journal of Dress, Body and Culture* 4/2 (2000): 179–99.
16. Ibid., 181.
17. Quotation and translation taken from Carl Piepkorn, *The Survival of the Historic Vestments in the Lutheran Church after 1555* (St. Louis, MO: Concordia Press, 1958), 9.
18. Ibid., 9.
19. Bodo Nischan, "The Second Reformation in Brandenburg: Aims and Goals," *The Sixteenth Century Journal* 14/2 (1983): 181–2.
20. Piepkorn, *The Survival*, 8.
21. Ibid., 12–30.
22. Patrick Collinson, *The Elizabethan Puritan Movement* (Oxford: Clarendon Press, 1990, 1st ed. 1967), 67–96.
23. The instruction is given before the order for morning prayer in chapter VI of the *Book of Common Prayer printed by Whitchurch 1552, commonly called the Second Book of Edward VI*, (London: William Pickering, 1844). I have modernized the spelling.
24. Janet Mayo, *A History of Ecclesiastical Dress* (New York: Holmes & Meier, 1984), 67.
25. Ibid., 68.
26. Ibid., 69.
27. Diane Cole Ahl, "Benozzo Gozzoli's Frescoes of the Life of Saint Augustine in San Gimignano: Their Meaning in Context," *Artibus et Historiae* 7/13 (1986): 35–53.
28. Kaspar Elm, "Augustinus Canonicus—Augustinus Eremita: A Quattrocento Cause Célèbre," in *Christianity and the Renaissance: Image and Religious Imagination in the Quattrocentro*, eds Timothy Verdon and John Henderson (Syracuse, NY: Syracuse University Pres, 1990), 83–107.
29. For a discussion of importance of the representation of the habit of the Augustinian Hermits in visual art between the fourteenth and the fifteenth century, see Cordelia Warr, "Hermits, Habits and History," in *Art and the Augustinian Order in Early Renaissance Italy*, eds Louise Bourdua and Anne Dunlop (Aldershot: Ashgate, 2007), 17–28, republished in Cordelia Warr, *Dressing for Heaven: Religious Clothing in Italy, 1215–1545* (Manchester: Manchester University Press, 2010), 117–30.
30. The rule is published in *Seraphicae legislationis textus originales*, Typographia Collegii S. Bonaventurae: Quaracchi (1897), 35–47. Translation taken from Paschal Robinson, *The Writings of Saint Francis* (London: J.M. Dent and Co., 1906), 66.
31. Duncan Nimmo, *Reform and Division in the Medieval Franciscan Order: From Saint Francis to the Foundation of the Capuchin* (Rome: Capuchin Historical Institute, 1987), 100.
32. Ibid., 121, 133, 157–8.
33. Father Cuthbert (ed. and trans.), *A Capuchin Chronicle* (London: Sheed & Ward, 1931), vii–ix.
34. Ibid., 2–3.
35. Father Cuthbert, *The Capuchins: A Contribution to the History of the Counter Reformation*, 2 vols. (London: Sheed & Ward, 1928 and 1929), 1:21.

36. Cuthbert, *A Capuchin Chronicle*, 3.
37. Ibid., 3–4.
38. Eric Young, "An Unknown Saint Francis by Francisco de Zurbarán," in *The Burlington Magazine* 115/841 (1973): 245–7.
39. Norman P. Tanner, *Decrees of the Ecumenical Councils*, 2 vols. (London: Sheed & Ward, 1990), 2: 774–6.
40. John Harvey, *Men in Black* (London: Reaktion, 1995), 83.
41. John W. O'Malley, *The First Jesuits* (Cambridge MA and London: Harvard University Press, 1993), 341–2.
42. Harvey, *Men in Black*, 84.
43. Jennifer Woodward, *The Theatre of Death: The Ritual Management of Royal Funerals in Renaissance England, 1570–1625* (Woodbridge: Boydell Press, 1997), 19.
44. Juan Luis Vives, *The Education of a Christian Woman*, ed. and trans. Charles Fantazzi (Chicago and London: University of Chicago Press, 2000), 311.
45. Lou Taylor, *Mourning Dress* (London: George Allen & Unwin, 1983), 86.
46. Cesare Vecellio, *Cesare Vecellio's Habiti Antichi e Moderni*, eds and trans. Margaret F. Rosenthal and Ann Rosalind Jones (London: Thames & Hudson, 2008), 186 (fol. 133 v and 134 r).
47. Luke Syson and Dora Thornton, *Objects of Virtue: Art in Renaissance Italy* (London: British Museum Press, 2001), 32.
48. Thomas Tuohy, *Herculean Ferrara* (Cambridge: Cambridge University Press, 1996), 9–10.
49. Michel Pastoureau, *Black: The History of a Colour* (Princeton and Oxford: Princeton University Press, 2008), 102–3; Harvey, *Men in Black*, 52–8.
50. Pastoureau, *Black*, 103; Gabriel Guarino, "Regulation of Appearances during the Catholic Reformation: Dress and Morality in Spain and Italy," in *Le deux réformes chrétiennes: propagation et diffusion*, eds Ilan Zinguer and MyriamYardeni (Leiden and Boston: Brill, 2004), 501.
51. Baldassare Castiglione, *The Book of the Courtier: The Singleton Translation*, ed. Daniel Javitch (New York and London: W.W. Norton & Company, 2002), 89 (Book 2, para. 27).
52. Ibid., 90.
53. Ibid., 88.
54. Ulrike Ilg, "The Cultural Significance of Costume Books in Sixteenth-Century Europe," in *Clothing Culture, 1350–1650*, ed. Catherine Richardson (Aldershot: Ashgate, 2004), 29.
55. Ibid., 40.
56. Ibid., 43.
57. Translation in ibid., 40.
58. A translation and facsimile of the 1562 edition has been published by Sara Shannon (ed. and trans.) and Carol Urness (intro.): François Deserps, *François Deserps, A Collection of the Various Styles of Clothing* (Minneapolis: University of Minnesota Press, 2001).
59. Translation given by Ilg, "The Cultural Significance," 45, from the 1564 edition (*Receuil*, fol. A3-A3 verso).
60. Translation from *Cesare Vecellio's Habiti Antichi e Moderni*, ed. and trans. Rosenthal and Jones, 88 (fol. 35 v and 35 r).
61. Tessa, Storey, "Clothing Courtesans: Fabric, Signals and Experiences," in *Clothing Culture*, ed. Richardson, 104.
62. Ilg, "The Cultural Significance," 46–7.
63. A.L. Beier, *Masterless Men: The Vagrancy Problem in England, 1560–1640* (London: Methuen & Co. Ltd, 1985), 131.
64. Claire Bartram, "Social Fabric in Thynne's *Debate between Pride and Lowliness*," in *Clothing Culture*, ed. Richardson, 137–49.
65. John Block Friedman, "The Iconography of Dagged Clothing and its Reception by Moralist Writers," *Medieval Clothing and Textiles* 9 (2013): 121–38.

66. John Bulwer, *Anthropometamorphosis: Man transformed: or, the artificial changling* (London: William Hunt, 1653, 2nd edition).
67. Rublack, *Dressing Up*, 9.
68. Bulwer, *Anthropometamorphosis*, 458.
69. Joel Konrad, "'Barbarous Gallants': Fashion, Morality, and the Marked Body in English Culture, 1590–1660," *Fashion Theory* 15/1 (2011), 29–48.
70. Aileen Ribeiro, *Dress and Morality* (Oxford: Berg, 2003), 62–3.
71. David Lindsay, *The Minor Poems of Lyndesay*, ed. J.A.H. Murray (London: Trübner, 1871), 574–9.
72. Ribeiro, *Dress and Morality*, 68–9.
73. Philip Stubbes, *The Anatomie of Abuses*, ed. Margaret Jane Kidnie, Renaissance English Text Society, 7th series, vol. 27, Arizona Center for Medieval and Renaissance Studies (Arizona: Tempe, 2002), 66–7, lines 536–54.
74. Stubbes, *The Anatomie of Abuses*, 90–128, lines 1386–2270.
75. Margaret Jane Kidnie, "Introduction," in Stubbes, *The Anatomie of Abuses*, 28–35.
76. Vives, *The Education*, 107.
77. Ibid., 236.
78. Ibid., 311.
79. Rudolph M. Bell, *How To Do It: Guides to Good Living for Renaissance Ladies* (Chicago and London: University of Chicago Press, 1999), 265.
80. Savonarola, *De Simplicitate*, 70–8 (liber III, conclusio VII).
81. See the discussion by Diane Owen Hughes, "Sumptuary Law and Social Relations in Renaissance Italy," in *Disputes and Settlements: Law and Human Relations in the West*, ed. John Bossy (Cambridge: Cambridge University Press, 1983), 69–100.
82. Translation in John Martin Vincent, *Costume and Conduct in the Laws of Basel, Bern and Zurich, 1370–1800* (New York: Greenwood Press, 1969, first published 1935), 141.
83. Alonso Carranza, *Discurso contra malos trajes y adornos lascivos*, Francisco Martinez: Madrid (1639). Translation taken from Amanda Wunder, "Dress (Spain)," in *A Lexicon of the Hispanic Baroque: Transatlantic Exchange and Transformation*, eds Evonne Levy and Kenneth Mills (Austin: University of Texas Press, 2013), 108.
84. Eugenia Paulicelli, *Writing Fashion in Early Modern Italy: From Sprezzatura to Satire* (Farnham: Ashgate, 2014), 215–20.
85. Guarino, "Regulation of Appearances," 507.
86. Michael Carter, "Remembrance, Liturgy and Status in a late medieval English Cistercian Abbey: The Mourning Vestment of Abbot Robert Thornton of Jervaulx," *Textile History* 41/2 (2010), 145–60.
87. Maria Hayward, *Rich Apparel: Clothing and the Law in Henry VIII's England* (Aldershot: Ashgate, 2009), 12.
88. Sharon Strocchia, *Death and Ritual in Renaissance Florence* (Baltimore: Johns Hopkins University Press, 1992), 39–43.
89. Ibid., 21.
90. Sally J. Cornelison, *Art and the Relic Cult of St. Antoninus in Renaissance Florence* (Farnham: Ashgate, 2012), 17–18.
91. Carlos M.N. Eire, *From Madrid to Purgatory: The Art and Craft of Dying in Sixteenth-Century Spain* (Cambridge: Cambridge University Press, 2002), 105–7.
92. Antonio Daza, *Historia de las Llagas de Nuestro Seráfico Padre San Francisco, colegida del Martirologio y Breviario Romano y Treynta Bulas y Dozientos Autores y Santos* (Valladolid, 1617), fols 57 recto – 64 recto.
93. Richard C. Trexler, "Dressing and Undressing Images: An Analytic Sketch," in *Religion and Social Context in Europe and America, 1200–1700*, Richard C. Trexler, Arizona Center for Medieval and Renaissance Studies (Arizona: Tempe, 2002), 381.
94. Christiane Klapisch-Zuber, *Women, Family and Ritual in Renaissance Italy* (Chicago and London: University of Chicago Press, 1985), 324.

95. Trexler, "Dressing and Undressing," 400.
96. Placido Tommaso Lugano, *I processi inediti per Francesca Bussa dei Ponziani* (Città del Vaticano: Bibliotheca Apostica Vaticana, 1945), 257–8.
97. Ibid., 288.

Chapter 5

1. *Hic Mulier* and *Haec Vir* [1620] 1985, in *Half Humankind: Contexts and Texts of the Controversy about Women in England, 1540–1640*, eds Katherine Usher Henderson and Barbara McManus (Urbana: University of Illinois Press, 1985), 265.
2. Janet Winter and Carolyn Savoy, index of "Unisex Clothing," in *Elizabethan Costuming for the Years 1550–1580*. (Oakland, CA: Other Times Publications, 1987).
3. Ulinka Rublack, *Dressing Up: Cultural Identity in Renaissance Europe* (Oxford: Oxford University Press, 2010), 248.
4. Maria Hayward, *Rich Apparel: Clothing and the Law in Henry VIII's England* (Burlington, VT: Ashgate, 2009), 125.
5. Evelyn Welch, "Scented Buttons and Perfumed Gloves: Smelling Things in Renaissance Italy," in *Ornamentalism: The Art of the Renaissance Accessory*, ed. Bella Mirabella (Ann Arbor: University of Michigan Press, 2011), 24–8.
6. Doretta Davanzo Poli, *Il Merletto Veneziano* (Venice: Novara, 1998); Santina Levey, *Lace: A History* (London: Victoria & Albert Museum in association with W.S. Maney & Son, 1983).
7. Eugenia Paulicelli, *Writing Fashion in Early Modern Italy: From Sprezzatura to Satire*, (Burlington, VT: Ashgate, 2014), 145.
8. Ibid., 144–5.
9. Karen Raber, "Chains of Pearls: Gender, Property, Identity," in *Ornamentalism: The Art of the Renaissance Accessory*, ed. Bella Mirabella (Ann Arbor: University of Michigan Press, 2011), 165.
10. Anthony Holden, 2002. "That's no lady, that's . . ." *The Guardian* (April 21, 2002): 15.
11. Jane Ashelford, *A Visual History of Costume in the Sixteenth Century* (London: Batsford, 1993), 15.
12. Ibid., 14.
13. Anne H. Van Buren, with Roger S. Wieck, *Illuminating Fashion: Dress in the Art of Medieval France and the Netherlands, 1325–1515* (London: Giles/New York: The Morgan Library and Museum, 2001). 7; Hayward, *Rich Apparel*, 135.
14. Timothy McCall, "Brilliant Bodies: Material Culture and the Adornment of Men's Bodies in North Italy's Quattrocento Courts," *I Tatti Studies in the Italian Renaissance* 16 (1 & 2) (2013): 451.
15. Hayward, *Rich Apparel*, 119.
16. Baldasar Heseler, in *Andreas Vesalius' First Public Anatomy at Bologna, 1540: An Eyewitness Report*, ed. and trans., Ruben Eriksson (Uppsala: Almqvist & Wiksells, [1540] 1959), 181.
17. Katharine Park, "Was there a Renaissance Body?" in *The Italian Renaissance in the Twentieth Century: Acts of an International Conference, Florence, Villa I Tatti, June 9–11, 1999*, eds Allen J. Grieco, Michael Rocke, and Fiorella Giofreddi Superbi (1999): 325; Gianna Pomata, "Knowledge-Freshening Wind: Gender and the Renewal of Renaissance Studies," in *The Italian Renaissance in the Twentieth Century: Acts of an International Conference, Florence, Villa I Tatti, June 9–11, 1999*, eds Allen J. Grieco, Michael Rocke, and Fiorella Giofreddi Superbi, (Florence: Olschki, 2002), 186–8.
18. Patricia Simons, *The Sex of Men in Premodern Europe: A Cultural History* (Cambridge: Cambridge University Press, 2011), 16.
19. Claude Dubois, "Introduction to Artus Thomas" [1605], *Les Hermaphrodites* (Geneva: Droz, 1996), 18–22.
20. Ann Rosalind Jones and Peter Stallybrass, "Fetishizing Gender: Constructing the Hermaphrodite in Renaissance Europe," in *Body Guards: The Cultural Politics of Gender*

Ambiguity, eds Julia Epstein and Kristina Straub (New York and London: Routledge, 1991), 92.
21. Van Buren, *Illuminating Fashion*, 56.
22. Rublack, *Dressing Up: Cultural Identity in Renaissance Europe*, 17.
23. Ibid., 16.
24. Cesare Vecellio, *Degli Habiti antichi et moderni di diverse parti del Mondo*, trans. Margaret F. Rosenthal and Ann Rosalind Jones (London: Thames & Hudson [1590] 2008), 274.
25. Ann Rosalind Jones and Peter Stallybrass, "Busks, Bodices, Bodies," in *Ornamentalism: The Art of the Renaissance Accessory*, ed. Bella Mirabella (Ann Arbor: University of Michigan Press, 2011), 90.
26. Paulicelli, *Writing Fashion in Early Modern Italy*, 16.
27. Graeme Murdock, "Dress, Nudity and Calvinist Culture in Sixteenth-Century France," in *Clothing Culture, 1350–1650*, ed. Catherine Richardson (Burlington, VT: Ashgate, 2004), 131.
28. Vecellio, *Degli Habiti antichi et moderni*, fol. 145v.
29. Simons, *The Sex of Men in Premodern Europe*, 98.
30. Ibid.
31. Konrad Eisenblicher, "Bronzino's Portrait of Guidobaldo II dellaRovere," Renaissance and Reformation, Vol. 24 (1) (1988): 21–33.
32. Rublack, *Dressing Up*, 135.
33. Michel Eyquem de Montaigne, *Essais*, 1575, quoted in Jeffery Persels, "Bragueta Humanistica, or Humanism's Codpiece," *Sixteenth Century Journal*, 28(1) (1997): 83.
34. Paulicelli, *Writing Fashion in Early Modern Italy*, 104.
35. Will Fisher, "'Had it a codpiece, 'twere a man indeed': The Codpiece as Constitutive Accessory in Early Modern Culture," in *Ornamentalism: The Art of the Renaissance Accessory*, ed. Bella Mirabella (Ann Arbor: University of Michigan Press, 2011), 103.
36. François Rabelais, *Gargantua*, trans. J.M. Cohen (Harmondsworth: Penguin, [1532] 1955), 55.
37. Fisher, "Had it a codpiece," pp. 120–1.
38. Tessa Storey, "Clothing Courtesans: Fabrics, Signals and Experiences," in *Clothing Culture 1350–1650*, ed. Catherine Richardson (Aldershot: Ashgate, 2004), 98.
39. Ibid., 99.
40. Richard Trexler, "La prostitution florentine au XVe siècle: patronage et clientele," *Annales*, Year 36 (6) (1981): 995.
41. Ibid., 996.
42. Ibid., 997–8.
43. Patrizia Cibin, "Meretrici e cortigiane a Venezianel '500," *Donna Woman Femme, Quaderni internazionali di studi sulla donna* 25 (6) (1985): 99.
44. Margaret F. Rosenthal, *The Honest Courtesan: Veronica Franco, Citizen and Writer in Renaissance Venice* (Chicago: University of Chicago Press, 1992), 291 n. 29, 327; Jennifer Haraguchi, "Debating Women's Fashion in Renaissance Venice," in *A Well-Fashioned Image: Clothing and Costume in European Art, 1500–1850*, eds Elizabeth Rodini and Elissa B. Weaver (Chicago: The David and Alfred Smart Museum/University of Chicago, 2002), 30.
45. Vecellio, *Degli Habiti antichi et moderni*, fol. 145v.
46. Henderson and McManus, *Half Humankind*, 267 n. 12; Ann Rosalind Jones and Peter Stallybrass, *Renaissance Clothing and the Materials of Memory* (Cambridge: Cambridge University Press, 2000), 80–1.
47. Ibid., 135.
48. Ibid., 41.
49. Ibid., 41.
50. Susan Vincent, *Dressing the Elite: Clothes in Early Modern England* (Oxford and New York: Berg, 2003), 171–2.

51. In Henderson and McManus, *Half Humankind*, p. 267.
52. Ibid., 282.
53. Ibid., 283–4.
54. Peter Goodrich, "Signs taken for wonders: Community, Identity and a History of Sumptuary Law," *Law and Social Inquiry*, 23 (3) (1998): 715.
55. Van Buren, *Illuminating Fashion*, 4.
56. Hayward, *Rich Apparel*, 29–39.
57. Marzia Cataldi Gallo, "Per una storia del costume genovese nel primo quarto del seicento," in *Van Dyck 350*, eds Susan Barnes and Arthur Wheelock, Jr. (Washington DC and Hanover, NH: National Gallery of Art/University of New England Press, 1994), 119–20.
58. Cataldi Gallo, "Per una storia del costume genovese", 119.
59. Maria Giuseppina Muzzarelli, "Reconciling the Privilege of a Few with the Common Good: Sumptuary Laws in Medieval and Early Modern Europe," *Journal of Medieval and Early Modern Studies* 39 (3), special issue (2009) ed. Margaret F. Rosenthal, *Cultures of Clothing in Later Medieval and Early Modern Europe*: 609.
60. Patricia Fortini Brown, "The Venetian Casa," in *At Home in Renaissance Italy* eds Marta Ajmar-Wollheim and Flora Dennis (London: V&A Publications, 2006) 60.
61. Giacomo Franco, *Habiti delle donne veneziane*, ed. Lina Urban (Venice: Centro Internazionale della Grafica di Venezia, [1610] 1990), 3.
62. Rita Casagrande di Villaviera, *Le cortigiane venetiane nel Cinquecento* (Milan: Longanesi, 1986), 60–1.
63. Christine Varholy, "'Rich like a Lady': Cross-class Dressing in the Brothels and Theaters of Early Modern London Authors," *Journal for Early Modern Cultural Studies*, 8 (1) (2008): 9.
64. Will Fisher, "Making most solemne love to a petticote": Clothing Fetishism in Early Modern English Culture," Renaissance Society of America conference, Berlin, March 27, 2015.
65. Thomas Nashe, "A choise of valentines (1592–3), in *The Penguin Book of Renaissance Verse*, H.R. Wudhuysen (ed.), David Norbrook (ed. intro), (London: Allen Lane/Penguin, 1992), 255.
66. Kathleen Brown, "'Changed into the Fashion of a Man': The Politics of Sexual Difference in a Seventeenth-Century Anglo-American Settlement," *Journal of the History of Sexuality* 6 (2) (1995): 171.
67. Ibid., 176.
68. Ibid., 175.

Chapter 6

1. Thomas Kemp, ed., *The Black Book of Warwick* (Warwick, n.d.), 1.
2. Key works on English clothing and social hierarchies include Maria Hayward, *Rich Apparel: Clothing and the Law in Henry VIII's England* (Aldershot: Ashgate, 2009); Alan Hunt, *Governance of the Consuming Passions: A History of Sumptuary Law* (London: Palgrave Macmillan, 1996), especially chapter 12; Negley Harte, "State Control of Dress and Social Change in Pre-Industrial England," in *Trade, Government and Economy in Pre-Industrial England*, eds D.C. Coleman and A.H. John (London: Weidenfeld & Nicolson, 1976); F.E. Baldwin, *Sumptuary Legislation and Personal Regulation in England* (Baltimore: Johns Hopkins University Press, 1926); Susan Vincent, *Dressing the Elite, Clothes in Early Modern England* (Oxford: Berg, 2003); Roze Hentschell, *The Culture of Cloth in Early Modern England: Textual Construction of a National Identity* (Aldershot: Ashgate, 2008); Section 3, plus chapters by Bartram and Hentschell in *Clothing Culture 1350–1650*, ed. Catherine Richardson (Aldershot: Ashgate, 2004).
3. Hunt, *Governance of the Consuming Passions*, 36, tables on 29–33; he argues that "the discourses of sumptuarism became integrated within and then submerged by those of protectionism" in the seventeenth century, offering another route for "the sumptuary spirit," 324.

4. Hayward, *Rich Apparel*, 17.
5. See Baldwin, *Sumptuary Legislation and Personal Regulation in England*, chapters IV and V; summary in Hayward, *Rich Apparel*, Table 1.1, 29–39.
6. The 1563 act made clear its intention to stop individuals spending money they did not have, threatening, "whosoever shall sell or deliver to any person (having not in possession lands or fees to the clear yearly value of £3000) any foreign [clothing] wares . . . for which wares, or the workmanship thereof, the seller shall not have received the whole money or satisfaction in hand" or within twenty-eight days following—you had to have a supply of ready money to be served by the mercer or tailor, Baldwin, *Sumptuary Legislation and Personal Regulation in England*, 209.
7. Kemp, *The Black Book of Warwick*, xxvii–xxviii.
8. On the history of the order see Peter Begent ed., *The Most Noble Order of the Garter, 650 years* (London: Spink & Son, 1999).
9. Janet Arnold, *Queen Elizabeth's Wardrobe Unlock'd* (Leeds: Maney, 1988), 67. Henry VIII had owned a similar "mantell of clothe of Silver lyned withe white Satten" to wear when he celebrated the saint's day, his decorated "withe Scallopppe Shelles," and a gold collar of alternating paired cockle shells and friar's girdles; Maria Hayward, *Dress at the Court of King Henry* VIII (Leeds: Maney, 2007), 138.
10. Hayward, *Dress at the Court of King Henry VIII*, 129–31.
11. Arnold, *Queen Elizabeth's Wardrobe Unlock'd*, 76.
12. The bill for their wages and the cloth for their liveries in 1540 was "£6,121 14s 11½d for the king's side and £571 2s 3½d for the queen's," Hayward, *Rich Apparel*, 244, 246.
13. Simon Adams ed., *Household Accounts and Disbursement Books of Robert Dudley, Earl of Leicester*, Camden Society Fifth Series (No. 6), (Cambridge: Cambridge University Press, 1996), 426–8.
14. For a discussion of the mentality behind livery see A.R. Jones and P. Stallybrass, *Renaissance Clothing and the Materials of Memory* (Cambridge: Cambridge University Press, 2000). especially pp. 17–21.
15. Hayward, *Rich Apparel*, 33.
16. Hayward, *Dress at the Court of King Henry VIII*, 95, 10.
17. Arnold, *Queen Elizabeth's Wardrobe Unlock'd*, 93; Jane A. Lawson ed., *The Elizabethan New Year's Gift Exchanges, 1559–1603* (Records of Social and Economic History 51), (Oxford: Oxford University Press, 2013).
18. Janet Cox-Rearick, "Power-Dressing at the Courts of Cosimo de' Medici and François I: The 'moda alla spagnola' of Spanish Consorts Eléonore d'Autriche and Eleonora di Toledo," *Artibus et Historiae* 30: 60, 2009: 39. For the relationship between style and cloth in the construction of Florentine identity see Elizabeth Currie, "Clothing and a Florentine style, 1550–1620," *Renaissance Studies*, 23: 1, 2009: 33–52.
19. "'Living Dolls': François Ier Dresses His Women," *Renaissance Quarterly*, 60: 1, 2007: 94–130.
20. For further details of his life see N.G. Jones, "Puckering, Sir John," ODNB, xlv, 503–4; A. Thrush and J.P. Ferris, *History of Parliament, House of Commons, 1604–1629*, v (Cambridge: Cambridge University Press, 2010), 773–7.
21. See Ann Hughes, *Politics, Society and Civil War* (Cambridge: Cambridge University Press, 2002), 21–4.
22. J. Whittle and E. Griffiths, *Consumption and Gender in the Early Seventeenth-Century Household: the world of Alice Le Strange* (Oxford: Oxford University Press, 2012), 18, 21, 23.
23. Ibid., 51–2.
24. Hayward, *Dress at the Court of King Henry VIII*, 32–3.
25. For more on the development of the season see the pioneering article by F.J. Fisher, "The development of London as a centre of conspicuous consumption in the sixteenth and

seventeenth centuries," *Transactions of the Royal Historical Society*, 4th ser., 30, 1948: 37–50; on new shopping practices Linda Levy Peck, *Consuming Splendor: Society and Culture in Seventeenth-Century England* (Cambridge: Cambridge University Press, 2005), 71. She also comments that the "secondhand market in goods re-circulated aristocratic clothing to those of lower status," although this downwards circulation of fashionable dress was apparently much less prominent and widespread than it was in Italy, where "the diffuse practice of recirculating material goods ... brought people from across the social scale into contact with dealers"; Ann Matchette, "Credit and credibility: used goods and social relations in sixteenth-century Florence," in *The Material Renaissance*, eds Michelle O'Malley and Evelyn Welch (Manchester: Manchester University Press, 2007), 225–41.

26. Evelyn Welch, *Shopping in the Renaissance* (New Haven: Yale, 2005); for Germany see Ulinka Rublack, *Dressing Up: Cultural Identity in Renaissance Europe* (Oxford: Oxford University Press, 2010).

27. The purchases are listed in the account book, Shakespeare Centre Library and Archive DR 37/3/17, and a transcription and further analysis of his purchasing patterns can be found in *The Household Account Book of Sir Thomas Puckering of Warwick 1620: Living in London and the Midlands*, eds Mark Merry and Catherine Richardson (Stratford-upon-Avon: Dugdale Society, 2012), 6–72.

28. Whittle and Griffiths, *Consumption and Gender in the Early Seventeenth-Century Household*, 58, 61.

29. See Vincent, *Dressing the Elite, Clothes in Early Modern England*, 33 for the different forms of labor needed; for Elizabeth's dressing, Arnold, *Queen Elizabeth's Wardrobe Unlock'd*, 157, 112, 12.

30. My thanks to David Mitchell for this information, based on his work on the silk trades in Restoration London; see also Peck, *Consuming Splendor: Society and Culture in Seventeenth-Century England*, chapter 2, for English efforts to establish a native industry. The opening of foreign markets had an impact on elite dress across Europe, B. Lemire and G. Riello, "East and West: textiles and fashion in early modern Europe," *Journal of Social History*, 41: 4, 2008: 887–916. In France for instance, the Siamese Embassy of 1686 brought back appealingly distinctive ikats from Thailand which were quickly adopted by the French nobility, Ina Baghdiantz McCabe, *Orientalism in Early Modern France* (Oxford: Berg, 2008).

31. Margaret Spufford, "Fabric for Seventeenth-Century Children and Adolescents' Clothes," *Textile History* 34: 1 (2003): 48–9.

32. Danae Tankard, "A Pair of Grass-Green Woollen Stockings: The Clothing of the Rural Poor in Seventeenth-Century Sussex," *Textile History* 43:1 (2012): 9–13.

33. Canterbury Cathedral Archives and Library PRC 11.63.350. Tankard argues for the seventeenth century that "all but the truly indigent would have had a minimum of two sets" of clothing.

34. Spufford, "Fabric for Seventeenth-Century Children and Adolescents' Clothes": 51–2.

35. Ibid., 61; Tankard, "A Pair of Grass-Green Woollen Stockings": 10; Diana O'Hara, "Ruled by my friends: aspects of marriage in the diocese of Canterbury, c. 1540–1570," *Continuity and Change*, 6 (1991): 9–41; Catherine Richardson, "A very fit hat; personal objects and early modern affection," in *Everyday Objects*, eds C. Richardson and T. Hamling (Aldershot: Ashgate, 2010), 289–98.

36. Records in F.G. Emmison, *Elizabethan Life: Home, Work and Land* (Chelmsford: Essex Record Office Publication no. 69, 1976), 165, 92, 167.

37. For notions of credit in this period see Craig Muldrew, *The Economy of Obligation, the Culture of Credit and Social Relations in Early Modern England* (London: Palgrave Macmillan, 1998).

38. Sheila Sweetinburgh, "Clothing the Naked in Late Medieval East Kent," in *Clothing Culture, 1350–1650*, ed. Catherine Richardson (Aldershot: Ashgate, 2004), 110, 114, 117, 119.

39. William Dugdale, *The Antiquities of Warwickshire* (2nd edition, Rev. William Thomas, 1730), 417. Beier states that a quarter of the population were living in poverty in the town during challenging times, "The social problems of an Elizabethan country town: Warwick, 1580–90," in *Country Towns in Pre-Industrial England*, ed. Peter Clark (Leicester: Leicester University Press, 1981), 50.
40. Dugdale, *The Antiquities of Warwickshire*, 463.
41. Examples include the Common Chest of Leisnig in Saxony or the general almonries of Lyon, Rouen, Antwerp and the cities of Holland, Brian Pullan, "Catholics, Protestants, and the Poor in Early Modern Europe," *The Journal of Interdisciplinary History*, 35: 3(2005): 441–56.
42. A.S. Saunders, "Provision of apparel for the poor in London, 1630–1680," *Costume* 40, (2006): 22.
43. Ibid., 26.
44. Spufford sets £300 and above as the value of the goods of "the normal bottom of the range for inferior gentry," 53.
45. Keith Wrightson, "Sorts of People in Tudor and Stuart England," in *The Middling Sort of People: Culture, Society, and Politics in England, 1550–1800*, eds Jonathan Barry and Christopher Brooks (New York: St. Martin's Press, 1994), 30, 38, 37, 35, 40. For more on the materiality of English middling status see Henry French, *The Middle Sort of People in Provincial England 1600–1750* (Oxford: Oxford University Press, 2007), chapter 3; and Catherine Richardson and Tara Hamling, *A Day at Home in Early Modern England: The Materiality of Domestic Life, 1500–1700* (New Haven: Yale University Press, forthcoming 2015).
46. Barry and Brooks (eds), *The Middling Sort of People*, 15, 2.
47. Ibid., 14–15.
48. For Italy and Germany see, for instance, Caroline Collier Frick, *Dressing Renaissance Florence* (Baltimore: Johns Hopkins Press, 2002); Rublack, *Dressing Up*.
49. Quoted in Graham Durkin, "The Civic Government and Economy of Elizabethan Canterbury," unpublished PhD thesis (Canterbury Christchurch, 2001), 55.
50. See for instance Canterbury Cathedral Archives and Library, PRC 21.1.25, inventory of Christopher Scott, alderman, 1568, whose gown of scarlet with a velvet tippet is valued at £3 6s 8d; further analysis of the bequest of such items is being undertaken for a project on, "Material Communities: clothing and early modern urban space," on which I am currently working.
51. Towns usually paid for such portraits: see Robert Tittler, *The Face of the City* (Manchester: Manchester University Press, 2007), 120.
52. Joseph Meadows Cowper (ed.), *The Diary of Thomas Cocks, March 25th, 1607, to December 31st, 1610* (Cross and Jackson, 1901).
53. T.N. Brushfield, "The Financial Diary of a Citizen of Exeter, 1631–43," *Reports and Transactions of the Devonshire Association* 3 (1901).
54. Richardson, forthcoming 2016.
55. In Florence, mercantile time also went into "the minutiae of the marketplace," including negotiation over embellishments such as pearls, feathers, ribbons and spangles, Frick, *Dressing Renaissance Florence*, 222–3.
56. For comparative examples see Anne E.C. McCants, "Good at Pawn: the overlapping worlds of material possessions and family finance in Early Modern Amsterdam," *Social Science History* 31:2 (2007), where she argues that both shop credit and pawning were more available to the middling sort than those beneath them.
57. Brushfield, "The Financial Diary of a Citizen of Exeter, 1631–43," 199.
58. For details of Philip Henslowe's pawnbroking business, in which clothing made up 62.2 percent of pawns, see J. Boulton, *Neighbourhood and Society: A London Suburb in the Seventeenth Century* (Cambridge: Cambridge University Press, 1987), 87–97.
59. For the development of the early modern grocery trade see, Jon Stobart, *Sugar and Spice: grocers and groceries in Provincial England, 1650–1830* (Oxford: Oxford University Press, 2013).

60. See for comparison the inventory of Hans Dinesen of Odense in Denmark in the 1580s, which lists, among other contents of his daughter's chest, several goods given for weddings including two satin collars one of which was given to her "for her sister Anne's wedding" and a black cloak of English cloth that her mother gave her "for Doctor Peder's wedding." Project website "Fashioning the Early Modern," http://www.fashioningtheearlymodern.ac.uk/object-in-focus/the-probate-of-hans-dinesen/
61. Brushfield, "The Financial Diary of a Citizen of Exeter, 1631–43"; 208.
62. Ibid., 203.
63. Richardson, "'As my whole trust is in him': Jewellery and the Quality of Early Modern Relationships," in *Ornamentalism: The Art of Renaissance Accessories*, ed. Bella Mirabella (Ann Arbor: University of Michigan Press, 2011), 182–201.
64. Only "four of the 50 Elizabethan mayors came from outside the merchant class," Muldrew, *The Economy of Obligation*, 57.
65. Barry and Brooks, *The Middling Sort of People*, 17.
66. Hunt, *Governance of the Consuming Passions*, 105.
67. Brushfield, p. 243; for the significance of gloves in urban culture see Robert Titller, "Freemen's Gloves and Civic Authority: The Evidence from Post-Reformation Portraiture," *Costume* 40, 2006, 13–20.
68. For more on developing national and international markets see Keith Wrightson, *Earthly Necessities: Economic Lives in Early Modern Britain*, Yale University Press, 2000.

Chapter 7

1. Sydney Nettleton Fisher, *The Middle East: A History* (London: Routledge, 1971).
2. Salih Özbaran, *Bir Osmanlı Kimliği: 14.–17. Yüzyıllarda Rum/Rumi Aidiyetve İmgeleri* (İstanbul: Kitapevi, 2004).
3. Ibid.
4. Stephen Spencer, *Race and Ethnicity: Culture, Identity, and Representation* (London: Routledge, 2006).
5. Ibid.
6. Stephen Cornell and Douglas Hartmann, *Ethnicity and Race: Making Identities in a Changing World* (London: Pine Forge Press, 1998).
7. Robert Bartlett, "Medieval and Modern Concepts of Race and Ethnicity," *Journal of Medieval and Early Modern Studies* 31, no. 1 (2001): 39–56.
8. Spencer, *Race and Ethnicity*.
9. Cornell and Hartmann, *Ethnicity and Race*.
10. Spencer, *Race and Ethnicity*.
11. Margaret F. Rosenthal and Ann Rosalind Jones, *Cesare Vecellio's Habiti Antichi et Moderni: The Clothing of the Renaissance World* (London: Thomas & Hudson, 2008); Mehmet Genç, *Osmanlı İmparatorluğu'nda Devlet ve Ekonomi* (İstanbul: Ötüken, 2007).
12. Hans Dernschwam, *İstanbul ve Anadolu'ya Seyahat Günlüğü*, trans. Yaşar Önen (Mersin: Mersin İmar Basımevi, 1992).
13. The Nishava River flows from Bulgaria to Serbia, passing near the city of Nish.
14. Thorstein Veblen, *The Theory of Leisure Class* (New York: Dover Publications, [1899] 1994).
15. Eminegül Karababa, "Investigating Early Modern Ottoman Consumer Culture in the Light of Bursa Probate Inventories," *Economic History Review* 65, no. 1 (2012): 194–219; Suraiya Faroqhi, *Stories of Ottoman Men and Women* (İstanbul: Eren, 2002), 66–74. See these references for a more detailed explanation of Muslim women's clothing.
16. Dernschwam, *İstanbul ve Anadolu'ya Seyahat*, 338.
17. Stephen Gerlach, *Türkiye Günlüğü 1573–1576*, ed. Kemal Beydilli, trans. Turkis Noyan (İstanbul: KitapYayınevi, 2007), 825–6.
18. Ogier Chiselin de Busbecq, *Türkiye'yi Böyle Gördüm* (Ankara: Kesit, 2004), 21.

19. Ibid.
20. Ibid.
21. Gerlach, *Türkiye Günlüğü*, 821–6, 841.
22. Dernschwam, *İstanbul ve Anadolu'ya Seyahat*, 338; Solomon Schweigger, *Sultanlar Kentine Yolculuk (1578–1581)*, ed. Heidi Stein, trans. S. Türkis Noyan (İstanbul: Kitap Yayınevi, 2004), 46.
23. Dernschwam, *İstanbul ve Anadolu'ya Seyahat*, 31.
24. Ibid.
25. Busbecq, *Türkiye'yi Böyle Gördüm*, 21.
26. Gerlach, *Türkiye Günlüğü*, 841.
27. Bursa is a city located to the south of Istanbul, within Marmara region. It served as the first major capital city of the Empire, until Edirne was conquered in 1363.
28. Karababa, *Investigating Early Modern Ottoman Consumer Culture*.
29. Dernschwam, *İstanbul ve Anadolu'ya Seyahat*, 338.
30. Gerlach, *Türkiye Günlüğü*, 74.
31. Ibid.
32. Dernschwam, *İstanbul ve Anadolu'ya Seyahat*, 32.
33. Charles Schefer, *Antoine Galland: İstanbul'a Ait Günlük Hatıralar (1672–1673)* vol. 1, trans. Nahid Sırrı Örik (Ankara: Türk Tarih Kurumu, 1998), 102; Michael Heberer, *Osmanlı'da Bir Köle: Brettenli Michael Heberer'in Anıları (1585–1588)*, trans. Türkis Noyan (İstanbul: Kitap Yayınevi, 2003), 295; Nicolas de Nicolay, *Muhteşem Süleyman'ın İmparatorluğu'nda*, eds Marie-Christine Gomes-Geraud and Stefanos Yerasimos, trans. Şirin Tekeli and Menekşe Tokyay (İstanbul: KitapYayınevi, [1576] 2014), 182–3; Gerlach, *Türkiye Günlüğü*, 451.
34. In my analysis, I use a recent Turkish translation of Nicolas de Nicolay's book, *Muhteşem Süleyman'ın İmparatorluğu'nda*.
35. Nicolay, *Muhteşem Süleyman'ın İmparatorluğu'nda*, 182–3.
36. This engraving must have been colored at a later period in reference to his text: the original would have been in black and white. I would like to thank Dr. Ayşe Yetişkin Kubilay for providing the image of Nicolay's engraving of the *Greek Girl in Pera*.
37. See Sevgi Gürtuna, *Osmanlı Kadın Giysisi* (Ankara: T.C. Kültür Bakanlığı Yayınevi, 1999) for clothing styles of Ottoman Muslim women.
38. Gerlach, *Türkiye Günlüğü*, 250; Heberer, *Osmanlı'da Bir Köle*, 297.
39. Gerlach, *Türkiye Günlüğü*, 451.
40. Rosenthal and Jones, *Cesare Vecellio's Habiti*, 422.
41. Karababa, *Investigating Early Modern Ottoman Consumer Culture*.
42. Gerlach, *Türkiye Günlüğü*; Heberer, *Osmanlı'da Bir Köle*.
43. Karababa, *Investigating Early Modern Ottoman Consumer Culture*.
44. Edirne is a city in the Thrace region and remained the capital of the Empire until Istanbul was conquered in 1453.
45. Schefer, *Antoine Galland*.
46. Nicolay, *Muhteşem Süleyman'ın İmparatorluğu'nda*, 183; Heberer, *Osmanlı'da Bir Köle*, 295.
47. Chandra Mukerji, "Costume and Character in the Ottoman Empire: Design as Social Agent in Nicolay's Navigations," in *Early Modern Things*, ed. P. Findlen, (London: Routledge, 2013).
48. Nicolay, *Muhteşem Süleyman'ın İmparatorluğu'nda*, 182; Gerlach, *Türkiye Günlüğü*, 95; Heberer, *Osmanlı'da Bir Köle*, 297.
49. Gerlach, *Türkiye Günlüğü*, 95.
50. Ibid.
51. In 1550 and 1584, one Venetian ducat was worth 60 and 65 to 70 akçes respectively: Şevket Pamuk, *Osmanlı İmparatorluğu'nda Paranın Tarihi* (İstanbul: Tarih Vakfı Yurt Yayınları, 1999), 69.

52. Probate books dating back to mid-sixteenth-century Bursa provide us with information about the monetary value of jewelry. For example, in probate book number A71 of Bursa, record number 496 belongs to a Muslim woman from a high-status group. She had 17,000 akçes in total wealth, of which her jewelry was valued at 7,859 akçes. In probate book number A77 of Bursa, record number 152 belongs to another Muslim townswoman, of lower status. She had 33,547 akçes in total wealth, of which jewelry amounted to around 8,297 akçes.
53. Rosenthal and Jones, *Cesare Vecellio's Habiti*, 422
54. Gerlach, *Türkiye Günlüğü*, 95.
55. Karababa, *Investigating Early Modern Ottoman Consumer Culture*.
56. Anne Hollander, *Fabric of Vision: Dress and Drapery in Painting* (London: National Gallery, 2002).
57. Heberer, *Osmanlı'da Bir Köle*, 297.
58. Gülgün Üçel-Aybet, *Avrupalı Seyyahların Gözünden Osmanlı Dünyası ve İnsanları* (İstanbul: İletişim, 2003), 193.
59. Dernschwam, *İstanbul ve Anadolu'ya Seyahat*, 147; Nicolay, *Muhteşem Süleyman'ın İmparatorluğu'nda*, 288.
60. Nicolay, *Muhteşem Süleyman'ın İmparatorluğu'nda*, 288.
61. Ibid.
62. Amnon Cohen, *Jewish Life under Islam* (Cambridge, MA: Harvard University Press, 1984), 73.
63. Nicolay, *Muhteşem Süleyman'ın İmparatorluğu'nda*, 132, 316.
64. Üçel-Aybet, *Avrupalı Seyyahların Gözünden Osmanlı*, 205.
65. Ibid.
66. Dernschwam, *İstanbul ve Anadolu'ya Seyahat*, 151.
67. Ibid.
68. Ibid., 158.
69. Macit Kenanoğlu, *Osmanlı Millet Sistemi: Mit ve Gerçek* (İstanbul: Klasik, 2004), 342–6.
70. Gerlach, *Türkiye Günlüğü*. 633–4.
71. Ibid.
72. Ibid.
73. Ibid, 327.
74. Ahmet Refik Altınay, *Onaltıncı Asırda İstanbul Hayatı* (İstanbul: Enderun, 1988), 51.
75. Gerlach, *Türkiye Günlüğü*, 327.
76. Ibid., 613.
77. Karababa, *Investigating Early Modern Ottoman Consumer Culture*.
78. Rifa'at 'Ali Abou-El-Haj, *Formation of the Modern State: The Ottoman Empire, Sixteenth to Eighteenth Centuries* (Syracuse, NY: Syracuse University Press, 2005), 36.
79. Şerif Mardin, *Türkiye'de Toplum ve Siyaset: Makaleler 1* (İstanbul: İletişim, 2000), 97–101.
80. Donald Quataert, "Clothing Laws, State, and Society in the Ottoman Empire, 1720–1829," *International Journal of Middle East Studies* 29, no: 3 (1997): 403–25.
81. Altınay, *Onaltıncı Asırda İstanbul*; Mardin, *Türkiye'de Toplum ve Siyaset*, 182.
82. Suraiya Faroqhi, "The Ottoman Ruling Group and the Religions of its Subjects in the Early Modern Age: A Survey of Current Research," *Journal of Early Modern History* 14, no. 3 (2010): 259.
83. Altınay, *Onaltıncı Asırda İstanbul*; Kenanoğlu, *Osmanlı Millet Sistemi*, 349–50.
84. Kenanoğlu, *Osmanlı Millet Sistemi*, 342–50.
85. Ibid.
86. Ibid.
87. Kenanoğlu, *Osmanlı Millet Sistemi*, 342–5.
88. Altınay, *Onaltıncı Asırda İstanbul*, 51.

89. Mehmet Şeker, *Gelibolulu Mustafa 'Âli ve meva 'idu'n-nefais fi-kava 'idi'lmecalis* (Ankara: Türk Tarih Kurumu, 1992), 156.
90. Altınay, *Onaltıncı Asırda İstanbul*, 47.
91. *Tarama Sözlüğü* (Ankara: Türk Dil Kurumu Yayınları, 1996). *Tarama Sözlüğü* is a dictionary formed from an analysis of old Turkish texts that date back to the thirteenth century onwards. It is very useful in identifying terms and objects in old Turkish. Each item in the dictionary contains examples from these old texts.
92. Altınay, *Onaltıncı Asırda İstanbul*, 47.
93. Janice Denegri-Knott and Elizabeth Parsons, "Disordering Things," *Journal of Consumer Behavior* 13, no. 2 (2014): 89–98.

Chapter 8

1. Katlijne van der Stighelen, *De portretten van Cornelis de Vos (1584/5–1651): Een Kritische Catalogus* (Brussels: AWLSK, 1990), 71–2.
2. Mark Weiss, "Catherine Carey, Countess of Nottingham," *Tudor and Stuart Portraits* (London: Weiss Gallery, 2012), 32–7.
3. Anne Van Buren, *Illuminating Fashion: Dress in the Art of Medieval France and the Netherlands, 1325–1515* (London: D. Giles Ltd., 2011), 30.
4. Ann Jones and Peter Stallybrass, *Renaissance Clothing and the Materials of Memory* (Cambridge: Cambridge University Press, 2000), 40.
5. Lisa Monnas, *Merchants, Princes and Painters: Silk Fabrics in Italian and Northern Paintings, 1300–550* (New Haven: Yale University Press, 2008), 197.
6. Emilie Gordenker, *Anthony Van Dyck (1599–1641) and the Representation of Dress in Seventeenth-Century Portraiture* (Belgium: Brepols Publishers, 2001), 22.
7. Van Buren, *Illuminating Fashion*, 29.
8. Jones and Stallybrass, *Renaissance Clothing and the Materials of Memory*, 42–5.
9. Dirk De Vos, *Hans Memling: The Complete Works* (London: Harry N. Abrams, 1994), 241.
10. Van Buren, *Illuminating Fashion*, 242.
11. De Vos, *Hans Memling*, 241.
12. Susan Broomhall, *Early Modern Women in the Low Countries: Feminizing Sources and Interpretations of the Past* (Aldershot: Ashgate, 2011), 54.
13. Todd Richardson, *Pieter Bruegel the Elder: Art Discourse in the Sixteenth-Century Netherlands* (Farnham: Ashgate, 2011), 84.
14. Anna Reynolds, *In Fine Style: The Art of Tudor and Stuart Fashion* (London: Royal Collection Trust, 2013), 270–6.
15. Isaac Oliver, *Anne of Denmark*, c. 1610, Royal Collection Trust (RCIN 420025).
16. John Hoskins, *Henrietta Maria*, c. 1632, Royal Collection Trust (RCIN 420891).
17. Jean Cadogan, *Domenico Ghirlandaio: Artist and Artisan* (New Haven: Yale University Press, 2000), 90.
18. Carole Collier Frick, *Dressing Renaissance Florence: Families, Fortunes and Fine Clothing* (Baltimore: Johns Hopkins University Press, 2002), 210.
19. Elizabeth Birbari, *Dress in Italian Painting 1460–1500* (London: John Murray, 1975), 25.
20. Frick, *Dressing Renaissance Florence*, 297.
21. The authorship of this painting is disputed. In some publications it is described as Haarlem School but the Frans Hals Museum currently attributes it to Hendrick Gerritsz Pot.
22. Margriet Van Eikema Hommes, *Changing Pictures: Discoloration in 15th-17th Century Oil Paintings* (London: Archetype Books, 2004), 91.
23. Margaret Scott, *Fashion in the Middle Ages* (Los Angeles: J. Paul Getty Museum, 2011), 109.
24. Ibid.
25. Annamaria Petrioli Tofani et al, *Drawing: Forms, Techniques, Meanings* (Turin: Istituto Bancario San Paolo di Torino, 1991), 198.

26. For example, Inigo Jones's costume design for Queen Henrietta Maria as *Divine Beauty and the Stars* in Tempe Restor'd of 1632 at Chatsworth House, Derbyshire. This includes a flap of paper which offers two choices for the design of the skirt.
27. Jean Michel Massing, "Albrecht Dürer's Irish Warriors and Peasants," *Irish Arts Review Yearbook*, Vol. 10 (1994): 223–6.
28. Another version is in the Albertina in Vienna. For the relationship between the two see Walter Strauss, *The Complete Drawings of Albrecht Dürer. Volume II* (New York: Abaris Books, 1974), 506.
29. Agathe Lewin, *Dürer and Costume: A Study of the Dress in some of Dürer's paintings and drawings* (London, 1993), PhD thesis, 107–10.
30. Carl Goldstein, *Print Culture in Early Modern France: Abraham Bosse and the Purposes of Print* (Cambridge: Cambridge University Press, 2012), 58.
31. George Duplessis, *Catalogue de l'oeuvre de Abraham Bosse*, Nos. 1044–6. (Paris, 1859).
32. Linda Levy Peck, *Consuming Splendor: Society and Culture in Seventeenth-Century England* (Cambridge: Cambridge University Press, 2005), 25–72.
33. Jo Anne Olian, "Sixteenth-Century Costume Books," *Dress: The Journal of the Costume Society of America* 3 (1977), 20–48.
34. Margaret Rosenthal and Ann Jones (eds), *The Clothing of the Renaissance world: Europe, Asia, Africa, the Americas: Cesare Vecellio's Habiti Antichi et Moderni* (London: Thames & Hudson, 2008), 21.
35. Margaret Beam Freeman, *The Unicorn Tapestries* (New York: E.P. Dutton, 1976), 96.
36. Keith Christiansen (ed.), *The Renaissance Portrait: from Donatello to Bellini* (New York: Yale, 2011), 166.
37. John Pope-Hennessy, *Italian Renaissance Sculpture* (London: Phaidon Press, 1996), 181–2.
38. *Giovanni de Medici*, Mino da Fiesole, c. 1455, Museo Nazionale del Bargello, Florence.
39. Peter and Ann Mactaggart, "The Rich Wearing Apparel of Richard, 3rd Earl of Dorset," *Costume*, vol. 14 (1980), 44–7.
40. Sara Stevenson and Helen Bennet, *Van Dyck in Check Trousers: Fancy Dress in Art and Life* (Edinburgh; Scottish National Portrait Gallery, 1978), 19–27.
41. Ibid., 83–5.

Chapter 9

1. Roland Barthes, *The Fashion System*, trans. Matthew Ward and Richard Howard (New York: Hill and Wang, 1983) and *The Language of Fashion*, ed. and trans. Andy Stafford (New York: Berg, 2006). For a history of two centuries of fashion theory see Michael Carter, *Fashion Classics from Carlyle to Barthes* (New York: Berg, 2003).
2. Eugenia Paulicelli, *Writing Fashion: From Sprezzatura to Satire* (Farnham: Ashgate, 2014), 3.
3. Agostino Lampugnani, *La carrozza da nolo. Ovvero del vestire e usanze alla moda* (Bologna and Milan, 1648). On etymology of "moda" see Doretta Davanzo Poli, *Il sarto*, in *Storia d'Italia: La Moda*, eds C. Marco Belfanti and F. Giusberti (Turin: Einaudi, 2003), 541–3.
4. On Italy see Paulicelli, *Writing Fashion*. See also Ann Rosalind Jones and Peter Stallybrass, *Renaissance Clothing and the Material of Memory* (Cambridge: Cambridge University Press, 2000).
5. English translation in Petrarch, *Letters of Old Age*, trans. Aldo Bernardo, Saul Levin, and Rita Bernardo, 2 vols. (Baltimore: Johns Hopkins University Press, 1992).
6. English and Italian texts can be found in Francesco Petrarch, *Canzoniere*, ed. and trans. Mark Musa (Bloomington: Indiana University Press, 1996), 196–7 (translation of poem 126 slightly altered). On Petrarch's personification of literature in the clothing of vernacular or Latin see Jane Tylus, "Petrarch's Griselda and the Sense of an Ending," *Nottingham Medieval Studies* 56 (2012): 421–45.

7. John Florio's Italian–English dictionary of 1598 defines *tela* as any woven cloth that is not made of wool, *A Worlde of Words* (London: Arnold Hatfield, 1598), 414.
8. On the metaphor of the tapestry in Ariosto see Louis C. Pérez, "The Theme of the Tapestry in Ariosto and Cervantes," *Revista de Estudios Hispánicos* 7 (1973): 289–98; Peter De Sa Wiggins, *Figures in Ariosto's Tapestry: Character and Design in the "Orlando Furioso"* (Baltimore: Johns Hopkins University Press, 1986).
9. All translations of Ariosto, unless indicated, are from Ludovico Ariosto, *Orlando Furioso*, trans. Guido Waldman (Oxford: Oxford University Press, 1983).
10. See Ornella Moroni, "Il velo: un excursus nella letteratura italiana," in *Abito e identità: Ricerche di storia letteraria e culturale,* ed. Cristina Giorcelli (Palermo: Ila Palma, 2009); Andrea Busto (ed.), *Il velo tra mistero, seduzione, misticismo, sensualità, potere e religione* (Milan: Silvana editoriale, 2007).
11. Dante Alighieri, *Inferno*, ed. and trans. Mark Musa (Bloomington: Indiana University Press, 1996), 85.
12. Leon Battista Alberti, *On Painting*, ed. and trans. Rocco Sinisgalli (New York: Cambridge University Press, 2011), 51–3.
13. Margaret Brose, "Fetishizing the Veil: Petrarch's Poetics of Rematerialization," *The Body in Early Modern Italy,* eds Julia L. Hairston and Walter Stephens (Baltimore: Johns Hopkins University Press, 2010), 23.
14. Eugenia Paulicelli, "From the Sacred to the Secular: The Gendered Geography of Veils in Italian Cinquecento Fashion," in *Ornamentalism: The Art of Renaissance Accessories,* ed. Bella Mirabella (Ann Arbor: University of Michigan Press, 2011), 40–58.
15. Translation Musa 83.
16. See also Paul Hills, "Titian's Veils," *Art History* 29 (2006).
17. Othello demands "ocular proof" of Desdemona's infidelity (3.3.365). On the handkerchief see Bella Mirabella, "Embellishing Herself with a Cloth: The Contradictory Life of the Handkerchief," in *Ornamentalism,* ed. Mirabella, 59–84.
18. Jane Tylus, *Writing and Vulnerability in the Late Renaissance* (Stanford: Stanford University Press, 1993).
19. Ibid., 84.
20. Translation from ibid., 89.
21. Translation from ibid., 85.
22. Ibid., 91.
23. Cited in Paulicelli, "From the Sacred to the Secular," 51.
24. Ibid.
25. On the color yellow see Michel Pastoreau and Dominique Simonnet, *Il piccolo libro dei colori* (Milan: Ponte delle Grazie, 2006). On Tullia d'Aragona who resisted the Florentine law requiring prostitutes to wear a yellow veil, see Paul Larivaille, *La vita quotidiana nell'Italia del Rinascimento* (Milan: Biblioteca Universale Rizzoli, 1983), 9; Salvatore Bongi, "Il velo giallo di Tullia d'Aragona," *Rivista critica della letteratura italiana* III (March 1886): 85–6.
26. Ann Rosalind Jones and Margaret Rosenthal, *The Clothing of the Renaissance World: Cesare Vecellio's Habiti Antichi et Moderni* (New York: Thames & Hudson, 2008), 36, 88.
27. For an analysis of the social anxieties created by the veiled woman in the Hispanic world see Laura R. Bass and Amanda Wunder, "The Veiled Ladies of the Early Modern Spanish World: Seduction in Seville, Madrid, and Lima," *Hispanic Review* 77:1 Winter (2009): 97–144.
28. Giovanni Boccaccio, *The Corbaccio*, trans. and ed. Anthony K. Cassell (Urbana: University of Illinois Press, 1975), 59.
29. Stefano Guazzo, *Civile Conversazione*, Book III (Venice: Gio. Battista Somasco, 1580), 464. (Translation mine.)
30. Arcangela Tarabotti, *Paternal Tyranny*, ed. and trans. Letizia Panizza (Chicago: University of Chicago Press, 2004), 130.
31. See Jerome's "Letter to Eustochium" for his advice on the proper dress of Christian women.

32. Judith 10:4 as cited in Elena Ciletti, "Patriarchal Ideology in the Renaissance Iconography of Judith," in *Refiguring Woman: Perspectives on Gender and the Italian Renaissance*, ed. Marilyn Migiel and Juliana Schiesari (Ithaca: Cornell University Press, 1991), 45. On Jerome and Judith see Elena Ciletti and Henrike Lähnemann, "Judith in the Christian Tradition," in *The Sword of Judith; Judith Studies Across the Disciplines*, eds Kevin R. Brine, Elena Ciletti, and Henrike Lähnemann (Cambridge: Open Book Publishers, 2010), 41–65.
33. For a study on developments in sixteenth-century artistic representations of Judith's fashions, particularly ornaments and jewelry, see Diane Apostolos-Cappadona, "Costuming Judith in Italian Art of the Sixteenth Century," in *The Sword of Judith* eds Brine, Ciletti, and Lähnemann, 325–43.
34. Translations of *Judith* and *Esther* found in Lucrezia Tornabuoni, *Sacred Narratives*, ed. and trans. Jane Tylus (Chicago: University of Chicago Press, 2001), 193. See also Gerry Milligan, "Unlikely Heroines in Lucrezia Tornauoni's *Judith* and *Esther*," *Italica* 88:4 (2011), 538–64.
35. Adrian W.B. Randolph, "Performing the Bridal Body in Fifteenth-Century Florence," *Art History* 21:2 (1998).
36. Randolph cites the 1472 Florentine sumptuary law declaring women should wear bridal jewels for a limited period (three years) after their wedding, 189.
37. Tornabuoni, *Sacred Narratives*, 147.
38. Ibid.
39. On the episode of Tristan's castle see Deanna Shemek, *Ladies Errant: Wayward Women and Social Order in Early Modern Italy* (Durham, N.C.: Duke University Press, 1998).
40. Trans. from ibid., 83.
41. Ibid., 103.
42. On supplementarity in Ariosto see ibid., 109–24.
43. Trans. from ibid., 99.
44. On the power of transvestism to create a third, androgynous figure see Gerry Milligan, "Behaving Like a Man: Performed Masculinities in *Gl'ingannati*," *Forum Italicum*, March 41 (2007): 23–42.
45. In *The Deceived*, a male character Fabrizio, dressed in men's clothing, is believed to be a girl dressed in men's clothing. On the use of transvestism in Italian comedy see Laura Giannetti, *Lelia's Kiss: Imagining Gender, Sex and Marriage in Italian Renaissance Comedy* (Toronto: University of Toronto Press, 2009).
46. Ilaria Taddei, *Fanciulli e giovani: crescere a Firenze nel Rinascimento* (Florence: Olschki, 2001), 58.
47. Francesco Pontano, "Dello integro e perfetto stato delle donzelle," *Raccolta di scritture varie pubblicata nell'occasione delle nozze Riccomanni-Fineschi*, ed. Cesare Riccomanni (Turin: Vercellino, 1863).
48. For a study on the positive reception of male ornament see Timothy McCall, "Brilliant Bodies: Material Culture and the Adornment of Men in North Italy's Quattrocento Courts," *I Tatti Studies* 16, 1–2 (2013): 445–90.
49. Silvio Antoniano, *Tre libri dell'educazione cristiana de'figliuoli* (Verona: Sebastiano dalle Donne & Girolamo Stringari, 1584), 1.3, 408–410.
50. See also Antoniano's chapter dedicated to ornaments, 228 (quoted in Taddei, 91).
51. Anton Francesco Doni, *I Marmi*, 167–8. Doni's *I marmi* is also available in digital form through www.liberliber.it. Pages given are from the digital format.
52. On the internalization of the dissimulated self see Jon R. Snyder, *Dissimulation and the Culture of Secrecy in Early Modern Europe* (Berkeley: University of California Press, 2009).
53. Jane Bridgeman, "'Condecenti et netti . . .': Beauty, Dress and Gender in Italian Renaissance Art," in *Concepts of Beauty in Renaissance Art*, eds Francis Ames-Lewis and Mary Rogers (Aldershot: Ashgate, 1998), 44–51.
54. Translation of Leon Battista Alberti's *Vita*, Renée Watkins, "L.B. Alberti in the Mirror: An Interpretation of the *Vita*, with a New Translation," *Italian Quarterly* 30 (1989): 9.

55. Baldesare Castiglione, *The Book of the Courtier*, trans. Charles Singleton, ed. Daniel Javitch (New York: Norton, 2002), I.XXVI.32. On the reception of the *Courtier* see Peter Burke, *The Fortunes of the Courtier* (University Park, PA: Penn State University Press, 1996).
56. Castiglione, *The Book of the Courtier,* 49.
57. Paulicelli, *Writing Fashion,* 52–5.
58. On cosmetics throughout history see Michelle A. Laughran, "Oltre la pelle: I cosmetici e il loro uso," in *Storia d'Italia: Annali. La moda* (Turin: Einaudi, 2003), 43–82.
59. On Alberti see Carla Freccero, "Loving the Other: Masculine Subjectivity in Early Modern Europe," in *The Poetics of Early Modern Masculinity*, eds Gerry Milligan and Jane Tylus, (Toronto: Centre for Renaissance and Reformation Studies, 2010), 101–18.
60. Amadeo Quondam, *Questo povero cortegiano: Castiglione, il libro, la storia* (Rome: Bulzoni, 2000), 386; Paulicelli, *Writing*, 51–88; Gerry Milligan, "The Politics of Effeminacy in *Il Cortegiano*," *Italica* 83:3–4 (2006), 347–69.

BIBLIOGRAPHY

Archival Sources

Archivio di Stato di Firenze, *Decima Grand ducale* 3784.
Canterbury Cathedral Archives and Library PRC 11.63.350 and 21.1.25.
Public Record Office, State Papers Domestic, Charles I, SP16/479/78.
Shakespeare Centre Library and Archive DR 37/3/17.
The National Archives, Kew, E101/417/4.

Websites

http://www.fashioningtheearlymodern.ac.uk/object-in-focus/the-probate-of-hans-dinesen/
www.concealedgarments.org

Abou-El-Haj, R.A.A. (2005), *Formation of the Modern State: The Ottoman Empire, Sixteenth to Eighteenth Centuries,* Syracuse, New York: Syracuse University Press.
Adams, S., ed. (1996), *Household Accounts and Disbursement Books of Robert Dudley, Earl of Leicester*, Camden Society Fifth Series (No. 6), Cambridge: Cambridge University Press.
Adshead, S.A.M. (1997), *Material Culture in Europe and China 1400–1800*, Basingstoke: Macmillan.
Ahl, D. Cole (1986), "Benozzo Gozzoli's frescoes of the life of Saint Augustine in San Gimignano: their meaning in context," *Artibus et Historiae* 7/13: 35–53.
Ajmar-Wollheim, M. and L. Molà (2011), "The Global Renaissance: Cross-Cultural Material Culture," in G. Adamson, G. Riello and S. Teasley (eds), *Global Design History*, London: Taylor & Francis.
Alberti, L.B. (2011), *On Painting*, ed. and trans. Rocco Sinisgalli, New York: Cambridge University Press.
Alcega, J. De (1580), *Libro de geometria, práctica y traça, el cual trata de lo tocante al officio del sastre*, Madrid: Guillermo Drouy.
Alighieri, D., *Inferno* (1996), ed. and trans. Mark Musa, Bloomington: Indiana University Press.
Allerston, P. (1993), "Reconstructing the Second-Hand Clothes Trade in Sixteenth- and Seventeenth-Century Venice." *Costume* 33: 46–56.
—— (2010), "Clothing and Early Modern Venetian Society," in Giorgio Riello and Peter McNeil (eds), *The Fashion History Reader: Global Perspectives*, London and New York: Routledge.
Allison, K.J. (1958), "Flock management in the sixteenth and seventeenth centuries," *Economic History Review*, 2nd series, 11: 98–112.
Altınay, A.R. (1988), *On altıncı Asırda İstanbul Hayatı*, İstanbul: Enderun Yayınevi.
Amman, J. (1586), *Gynaeceum, siue, Theatrum mulierum*, S. Feyrabend: Frankfurt.
Andersson, E.I. (2014), "Foreign Seductions: Sumptuary laws, consumption and national identity in early modern Sweden," in T. Engelhardt Mathiassen, M.-L. Nosch, M.

Ringgaard, K. Toftegaard, M. Venborg Pedersen (eds), *Fashionable Encounters: Perspectives and Trends in Textile and Dress in the Early Modern Nordic World*, Oxford and Oakville: Oxbow Books.
Anthony, I.E. (1980), "Clothing Given to a Servant of the Late Sixteenth Century in Wales," *Costume* 14: 32–40.
Antoniano, Silvio (1584), *Tre libri del'educazione cristiana de'figliuoli,* Verona: Sebastiano dalle Donne & Girolamo Stringari.
Apostolos-Cappadona, Diane (2010), "Costuming Judith in Italian Art of the Sixteenth Century," in Kevin R. Brine, Elena Ciletti, and Henrike Lähnemann (eds), *The Sword of Judith: Judith Studies across the Disciplines*, Cambridge: Open Book Publishers, 325–43.
Aribaud, C. (2006), "Les taillades dans le vêtement de la Renaissance: l'art des nobles écritures," in *Paraître et se vêtir*, Sainte-Etienne: PU Sainte-Etienne.
Ariès, P. (1975), *L'Enfant et la vie familiale*, Paris: Seuil, 79.
Ariosto, L. (1983), *Orlando Furioso*, trans. Guido Waldman, Oxford: Oxford University Press.
Arnold, J. (1978), *A Handbook of Costume*, London: Macmillan.
—— (1985), *Patterns of Fashion: The Cut and Construction of Clothes for Men and Women c. 1560–1620*, London: Macmillan.
—— (1988), *Queen Elizabeth's Wardrobe Unlock'd,* Leeds: Maney.
—— (2000), *Make or Break: The Testing of Theory by Reproducing Historic Techniques*, in M.M. Brooks (ed.), *Textiles Revealed*, London: Archetype Publications.
—— (2008), *Patterns of Fashion 4: The Cut and Construction of Linen Shirts, Smocks, Neckwear, Headwear and Accessories for Men and Women, c. 1540–1660*, completed by Jenny Tiramani and Santina Levey, London: Macmillan.
Ashelford, J. (1988), *Dress in the Age of Elizabeth*, London: Batsford.
—— (1993), *A Visual History of Costume in the Sixteenth Century*, London: Batsford.
—— (1996), *The Art of Dress: Clothes and Society 1500–1914*, London: National Trust.
Ashley, K. (2004), "Material and Symbolic Gift-Giving: Clothes in English and French Wills," in E. Jane Burns (ed.), *Medieval Fabrications: Dress, Textiles, Cloth Work, and Other Cultural Imaginings*, New York: Palgrave Macmillan.
Bailey, A. (2001), "Monstrous Manner: Style and the Early Modern Theater," *Criticism*, vol. 43, no. 3, Summer: 249–84.
Bald, R.C. (1986), *Donne and the Drurys*, Westport CT: Greenwood Press.
Baldwin, F.E. (1926), *Sumptuary Legislation and Personal Regulation in England*, Baltimore: Johns Hopkins University Press.
Bardiès-Fronty, I. and M. Bimbenet-Privat, eds (2009), *Le bain et le miroir: soins du corps et cosmétique de l'Antiquité à la Renaissance*, Paris: Gallimard.
Barthes, R. (1983), *The Fashion System,* trans. Matthew Ward and Richard Howard, New York: Hill & Wang.
—— (2006), *The Language of Fashion*, ed. and trans. Andy Stafford, New York: Berg.
Bartlett, R. (2001), "Medieval and Modern Concepts of Race and Ethnicity," *Journal of Medieval and Early Modern Studies* 31, no. 1: 39–56.
Bartram, C. (2004), "Social fabric in Thynne's *Debate between Pride and Lowlines*," in *Clothing Culture 1350–1650*, Aldershot: Ashgate.
Bass, L.R. (2008), *The Drama of the Portrait*, University Park: Penn State Press.
Bass, L.R. and A. Wunder (2009), "The Veiled Ladies of the Early Modern Spanish World: Seduction in Seville, Madrid, and Lima," *Hispanic Review* 77:1 Winter: 97–144.
Begent, P., ed. (1999), *The most noble Order of the Garter, 650 years*, London: Spink & Son Ltd.

Beier, A.L. (1981), "The social problems of an Elizabethan country town: Warwick, 1580–90," in Peter Clark (ed.), *Country Towns in Pre-Industrial England*, Leicester: Leicester University Press.

—— (1985), *Masterless men: the vagrancy problem in England, 1560–1640*, London: Methuen & Co. Ltd.

Belfanti, C.M. and F. Giusberti (2000), "Clothing and Social Inequality in Early Modern Europe: Introductory Remarks," in *Continuity and Change* 15.3, 359–65.

Bell, R.M. (1999), *How To Do It: guides to good living for renaissance ladies*, Chicago and London: University of Chicago Press.

Benedetto, A. Di, ed. (1991), *Prose di Giovanni Della Casa e altri trattatisti cinequecenteschi di comportamento*, Turin: Utet.

Berger, H. (2000), *The Absence of Grace: Sprezzatura and Suspicion in Two Renaissance Courtesy Books*, Stanford: Stanford University Press.

Berger, R.M. (1993), *The Most Necessary Luxuries: The Mercers' Company of Coventry, 1550–1680*. University Park: Penn State Press.

Bernis, C. (1962), *Indumentaria española en tiempos de Carlos V*, Madrid: Instituto Diego Velázquez.

Bertelli, P. (1589), *Diversarum Nationum Habitus Gentum*, Padua: Alci.

Blanc, O. (1997), *Parades et parures. L'invention du corps de mode à la fin du Moyen Age*, Paris: Gallimard.

Blum, S. Neilsen (1969), *Early Netherlandish Triptychs: A Study in Patronage*, Berkeley: University of California Press.

Boccaccio, G. (1975), *The Corbaccio*, ed. and trans. Anthony K. Cassell, Urbana: University of Illinois Press.

Bongi, S. (1889), "Il velo giallo di Tullia d'Aragona," *Rivista critica della letteratura italiana* III (March 1886): 85–6.

Bolton, J.L. (1980), *The Medieval English Economy 1150–1500*, London: J.M. Dent Ltd.

Boucher, J. (1981), *Société et mentalités autour de Henri III*, Lille: Atelier de reproduction des theses.

Boulton, J. (1987), *Neighbourhood and Society: A London Suburb in the Seventeenth Century*, Cambridge: Cambridge University Press.

Bourdieu, P. (1979), *La distinction, Critique sociale du jugement*, Paris, Minuit.

Boverius, Z. (1632–39), *Annalium seu sacrarum historiarum ordinis minorum S. Francisci qui Capucini nuncupantur*, 2 vols., Claudius Landry: Lyons.

Brandi, E. Tosi (2002), *Introduzione a Cesena*, in M.G. Muzzarelli (ed.), *La Legislazione Suntuaria Secoli XIII–XVI, Emilia Romagna*, Rome: Ministero per i beni e le attività culturali.

Brantôme (1991), *Recueil des Dames*, Paris: Gallimard.

Braudel, F. (1981), *The Structure of Everyday Life: Civilization and Capitalism 15th to 18th Century*, vol. 1, London: Harper Collins Ltd.

Braunstein, Ph., ed. (1992), *Un banquier mis à nu. Autobiographie de Matthäus Schwarz, bourgeois d'Augsbourg*, Paris, Gallimard.

Bridgeman, J. (1998), "'Condecenti et netti . . .': Beauty, Dress and Gender in Italian Renaissance Art," in Francis Ames-Lewis and Mary Rogers (eds), *Concepts of Beauty in Renaissance Art*, Aldershot: Ashgate.

—— (2000), "Dress in Moroni's Portraits," in Peter Humfrey (ed.), *Giovanni Battista Moroni: Renaissance Portraitist*, Fort Worth: Kimbell Art Museum.

Broomhall, S. (2008), "Women, Work, and Power in Female Guilds of Rouen," in Megan Cassidy-Welch and Peter Sherlock (eds), *Practices of Gender in Late Medieval and Early Modern Europe*, Turnhout: Brepols.

—— (2011), *Early Modern Women in the Low Countries: Feminizing Sources and Interpretations of the Past*, Aldershot: Ashgate.

Brose, M. (2010), "Fetishizing the Veil: Petrarch's Poetics of Rematerialization," in Julia L. Hairston and Walter Stephens (eds), *The Body in Early Modern Italy*, Baltimore: Johns Hopkins University Press.

Brown, H.F., ed. (1894), *Calendar of State Papers Venetian, vol. 2, 1607–1610*, London: HMSO.

Brown, J. (1987), "Patronage and piety: religious imagery in the art of Francisco de Zurbáran," in Jeannine Baticle, *Zurbarán*, Abrams: New York, 1–24.

Brown, K. (1995), "'Changed into the Fashion of a Man': The Politics of Sexual Difference in a Seventeenth-Century Anglo-American Settlement," *Journal of the History of Sexuality*, 6 (2): 171–93.

Brown, P. Fortini (2006), "The Venetian Casa," in Marta Ajmar-Wollheim and Flora Dennis (eds), *At Home in Renaissance Italy*, London: V&A Publications.

Brushfield, T.N. (1901), "The Financial Diary of a Citizen of Exeter, 1631–43," *Reports and Transactions of the Devonshire Association 3*.

Buck, A. (2000), "Clothing and Textiles in Bedfordshire Inventories, 1617–1620," *Costume* 34: 25–37.

Bulwer, J. (1650 and 1653), *Anthropometamorphosis: man transformed: or, the artificial changeling*, London: J. Hardesty and London: William Hunt.

Burke, P. (1987), *The Historical Anthropology of Early Modern Italy*, Cambridge: Cambridge University Press.

—— (1996a), *The Fortunes of the Courtier*, University Park: Penn State Press.

—— (1996b), "Representations of the Self from Petrarch to Descartes," in Roy Porter (ed.), *Re-writing the Self*, London and New York: Routledge.

Burkholder, K.M. (2005), "Threads Bared: Dress and Textiles in Late Medieval English Wills," in Robin Netherton and Gale Owen-Crocker (eds), *Medieval Clothing and Textiles* 1, Woodbridge: Boydell Press.

Busbecq, O.C. De (2004), *Türkiye'yi Böyle Gördüm*, Ankara: Kesit.

Buss, C. (2009), "Silk, Gold, Crimson," in C. Buss (ed.), *Silk, Gold, Crimson: Secrets and Technology at the Visconti and Sforza Courts*, Milan: Silvana Editoriale.

Busto, A., ed. (2007), *Il velo tra mistero, seduzione, misticismo, sensualità, potere e religione*, Milan: Silvana editoriale.

Butazzi, G. (rev edn. 1997), "'The Scandalous Licentiousness of Tailors and Seamstresses': Considerations on the Profession of the Tailor in the Republic of Venice," in *I Mestieri della Moda a Venezia: The Arts and Crafts of Fashion in Venice, from the 13th to the 18th Century*, Exhibition Catalogue.

Butler Greenfield, A. (2005), *A Perfect Red: Empire, Espionage and the Quest for the Colour of Desire*, London: Doubleday.

Cadogan, J. (2000), *Domenico Ghirlandaio: Artist and Artisan*, New Haven: Yale University Press.

Carleton, D. (1972), *Dudley Carleton to John Chamberlain 1603–1624: Jacobean Letters*, ed. Maurice Lee, New Brunswick: Rutgers University Press.

Canny, N. (1998), *The Oxford History of the British Empire: Volume 1. The Origins of Empire, British Overseas Enterprise to the Close of the Seventeenth Century*, Oxford: Oxford University Press.

Caracausi, A. (2014), "Beaten Children and Women's Work in Early Modern Italy," *Past and Present*, no. 222, Feb.: 95–128.

Carnesecchi, C. (1902), *Cosimo I e la legge suntuaria del 1562*, Florence: Stabilimento Pellas.

Carranza, A. (1639), *Discurso contra malos trajes y adornos lascivos*, Francisco Martinez: Madrid.
Casagrande di Villaviera, R. (1986), *Le cortigiane venetiane nel Cinquecento*, Milan: Longanesi.
Castiglione, B. (1528), *Il Libro del Cortegiano*, Venice: Aldo Manuzio.
—— (2002), *The Book of the Courtier: the Singleton translation*, trans. Charles Singleton, ed. Daniel Javitch, New York and London: W.W. Norton & Company.
Cataldi Gallo, M. (1994), "Per una storia del costume genovese nel primo quarto del seicento," in Susan Barnes and Arthur Wheelock, Jr. (eds), *Van Dyck 350*, Washington DC and Hanover, NH: National Gallery of Art/University of New England Press.
Cavallo, A. (1998), *The Unicorn Tapestries at the Metropolitan Museum of Art*, New York: Harry N. Abrams.
Cavallo, S. and T. Storey (2013), *Healthy Living in Late Renaissance Italy*, Oxford: Oxford University Press.
Céard, J. et al., eds (1990), *Le corps à la Renaissance, Actes du colloque de Tours, 1987*, Paris: Amateurs de livres.
Cerri, M. (1995), "Sarti toscani nel seicento: attività e clientela," in Anna Giulia Cavagna and Grazietta Butazzi (eds), *Le Trame della moda*, Rome: Bulzoni.
Channing Linthicum, M. (1936), *Costume in the Drama of Shakespeare and his Contemporaries*, Oxford: Clarendon Press.
Cherry, J. (1991), "Leather," in J. Blair and N. Ramsey (eds), *English Medieval Industries: Craftsmen, Techniques, Products*, London: A.&C. Black Publishers, 295–318.
Chirelstein, E. (1995), "Emblem and Reckless Presence: The Drury Portrait at Yale," in L. Gent (ed.), *Albion's Classicism: The Visual Arts in Britain, 1550–1660*, New Haven and London: Yale University Press.
Chojnacki, S. (1980), "La Posizione della Donna a Venezia nel Cinquecento," in M. Gemin and G. Paladini (eds), *Tiziano e Venezia*, Vicenza: Neri Pozza.
Christiansen, K., ed. (2011), *The Renaissance Portrait: from Donatello to Bellini*, New York: Metropolitan Museum of Art.
Cibin, P. (1985), "Meretrici e cortigiane a Venezia nel '500," *Donna Woman Femme, Quaderni internazionali di studi sulla donna* 1985, 25 (6): 79–102.
Ciletti, E. (1991), "Patriarchal Ideology in the Renaissance Iconography of Judith," in Marilyn Migiel and Juliana Schiesari (eds), *Refiguring Woman: Perspectives on Gender and the Italian Renaissance*, Ithaca: Cornell University Press.
Ciletti, E. and Henrike Lähnemann (2010), "Judith in the Christian Tradition," in Kevin R. Brine, Elena Ciletti, and Henrike Lähnemann (eds), *The Sword of Judith; Judith Studies Across the Disciplines,* Cambridge: Open Book Publishers, 41–65.
Clark, P. and P. Slack (1976), *English Towns in Transition 1500–1700*, Oxford: Oxford University Press.
Clark, S. (1985), "'Hic Mulier,' 'Haec Vir,' and the Controversy over Masculine Women," *Studies in Philology*, vol. 82 (2): 157–83.
Clarkson, L. (2003), "The linen industry in early modern Europe," in D. Jenkins (ed.), *The Cambridge History of Western Textiles*, vol. 1, Cambridge: Cambridge University Press, 476–7.
Clifford, A. *The Diaries of Lady Anne Clifford*, ed. D.J.H. Clifford. Stroud: Sutton, 1990.
Clunas, C. (2004), *Superfluous Things: Material Culture and Social Status in Early Modern China*, Honolulu: University of Hawai'i Press.
Cockayne, E. (2007), *Hubbub: Filth, Noise and Stench in England, 1600–1770*, New Haven and London: Yale University Press.
Cohen, A. (1984), *Jewish Life under Islam*, Cambridge, MA: Harvard University Press.
Collinson, P. (1990), *The Elizabethan Puritan Movement*, Oxford: Clarendon Press.

Colomer, J.L. (1990, first ed. 1967) and A. Descalzo, eds, *Spanish Fashion at the Courts of Early Modern Europe*, vols. I & II, London: Paul Holberton.
Cornelison, S.J. (2012), *Art and the Relic Cult of St. Antoninus in Renaissance Florence*, Aldershot: Ashgate.
Cornell, S., and D. Hartmann (1998), *Ethnicity and Race: Making Identities in a Changing World*, London: Pine Forge Press.
Costa, D. (1998), "La Raffaella di Alessandro Piccolomini: un'armonia nella disarmonia?" in L. Rotondi Secchi Tarugi (ed.), *Disarmonia, bruttezza e bizzarria nel Rinascimento*, Florence: F. Cesati.
Cowper, J. Meadows, ed. (1901), *The Diary of Thomas Cocks, March 25th, 1607, to December 31st, 1610*, Canterburg: Cross and Jackson.
Cox-Rearick, J. (2009), "Power-Dressing at the Courts of Cosimo de' Medici and François I: The 'moda alla spagnola' of Spanish Consorts Eléonore d'Autriche and Eleonora di Toledo," *Artibus et Historiae* vol. 30, no. 60: 39–69.
Crawford, J. (2004), "Clothing Distributions and Social Relations c. 1350–1500," in C. Richardson (ed.), *Clothing Culture 1350–1650*, Aldershot: Ashgate.
Croizat, Y. (2007), "'Living Dolls': François Ier Dresses His Women," *Renaissance Quarterly* 60: 94–130.
Cronin, J.M. (1990), *The Elements of Archaeological Conservation*, London: Routledge.
Crouzet, Denis (1974), "Imaginaire du corps et violence au temps des troubles de Religion," in P.E. Cunnington, *Costume of Household Servants*, London: A.&C. Black Publishers.
Currie, E. (2000), "Prescribing Fashion: Dress, Politics, and Gender in Sixteenth Century Conduct Literature," *Fashion Theory* 4: 157–78.
—— (2007), "Diversity and Design in the Florentine Tailoring Trade, 1550–1620," in Michelle O'Malley and Evelyn Welch (eds), *The Material Renaissance*, Manchester: Manchester University Press.
—— (2009), "Fashion Networks: Consumer Demand and the Clothing Trade in Florence from the mid-Sixteenth to Early Seventeenth Century," *Journal of Medieval and Early Modern Studies* 39: 483–509.
Cuthbert, Father, ed. and trans. (1931), *A Capuchin chronicle*, London: Sheed and Ward.
Damme, I. van (2010), "Middlemen and the Creation of a 'Fashion Revolution': The Experience of Antwerp in the Late Seventeenth and Eighteenth Centuries," in B. Lemire (ed.), *The Force of Fashion in Politics and Society*, Ashford: Ashgate.
Dasent, J. R., ed. (1897), *Acts of the Privy Council of England*, 1586–87, vol. 14, London: HMSO.
Davanzo Poli, D. (1998), *Il Merletto Veneziano*, Venice: Novara.
—— (2003), *Il sarto*, in C. Marco Belfanti and F. Giusberti (eds), *Storia d'Italia: La Moda*, Turin: Einaudi.
Davidsohn, R. (1965), *Storia di Firenze*, vol. 7, Florence: Sansoni.
Davidson, N. (1994), "Theology, Nature and the Law," in T. Dean and K.J.P. Lowe (eds), *Crime, Society and the Law in Renaissance Italy*, Cambridge: Cambridge University Press.
Davies, M. and Ann Saunders (2004), *The History of the Merchant Taylors' Company*, Leeds: Maney.
Davis, F. (1992), *Fashion, Culture and Identity*, Chicago: University of Chicago Press.
Daza, A. (1617), *Historia de las llagas de nuestro seráfico Padre San Francisco, colegida del martirologio y breviario romano y treynta bulas y dozientos autores y santos*, Luis Sánchez: Valladolid.
Dean, T. (2001), *Crime in Medieval Europe 1200–1550*, Harlow and London: Longman.

Deceulaer, H. (2000), "Entrepreneurs in the Guilds: Ready-to-wear Clothing and Subcontracting in Late Sixteenth- and Early Seventeenth-Century Antwerp," *Textile History* 31: 133–49.

—— (2008), "Second-Hand Dealers in the Early Modern Low Countries: Institutions, Markets and Practices," in Laurence Fontaine (ed.) *Alternative Exchanges: Second-Hand Circulations from the Sixteenth Century to the Present*, New York and Oxford: Berghahn Books.

Dee, J. (1842), *The Private Diary of Dr. John Dee*, ed. James Orchard Halliwell, Camden Society, o.s. 19.

Dekker, T. (1606), *The Seven Deadly Sinnes of London*, London.

Denegri-Knott, J., and E. Parsons (2014), "Disordering Things," *Journal of Consumer Behavior* 13, no. 2: 89–98.

Denny-Brown, A. (2009), "Old habits die hard: vestimentary change in William Durandus' *Rationale divinorum officiorum*," *The Journal of Medieval and Early Modern Studies* 39/3: 545–70.

Dernschwam, H. (1992), *İstanbul ve Anadolu'ya Seyahat Günlüğü*, trans. Yaşar Önen, Mersin: Mersin İmar Basımevi.

Deserps, F. (1562), *Receuil de la diversité des habits qui sont de present en usaige tant es pays d'Europe, Asie, Affrique & Illes sauvages, le tout fait apres le naturel*, Paris: Richard Breton.

De Vos, D. (1994), *Hans Memling: The Complete Works*, London: Thames & Hudson.

Dubois, C. (1996), Introduction to Artus Thomas [1605], *Les Hermaphrodites*, Geneva: Droz.

Dugdale, W. (1730), *The Antiquities of Warwickshire*, 2nd ed. rev. William Thomas.

Duplessis, G. (1859), *Catalogue de l'oeuvre de Abraham Bosse*, Paris.

Durand, W. (2010), *On the clergy and their vestments*, (trans. and intro.) Timothy M. Thibodeau, Chicago: University of Scranton Press.

Durkin, G. (2001), *The Civic Government and Economy of Elizabethan Canterbury*, unpublished PhD thesis, Canterbury Christchurch.

Eastop, D. (2000), "Textiles as Multiple and Competing Histories," in M.M. Brooks, (ed.), *Textiles Revealed*, London: Archetype Publications.

Egan, G. (2005), *Material Culture in London in an Age of Transition: Tudor and Stuart Period Finds c. 1450–c. 1700 from Excavations at Riverside Sites in Southwark*, MoLAS Monograph 19, London: Museum of London.

Eikema Hommes, M. van (2004), *Changing Pictures: Discoloration in 15th–17th Century Oil Paintings*. London: Archetype Books.

Eire, C.M.N. (2002), *From Madrid to Purgatory: the art and craft of dying in sixteenth-century Spain*, Cambridge: Cambridge University Press.

Eisenblicher, Konrad (1988), "Bronzino's Portrait of Guidobaldo II della Rovere," *Renaissance and Reformation*, vol. 24 (1): 21–33.

Elm, K. (1990), "Augustinus canonicus—Augustinus eremita: a quattrocento *cause célèbre*," in T. Verdon and J. Henderson (eds), *Christianity and the Renaissance: image and religious imagination in the quattrocento*, Syracuse: Syracuse University Press, 83–107.

Emmison, F.G. (1976), *Elizabethan Life: Home, Work and Land*, Essex Record Office Publication no. 69, Chelmsford: Essex Record Office.

Entwistle, J. (2000), *The Fashioned Body. Fashion, Dress and Modern Social Theory*, Cambridge: Polity.

Erasmus, D. (1997), *Collected Works of Erasmus: Colloquies*, vol. I, (trans. and annotated) Craig R. Thompson, Toronto: University of Toronto Press.

Erondelle, P. (1605), *The French Garden*, London: Edward White.

Evelyn, J. (1897), *Memoirs of John Evelyn*, ed. William Bray, London: Frederick Warne & Co.

Faroqhi, S. (2002), *Stories of Ottoman Men and Women*, İstanbul: Eren.
—— (2010), "The Ottoman Ruling Group and the Religions of Its Subjects in the Early Modern Age: A Survey of Current Research," *Journal of Early Modern History* 14, no. 3: 239–66.
Farr, J.R. (1997), "Cultural Analysis and Early Modern Artisans," in G. Crossick (ed.), *The Artisan and the European Town 1500–1900*, Aldershot: Scolar Press.
—— (2000), *Artisans in Europe, 1300–1914*, Cambridge: Cambridge University Press.
Finucci, V. (1994), "The Female Masquerade: Ariosto and the Game of Desire," in Valeria Finucci and Regina Schwartz (eds), *Desire in the Renaissance: Psychoanalysis and Literature*, Princeton: Princeton University Press.
Fisher, F.J. (1948), "The development of London as a centre of conspicuous consumption in the sixteenth and seventeenth centuries," *Transactions of the Royal Historical Society*, 4th ser., 30: 37–50.
Fisher, S.N. (1971), *The Middle East: A History*, London: Routledge.
Fisher, W. (2011), "Had it a codpiece, 'twere a man indeed," in B. Mirabella (ed.), *Ornamentalism: The Art of Renaissance Accessories*, Ann Arbor: University of Michigan Press.
—— (2015), "Making most solemne love to a petticote: Clothing Fetishism in Early Modern English Culture," Unpublished conference paper, Berlin: RSA.
Florio, J. (1598), *A Worlde of Words*, London: Arnold Hatfield, 1598.
Franco, G. (1990), *Habiti delle donne veneziane* (1610), ed. Lina Urban, Venice: Centro Internazionale dell Grafica di Venezia.
Freccero, C. (2010), "Loving the Other: Masculine Subjectivity in Early Modern Europe," in Gerry Milligan and Jane Tylus (eds), *The Poetics of Early Modern Masculinity*, Toronto: Centre for Renaissance and Reformation Studies, 101–18.
Freeman, M. Beam (1976), *The Unicorn Tapestries*, New York: E.P. Dutton.
French, H. (2007), *The Middle Sort of People in Provincial England 1600–1750*, Oxford: Oxford University Press.
Frick, C. Collier (2002), *Dressing Renaissance Florence: Families, Fortunes, and Fine Clothing*, Baltimore: Johns Hopkins University Press.
—— (2004), "The Florentine 'Rigattieri': Second Hand Clothing Dealers and the Circulation of Goods in the Renaissance," in Alexandra Palmer and Hazel Clark (eds), *Old Clothes, New Looks: Second-Hand Fashion*, Oxford: Berg.
Friedman, J. Block (2013), "The iconography of dagged clothing and its reception by moralist writers," *Medieval Clothing and Textiles* 9: 121–38.
Gage, J. (1993), *Colour and Culture*, London: Thames & Hudson.
Gawdy, P. (1906), *Letters of Philip Gawdy*, ed. Isaac Herbert Jeayes, London: J.B. Nichols & Sons.
Geffe, N. (1607), *The Perfect Use of Silk-Wormes and their Benefit*, London.
Genç, M. (2007), *Osmanlı İmparatorluğu'nda Devlet ve Ekonomi*, İstanbul: Ötüken.
Gerlach, S. (2007), *Türkiye Günlüğü 1573–1576*, ed. K. Beydilli, trans. T. Noyan, İstanbul: Kitap Yayınevi.
Giannetti, L. (2009), *Lelia's Kiss: Imagining Gender, Sex and Marriage in Italian Renaissance Comedy*, Toronto: University of Toronto Press.
Gilbert, D. (2000), "Urban Outfitting: The City and the Spaces of Fashion Culture," in S. Bruzzi and P. Church-Gibson (eds), *Fashion Cultures: Theories, Explanations and Analysis*, London: Routledge.
Goffman, E. (1959), *The Presentation of Self in Everyday Life*, New York: Anchor Books.

Gohl, E.P.G. and L.D. Vilensky (1980), *Textile Science: An Explanation of Fibre Properties*, Melbourne: Longman Cheshire.

Goldstein, C. (2012), *Print Culture in Early Modern France: Abraham Bosse and the Purposes of Print*, Cambridge: Cambridge University Press.

Goldthwaite, R.A. (2009), *The Economy of Renaissance Florence*, Baltimore: Johns Hopkins University Press.

Goodrich, P. (1998), "Signs taken for wonders: Community, Identity and a History of Sumptuary Law," *Law and Social Inquiry*, 23(3): 707–28.

Gordenker, E. (2001), *Van Dyck (1599–1641) and the Representation of Dress in Seventeenth-Century Portraiture*, Turnhout: Brepols.

Goulemot, J.M. et al, eds (1995), "Voyage de J. Lippomano, ambassadeur de Venise en France en 1577," in *Le Voyage en France. Anthologie des voyageurs européens en France, du Moyen Age à la fin de l'Empire* Montaigne, *Journal de voyage en Italie*, in *Oeuvres complètes*, Paris: Laffont.

Greenblatt, S. (1980), *Renaissance Self-Fashioning: From More to Shakespeare*, Chicago: University of Chicago Press.

Greenblatt, S. (1997), "Mutilation and Meaning," in D. Hillman, and C. Mazzio (eds), *The Body in Parts*, London: Routledge.

Grieco, A.J. (2006), "Meals," in *At Home in Renaissance Italy*, Marta Ajmar-Wollheim and Flora Dennis (eds), London: V&A Publications.

Grimes, K.I. (2002), "Dressing the World: Costume Books and Ornamental Cartography in the Age of Exploration," in E. Rodini and E.B. Weaver (eds), *A Well-Fashioned Image: Clothing and Costume in European Art, 1500–1850*, Chicago: University of Chicago.

Guarino, G. (2004), "Regulation of appearances during the Catholic reformation: dress and morality in Spain and Italy," in Ilan Zinguer and Myriam Yardeni (eds), *Le deux réformes chrétiennes: propagation et diffusion*, Leiden and Boston: Brill, 492–510.

Guazzo, S. (1580), *La Civil Conversazione* Book III, Venice: Gio. Battista Somasco.

—— (1993), *La Civil Conversazione*, ed. A. Quondam, Modena: Panini.

Guérer, A. Le. (2005), *Le parfum des origines à nos jours*, Paris: Odile Jacob.

Gürtuna, S. (1999), *Osmanlı Kadın Giysisi*, Ankara: T.C. Kültür Bakanlığı Yayınevi.

Guy, J. (1998), *Woven Cargoes: Indian Textiles in the East*, London: Thames & Hudson.

Haigh, C. (1981), "The continuity of Catholicism in the English reformation," *Past and Present* 93: 37–69.

Hamling, T. and Catherine Richardson (forthcoming), *A Day at Home in Early Modern England: The Materiality of Domestic Life, 1500–1700*. New Haven and London: Yale University Press.

Haraguchi, J. (2002), "Debating Women's Fashion in Renaissance Venice," in Elizabeth Rodini and Elissa B. Weaver (eds), *A Well-Fashioned Image: Clothing and Costume in European Art, 1500–1850*. Chicago: The David and Alfred Smart Museum/University of Chicago.

Harley, Lady B. (1854), *Letters of the Lady Brilliana Harley*, ed. Thomas Taylor Lewis, London: Camden Society, 58.

Harman, T. (1567), *A caueat for common cursetors vvlgarely called uagaboes*, London: Wylliam Gryffith.

Harris, J., ed. (1993), *Textiles: 5000 Years*, London: Harry N. Abrams.

Harrison, W. (1994), *Description of England*, Washington: Folger Shakespeare Library.

Harte, N. (1976), "State Control of Dress and Social Change in Pre-Industrial England," in D.C. Coleman and A.H. John (eds), *Trade, Government and Economy in Pre-Industrial England*, London.

Harvey, J. (1995), *Men in Black*, London: Reaktion.

Hayward, M.A. (2002), "Reflections on gender and status distinctions: an analysis of the liturgical textiles recorded in mid-sixteenth century London," *Gender and History* 14/3, 403–25.

—— (2004), "Fashion, Finance, Foreign Politics and the Wardrobe of Henry VIII," in *Clothing Culture 1350–1650*, ed. C. Richardson, Aldershot: Ashgate.

—— (2007), *Dress at the Court of King Henry VIII*, Leeds: Maney Publishing.

—— (2009), *Rich Apparel: Clothing and the Law in Henry VIII's England*, Aldershot: Ashgate.

Hayward, M.A., ed. (2012), *The Great Wardrobe Accounts of Henry VII and Henry VIII*, London Record Society, 47, Woodbridge: Boydell and Brewer.

Heberer, M. (2003), *Osmanlı'da Bir Köle: Brettenli Michael Heberer'in Anıları (1585–1588)*, trans. T. Noyan, İstanbul: Kitap Yayınevi.

Henderson K. Usher and B. McManus, eds (1985), *Half Humankind: Contexts and Texts of the Controversy about Women in England, 1540–1640*. Urbana: University of Illinois Press.

Hentschell, R. (2008), *The Culture of Cloth in Early Modern England: Textual Constructions of a National Identity*, Aldershot: Ashgate.

Herald, J. (1981), *Renaissance Dress in Italy 1400–1500*, London: Bell & Hyman.

Heseler, B. (1959), *Andreas Vesalius' First Public Anatomy at Bologna, 1540: An Eyewitness Report*, ed. and trans. Ruben Eriksson, Uppsala: Almqvist & Wiksells.

Hillman, D. and Carla Mazzio, eds (1997), *The Body in Parts: Fantasies of Corporeality in Early Modern Europe*, London: Routledge.

Hills, P. (2006), "Titian's Veils," *Art History* 29.

Hofenk de Graaff, J.H. (2004), *The Colourful Past: Origins, Chemistry and Identification of Natural Dyestuffs*, Berne: Abegg-Stiftung Foundation.

Holden, A. (2002), "That's no lady, that's . . ." *The Guardian*, Sunday April 21.

Hollander, A. (2002), *Fabric of Vision: Dress and Drapery in Painting*, London: National Gallery Company.

Hoskins, W.G. (1976), *The Age of Plunder: The England of Henry VIII 1500–1547*, London: Longman.

Howell, M.C. (2010), *Commerce Before Capitalism*, Cambridge: Cambridge University Press.

Huggett, J.E. (1999), "Rural Costume in Elizabethan Essex: A Study Based on the Evidence of Wills," *Costume* 33: 74–88.

Hughes, A. (2002), *Politics, Society and Civil War*, Cambridge: Cambridge University Press.

Hughes, D. Owen (1983), "Sumptuary Law and Social Relations in Renaissance Italy," in John Bossy (ed.), *Disputes and Settlements: Law and Human Relations in the West*, Cambridge: Cambridge University Press, 69–99.

Hunt, A. (1996), *Governance of the Consuming Passions: A history of sumptuary law*, Basingstoke: Macmillan.

Hutchinson, L. (1995), *Memoirs of the Life of Colonel Hutchinson*, ed. N.H. Keeble, London: Dent.

Innocent III (1846) *De sacro altaris mysterio*, Sylvae-Ducum: Verhoeven, 86–92.

Izbicki, T.M. (2005), "Forbidden colors in the regulation of clerical dress from the Fourth Lateran Council (1215) to the time of Nicholas of Cusa (d. 1464)," *Medieval Dress and Textiles* 1: 105–14.

Jacobs, F. (2012), "Sexual Variations: Playing with (Dis)similitude," in B. Talvacchia (ed.), *A Cultural History of Sexuality in the Renaissance*, London: Bloomsbury.

Jones, A.R. (2011), "Busks, Bodices, Bodies," in B. Mirabella (ed.), *Ornamentalism: The Art of Renaissance Accessories*, Ann Arbor: University of Michigan Press.

Jones, A.R., and M. Rosenthal (2008), *The Clothing of the Renaissance World: Cesare Vecellio's Habiti Antichi et Moderni*, New York: Thames & Hudson.

Jones, A.R. and Peter Stallybrass (1991), "Fetishizing Gender: Constructing the Hermaphrodite in Renaissance Europe," in Julia Epstein and Kristina Straub (eds), *Body Guards: The Cultural Politics of Gender Ambiguity*, New York and London: Routledge, 1991.

—— (2000), *Renaissance Clothing and the Materials of Memory*, Cambridge: Cambridge University Press.

Jones, N.G. (2007), "Puckering, Sir John," *ODNB*, xlv, 503–4.

Karababa, E. (2012), "Investigating Early Modern Ottoman Consumer Culture in the Light of Bursa Probate Inventories," *Economic History Review* 65, no: 1: 194–219.

Kay-Williams, S. (2013), *The Story of Colour in Textiles*, London: Bloomsbury.

Kelsey Staples, K. (2010), "Fripperers and the Used Clothing Trade in Late Medieval London," in Robin Netherton and Gale Owen-Crocker (eds), *Medieval Clothing and Textiles 6*, Woodbridge: Boydell Press.

Kemp, T., ed. (n.d.), *The Black Book of Warwick*, Warwick.

Kenanoğlu, M. (2004), *Osmanlı Millet Sistemi: Mitve Gerçek*, İstanbul: Klasik.

Kerridge, E. (1985), *Textile Manufactures in Early Modern England*, Manchester: Manchester University Press.

Kidnie, M.J. (2002), "Introduction," in P. Stubbes, *The anatomie of abuses*, ed. Margaret Jane Kidnie, Renaissance English Text Society, seventh series, vol. 27. Arizona Center for Medieval and Renaissance Studies: Tempe, Arizona, 2002, 1–35.

Killerby, C. Kovesi (2002), *Sumptuary Law in Italy 1200–1500*, Oxford: Clarendon Press.

King, M. and D. King, eds (1990), *European Textiles in the Kerr Collection 400 BC to 1800 AD*, London and Boston: Faber & Faber.

Klapisch-Zuber, C. (1985), *Women, Family and Ritual in Renaissance Italy*, London: University of Chicago Press, 1985.

Köhler, Neeltje (2006), *Painting in Haarlem 1500–1850: The collection of the Frans Hals Museum*, Gent: Ludion Editions.

Konrad, J. (2011), "'Barbarous Gallants': fashion, morality, and the marked body in English culture, 1590–1660," *Fashion Theory* 15/1: 29–48.

Kren, T., ed. (1997), *Masterpieces of the J. Paul Getty Museum. Illuminated Manuscripts*, Oxford: Oxford University Press.

—— (2003), *Illuminating the Renaissance: The Triumph of Flemish Manuscript Painting in Europe*, Los Angeles: J. Paul Getty Museum.

Lambin, R. (1999), *Le voile des femmes. Un inventaire historique, social et psychologique*, Bern: Peter Lang.

Lampugnani, A. (1648), *La carrozza da nolo. Ovvero del vestire e usanze alla moda*, Bologna and Milan.

Landini, R. Orsi and B. Niccoli (2005), *Moda a Firenze 1540–1580: lo stile di Eleonora di Toledo e la sua influenza*, Florence: Polistampa.

Larivaille, P. (1983), *La vita quotidiana nell'Italia del Rinascimento*, Milan: Biblioteca Universale Rizzoli.

Larkin, J.F. and P.L. Hughes, eds (1969), *Tudor Royal Proclamations: The Later Tudors 1553–1587*, vol. II, Oxford: Clarendon Press.

Larkin, J.F. and P.L. Hughes, eds (1973), *Stuart Royal Proclamations: Royal Proclamations of King James I, 1603–1625*, vol. I, Oxford: Clarendon Press.

Laughran, M.A. (2003), "Oltre la pelle: I cosmetici e il loro uso," in *Storia d'Italia: Annali. La moda*, Turin: Einaudi.

Lawson, J.A., ed. (2013), *The Elizabethan New Year's Gift Exchanges, 1559–1603*, Records of Social and Economic History 51, Oxford: Oxford University Press.

Legg, J. Wickham (1882), *Notes on the History of the Liturgical Colours*, London: John S. Leslie.

Leibacher-Ouvrard, L. (2000), "Decadent Dandies and Dystopian Gender-Bending: Artus Thomas's L'Isle des hermaphrodites (1605)," *Utopian Studies*, 11(1): 124–31.

Lemire, B. (2003), "Fashioning cottons: Asian trade, domestic industry and consumer demand, 1660–1780," in D. Jenkins (ed.), *The Cambridge History of Western Textiles*, vol. 1, Cambridge: Cambridge University Press.

—— (2004), "Shifting Currency: The Culture and Economy of the Second Hand Trade in England, c. 1600–1850," in Alexandra Palmer and Hazel Clark (eds), *Old Clothes, New Looks: Second-Hand Fashion*, Oxford: Berg.

—— (2006), "Plebeian Commercial Circuits and Everyday Material Exchange in England, c. 1600–1900," in Bruno Blondé, Peter Stabel, Jon Stobart, and Ilja Van Damme (eds), *Buyers and Sellers: Retail Circuits and Practices in Medieval and Early Modern Europe*, Turnhout: Brepols.

Lemire, B. and G. Riello (2008), "East and West: textiles and fashion in early modern Europe," *Journal of Social History*, 41: 4: 887–916.

Léry, J. de (1990), *History of a voyage to the land of Brazil, otherwise called America* (1578), ed. J. Whatley, Berkeley: University of California Press.

Lestringant, F., ed. (1997), *Le Brésil d'André Thévet. Les singularités de la France Antartique (1557)*, Paris: Chandeigne.

Levey, S. (1990), *Lace: a History*, Leeds: Maney.

—— (2003), "Lace in the early modern period, c. 1500–1780," in D. Jenkins (ed.), *The Cambridge History of Western Textiles*, vol. 1, Cambridge: Cambridge University Press, 585–96.

Levine, L. (1994), *Men in Women's Clothing: Anti-Theatricality and Effeminization, 1579–1642*. Cambridge: Cambridge University Press.

Lewin, A. (1993), *Dürer and Costume: A Study of the Dress in some of Dürer's paintings and drawings*, London, PhD Thesis.

Lindsay, D. (1871), *The minor poems of Lyndesay*, ed. J.A.H. Murray, London: Trübner.

Llewellyn, N. (2000), *Funeral Monuments in Post-Reformation England*, Cambridge: Cambridge University Press.

Lockyer, R. (1974), *Habsburg and Bourbon Europe 1470–1720*, Harlow: Longman.

Luders, A., ed. (1810–20), *The Statutes of the Realm*, 11 vols., London: Records Commission.

Lugano, P.T. (1945), *I processi inediti per Francesca Bussa dei Ponziani*, Città del Vaticano: Bibliotheca Apostica Vaticana.

Lüttenberg, T. (2005), "The Cod-piece. A Renaissance Fashion between Sign and Artefact," *The Medieval History Journal*, vol. 8, no. 1,: 49–81.

MacKinnon, D. (2008), "Charitable Bodies: Clothing as Charity in Early-Modern Rural England," in Megan Cassidy-Welch and Peter Sherlock (eds), *Practices of Gender in Late Medieval and Early Modern Europe*, Turnhout: Brepols.

Mactaggart, P. and A. Mactaggart (1980), "The Rich Wearing Apparel of Richard, 3rd Earl of Dorset," *Costume* 14: 44–7.

Malanima, P. (1990), *Il Lusso dei Contadini, consumi e industrie nelle campagne toscane del sei e settecento*, Bologna: Il Mulino Ricerca.

Mann, C. (2005), "Clothing Bodies, Dressing Rooms: Fashioning Fecundity in The Lisle Letters," *Parergon*, vol. 22, no. 1, January, 137–57.

Mardin, Ş. (2000), *Türkiye'de Toplum ve Siyaset: Makaleler 1*, İstanbul: İletişimYayınevi.

Marly, D. de (1986), *Working Dress: A History of Occupational Clothing*, London: B.T. Batsford Ltd.

Marouby, C. (1990), *Utopie et primitivisme. Essai sur l'imaginaire anthropologique à l'âge classique*, Paris: Seuil.

Matchette, A. (2007), "Credit and Credibility: Used Goods and Social Relationships in Sixteenth-Century Florence," in Michelle O'Malley and Evelyn Welch (eds), *The Material Renaissance*, Manchester: Manchester University Press.

Mauss, M. (1936), "Les techniques du corps," *Journal de Psychologie*, XXXII, mars-avril: 363–86

Mayo, J. (1984), *A History of Ecclesiastical Dress*, London: Batsford.

McCabe, I. Baghdiant (2008), *Orientalism in Early Modern France*, Oxford: Berg.

McCall, T. (2013), "Brilliant Bodies: Material Culture and the Adornment of Men in North Italy's Quattrocento Courts," *I Tatti Studies* 16, 1–2: 445–490.

McCants, A.E.C. (2007), "Good at Pawn: the overlapping worlds of material possessions and family finance in Early Modern Amsterdam," *Social Science History* 31:2.

Mendelson, S. and P. Crawford (1998), *Women in Early Modern England 1530–1720*, Oxford: Clarendon Press.

Merry, M. and C. Richardson, eds (2012), *The Household Account Book of Sir Thomas Puckering of Warwick 1620: Living in London and the Midlands*, Stratford-upon-Avon: Dugdale Society.

Meteren, E. van (1614), *Nederlandtsche Historie*, Delft.

Middleton, T. (2007), *Thomas Middleton: The Collected Works*, eds Gary Taylor and John Lavagnino, Oxford: Oxford University Press.

Mikhaila, N. and J. Malcolm-Davies (2006), *The Tudor Tailor: Reconstructing Sixteenth-Century Dress*. London: Batsford.

Miller, O. (1963), *The Tudor and Stuart Paintings in the Collection of Her Majesty The Queen*, London: Royal Collection Trust.

Milligan, G. (2006), "The Politics of Effeminacy in *Il Cortegiano*," *Italica* 83:3–4: 347–69.

—— (2007), "Behaving Like a Man: Performed Masculinities in *Gl'ingannati*," *Forum Italicum*, March 41:23–42.

—— (2011), "Unlikely Heroines in Lucrezia Tornauoni's *Judith* and *Esther*," *Italica* 88:4: 538–64.

Mirabella, B. (2011), "Embellishing Herself with a Cloth: The Contradictory Life of the Handkerchief," in B. Mirabella (ed.), *Ornamentalism: The Art of Renaissance Accessories*, Ann Arbor: University of Michigan Press.

Molà, L. (2000), *The Silk Industry of Renaissance Venice*, Baltimore and London: Johns Hopkins University Press.

Molli, G. Baldissin (2006), *Fioravante, Nicolò e altri artigiani del lusso nell'età di Mantegna: ricerche di archivio a Padova*, Saonora: Il Prato.

Monnas, L. (1989), "New documents for the vestments of Henry VII at Stonyhurst College," *Burlington Magazine*, 131: 345–9.

—— (2008), *Merchants, Princes and Painters: Silk Fabrics in Italian and Northern Paintings 1300–1550*, New Haven and London: Yale University Press.

Monson, C.A. (2002), "The Council of Trent revisited," *Journal of the American Musicological Society* 55/1: 1–37.

Montaigne, M. de (1962), *Oeuvres completes*, Paris: Gallimard.

—— (1989), *Essais (1575)*, trans. Donald M. Frame, Stanford: Stanford University Press.

Morison, F. (1617), *An Itinerary*, London.

Moroni, O. (2009), "Il velo: un excursus nella letteratura italiana," in Cristina Giorcelli (ed.), *Abito e identità: Ricerche di storia letteraria e culturale,* Palermo: Ila Palma.

Mukerji, C. (2013), "Costume and Character in the Ottoman Empire: Design as Social Agent in Nicolay's Navigations," in P. Findlen (ed.), *Early Modern Things,* London: Routledge.

Muldrew, C. (1998), *The Economy of Obligation, the Culture of Credit and Social Relations in Early Modern England,* New York: Palgrave.

Mullins, W.G. (2009), *Felt,* Oxford and New York: Berg.

Murdock, G. (2000), "Dressed to repress? Protestant clerical dress and the regulation of morality in early modern Europe," *Fashion Theory: The Journal of Dress, Body and Culture* 4/2: 179–99.

—— (2004), "Dress, Nudity and Calvinist Culture in Sixteenth-Century France," in C. Richardson (ed.), *Clothing Culture 1350–1650,* Aldershot: Ashgate, 2004.

Muzzarelli, M.G. (2000), "Seta posseduta e seta consentita: dalle aspirazioni individuali alle norme suntuarie nel basso Medioevo," in L. Molà, R.C. Mueller, and C. Zanier (eds), *La seta in Italia dal Medioevo al Seicento: dal baco al drappo,* Venice: Marsilio.

—— (2006), "Nuovo, moderno e moda tra Medioevo e Rinascimento," in Eugenia Paulicelli (ed.), *Moda e Moderno,* Rome: Meltemi, 17–38.

—— (2009), "Reconciling the Privilege of a Few with the Common Good: Sumptuary Laws in Medieval and Early Modern Europe," *Journal of Medieval and Early Modern Studie,* 39 (3), special issue, Margaret F. Rosenthal (ed.), *Cultures of Clothing in Later Medieval and Early Modern Europe*: 597–617.

Nashe, T. (1992), "A choise of valentines (1592–3)," in David Norbrook (intro) and H.R. Wudhuysen (ed.), *The Penguin Book of Renaissance Verse,* London: Allen Lane/Penguin, 253–63.

Newman, K. (1991), *Fashioning Femininity and English Renaissance Drama,* Chicago: University of Chicago Press.

—— (2007), *Cultural Capitals: Early Modern London and Paris,* Princeton: Princeton University Press.

Nevinson, J. (1978), "The Dress of the Citizens of London," in Joanna Bird, Hugh Chapman, John Clark (eds), *Collectanea Londiniensia: Studies in London Archaeology and History,* London: London and Middlesex Archaeological Society.

Nevola, F. (2006), "Più honorati et suntuosi ala Republica': botteghe and luxury retail along Siena's Strada Romana," in B. Blondé, P. Stabel, J. Stobart, I. Van Damme (eds), *Buyers and Sellers, Retail Circuits and Practices in Medieval and Early Modern Europe,* Turnhout: Brepols.

Nicolay, N. de (2014), *Muhteşem Süleyman'ın İmparatorluğu'nda* (1576), eds M.C. Gomes-Geraud and S. Yerasimos, trans. Ş. Tekeli and M. Tokyay, İstanbul: Kitap Yayınevi.

Nieuwdorp, Hans (2006), *A Publication on the Portrait of Jan Vekemans by the Celebrated Portrait Artist Conelis De Vos,* Antwerp: Cultural Heritage Fund.

Nimmo, D. (1987), *Reform and Division in the Medieval Franciscan Order: From Saint Francis to the Foundation of the Capuchins,* Rome: Capuchin Historical Institute.

Nischan, B. (1983), "The second reformation in Brandenburg: aims and goals," *The Sixteenth Century Journal* 14/2: 173–87.

North, S. and J. Tiramani, eds (2011), *Seventeenth-Century Women's Dress Patterns: Book One.* London: V&A Publishing.

O'Hara, D. (1991), "'Ruled by my friends': aspects of marriage in the diocese of Canterbury, c. 1540–1570," *Continuity and Change,* 6: 9–41.

Olian, J.A. (1977), "Sixteenth Century Costume Books," *Dress* 3: 20–48.

O'Malley, J.W. (1993), *The First Jesuits*, Cambridge, MA, and London: Harvard University Press.
Özbaran, S. (2004), *Bir Osmanlı Kimliği: 14.–17. Yüzyıllarda Rum/Rumi Aidiyetveİmgeleri*, İstanbul: Kitapevi.
Pacheco, F. (1956), *Arte de la pintura*, 2 vols., ed. F.J. Sanchez Canton, Madrid: Instituto de Valencia de Don Juan.
Pamuk, Ş. (1999), *Osmanlı İmparatorluğu'nda Paranın Tarihi*, İstanbul: TarihVakfı Yurt Tatınları.
Paresys, I. (2007), "The Dressed Body: the Moulding of Identities in 16th Century France," in H. Roodenburg (ed.), *Cultural Exchange in Early Modern Europe*, vol. 4, *Forging European Identities, 1400–1700*, Cambridge: Cambridge University Press/European Science Foundation.
—— (2011), "Vêtir les souverains français à la Renaissance: les garde-robes d'Henri II et de Catherine de Médicis en 1556 et 1557," in I. Paresys and N. Coquery (eds), *Se vêtir à la cour en Europe (1400–1815)*, Villeneuve d'Ascq: Centre de recherche du château de Versailles-IRHiS-CEGES Lille 3.
—— (2012), "A profusion of ruffs," in S. Boucher, A-C Laronde and I. Paresys, (ed.), *A Feast for the Eyes: Spectacular Fashions*, Milan: Silvana Editoriale.
Park, K. (1999), "Was there a Renaissance Body?" in A.J. Grieco, M. Rocke, and F. Giofreddi Superbi (eds), *The Italian Renaissance in the Twentieth Century: Acts of an International Conference, Florence, Villa I Tatti, June 9–11, 1999*, Florence: Olschki.
Pastoureau, M. (2001), *Blue: the History of a Colour*, Princeton: Princeton University Press.
—— (2008), *Black: the history of a colour*, Princeton and Oxford: Princeton University Press.
Pastoreau, M. and Dominique Simonnet (2006), *Il piccolo libro dei colori*, Milan: Ponte delle Grazie.
Paulicelli, E. (2011), "From the Sacred to the Secular: The Gendered Geography of Veils in Italian Cinquecento Fashion," in B. Mirabella (ed.), *Ornamentalism: The Art of Renaissance Accessories*, Ann Arbor: University of Michigan Press.
—— (2014), *Writing Fashion in Early Modern Italy: from sprezzatura to satire*, Aldershot: Ashgate.
Peck, L. Levy (2005), *Consuming Splendor: Society and Culture in Seventeenth-Century England*, Cambridge: Cambridge University Press.
Pérez, L.C. (1973), "The Theme of the Tapestry in Ariosto and Cervantes," *Revista de Estudios Hispánicos* 7: 289–98.
Perouse, G.A. (1990), "La Renaissance et la beauté masculine," in J. Céard et al (eds), *Le Corps à la Renaissance. Actes du XXXe colloque de Tours 1987*, Paris: Amateurs de Livres.
Perrot, P. (1981), *Les dessus et le dessous de la bourgeoisie, une histoire du vêtement au XIX$^{es.}$*, Paris: Fayard.
Persels, J.C. (1997), "Bragueta Humanistica, or Humanism's Codpiece," *Sixteenth-Century Journal* 28 (1).
Petrarch, F. (1992), *Letters of Old Age*, 2 vols., trans. Aldo Bernardo, Saul Levin, and Rita Bernardo, Baltimore: Johns Hopkins University Press.
—— (1996), *Canzoniere*, ed. and trans. Mark Musa, Bloomington: Indiana University Press.
Piepkorn, C. (1958), *The Survival of the Historic Vestments in the Lutheran Church After 1555*, St. Louis, MO: Concordia Press.
Poli, D. Davanzo (2003), "Il sarto," *Storia d'Italia, Annali 19, La moda*, ed. M. Belfanti and F. Giusberti, Torino: Einaudi.
Pomata, G. (2002), "Knowledge-Freshening Wind: Gender and the Renewal of Renaissance Studies," in A.J. Grieco, Michael Rocke, and F. Giofreddi Superbi (eds), *The Italian*

Renaissance in the Twentieth Century: Acts of an International Conference, Florence, Villa I Tatti, June 9–11, 1999, Florence: Olschki.

Pontano, F. (1863), "Dello integro e perfetto stato delle donzelle," *Raccolta di scritture varie pubblicata nell'occasione delle nozze Riccomanni-Fineschi,* ed. Cesare Riccomanni, Turin: Vercellino.

Pope-Hennessy, J. (1996), *Italian Renaissance Sculpture,* London: Phaidon.

Pullan, B. (2005), "Catholics, Protestants, and the Poor in Early Modern Europe," *The Journal of Interdisciplinary History,* 35: 3: 441–56.

Quataert, D. (1997), "Clothing Laws, State, and Society in the Ottoman Empire, 1720–1829," *International Journal of Middle East Studies* 29, no. 3: 403–25.

Quondam, A. (2000), *Questo povero cortegiano: Castiglione, il libro, la storia.* Rome: Bulzoni.

Rabelais, F. (1955), *Gargantua,* trans. J.M. Cohen, Harmondsworth: Penguin.

—— (1968) *Gargantua,* Paris: Garnier-Flammarion.

Raber, K. (2011), "Chains of Pearls: Gender, Property, Identity," in B. Mirabella (ed.), *Ornamentalism: The Art of Renaissance Accessories,* Ann Arbor: University of Michigan Press.

Randolph, A.W.B. (1998), "Performing the Bridal Body in Fifteenth-Century Florence," *Art History* 21:2.

Reichman, E. (2010), "Anatomy and the Doctrine of the Seven-chamber Uterus in Rabbinic Literature," *Hakira,* The Flatbush Journal of Jewish Law and Thought, 9: 245–265.

Reynolds, A. (2013), *In Fine Style,* London: Royal Collection Trust.

Ribeiro, A. (2003) *Dress and Morality,* Oxford: Berg.

Richardson, C., ed. (2004), *Clothing Culture, 1350–1650,* Aldershot: Ashgate.

Richardson, C. (2011), "'As my whole trust is in him': Jewellery and the Quality of Early Modern Relationships," in B. Mirabella (ed.), *Ornamentalism: The Art of Renaissance Accessories,* Ann Arbor: University of Michigan Press.

Richardson, C. and T. Hamling, eds (2010), *Everyday Objects,* Aldershot: Ashgate.

Richardson, T.M. (2007), *Pieter Bruegel the Elder: Art Discourse in the Sixteenth Century Netherlands,* Ph.D. thesis, Leiden University, https://openaccess.leidenuniv.nl/bitstream/handle/1887/12377/03.pdf?sequence=10.

Ridderbos, B., ed. (2005), *Early Netherlandish Paintings: Rediscovery, Reception, and Research,* Amsterdam: Amsterdam University Press.

Riello, G. (2012), "From Renaissance Platforms to Modern High Heels: Disequilibrium of gait," in A.C. Laronde, S. Boucher and I. Paresys (eds), *A Feast for the Eyes! Spectacular Fashions,* Milano: Silvana Editoriale.

—— (2013), *Cotton: The Fabric that Made the Modern World,* Cambridge: Cambridge University Press.

Roberts, B.B. (2012), *Sex and Drugs before Rock 'n' Roll: Youth Culture during Holland's Golden Age,* Chicago: University of Chicago Press.

Robinson, P. (1906), *The Writings of Saint Francis,* London: J.M. Dent & Co.

Rocha Burguen, F. de la (1618), *Geometria y Traça perteneciente al officio de Sastres,* Valencia: Pedro Patricio Mey.

Roche, D. (1996), *The Culture of Clothing: Dress and Fashion in the Ancien Régime,* Cambridge: Cambridge University Press.

Rogers, J.M. and R.M. Ward (1988), *Süleyman the Magnificent,* London: The British Museum Press.

Rogers, M. and P. Tinagli, eds (2005), *Women in Italy, 1350–1650: Ideals and Realities*, Manchester: Manchester University Press.

Rosenthal, M.F. (1992), *The Honest Courtesan: Veronica Franco, Citizen and Writer in Renaissance Venice*, Chicago: University of Chicago Press.

—— (2013), "Clothing, Fashion, Dress, and Costume in Venice (c. 1450–1650)," in Eric R. Dursteler (ed.), *A Companion to Venetian History, 1400–1797*, Leiden and Boston: Brill.

Rublack, U. (2010), *Dressing Up: Cultural Identity in Renaissance Europe*, Oxford: Oxford University Press.

—— (2013), "Matter in the Material Renaissance," *Past and Present*, no. 219, May: 41–85.

Rye, W. Brenchley (1967), *England as Seen by Foreigners in the Days of Elizabeth and James I*, New York: B. Bloom.

Salisbury, W.N., ed. (1860), *Calendar of State Papers, Colonial America and West Indies*, I, 1574–1660, London: HMSO.

Salter, E. (2004), "Reworked Material: Discourses of Clothing Culture in Early Sixteenth-Century Greenwich," in Catherine Richardson (ed.), *Clothing Culture 1350–1650*, Aldershot: Ashgate.

Sanbenedetti, B. (1643), *Annali dell'ordine de'Frati Minori Cappuccini*, Venice: Giunti.

Saunders, A.S. (2006), "Provision of apparel for the poor in London, 1630–1680," *Costume* 40: 21–7.

Savonarola, G. (1959), *De simplicitate christianae vitae*, ed. Pier Giorgio Ricci, Rome: Angelo Belardetti Editore.

Schefer, C. (1998), *Antoine Galland: İstanbul'a Ait Günlük Hatıralar (1672–1673)*, vol. 1, trans. N.S. Örik, Ankara: Türk Tarih Kurumu.

Schuessler, M. (2009), "French Hoods: Development of a Sixteenth-Century Court Fashion," in R. Netherton and G. R. Owen-Crocker (eds), *Medieval Clothing and Textiles*, vol. 5, Woodbridge: Boydell & Brewer.

Scott, M. (2011), *Fashion in the Middle Ages*, Los Angeles: J. Paul Getty Museum.

Seiler-Baldinger, A. (1994), *Textiles: A Classification of Techniques*, Bathurst: Crawford House Press.

Şeker, M. (1997), *Gelibolulu Mustafa 'Âlivemeva 'idu'n-nefais fi-kava 'idi'lmecalis*, Ankara: Türk Tarih Kurumu.

Sella, D. (1968), "The rise and fall of the Venetian woollen industry," in B. Pullan (ed.), *Crisis and Change in the Venetian Economy in the 16th and 17th Centuries*, London: Methuen & Co.

Seraphicae Legislationis Textus Originales, (1897), Quaracchi: Typographia Collegii S. Bonaventurae.

Shemek, D. (1998), *Ladies Errant: Wayward Women and Social Order in Early Modern Italy*, Durham, NC: Duke University Press.

Sherrill, T. (2006), "Fleas, fur and fashion: Zibellini as luxury accessories of the Renaissance," *Medieval Clothing and Textiles*, 2, London: Boydell Press: 121–50.

Simons, P. (2011), *The Sex of Men in Premodern Europe: A Cultural History*, Cambridge: Cambridge University Press.

Smith, W.D. (2002), *Consumption and the Making of Respectability, 1600–1800*, New York and London: Routledge.

Snyder, J.R. (2009), *Dissimulation and the Culture of Secrecy in Early Modern Europe*, Berkeley: University of California Press.

Spencer, S. (2006), *Race and Ethnicity: Culture, Identity, and Representation*, London: Routledge.

Spufford, M. (1984), *The Great Reclothing of Rural England: Petty Chapmen and their Wares in the Seventeenth Century*, London: Hambledon Press.

—— (2003), "Fabric for Seventeenth-Century Children and Adolescents' Clothes," *Textile History* 34: 1: 47–63.

Spufford, P. (2002), *Power and Profit: The Merchant in Medieval Europe*, London: Thames & Hudson.

Steinberg, S. (2001), *La Confusion des sexes. Le travestissement de la Renaissance à la Révolution*, Paris: Fayard.

Stevens, S. Manning (2003), "New World Contacts and the Trope of the 'Naked Savage'," in Elizabeth D. Harvey (ed.), *Sensible Flesh: On Touch in Early Modern Culture*, Philadelphia: University of Pennsylvania Press.

Stevenson, S. and Helen Bennet (1978), *Van Dyck in Check Trousers: Fancy Dress in Art and Life, 1700–1900*, Edinburgh: Scottish National Portrait Gallery.

Stobart, J. (2004), *Sugar and Spice: grocers and groceries in Provincial England, 1650–1830*, Oxford: Oxford University Press.

Storey, T. (2004), "Clothing courtesans: fabric, signals and experiences," in C. Richardson (ed.), *Clothing culture 1350–1650*, Aldershot: Ashgate, 95–108.

Stowe, J. [1598, 1603], *The Survey of London*, London: Nicholas Bourn.

Strauss, W.L. (1974), *The Complete Drawings of Albrecht Dürer. Volume II*, New York: Abaris Press.

Strocchia, S. (1992), *Death and Ritual in Renaissance Florence*, Baltimore: Johns Hopkins University Press.

Strong, R. (1983), *Artists of the Tudor Court: The Portrait Miniature Rediscovered 1520–1620*, London: Victoria & Albert Museum.

Stuard, S. Mosher (2006), *Gilding the Market: Luxury and Fashion in Fourteenth-Century Italy*, Philadelphia: University of Pennsylvania Press.

Stubbes, P. (1595), *The anatomie of abuses*, London: Richard Iohnes, at the sign of the Rose and Crowne.

—— (2002), *The anatomie of abuses*, ed. Margaret Jane Kidnie, Renaissance English Text Society, seventh series, vol. 27, Tempe, Arizona: Arizona Center for Medieval and Renaissance Studies.

Styles, J. (2007), *The Dress of the People: Everyday Fashion in Eighteenth-Century England*, New Haven and London: Yale University Press.

Sutton, A. (2005), *The Mercery of London: Trade, Goods and People, 1130–1578*, Aldershot: Ashgate.

Sutton, E. (2012), *Early Modern Dutch Prints of Africa*, Aldershot: Ashgate.

Syson, L. and D. Thornton (2001), *Objects of Virtue: art in renaissance Italy*, London: British Museum Press.

Swann, J. (2001), *History of Footwear in Norway, Sweden and Finland*, Stockholm: The Royal Academy of Letters, History and Antiquities.

Swanson, H. (1989), *Medieval Artisans: An Urban Class in Late Medieval England*, Oxford: Blackwell.

Sweetinburgh, S. (2004), "Clothing the Naked in Late Medieval East Kent," in C. Richardson (ed.), *Clothing Culture, 1350–1650*, Aldershot: Ashgate.

Sweigger, S. (2004), *Sultanlar Kentine Yolculuk (1578–1581)*, ed. H. Stein, trans. S.T. Noyan, İstanbul: Kitap Yayınevi.

Taddei, I. (2001), *Fanciulli e giovani: crescere a Firenze nel Rinascimento*, Florence: Olschki.

Tankard, D. (2012), "'A Pair of Grass-Green Woollen Stockings': The Clothing of the Rural Poor in Seventeenth-Century Sussex," *Textile History* 43:1.

Tanner, N.P. (1990), *Decrees of the Ecumenical Councils*, 2 vols., London: Sheed & Ward.

Tarabotti, A. (2004), *Paternal Tyranny*, ed. and trans. Letizia Panizza, Chicago: University of Chicago Press.

Tarama Sözlüğü (Turkish language dictionary) (1996), Ankara: Türk Dil Kurumu Yayınları6.

Taylor, L. (1983), *Mourning Dress*, London: George Allen & Unwin.

—— (2001a), *The Study of Dress History*, Manchester: Manchester University Press.

—— (2001b), "Dangerous Vocations," in L. Taylor (ed.), *Preachers and People in the Reformations and Early Modern Period*, Leiden and Boston: Brill, 2001, 91–124.

The Lisle Letters (1981), ed. Muriel St. Clare Byrne, 6 vols., Chicago and London: University of Chicago Press.

The Paston Letters: A Selection in Modern Spelling (1983), ed. Norman Davies, Oxford: Oxford University Press.

Thirsk, J. (1973), "The fantastical folly of fashion: the English stocking knitting industry, 1500–1700," in N.B. Harte and K.G. Ponting (eds), *Textile History and Economic History: Essays in Honour of Miss Julia de Lacy Mann*, Manchester: Manchester University Press.

—— (2003), "Knitting and knitware c. 1500–1780," in D. Jenkins (ed.), *The Cambridge History of Western Textiles*, vol. 1, Cambridge: Cambridge University Press, 565–6.

Thrush, A. and J.P. Ferris (2010), *History of Parliament, House of Commons, 1604–1629*, v, Cambridge: Cambridge University Press.

Thomas, Artus (previously known as Thomas Artus) (1996), *Les Hermaphrodites* (1605), ed. Claude Dubois, Geneva: Droz.

Thomson, R. (1981), "Leather manufacture in the post-medieval period with special reference to Northamptonshire," *Post Medieval Archaeology*, 15: 161–75.

Tiramani, J. (2010), "Pins and Aglets," in T. Hamling & C. Richardson (eds), *Everyday Objects: Medieval and Early Modern Material Culture and its Meanings*, Aldershot: Ashgate.

Tittler, R. (2006), "Freemen's Gloves and Civic Authority: The Evidence from Post-Reformation Portraiture," *Costume* 40: 13–20.

—— (2007), *The Face of the City*, Manchester: Manchester University Press.

Tornabuoni, L. (2001), *Sacred Narratives*, ed. and trans. Jane Tylus, Chicago: University of Chicago Press.

Trexler, R. (1981), "La prostitution florentine au XVe siècle: patronage et clientele," *Annales*, Year 36 (6): 983–1015.

—— (2002), "Dressing and undressing images: an analytic sketch," in Richard Trexler, *Religion and Social Context in Europe and America, 1200–1700*, Tempe, Arizona: Arizona Center for Medieval and Renaissance Studies: 374–408.

Tuohy, T. (1996), *Herculean Ferrara*, Cambridge: Cambridge University Press.

Tylus, J. (1993), *Writing and Vulnerability in the Late Renaissance*, Stanford: Stanford University Press.

—— (2012), "Petrarch's Griselda and the Sense of an Ending," *Nottingham Medieval Studies* 56: 421–45.

Üçel-Aybet, G. (2003), *Avrupalı Seyyahların Gözünden Osmanlı Dünyasıve İnsanları (1530–1699)*, İstanbul: İletişim.

Ulg, U. (2004), "The cultural significance of costume books in sixteenth-century Europe," in C. Richardson (ed.), *Clothing Culture, 1350–1650*, Aldershot: Ashgate.

Van Buren, A. (2011), *Illuminating Fashion: Dress in the Art of Medieval France and the Netherlands, 1325–1515*, London: Giles; New York: The Morgan Library and Museum.

Varholy, C. (2008), "'Rich like a Lady': Cross-class Dressing in the Brothels and Theaters of Early Modern London Authors," *Journal for Early Modern Cultural Studies*, 8(1): 4–34.

Veale, E. (2003), *The English Fur Trade in the Later Middle Ages*, London Record Society, Woodbridge: Boydell & Brewer.

—— (2012), "From sable to mink," in M. A. Hayward and P. Ward (eds), *The 1547 Inventory of King Henry VIII: Volume 2 Textiles and Dress*, London: Harvey Miller for the Society of Antiquaries, 335–43.

Veblen, T. (1994), *The Theory of Leisure Class*, New York: Dover Publications.

Vecellio, C. (1590), *De gli habit antichi e moderni di diverse parti del mondo*, Venice: Damiano Zenaro.

Verney, F.P. (1892), *Memoirs of the Verney Family During the Civil War*, 4 vols., London: Longmans.

Verville, B. de (2002), *Le Moyen de parvenir (1617)*, Albi: éd. du Passage.

Vicary, G.Q. (1989), "Visual Art as Social Data: The Renaissance Codpiece," *Cultural Anthropology*, vol. 4 (1): 8–9.

Vigarello, G. (1978), *Le corps redressé. Histoire d'un pouvoir pédagogique*, Paris: Delarge.

—— (1988), *Concepts of Cleanliness: changing attitudes in France since the Middle Age*, Cambridge: Cambridge University Press.

Villiers, H. de (1824), *Essais historiques sur les modes et la toilette française par le chevalier de***, tome premier*, Paris: Librairie universelle Pierre Mongie.

Vincent, J.M. ([1935] 1969), *Costume and Conduct in the Laws of Basel, Bern and Zurich, 1370–1800*, New York: Greenwood Press.

Vincent, S.J. (2003), *Dressing the Elite: Clothes in Early Modern England*, Oxford: Berg.

—— (2009), *The Anatomy of Fashion: Dressing the body from the Renaissance to today*, Oxford: Berg.

—— (2013), "From the cradle to the grave. Clothing the early modern body," in Sarah Toulalan and Kate Fisher (eds), *The Routledge History of Sex and the Body, 1500 to the Present*, London and New York: Routledge.

Vives, J.L. (2000), *The Education of a Christian Woman*, ed. and trans. Charles Fantazzi, Chicago and London: University of Chicago Press.

Walsh, C. (2006), "The Social Relations of Shopping in Early Modern England," in Bruno Blondé, Peter Stabel, Jon Stobart, and Ilja Van Damme (eds), *Buyers and Sellers: Retail Circuits and Practices in Medieval and Early Modern Europe*, Turnhout: Brepols.

Warr, C. (2007), "Hermits, habits and history," in Louise Bourdua and Anne Dunlop (eds), *Art and the Augustinian Order in Early Renaissance Italy*, Aldershot: Ashgate.

—— (2010), *Dressing for Heaven: religious clothing in Italy, 1215–1545* Manchester: Manchester University Press.

Watkins, R. (1989), "L.B. Alberti in the Mirror: An Interpretation of the *Vita*, with a New Translation," *Italian Quarterly* 30.

Wee, H. van der (in collaboration with John Munro) (2003), "The western European woollen industries, 1500–1750," in D. Jenkins (ed.), *The Cambridge History of Western Textiles*, vol. I, Cambridge: Cambridge University Press.

Weiss, M. (2012), "Catherine Carey, Countess of Nottingham," *Tudor and Stuart Portraits*, London: 32–7.

Welch, E. (2000), "New, Old and Second hand Culture: the Case of the Renaissance Sleeve," in G. Neher and R. Shepherd (eds), *Revaluing Renaissance Art*, Aldershot: Ashgate.

—— (2005), *Shopping in the Renaissance*, New Haven and London: Yale University Press.

Whitelocke, J. (1858), *Liber Famelicus of Sir James Whitelocke*, ed. John Bruce, London: Camden Society 70.

Whittle, J. and E. Griffiths (2012), *Consumption and Gender in the Early Seventeenth-Century Household: the world of Alice Le Strange*, Oxford: Oxford University Press.

Wiggins, P. DeSa (1986), *Figures in Ariosto's Tapestry: Character and Design in the "Orlando Furioso,"* Baltimore: Johns Hopkins University Press.

Willan, T.S. (1962), *A Tudor Book of Rates*, Manchester: Manchester University Press.

Winkel, M. de (2006), *Fashion and Fancy: Dress and Meaning in Rembrandt's Paintings*, Amsterdam: Amsterdam University Press.

Winter, J. and C. Savoy (1987), Index of "Unisex Clothing," in *Elizabethan Costuming for the Years 1550–1580*, Oakland, CA: Other Times Publications.

Woodward, J. (1997), *The Theatre of Death: the ritual management of royal funerals in renaissance England, 1570–1625*, Woodridge: Boydell Press.

Wright, A. (2005), *The Pollaiuolo Brothers: the arts of Florence and Rome*, New Haven and London: Yale University Press.

Wrightson, K. (1994), "'Sorts of People' in Tudor and Stuart England," in J. Barry and C. Brooks (eds), *The Middling Sort of People: Culture, Society, and Politics in England, 1550–1800*, New York: St. Martin's Press.

Wunder, A. (2013), "Dress (Spain)," in Evonne Levy and Kenneth Mills (eds), *A Lexicon of the Hispanic Baroque: transatlantic exchange and transformation*, Austin: University of Texas Press.

—— (2015), "Seventeenth-Century Spain: The Rise and Fall of the *Guardainfante*," *Renaissance Quarterly*, vol. 68 no. 1, Spring.

Young, E. (1973), "An unknown Saint Francis by Francisco de Zurbarán," *The Burlington Magazine* 115/841: 245–7.

NOTES ON CONTRIBUTORS

Elizabeth Currie is a lecturer and author specializing in early modern dress and textile history. She was formerly a research fellow at the Royal College of Art and an assistant curator in the Fashion, Textiles and Furniture Department of the Victoria and Albert Museum. Her articles have appeared in *Fashion Theory*, *Renaissance Studies*, and the *Journal of Medieval and Early Modern Studies* and she has recently completed a monograph, *Fashion and Masculinity in Renaissance Florence* (2016).

Maria Hayward is Professor of Early Modern History at the University of Southampton. Her research interests include textiles and dress in the medieval and early modern periods with a particular focus on the Tudor and Stuart courts. Her books include *Dress at the Court of King Henry VIII* (2007), *Rich Apparel: Clothing and the Law in Henry VIII's England* (2009) and with Ulinka Rublack, *The First Book of Fashion: The Book of Clothes of Mattaeus and Veit Konrad Schwarz of Augsburg* (2015).

Ann Rosalind Jones, Esther Cloudman Dunn Professor Emerita of Comparative Literature at Smith College, has written on the history of dress since the 1980s. Her publications include *Renaissance Clothing and the Materials of Memory* (2000) with Peter Stallybrass, and, with Margaret F. Rosenthal, a translation, *The Clothing of the Renaissance World (Europe, Asia, Africa, America): Cesare Vecellio's Habiti Antichi et Moderni* (2008), republished in Italy as *Habiti antichi et moderni: La Moda nel Rinascimento*. Her current project is *Global Habits: The Early Modern Costume Book.*

Eminegül Karababa is an associate professor of Marketing at the Middle East Technical University in Turkey. Her publications have appeared in *Economic History Review*, *Journal of Consumer Research*, *Marketing Theory*, *Consumption Markets and Culture*, and *Journal of Historical Research in Marketing*. Her research explores the historical development of markets, consumer cultures and consumer subjectivities, with a focus on Ottoman history. She also publishes on value theory and is currently working on the contributions of alternative historical approaches to Consumer Culture Theory.

Gerry Milligan is Associate Professor of Italian Literature at the College of Staten Island, City University of New York. His publications include (as co-editor) *The Poetics of Masculinity in Early Modern Italy and Spain* (2010) and articles on masculinity, women writers, and theater of the Italian Renaissance. He has recently completed a monograph on gender and war in Renaissance Italy and is currently working on a new project on effeminacy, fashion, and warfare.

Isabelle Paresys is Associate Professor of Cultural History at the University of Lille in France and has mainly published on dress and fashion history in Renaissance France and Europe. She edited *Paraître et apparences du Moyen Âge à nos jours* (2008), co-edited *Se vêtir à la cour en Europe (1400–1815)* (2011) and *A Feast for the Eyes: Spectacular*

Fashions (2012). She runs the online journal *Apparence(s). Histoire et culture du paraître*. She is currently researching Renaissance costumes in French cinema.

Anna Reynolds is Deputy Surveyor of Painting at Royal Collection Trust, with curatorial responsibility for temporary exhibitions at The Queen's Gallery in London and the permanent display of approximately 8,000 paintings across royal residences including Buckingham Palace, Windsor Castle and the Palace of Holyroodhouse. Her exhibitions and accompanying publications include *In Fine Style: The Art of Tudor and Stuart Fashion* (2013), *Royal Childhood* (2014), *A Royal Welcome* (2015), and *Portrait of the Artist* (2016).

Catherine Richardson is reader in Renaissance Studies at the University of Kent. She is author of *Domestic Life and Domestic Tragedy in Early Modern England* (2006), *Shakespeare and Material Culture* (2011) and, with Tara Hamling, *A Day at Home in Early Modern England, The Materiality of Domestic Life, 1500–1700* (2016); editor of *Clothing Culture 1350–1650* (2004) and, also with Tara Hamling, *Everyday Objects: Medieval and Early Modern Material Culture and its Meanings* (2010).

Susan Vincent is a research associate at the Centre for Renaissance and Early Modern Studies (CREMS) at the University of York. While working primarily on the cultural history of dress in the early modern period, she has expanded her research interests to include dress practices up to the present day. Her publications include *Dressing the Elite: Clothes in Early Modern England* (2003) and *The Anatomy of Fashion: Dressing the Body from the Renaissance to Today* (2009).

Cordelia Warr is Senior Lecturer in Art History and Visual Studies at the University of Manchester. She has published extensively on the history of dress in the Middle Ages and Renaissance, including *Dressing for Heaven: Religious Clothing in Italy, 1215–1545* (2010) and, most recently, "The Devil on my Tail: Clothing and Visual Culture in the Camposanto *Last Judgement*," in *Medieval Clothing and Textiles* 11 (2015).

INDEX

Alberti, Leon Battista 178, 190, 191
Alçega, Juan de 66
Alexander IV (Pope) 80
Alexander VI (Pope) 76
Alfonso, King of Naples 83
Amman, Jost 41, 43, 46, 87, 139
Anjou, Duke of 70
Anne of Austria 8, 60, 71
Anne of Brittany 8
Anne of Denmark 162
Anthony of Padua 82
Aquinas, Thomas 75, 76
Aretino, Pietro 15
Ariosto, Ludovico 176, 187
Armenian dress 135, 146–50
artisans 40–1, 45–6, 53–4, 125
    clothing of 7, 15
    entrepreneurship 17
    migration of 29, 31

Basset, Katharine 52
Bassett, Anne 8
Battiferri, Laura 177
bents 27
bequests 11, 52, 127–8, 214
Bertelli, Pietro 61–2, 70, 106–7
black 31, 33, 35, 83–5, 88, 98, 102, 112, 147, 160, 161, 183
Boccaccio, Giovanni 176, 182
bombast 27
Bosse, Abraham 169–70
Brant, Sebastian 105
Brantôme, Pierre de Bourdeille 61, 67
breeches 70, 88, 101, 105–6, 109
Bruegel, Pieter the Elder 161–2
Bruyn, Cornelis de 145
Bulgarian dress 136–8
Bulwer, John 2–3, 73, 88–9
Burguen, Francisco de la Rocha 66
Bursa 24, 139, 140–1, 143
Busbecq, Ogier Ghiselin de 136, 138, 150
Busby, Elizabeth 52–3

Calley, William 54

camel hair 21, 23
Cappella, Giovanni da 83
Capuchins 80–2
Carducho, Vicente 15
Carey, Catherine, Countess of Nottingham 155–6
Carleton, Dudley 54
Carr, Thomas, Duke of Somerset 109
Carranza, Alonso 91
Castiglione, Baldassare 13, 67, 85–6, 175, 190–1
Catherine of Aragon 39
Catherine Howard 26
Chardin, John 22
charitable provisions 127–8
Charles V 5, 59, 85, 122
chasuble 75, 77, 79, 91–2
children's clothing 59–61, 98
China 21, 24
Chivalric Orders 119–20, 164
cioppa 164
civility 67, 70
cleanliness 31, 37–8, 70–2
cloth of gold 11, 21, 24, 67, 118, 157, 171
Cocks, Thomas 130–2
codpieces 19, 28, 58, 64, 69–70, 104–5, 171
color symbolism 76, 85, 157
construction 26–8, 40, 42–3, 45, 66, 122, 157, 162, 171
consumers
    conspicuous 50, 90–1, 112, 118, 148
    discerning 42–5
    economising 49, 126
    recycling 49–50
cope 24, 75–9
Corsuccio, Giovan Andrea 33
costume books 1, 9, 57, 61–2, 67, 70, 86–9, 101, 107, 143, 151, 170
cotton 19, 22, 23, 24, 25, 27, 29, 32, 33, 34, 106, 113, 149
courtiers 8, 13, 51, 61, 66–7, 83, 85–6, 101, 122, 190–1
Cristoforus of Padua 78
Croatian dress 139, 140
cross-dressing 105–7, 109–12

dalmatic 75–7
Dante Alighieri 177–8
Daza, Antonio 92
Dee, John 48
Dekker, Thomas 19
Della Porta, Giambattista 59
Dernschwam, Hans 136–40, 143, 145
Deserps, François 87
di Toledo, Eleonora 8, 16, 122
domestic production 38–9
Doni, Anton Francesco 189
doublets 26, 27, 46, 58, 66, 96, 98, 101, 106, 162
dowry 11, 164, 185
draperies, old and new 23, 25
draw loom 22
drawings 167–8
Drebbel, Cornelis 33
Dudley, Robert, Earl of Leicester 119–20, 129
Durandus, William 75
Dürer, Albrecht 96, 167–8
Dutch Republic 6, 29, 53
dyes 31–5, 154, 165

Edward III 118
Edward VI 39, 79
effeminacy 101, 181, 188, 189, 191–2
Elizabeth I 5, 14, 39, 44, 48, 79, 111, 118, 122, 129, 155
embroidery 18, 27, 28, 39, 77, 88–9, 101, 118, 138, 147, 155
Erasmus, Desiderius 1, 9, 57, 67
Este, Beatrice d' 5
Este, Ercole d' 83
Este, Isabella d' 9, 122
Esther (Old Testament) 184
Evelyn, John 10–11, 63

farthingales 15, 27, 60, 63, 91
fashion
    cities 9–11
    critiques of 6–7, 50, 71, 73, 75, 87, 88, 89–91, 106, 112, 118, 188–9
    decorum 5, 90, 119, 161
    dissemination of 7–12, 29–31, 44, 51–4, 113
    dolls 44
    foreign 1, 10, 16, 19, 118, 122, 125, 191
    moderation 83–6
    morality 70–1, 89–91, 101–3, 142, 191
    and politics 29, 58, 67, 101, 109, 117–18, 122, 191

felt 23, 26
female workforce 38–40
fetish 178–9
fibers 19–22
finials 138, 140
flax 21–2, 25–6
Franciscans 13, 80, 81–3, 92
Franco, Giacomo 9–10, 175
François I 9
frescoes 163–4
Fresne-Canaye, Philippe du 143
Fuller, Thomas 13
funerals 91–3, 127, 131
furs 19, 24, 26, 35, 118

Galen 69, 99
Galland, Antoine 141
Gamage, William 105
Gawdy, Philip 44, 45, 47
Geffe, Nicholas 29
gender 15, 58, 95–116, 176, 187–90
genre painting 160–2
Gerlach, Stephan 138–48
gifts 14, 16, 19, 51–3, 71, 121–2, 127, 131–2, 162, 185
gloves 71, 76–7, 101, 132–3, 169, 190
Gonzaga, Federico 9
Gozzoli, Benozzo 80–1
Guazzo, Stefano 7, 182

haberdashery 11, 26, 28, 45
hairstyles 61, 71, 73, 101, 106–7, 109–10, 122, 139, 140, 142–3, 145, 162, 188–9
Hardwick Hall 18
Harley, Brilliana 39–40
Harman, Thomas 54
Harrison, William 1, 16
Hayne, John 130–2
headwear 138, 141, 162, 167
    bourrelet 167
    cappuccio 81–2
    French hood 8, 61
    hennin 4, 61, 167
    sugarloaf hats 2, 61
health 16, 71, 73, 93
    see also medical theories
Heberer, Michael 142–3
Henri IV 87
Henrietta Maria 162
Henry VII 24
Henry VIII 5, 16, 19, 22, 26, 39, 51, 79, 96, 112, 118, 120, 121–3

hermaphrodites 100–1, 114
Holbein, Hans 157
Howard, Frances, Baroness Cobham 96, 107–9
Huguenots 17, 70
Hungarian dress 137
Hutchinson, Lucy 13, 45

identity, mistaken 7, 12–13, 112
il Moro, Ludovico 5
India 21, 22, 24, 28, 29, 32, 34, 109
Innocent III (Pope) 76
Istanbul 29, 136, 140, 141, 144–6, 148

James I 29, 136, 140, 144, 145–6, 148
Jesuits 83
Jewish clothing 13, 143, 145–9, 184
John XXII (Pope) 82
Jonson, Ben 113, 170
Judith (Old Testament) 184–6

knitting 18, 23, 29, 119, 141, 158

lace 17, 28, 45, 90, 117, 126, 131–3, 155, 173
Lampugnani, Agostino 175
Lanteri, Giacomo 102, 181
leather 26, 30, 35, 51, 88, 149, 158, 168
Lee, Anne 44–5
Lee, William 29
Léry, Jean de 67
Le Strange family 11, 123–4
linen 19, 21–2, 24–5, 27–8, 30–1, 37–40, 45, 52–3, 59, 68, 70–1, 90, 96, 112, 125, 138, 140, 155, 158, 160, 168
Lisle, Honor 9, 42–3, 52
livery 48, 121–2, 126–8, 130
Lodge, Thomas 7
London 7, 9, 11, 26, 27, 29, 30, 31, 32, 53, 54, 106–7, 113, 122–4, 127–8, 131
Louis XIII 61
Louis XIV 60
Luther, Martin 79

manuscripts, illuminated 166–7
Margaret of Austria, Duchess of Savoy 8
Margaret of Austria, Queen of Spain 5
Margaret of Valois 66
Marie of Cleves 70
Mary, Queen of Scots 83–4
Mary Tudor 79, 98
Maximilian II 138
medical theories 61, 69, 99
Memling, Hans 159–60

Menot, Michel 18
mercers 9, 11, 41, 169
merchants 7, 30, 31, 32, 47, 48, 54, 122, 130, 131, 132, 153
Methwold, William 34
milliners 45
miniatures 8, 39, 42, 64, 162
monastic dress 80
Montaigne, Michel de 67
Morrison, Fynes 22
mourning dress 80–3
Mundy, Peter 146–7
Muslim clothing 136–7, 140–9

nakedness 67–70
Nashe, Thomas 102, 113
national identities 16, 118, 122, 129, 135, 191
Nicholas of Cusa 75
nuns 77, 83, 181, 183

Oliver, Isaac 64, 162, 173
Ottoman empire 33, 135–51
Overbury, Thomas 109

padding 19, 22, 26, 27, 58, 63, 64, 66, 96, 155
pamphlets
    Haec Vir 109–12
    Hic Mulier 109–12
Parenti, Marco 48, 53
Paul III (Pope) 78
pawning 52–3
pearls 4, 16, 96, 97, 101, 105, 112, 132, 138, 140, 143, 162, 164, 165
pedlars 38, 45
Pera 140–1, 143
performance 13, 61, 66–7, 113, 187, 190–2
perfume 16, 45, 71–2, 95, 101, 190
Petrarch 176–9
Pezzen, Bartolomeo von 136
Philip II of Spain 85, 98
Philip III of Spain 5, 91
Philip IV of Spain 91
Piccolomini, Alessandro 15
pigments 158, 164–5
Pius II 75–6
Pollaiuolo, Antonio del 77–8
pomegranate motif 33, 171, 172
Pontano, Francesco 188
Portinari, Maria 4
portraiture 154–6, 158–60
pride 73, 88, 90–1, 102, 111
printed textiles 34

probate inventories 125–6, 137, 139, 141, 143
prostitutes 87–8, 91, 103, 105, 112–13, 181
Puckering, Thomas 122–4, 127

Rabelais, François 70, 105
ready-made clothing 11, 39, 45–6, 54
Reformation 52, 75, 78, 79, 80, 83, 93, 127
Rosetti, Giovanventura 33
Rovere, Guidobaldo della 104
Royal Exchange 11
Ruffino da Siena, Fra 82–3
ruffs 45, 53, 64–6, 69, 70, 73, 98, 101, 106, 109, 110, 112, 114, 115

Sackville, Richard 64, 173
Savonarola, Girolamo 76–7, 90
Schwarz, Matthäus 69
sculpture 172
seamstresses 45, 54, 109, 169
second-hand trade 39, 46, 53–4, 58, 113
Serbian dress 136, 139–40
sericulture 21
sexuality 95–115, 140, 179–83, 187–90
Seymour, Jane 8
Shakespeare, William 179
shirts, *see* undergarments
shoes 61
shopping 10–11, 45–8, 123–4, 169–70
Siena 11
silk guild 15–16
silk weaving 17, 22, 24, 25, 29, 33
Sixtus IV (Pope) 80
slashing 50–1, 69, 88
spinning 22, 77
sprezzatura 190–1
stays 66, 96
stockings 11, 18, 46–7, 190
Stowe, John 54
Stubbes, Philip 15, 17, 37, 55, 90
sumptuary legislation 5, 15, 90–1, 112, 117–19, 125–6, 128–9, 131, 188

tailors 15, 26, 40–6, 54, 66, 101, 109, 113, 122, 126, 128, 130, 131
talismans 16
tapestry 170–1
Tarabotti, Arcangela 183
Tasso, Torquato 179–81, 188
Teellinck, Willem 6

theatre 13
thefts of clothing 54–5, 88
Thévenot, Melchisédech 145
Thomas, Artus 100–1
thread 26–7
Tornabuoni, Giovanni 163
Tornabuoni, Lodovica 164
Tornabuoni, Lucrezia 185
trains 89–90
Trent, Council of 78, 83
tunic 66, 75, 77, 79, 80–2
Turkey 17, 21, 24
   Turkish dress 1, 2, 10, 61, 87, 135–6, 139, 140, 142–9, 191

undergarments 37, 45, 66, 68, 96–7, 138, 164

Van Dyck 173
vanity 83, 87–8, 90, 188, 191
Vecellio, Cesare 7, 8, 13, 17, 70, 71, 83, 84, 88, 101, 102, 103, 106, 140, 143, 151, 170, 175, 181–2
veils 71, 91, 143, 147, 162, 168, 178–81
velvet 11, 21, 24, 29, 33, 52, 88, 113–14, 119, 140, 145, 172, 173
Verney, Mary 44–5
Vesalius, Andreas 99
Vespasiano da Bisticci 83
vestiarian controversy 79–80
vestments, clerical 75–89, 91–2
Visconti, Gian Galeazzo 80
Vives, Juan Luis 90
Vos, Lambert de 144

wedding feast 161
whalebone 27, 66, 96
Whitelocke, James 52
widows 83–4, 90, 111–12, 181–2
Wise, Christopher 130
wool 19–23, 25, 26–7, 29, 31, 35, 37, 66, 76, 90, 95, 112, 117, 140, 161
working dress 125–6

yellow 5, 13, 14, 31, 109, 113, 144–5, 148, 181
York 30, 40

zibellino 26